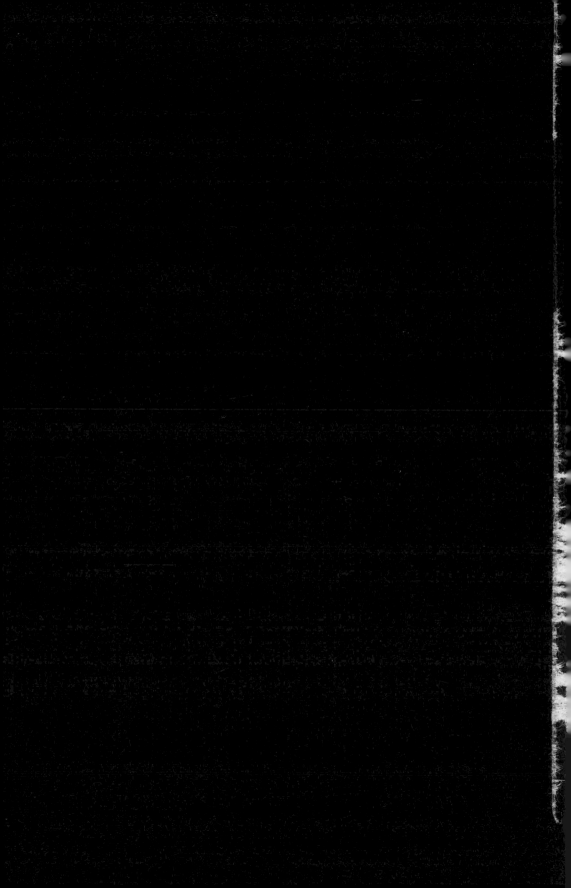

HOWDUNIT

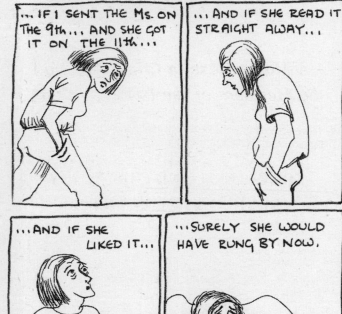

How not to do it? A Detection Club cartoon by Clewsey.

Howdunit

A Masterclass in Crime Writing
by Members of the Detection Club

CONCEIVED AND EDITED BY
MARTIN EDWARDS

COLLINS
CRIME
CLUB

COLLINS CRIME CLUB
An imprint of HarperCollins*Publishers*
1 London Bridge Street
London SE1 9GF
www.harpercollins.co.uk

Published by Collins Crime Club 2020
1

A catalogue record for this book
is available from the British Library

ISBN 978-0-00-838013-7

Typeset by Palimpsest Book Production Ltd, Falkirk, Stirlingshire

Printed and bound in Great Britain by
CPI Group (UK) Ltd, Croydon CR0 4YY

MIX
Paper from
responsible sources
FSC® C007454

This book is produced from independently certified FSC™ paper
to ensure responsible forest management.

For more information visit: www.harpercollins.co.uk/green

Dedicated to Len Deighton,
elected to membership of the Detection Club in 1969

Contents

Premise

Introduction

In *Howdunit*, no fewer than ninety leading crime novelists offer personal perspectives on their approach to their craft – and on the writing life. There are countless valuable insights for would-be writers, but our overriding aim is to entertain and inform *anyone* who enjoys crime fiction. And perhaps even some people who don't regard themselves as crime fans – at least not yet – but who are fascinated by the way authors work.

Each contributor is a past or present member of the Detection Club, the world's oldest social network of crime writers. Publication of *Howdunit* coincides with the Club's ninetieth birthday, so there is one essay for each year of the Club's life to date. Over the past nine decades, many of Britain's pre-eminent authors in the genre have belonged to the Club. Their work includes spy, thriller, and adventure fiction, as well as traditional detective stories and novels of psychological suspense. It is high time that their collective wisdom appeared in a single volume. The emphasis is on present-day writing and writers, but our predecessors' thoughts remain of interest. This is partly because they illustrate how much the writing life and literary fashions have changed, and partly because they show that quite a few challenges remain the same. Detection

Club members take their work seriously – but we also take joy from it. That sense of pleasure ripples through the contributions, from Lindsey Davis's thoughts on literary style to Simon Brett's rueful reflections about the prospect of having one's masterpiece adapted by other hands.

A century ago, the Club's first President, G. K. Chesterton, wrote with pungent wit, 'It is a well-known fact that people who have never succeeded in anything end by writing books about how to succeed; and I do not see why this principle should not be applied to success in the writing of detective stories as well as in lower and less glorious walks of life.' But I like to think that Chesterton would have approved of this book, and would be delighted to see his own opinions appear alongside those of his contemporaries and successors.

From the Club's formation in 1930, Detection Club members, with Anthony Berkeley Cox and Dorothy L. Sayers taking a vigorous lead, set about raising the literary standards of the genre. In those early days, bestselling thrillers tended to be shoddily written and jingoistic, so membership was confined to authors who had produced at least two detective novels of 'acknowledged merit', a standard occasionally applied in a rather haphazard manner. Thriller writers were excluded unless they also wrote detective stories in the classic vein. After the Second World War, when it became obvious even to the diehards that first-rate authors such as Eric Ambler were writing thrillers, the absurdity of continuing the exclusion was recognized and it was abandoned.

In its infancy, the Club was popularly associated with the idea of laying down 'rules' about how to write detective stories. The rules and their purpose have been shrouded in myths and misunderstandings. For a start, the rules were conceived by Ronald Knox, renowned as a satirist, before the Club was founded. And they were written tongue-in-cheek: an ordained priest, Knox presented them as a gentle skit on the Ten Commandments. Some of the 'rules', such as 'The detective must not himself commit the crime', were futile, taking the idea of 'fair play' towards the reader too far and for no good reason.

He made one or two sensible points: for instance, when he says that twin brothers and doubles 'must not appear unless we have been duly prepared for them', he was simply arguing against the use of inelegant trickery that might fool readers but only at the cost of exasperating them. Above all, he was arguing for common sense in the writing of mysteries, urging practitioners to shun the absurd plot contrivances and racial stereotypes that abounded in early twentieth-century crime writing.

Cox, who founded the Club, and wrote innovative and influential crime fiction as Anthony Berkeley and Francis Iles, delighted in breaking the so-called 'rules' in his work, and so did many of his fellow members. But over the years, the joke got lost. One often-repeated canard is that Agatha Christie came close to being drummed out of the Club because *The Murder of Roger Ackroyd* was deemed to breach its rules. This is pure invention; the truth is that the novel was published four years before the Club came into existence, and it was much admired by Cox, Sayers, and Christie's other colleagues.

It's tempting to go to the other extreme, and suggest that the only rule for crime writers is that there are no rules. Writing is a process of trial and error, and each person has to work out what suits them best. Even so, the experiences of skilled practitioners, past and present, are instructive as well as intriguing. And who better, in Britain at least, to compile such a book than members of the Detection Club?

When I proposed, at the Club's AGM in February 2019, that we collaborate on a book of this kind in order to boost our finances, I was unsure of the likely reaction. As it turned out, everyone was highly enthusiastic. The meeting also agreed to dedicate the book to Len Deighton, our longest-serving member, as a way of celebrating the golden anniversary of his election to the Club. As for the guiding concept of the book, Felix Francis summed it up as 'How *we* dunit'. In other words, we'd talk about our own experiences, expressing personal views rather than laying down an earnest update of Knox's jokey commandments. The Club's publishers, HarperCollins, loved the idea, and in the months that followed, *Howdunit* took shape.

The result is not a textbook or manual; readers wishing to delve into the minutiae of police and courtroom procedure, forensic science, and the law of libel should look elsewhere. Instead the contributors offer a treasure trove of wit, wisdom, and anecdotes. You will find out here which author was the first novelist to use a word processor, who wrote what has been described as the first 'electronic novel', how a Booker Prize nomination led to a commission to revive a great detective of the Golden Age, and a good deal more. There is even a step-by-step case study in correspondence of the making of a collaborative crime classic, which illustrates that the creative process is an extraordinary mixture of pleasure and pain. And because there is no limit to the talents in the Detection Club, there are also several cartoons by 'Clewsey', whose name conceals a collaboration of three members, one of whom trained in graphic design . . .

I suggested broad topics that members might like to write about, and offered more detailed ideas to anyone who asked for them, but I didn't try to impose conformity of approach or message or to eliminate contradictions. I wanted contributors to express themselves without feeling constrained by editorial diktats. When you are lucky enough to have the chance to work with such a gifted group of authors, it would be crazy not to give them free rein. The genre is a broad church, encompassing so many types of story, and it would be strange if all crime writers had same opinions or went about their task in the same way. As will become evident, they don't. In these pages you can hear (just as you can if you attend a major literary festival) many different voices. The contributors have diverse opinions about everything from writer's block to the crime novelist's mission.

Some writers plot or outline in advance before writing the first word of a story, while others write from the seat of their pants, setting off on the journey of novel writing without having the faintest idea of where it will take them. Both approaches are explored in *Howdunit*, along with many other areas where there is room for divergent attitudes and approaches. To suggest

that one view is invariably 'right' and another is 'wrong' is
naive. Just as different criminals favour different m.o.s, so
different crime novelists follow different paths when creating
their mysteries. They also favour different types of crime fiction;
this book aims to show the rich potential of the genre. The
value of the *personal* views expressed by contributors lies in
the way they illuminate the pros and cons, the choices that
any writer needs to make. We don't offer the false comfort of
definitive answers where none exist, although there are also
areas of widespread consensus – for instance, that writers with
fertile imaginations can find ideas anywhere. The question for
any individual is ultimately: what works for you?

I'm the eighth and current President of the Club, and my
predecessors include such legendary figures as Chesterton,
Dorothy L. Sayers, and Agatha Christie. The Club has a rich
history, and I charted its early years in *The Golden Age of
Murder*; suffice it to say here that the Club is simply a social
association, a small dining club with membership by invitation.
It's very different from the Crime Writers' Association, a much
larger professional organization for anyone who has published
a crime book, together with associates involved in the business
of crime writing. The two organizations are not competitors
and they enjoy a warm relationship; the four most recent
presidents of the Club also chaired the CWA. Although the two
organizations' archives are distinct, together they comprise the
British Crime Writing Archives, which for the past few years
have been celebrated by an annual summer festival at
Gladstone's Library in north Wales.

In contrast to the position with the CWA, the number of
members of the Club has always been limited, and as an
organization that exists to have occasional dinners in London,
its membership is predominantly British. There are no formal
restrictions, and several Americans, including such contrasting
authors as John Dickson Carr and Patricia Highsmith, have
been members; so was the New Zealander Ngaio Marsh. The
general principle is that membership is for life, and in fact
Sayers had abandoned writing detective novels a decade before

she became the Club's third President. The enduring appeal of
the Club has much to do with its small size, and with the spirit
of collegiality between everyone who attends the dinners. From
the Club's inception, the list of eminent guest speakers at the
main autumn dinner, currently held at the Ritz, has been
impressive and eclectic.

Right from the start of the Club's existence, it has subsidized
its activities – well, the consumption of those splendid but
rather pricey dinners – by producing crime stories. The first
two joint ventures were collaborative cross-media mysteries
broadcast by the infant BBC and published serially in *The
Listener*, and on 23 July 1930 the Corporation also aired
'Plotting a Detective Story', a fifty-minute talk given by Berkeley
and Sayers. The audience was reckoned to exceed twelve million
people – a reach that, today, any prime-time British TV show
or indeed publisher would kill for.

These groundbreaking initiatives were rapidly followed by
the Club's first novel, *The Floating Admiral*. This joint effort
was concocted by no fewer twelve authors and boasted a preface
by Chesterton. Almost ninety years on, it remains in print, and
has recently been translated into several foreign languages.
Further innovative books followed over the years, including
stories in which Club members wrote about each other's detectives, a collection of true-crime essays, and a set of stories
about supposedly perfect crimes solved by a superintendent
from Scotland Yard. The Club's most recent publications are
The Sinking Admiral, a twenty-first-century homage to its
famous forerunner masterminded by Simon Brett, and a short
story collection, *Motives for Murder*.

From the 1930s until the post-war era, these publications
helped to keep the Club solvent and even enabled the hire of
a couple of rooms in Soho, where the Club's library was kept.
But, as with most small membership organizations, the Club
has never been flush with cash, and Sayers' correspondence
contains occasional outpourings of anguish about the parlous
state of its finances. During the 1940s, and occasionally in
succeeding decades, the Club's very survival has been uncertain.

The rented rooms are long gone, and so is the library. And the march of time prompts another question: in the twenty-first century, is there really any need for the Detection Club? How can it still have value and relevance in the era of social media and innumerable festivals, conventions and other opportunities for crime writers to get together with each other, as well as with fans?

My own, far from unbiased, opinion, is that the Club is such an agreeable institution, and so historically significant, that it deserves to be cherished. Quite apart from the convivial nature of the dinners, there is a growing interest in the heritage of crime fiction around the world, and the Club and its members have made a major contribution to that heritage. The Honkaku Mystery Writers of Japan is a club modelled on ours, and I've had the pleasure of meeting its President, while over the past three years alone, the Club's history has been discussed and debated at events in countries as diverse as Estonia, the United States, Iceland, Canada, Dubai, Spain, and China. During the past twelve months it has also been celebrated by a BBC radio play and a French graphic novel. So if one looks beyond the superficial anachronisms, the Club is as 'relevant' as ever.

The real test is whether the small band of members considers that the Club remains worthwhile. If any doubt existed, this project has laid it to rest. Any editor will tell you that it's one thing for seasoned authors to express interest in writing something and quite another to persuade them to produce it in a short space of time. My task was to approach busy authors with deadlines aplenty to plague their consciences, and also – because the project was a Club fundraiser in that fine tradition dating back to *The Floating Admiral* – to inveigle them into writing for free. All of us have a strong belief that writers should be properly valued and paid, now more than ever, with widespread research suggesting that literary incomes are in decline around the world (something that the aspiring author needs to keep in mind). But as the response to *Howdunit* shows, writers are also warm and generous people, and members of the Detection Club want it to continue to thrive.

Bestselling superstars showed themselves willing to put aside their current work-in-progress to contribute to this book. Even veteran members who hadn't written a novel for years proved eager to participate. I found it thrilling to receive one manuscript after another and to marvel at the musings on so many different aspects of our craft. Members told me they were happy to contribute, first because of their enthusiasm for the Club, and secondly because they felt they had something worth saying about aspects of the writing process and the crime writer's life.

The aim was not merely to produce a snapshot of the state of play in contemporary crime writing. Including historical material and illustrations, even cartoons, gives the book an added texture, highlighting changing fashions as well as truths about writing that are timeless. Families and estates of deceased contributors, aware of the strength of the members' attachment to the Club, were remarkably supportive. The pieces by former members are usually shorter than those by current members, and I've written brief commentaries to link many of the contributions and to set certain pieces in context. Among other things, I hope readers will be tempted to read the books of contributors whose work they haven't previously encountered.

Women writers have always played a central role in the Detection Club. Agatha Christie wasn't by nature a 'joiner', but she became a member of the committee, and after Sayers' death she held the Presidency for the rest of her life. In the early days, Secretaries of the Club included Lucy Malleson, who wrote as Anne Meredith and Anthony Gilbert, and Carol Rivett, alias E. C. R. Lorac; their more recent successors have included Mary Kelly and Jessica Mann. In the early years of the twenty-first century, distinguished writers such as P. D. James and Margaret Yorke continued to be prominent and loyal members who regularly attended the dinners, and the tradition continues to this day. So it seemed fitting for Liza Cody to contribute thoughts about the female perspective in crime fiction.

I aimed to edit the contributions as lightly as possible, despite inevitable overlaps and constraints of space. Of course, in terms of subject matter, we wanted to round up the usual suspects – plotting, people, and place – but also to do much more. So, to take two examples out of many, we have Mark Billingham reflecting on the nexus between stand-up comedy and suspenseful fiction, and Stella Duffy drawing on her experience in the theatre to suggest ways in which writers can learn from the art of improvisation.

Without a huge amount of goodwill on the part of many people and organizations, *Howdunit* could never have come into existence. I'm grateful to everyone who has helped me to put the book together, not least those who have tracked down or helped me to assemble potential contributions, including Nigel Moss, John Curran, Tony Medawar, James Hallgate, Lady Denham, Denis Kendal, the numerous literary agents who have assisted in my efforts to secure the rights and the material, not least Georgia Glover of David Higham, the Club's own agent, and those who have contributed to the editorial process, including Mike Lewin, Dea Parkin and John Garth. David Brawn has proved (once again) to be a superb editor, and I greatly appreciate the support of David and his colleagues at HarperCollins who have worked on this book. Above all, my heartfelt thanks go to Len Deighton and my other friends and colleagues within the Detection Club for their kindness and generosity in making sure that the idea of this book became an exciting reality.

Martin Edwards

Motives

What is the value of crime fiction? Why bother to write it or read it? These old questions continue to be asked. Gilbert Keith Chesterton, who became the first President of the Detection Club, provided some answers. 'The Value of Detective Stories', published in *The Speaker* on 21 June 1901, from which this extract is taken, was subsequently retitled 'A Defence of Detective Stories' and is the first significant essay extolling the merits of the genre.

The Value of Detective Fiction
G. K. Chesterton

The first essential value of the detective story lies in this, that it is the earliest and only form of popular literature in which is expressed some sense of the poetry of modern life. Men lived among mighty mountains and eternal forests for ages before they realized that they were poetical; it may reasonably be inferred that some of our descendants may see the chimney-pots as rich a purple as the mountain-peaks, and find the lamp-posts as old and natural as the trees. Of this realization of a great city itself as something wild and obvious the detective story is certainly the *Iliad*.

No one can have failed to notice that in these stories the hero or the investigator crosses London with something of the loneliness and liberty of a prince in a tale of elfland, that in the course of that incalculable journey the casual omnibus assumes the primal colours of a fairy ship. The lights of the city begin to glow like innumerable goblin eyes, since they are the guardians of some secret, however crude, which the writer knows and the reader does not. Every twist of the road is like a finger pointing to it; every fantastic skyline of chimney-pots seems wildly and derisively signalling the meaning of the mystery.

Chesterton's argument about the role of the lonely urban detective has often been echoed or refashioned, with the gumshoe going down the mean streets most famously compared – by Raymond Chandler in 'The Simple Art of Murder' – to a knight errant.

Despite Chesterton's eloquence, scepticism about the detective story persisted. In 1924, Richard Austin Freeman, pioneering creator of the scientific detective Dr John Thorndyke and later a founder member of the Detection Club (and an author Chandler described as 'a wonderful performer') wrote a long essay in *The Nineteenth Century and After* to defend his craft. Here is an extract.

The Art of the Detective Story

R. Austin Freeman

The status in the world of letters of that type of fiction which finds its principal motive in the unravelment of crimes or similar intricate mysteries presents certain anomalies. By the critic and the professedly literary person the detective story – to adopt the unprepossessing name by which this class of fiction is now universally known – is apt to be dismissed contemptuously as outside the pale of literature, to be conceived of as a type of work produced by half-educated and wholly incompetent writers for consumption by office boys, factory girls, and other persons devoid of culture and literary taste.

That such works are produced by such writers for such readers is an undeniable truth; but in mere badness of quality the detective story holds no monopoly. By similar writers and for similar readers there are produced love stories, romances, and even historical tales of no better quality. But there is this difference: that, whereas the place in literature of the love story or the romance has been determined by the consideration of the masterpieces of each type, the detective story appears to have been judged by its failures. The status of the whole class has been fixed by an estimate formed from inferior samples.

What is the explanation of this discrepancy? Why is it that, whereas a bad love story or romance is condemned merely on its merits as a defective specimen of a respectable class, a detective story is apt to be condemned without trial in virtue of some sort of assumed original sin? The assumption as to the class of reader is manifestly untrue. There is no type of fiction that is more universally popular than the detective story . . .

This being the case, I again ask for an explanation of the contempt in which the whole genus of detective fiction is held by the professedly literary. Clearly, a form of literature which

4

Clues & evidence.

Envelope found in pocket. Given to Brodribb (to compare with correspondence) who gives it to Thorndyke.

Finger prints. Post Mark. Handwriting (a forgery of David's) with some foreign character. Greasy fingermarks. Character of envelope. (Jasper might find an envelope & take it to carry some small object from house from wh. he escaped).

_____

Herring scales found on body, in mouth, stomach & lungs. Also salt & nitre, & minute shred of cabbage.

Body found on Tuesday morning. Proved not to have been there on Sunday night. But Brodribb received sealed letter on Monday morning. It was ~~Thursday~~ posted (post mark) on Saturday evening.

_____

Rope tied to beam with fisherman's bend: noose with running bowline. Rope is marine type — deep-sea lead line or similar type. Foreign in origin: might be a left-handed rope. Knot at back of neck.

This rope identical with that wh. bound Stella & wh. Jasper brought away with him & kept.

over

An extract from Richard Austin Freeman's notebook detailing 'Clues & evidence' in the novel he was planning, Pontifex, Son and Thorndyke.

arouses the enthusiasm of men of intellect and culture can be
affected by no inherently base quality. It cannot be foolish,
and is unlikely to be immoral. As a matter of fact, it is neither.
The explanation is probably to be found in the great proportion of failures; in the tendency of the tyro and the amateur
perversely to adopt this difficult and intricate form for their
'prentice efforts; in the crude literary technique often associated with otherwise satisfactory productions; and perhaps in
the falling off in quality of the work of regular novelists when
they experiment in this department of fiction, to which they
may be adapted neither by temperament nor by training.

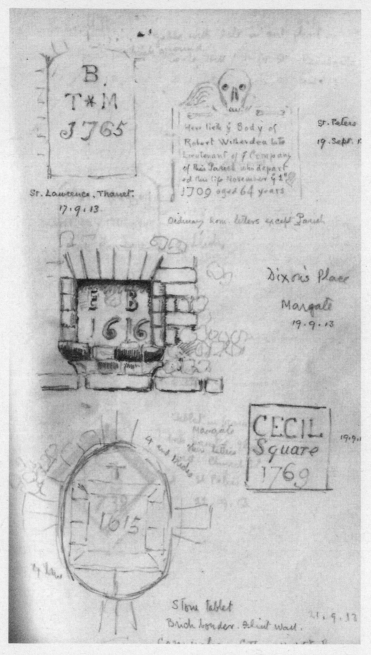

Richard Austin Freeman was a capable amateur artist and kept a sketchbook, which includes several pages like these of inscriptions on ancient gravestones.

An illustration of this type appears in Dr Thorndyke Intervenes
*and adds interest to a mystery about inheritance
and a missing body.*

Despite the flood of high-calibre crime novels over the years, some
people continue to express reservations about the genre, frequently
confusing their personal reading preferences with objective arguments about literary merit.

John Bingham, a Detection Club author who was also a spy (said
to have been used by his colleague John Le Carré as a model for
George Smiley) wrote a full-page article for the *TV Times* in the
summer of 1958 headed 'A Thriller a Day Keeps Crime at Bay'. He
highlighted what he saw as the sociological value of crime fiction,
suggesting that it may deter criminals, by showing the consequences
of law-breaking, and may help to recruit people to the police
(although several of Bingham's finest novels were notable for the
ruthless interrogations of innocent suspects; so much so that in
Murder Plan Six, he felt impelled to write a preface denying that
he was 'anti-police').

H. R. F. Keating, sixth President of the Club, said in *Writing Crime
Fiction* that the genre 'puts its reader first, not the writer' whilst
contending that, quite apart from its value as entertainment, 'the
crime story can, to a small extent or to quite a large extent, do what
the pure novel does. It can make a contemporary map for its readers
out of the chaos of their surroundings.'

In modern times, Ian Rankin has been a powerful and persuasive
advocate of the genre's quality and importance. In 1999, he gave a
lecture in Japan under the aegis of the British Council arguing that
crime fiction has real value. Developing and updating those arguments in this essay, he makes a formidable case.

Why Crime Fiction Is Good for You

Ian Rankin

Why is crime fiction good for you? Well, it is about tragedy and our emotional responses to tragedy. It is also about moral choices and questions. It can be utterly serious in intent, yet still entertaining. It is still occasionally dismissed by the literary establishment as mere genre fiction – fine if you need something to pass the time, but not quite important enough to merit serious study. Yet ironically many literary novels (past and present) use the exact same tropes as crime fiction.

In the widest sense, of course, all *fiction* is good for you. It relaxes and entertains; it moves the reader from his or her own consciousness into that of other people in what can often be very different cultures and circumstances. In doing so it broadens our appreciation of human nature and the world around us. At some point in history, however, genre fiction became separated from literary or mainstream fiction, which are apparently more 'serious' in their approaches and ambitions. Yet it can be argued that early pulp fiction, such as that published in cheap popular magazines by the likes of Raymond Chandler and Dashiell Hammett, is the child of the serials and stories written by Charles Dickens, Arthur Conan Doyle and others; stories which in their day were exemplars of mass entertainment, even sensationalist, like modern-day TV soaps, but are now regarded as literature. Dickens in his own day was not regarded as a particularly worthy writer; rather, he was a forerunner of the modern airport bestseller. This gives me hope that many of today's crime and thriller writers will in the future come to be regarded as powerful moralists and stylists as well as tellers of fascinating tales.

If we examine the canon of Western literature, especially the novel, we find that the main ingredients of crime fiction – violence, sudden reversals, mystery, deception, moral dilemmas and so on – can be found everywhere, from the Greek epics to contemporary Booker Prize winners. Ask yourself what keeps you reading a particular novel. It is the need to know what happens next. Novels need to pose questions and problems which will be resolved only if the reader keeps reading. If an author makes us curious, we will keep turning the pages. In a sense therefore all readers are detectives, and the crime novel merely codifies this essential aspect of the pleasure of reading.

The great crime writer and critic Julian Symons (one-time President of the Detection Club) once described the folk tale Little Red Riding Hood as an interesting case of disguise and attempted murder. Murder, suspense and betrayal can be found throughout folk literature and in the classic texts of most if not all civilizations – from *The Odyssey* through *Hamlet* and *King Lear* to the novels of Ruth Rendell and P. D. James. The poet and detective novelist C. Day-Lewis thought of the whodunit specifically as a twentieth-century form of folk tale, while for his fellow poet W. H. Auden the classical detective story seemed an allegory of the 'death' of happiness. In real life, we seldom know what specifically killed off our happiness, whereas in the novel the seemingly random nature of existence is given an explanation – in crime fiction, death never happens without good reason and the causes of death never go unexplained (and are seldom unpunished).

Auden of course was talking of the 'classical' English detective story. Things have been changing more recently, the crime novel becoming ever more elastic. Consider the various terms by which it is known: the crime novel, detective novel, whodunit, suspense novel, *roman noir*, hard-boiled, pulp, police procedural, mystery novel, domestic *noir*, Scandi *noir* . . . even tartan noir. The reason for this proliferation may lie in confusion about the basic identity of the crime novel. This is a genre after all that would seek to include everything from the most basic puzzle-style story up to the likes of Dostoevsky. P. D. James tried to have it both ways when she described a successfully realized crime novel as combining 'the old traditions of an exciting story and the satisfying exercise of rational deduction with the psychological subtleties and moral ambiguities of a good novel'. Certainly crime novels are intended to entertain. They are products of popular culture. As such they must turn a profit, for few institutions and publicly backed funders will subsidise them. Crime fiction may have literary aspirations, but its emphasis on entertainment ensures that these aspirations do not deter potential readers. Crime fiction is democratic in that it is accessible to all.

Before the Second World War, the crime novel in the UK reassured its readership that all would be well, that society might occasionally be shaken up (by some heinous crime such as murder) but that order would quickly be restored. A courteous and brilliant detective would bring elucidation and the guilty party or parties would be uncovered and sent for trial. The tight confines of this fictional universe, and the neat conclusions, provided pleasure to many but meant that the crime novel was considered as escapist literature, since real life seldom provided its own set of pat resolutions. In the United States, authors such as Raymond Chandler began to argue against such tidy (and mostly bloodless) confections. He wanted crime fiction to be a bit more cynical about human nature, creating a world of tarnished knights such as Philip Marlowe. Chandler sensed that what crime fiction really needed was a sense of the incomplete and of life's messy complexity. The reader should go to crime fiction to be challenged by these realities. Practitioners in the UK began to realize this, too – gritty urban settings competed with rural idylls; good did not always triumph over evil; evil couldn't always be explained away. In contemporary crime fiction the villains may escape justice altogether, or the reader may be invited to take sides with the criminal against the powers of law and order. There are even novels with no detectives and no mysteries, showing a world in which criminality, in the form of organized crime, operates openly and without apparent hindrance.

For many readers this came – and comes – as a refreshing change, because the crime novel has always been capable of so much more than simply telling a good story or playing an elaborate game with its audience. Crime writers throughout the world have known for years that the crime novel can be a perfect tool for the dissection of society. It's something I learned very early on in my Inspector Rebus novels. I wanted to explore the city of Edinburgh from top to bottom, but also wanted to use Edinburgh as a microcosm for the wider world. I wanted to discuss politics and economics and moral questions and the problems we all face as a society. I realized that my police detective gave me a sort of all-areas pass. He could visit the various seats of power but also investigate the worlds of the dispossessed and disenfranchised. This has allowed me to explore themes of racism and human trafficking, the drug trade, various political upheavals, changing social attitudes, the rise of new technologies, our increasingly surveillance-driven society and so forth, without my novels reading as tracts or treatises. The adventure, the thrill of the chase, underpins the whole, but the story is no longer 'just' about that chase.

In spite of its exaggerations and heightened effects, the contemporary crime novel often tells us more about the world around us than do literary novels, many of which can seem introspective or focused on a narrow remit (an individual life; or the lives of a small interconnected group). Crime fiction tackles big issues, from corporate corruption to child abuse, inviting its readers to consider why these crimes continue to affect us, while also warning those same readers of new types of crime – as evidenced by the rise of the crime novel where the internet and social media are seen as a potential source of malevolence. The shadowy figure who steps out of a darkened alley in front of us has been replaced by an equally shadowy figure who threatens us via our home computer or mobile phone.

Writers such as Val McDermid, Denise Mina, Sarah Hilary, Eva Dolan, Mark Billingham and Adrian McKinty challenge their readers with stories that seem torn from the pages of this week's newspapers and which make dramatic use of current technology, be it DNA analysis or CCTV. I'm not sure if they think of themselves as political writers, but there are certainly political elements to their themes and stories. These authors – and many others like them – see the roots of petty crime in abject poverty, in the current social problems of the UK. They also know how easily petty crime can escalate, and they often have a view to the larger (often invisible) crimes perpetrated by institutions and corporations. Their stories tend to be set in the urban here and now, allowing them to engage more readily with the world inhabited by their readers. Drug culture, youth problems and the alienation felt by many at the bottom of the pile are dealt with in their novels.

I chose Edinburgh as the setting for my books for similar reasons. It's a city that visitors feel they can get to know fairly quickly, being compact and on the surface safe and civilized, with a wealth of historic streets and artefacts. In fact, it can seem a single homogenous entity with a castle at its core. Some of this conceit was exploded by Irvine Welsh's novel *Trainspotting* – and more especially by the hugely successful film that came shortly after. In my own first novel *Knots and Crosses* a serial killer is stalking the Edinburgh of the mid–1980s, and locals gather together to share their astonishment and outrage – it's just not the sort of thing anyone associates with Edinburgh!

Except . . .

Well, the 25-year-old Ian Rankin who wrote that book had no grounding in the English whodunit. I had never read any Christie or Allingham or Sayers and had yet to discover Rendell and James. But I was doing a PhD on the novels of Muriel Spark, whose magnum opus, *The Prime of Miss Jean Brodie*, had taken me on an adventure into the world of the gothic, much of it Edinburgh-based and much of it grounded in reality. Miss Brodie tells us that she is descended from Deacon William Brodie, a noted gentleman. What she neglects to add is that William Brodie – a real-life historical figure – was a respected figure by day but a thief and rogue by night. He headed a gang which would break into homes, assaulting the unwary and stealing their valuables. Brodie was caught, tried and hanged – allegedly on a scaffold he had helped craft as Deacon of Wrights. Robert Louis Stevenson may have had Deacon Brodie's story in mind when he wrote *Dr Jekyll and Mr Hyde*, his short but potent novel focused on the question at the heart of all crime fiction – why do we humans continue throughout history to inflict terrible damage on each other? Stevenson chose (for whatever reason) to set his tale in London, but it is every bit as Scottish in its themes and tone as Spark's much later novel, and both books perhaps owe a debt to an earlier, lesser-known work, James Hogg's Edinburgh-based slice of psychological Grand Guignol, *Memoirs and Confessions of a Justified Sinner*. Just as Spark took me to Stevenson, so Stevenson led me to Hogg and his complex narrative concerning a young religious zealot who comes under the spell of a charismatic stranger; who convinces him that as a member of 'the elect' (and therefore bound for Heaven whatever he does on Earth) he should feel free to murder those he feels deserve it, including an elderly minister of the church and, eventually, his own brother.

We are never sure in Hogg's tale whether the charismatic stranger is a psychopath, the Devil incarnate, or a fever-dream conjured up by a religious maniac. This ambiguity is central to much of the best Scottish literature, along with an interest in the doppelgänger. All three books suggest that human beings have within them warring natures. Sometimes we're good, and sometimes bad. In my first Rebus novel I created an evil alter ego for the detective, in the shape of someone who had been almost like a brother but was now out to destroy him. I certainly had the battle between Jekyll and Hyde in mind as I planned the book. I even added clues that Rebus himself may be the serial killer terrorising Edinburgh. He suffers alcoholic blackouts and wakes in the morning unable to remember the night before, much as Jekyll does. In Rebus's second adventure, *Hide and Seek*, I even play with the name Hyde in the title. (The book was originally going to be called *Hyde and Seek*.)

Many of the best contemporary Scottish crime writers learned from the same books I did, their work owing as much to Hogg as to Christie or Chandler. But several of us also proclaim a debt to William McIlvanney, a literary novelist, poet and essayist who, in the late 1970s, created Jack Laidlaw, a tough, streetwise Glasgow detective with a penchant for philosophy. Those books emerged just as the Scottish novel was having fresh life breathed into it by the likes of James Kelman and Alasdair Gray, writers sustained by working-class city life and by the trials and vicissitudes of characters often not given a voice in literature. This is something I feel the Scottish crime novel has picked up on – giving a voice to the voiceless. Crime after all is more likely to strike those who have little or nothing than it is those who are protected by wealth and power.

The mechanics of the whodunit – its narrative conventions – do not really interest me as a writer. What interests me is the soul of the crime novel – what it tells us about ourselves and our society, what it is capable or uniquely qualified to discuss. My favourite crime novels tackle big issues, but always with reference to the effects of the investigation upon those doing the investigating and those affected by the crime, up to and including the initial victim. We are all inquisitive and curious animals, learning through questioning, and crime fiction touches this deep need both to ask the questions and (hopefully) to begin to touch on possible answers.

Crime fiction also enters dangerous territory – murder, rage, revenge – and so stirs up emotional responses we might not otherwise feel. Reading is not a passive experience in the way sitting through a film or TV show is. We watch violence on the screen, but seldom feel it in our heart. A well-executed narrative description can make us feel the pain of the sufferer, while also putting us inside the head of the inflicter. In a world made largely safe, crime fiction provides the sensation that we may be on the edge of danger. It heightens our basic survival instincts and gives us a primal reminder of the cave and the predator. And yet we read these books in our largely murder-free communities. There is little demand for crime fiction in a war zone. Once the conflict has died down, the crime fiction appears, to try to explain to us what just happened. You see this right now in Ireland, in the brilliant novels of Adrian McKinty, Stuart Neville, Brian McGilloway and many others. And in Africa, in everyone from Deon Meyer to Oyinkan Braithwaite. Just as the Scandinavian crime novel tells us so much about the social issues of that region, so writers in India such as Anita Nair are beginning to use the whodunit to explore issues such as child exploitation and sexual identity.

It seems to me there's not much that is out of bounds to the crime novel, which is perhaps fitting, since the spirit of the crime novel is anarchic. We are absurdist writers, writing in the realms of satire and irony, from the 'cosier' end of the spectrum (owing much to Jane Austen, as realized by authors such as Reginald Hill, P. D. James and Val McDermid) to the harsher, derisive ironies and dark exaggerations of a Derek Raymond, Philip Kerr or David Peace. In satire, prevailing vices and follies are held up to ridicule, and the crime novel is the perfect vehicle for this, dealing as it does with larger-than-life characters whose weaknesses will soon be revealed, all set in a society largely ill at ease with itself. Of course, this also makes the crime novel ripe for satirizing, and plenty of authors have had fun deconstructing the likes of Hercule Poirot or the hard-boiled gumshoe. Michael Dibdin's sublime *The Dying of the Light* comes to mind, as does Tom Stoppard's clever stage comedy *The Real Inspector Hound*. More recently, Anthony Horowitz (*The Magpie Murders*; *The Word Is Murder*) and Steve Cavanagh (*Twisted*) have played with the crime novelist as anti-hero. Literary authors, too, have been attracted to the crime genre down the ages, either by plundering or paying homage. Umberto Eco's *The Name of the Rose* is a favourite – the monk/detective's name is even William of Baskerville! Muriel Spark turns the conventions of crime fiction on their head in her short, shocking novel *The Driver's Seat*, which was itself influenced by the *nouveau roman*, especially in the hands of Alain Robbe-Grillet, several of whose experimental novels were shaped as whodunits. More recent literary successes include Eleanor Catton's Booker-winning *The Luminaries*, which has a murder mystery as its narrative engine. Nor is children's fiction immune. J. K. Rowling's Harry Potter novels are constructed as traditional whodunits, full of untrustworthy characters, reversals, mysteries, twists and revelations. Little surprise that Rowling, post-Potter, has gone on to fresh success as a writer of crime novels for adults.

The whodunit is, however, the broadest possible church, able to embrace the macho blood-and-guts nihilism of a James Ellroy and the gentle humanity of Alexander McCall Smith's Ramotswe stories. In the stories of the past, however, there was a tendency for the irruption of violence to lead to resolution (the unmasking of the culprit) and a return to the status quo. These days, it is harder to imagine everything settling back to 'normal' after an extreme act. Extremism has visited places we never imagined it would. Murderous acts seem to happen out of the blue – rare though they still are. The murder mystery these days seldom ignores this. As Muriel Spark herself once said, 'We should know ourselves better by now than to be under the illusion that we are all essentially aspiring, affectionate and loving creatures. We do have these qualities, but we are aggressive too.'

In dealing with these aggressive qualities in the human animal, crime fiction provides both a salutary warning and the catharsis common to all good drama. The tight three-act structure of the crime novel (crime–investigation–resolution) pays tribute to the fact that we humans hunger for form and a sense of closure. Yet within those confines all human life plays out. We readers can explore cultures of the past, present and (very occasionally) future. We can visit countries and regions new to us and see the world through the consciousnesses of myriad others. We can have a multitude of adventures, experiencing the danger of chaos and coming face to face with the ugliest manifestations of evil and depravity as we dice with danger and the threat of imminent demise. And, in the end, haven't we sentient creatures always been obsessed with death? It's coming for all of us in some shape or form. Crime fiction gives us a way of exploring some of the implications, while still managing to have fun in the process.

So you see, crime fiction really *is* good for you.

From Ian Rankin's belief in the soul of the crime novel, it's a natural step to consider the moral energy and compass of the genre, subjects that have preoccupied members of the Detection Club from the days of Chesterton and Ronald Knox to the present. James Runcie, son of a former Archbishop of Canterbury, has (like Chesterton) not merely created a hugely popular priest detective but also thought deeply about the implications of his writing.

Why Do It?

James Runcie

Since Aristotle there have been numerous attempts to provide a rulebook for crime writing. Most famously, Ronald Knox wrote his famous 'Ten Commandments', which recommended no twins, no undiscovered poisons, no supernatural agencies and no Chinamen. Dorothy L. Sayers wrote a historical survey in her introduction to *The Omnibus of Crime* published in 1928, outlining potential murders and possible plots: 'Here is a brief selection of handy short cuts to the grave. Poisoned tooth stoppings; shaving brushes inoculated with dread diseases; poisoned boiled eggs (a bright thought); poison gas; a cat with poisoned claws; poisoned mattresses; knives dropped through the ceiling; stabbing with a sharp icicle' (that melts – I recently noted melting ice in the drama series *Death in Paradise* on BBC One); 'electrocution by telephone; biting by plague-rats and typhoid carrying lice; boiling lead in the ears . . . air-bubbles injected into the arteries; explosion of a gigantic "Prince Rupert's drop" (that's molten glass dropped into cold water – a swimming pool might be ideal); frightening to death; hanging head downwards; freezing to atoms in liquid air; hypodermic injections shot from air-guns; exposure, while insensible, to extreme cold; guns concealed in cameras; a thermometer which explodes a bomb when the temperature of the room reaches a certain height; and so forth . . .'

Then, crucially, she adds, 'There certainly does seem a possibility that the detective story will some time come to an end, simply because the public will have learnt all the tricks. But it has probably many years to go yet, and in the meantime a new and less rigid formula will probably have developed, linking it more closely to the novel of manners and separating it more widely from the novel of adventure.'

Here, I think, she understands that what matters is not so much plot, but character. Crime fiction cannot work if we do not care about the people involved. The story has to be more than a puzzle. It can't just be a conjuring trick with people's lives, no matter how fictional they all are.

It's my belief that we use crime writing to test the limits of our capacity for good and evil and to make sense of the world – and, as the writer of *The Grantchester Mysteries*, I think we turn to crime to contemplate our own mortality.

Here's a thought . . .

One hundred years ago, in the United Kingdom, people used to recite the Book of Common Prayer at least twice a day, at morning and night.

Good Lord, deliver us from lightning and tempest, from plague, pestilence and famine; from battle and murder, and from sudden death.

Now, in a less Christian country, we think about death through crime writing. This has become the secular space in which we address our deepest fears and anxieties and, at the same time, we look for the consolation, justice and closure that is so often found wanting in real life.

As a result, I think crime writing has to be more than entertainment. It needs moral energy.

Think of Dostoevsky's *Crime and Punishment*. Raskolnikov's killing of both the old landlady, Alyona, and then her sister, Lizaveta, provokes the questions: How much is it true that a murder can be justified? Can it ever be explained or excused by the argument that the murderer claims he was possessed

by the devil? Can some individuals transcend cultural norms
or contemporary ethics? Is it true that 'without God everything
is permitted'? Should confession and regret lead to a lighter
sentence? Can a criminal ever truly repent of his crimes? Can
a Christian?

For Christians the answer is 'Yes', but this forgiveness is
dependent on the sincerity of penitence – and who, other than
God, is to judge that?

The issues can prove so complex and disturbing that many
writers bring the light of humour in to alleviate this moral
darkness – even Dostoevsky does it. Think of the cynical giggling
detective Porfiry Petrovich or Sonya's dreadful old drunk father
Marmeladov. They are the kind of figures you might find in
Dickens; and it could be argued that *Oliver Twist* is a crime
novel. Oliver is brought up 'in care' and is frequently kidnapped
and kept in a place against his will. Fagin runs a criminal
gang. Nancy is in an abusive relationship. Bill Sikes is a
murderer. Monks dies in prison. Fagin is sent to the gallows.
It's a crime novel, a satire and a grim fairy tale all in one; but
as with so much great fiction, the writer tests the characters
by exposing them to crime, malpractice and misadventure.

Crime writing, if it is to be any good, is necessarily ethical.
My own books are moral fables. You could even argue that
they are sermons dressed up as fiction and social history. My
hero, Canon Sidney Chambers, does not simply investigate. He
considers the moral implications of crime and its effect on its
victims. While keen to establish who dunnit, Sidney looks at
the aftermath as much as the felony itself, regarding all those
involved with compassion, bemusement and, sometimes, even
comic detachment. His task is fiercely Christian. The whydunit.
Hate the sin but love the sinner. There are traditional crime
motifs in the stories, plot turns, twists, and heroes who turn
out to be villains. There are several love interests. And while
there are also jokes in these mysteries, there is also a teasing
and tolerant humanity.

By the end of the series, I hope to have written a loving
portrayal of a man who moves between the world of the spirit

and the all-too-mortal world of the flesh, bicycling from Grantchester to Cambridge and back, attempting to love the unloveable, forgive the sinner, and lead a decent, good life.

I believe that detective fiction has to have this moral purpose and that, however lightly it is done, it should also enable people to think more deeply about the world and what matters within it. No crime is ever cosy. All good writing has to count. As Dorothy L. Sayers observed, 'The only Christian work is good work, well done.'

We write, and we read, not just to be entertained, but in order to work out who we are and how we might live a better and more meaningful existence on this frail earth. And then, in confronting death imaginatively and unflinchingly, we learn to contemplate what we believe in, what we value and what we cherish.

It should make us all the more glad to be alive.

Frances Fyfield's background is in the law rather than the church, and she has created two series characters, Helen West and Sarah Fortune, who are lawyers. Like her friend the late P. D. James, she is interested in detective fiction's moral dimension, and the calibre of her books prompted Ian Rankin to say, 'Her knowledge of the workings of the human mind – or more correctly the soul – is second to none.'

The Moral Compass of the Crime Novel

Frances Fyfield

Murder most foul! Read all about it! Distract yourself from daily boredom by reading of people whose lives are infinitely more dramatic and dangerous than your own.

The Victorians loved a good murder and the love of the reportage of same marks the beginning of this popular fiction. Read all about it, the more brutal the better. Revel in repugnance of dreadful deeds and personal tragedies and let the crime writers make money out of it. Is this really a high calling, or a base occupation? Is it exploitative, rather like being a salaried voyeur?

Once, when I was working in a legal office, a senior colleague came into my room and slammed one of my books down on the desk. 'Filth!' he roared. 'Absolute filth!' Fact is, some regard the fictionalization of murder as dirty work, while the majority of readers know better. Murder, that subject of universal fascination as being ranked the most abhorrent of crimes (I don't always agree with that; think there could be worse) is the best subject you could ever get for a novel. The crime novel explores extreme emotions, the root causes and the effects of untimely death. It reflects its own society, and in the case of historical crime fiction, other societies. There is nothing wrong with murder as entertainment. P. D. James, writing about Dorothy L. Sayers, said of her, 'She wrote to entertain and make money; neither is an ignoble aim.'

You may as well say, don't write about war, or anything involving pain. When P. D. James (my role model in all things) wrote and talked about the morality of writing about murder as a subject, she was never ambivalent. You wrote the truth was all; you wrote a story in which moral dilemmas were paramount, so that the morality of the thing was implicit in the text. In other words, she wrote about characters who made a choice either to kill or to engineer the death of another. With her characters, there had to be a choice. Maybe the decision to do it seemed irreversible at the time, because of the imperatives of revenge, survival, reputation, jealousy; a whole range of motives that lead to eradication by homicide as the only solution for the perpetrator. When really, with her characters, there was always another choice, i.e. to refrain and . . . take the consequences, however dire they might be. The worst consequence of all was to go ahead, because as P. D. James said in so many words, in the act of taking life, the thinking murderer is changed. He or she remains damned, haunted, guilty, unloved, on the run and lonely. Murder is akin to suicide.

Unless the perpetrator happens to be psychopathic, with no emotions on the normal register, who likes pulling wings off things and killing for fun. His choices are limited: his capacity for regret no more than damage limitation and evasion. An all-too-convenient device in a crime novel, but not, to my mind, nearly as interesting as the examination of choice and regret.

The crime novel always has a moral compass. It cannot be self-indulgent: the rule is, tell the story, and above all, add more than a dash of pity.

P. D. James wrote about choice and consequences; about retribution, revenge and the enduring power of love. She said in her memoir, 'The intention of any novelist must surely be to make that straight avenue to the human heart . . . every novelist writes what he or she needs to write, a subconscious compulsion to express and explain his unique view of reality.'

P. D. James again: 'The crime novelist needs to deal with the atavistic fear of death, to exorcize the terror of violence and to restore at least fictional peace and tranquillity after the disruptive terror of murder, and to affirm the sanctity of human life, and the possibility of justice, even if it is only the fallible justice of men.'

Most writers do not make a conscious decision, moral or otherwise, to write about crime. The subject matter chooses them. If you are going to write, write about what fascinates you, a matter of taste and compulsion. P. D. James never considered writing any other kind of novel than the detective kind and this was not because her career in forensic science gave her a taste for death, but because she saw the detective/ crime novel as the very best of all vehicles to write a good, strong novel about human passions. Of all writers, she is the most steeped in English Literature and the most rooted in Samuel Johnson, Austen, the Book of Common Prayer and more. And yet she wrote crime novels. She did not write romantic fiction, poetry, or novels of espionage, because murder chose her.

Murder chose me. I did not choose to write about crime, although I chose to write. During my day job which featured homicide on paper, I moonlighted with short stories of a romantic nature. In which boy and girl take a walk on the cliff path of an evening, hand in hand, happily contemplating the pretty sunset of their future. Only I could not let them do it; the pen failed. They argue; he pushes her over, and she falls, she falls, she falls.

I had sat through several trials of carefully prepared and honestly compiled evidence, only to conclude that facts alone don't do it. At the end of it all a compilation of facts and witness statements will not tell you exactly what went on that fateful night. I wanted to bring order into chaos and fill in the gaps that evidence alone cannot fulfil. Only imagination and putting yourself in the shoes of another can do that. Also, I wanted to write about good people as well as bad. I think the crime novel has to acknowledge and celebrate goodness as well as badness, and always allow for the possibility of redemption. Because good people outnumber the bad by a long, long way. Only problem is, they have the inhibitions of decency, whereas evil has none. Says Raymond Chandler, 'Down these mean streets a man must go who is not himself mean.'

There are no rules. The only moral compass is honesty, writing to the best of your ability.

A straight avenue to the heart.

Beginning

Deciding to write a crime story is one thing. To make a start and then keep going is quite another. Tackling the blank page demands drive and determination. How to banish the self-doubts and maintain confidence? Or, as Peter James puts it, to keep the dream?

Motivation

Peter James

One writer asks the other, 'What are you up to these days?'

He replies, 'I'm writing a novel.'

The first one says, 'Neither am I.'

The easiest thing in the world for a writer to do is to not write. Most novelists I've ever talked to could procrastinate for England. I'm just as much a culprit – I could captain the British Olympic Procrastination Team. Our motto would be *Anything but writing!*

Social media has been a wonderful boon for all of us procrastinators. We can avoid getting those first words down by checking email, Twitter, Facebook, Instagram, LinkedIn, whatever. When we've exhausted that, it's time to let the dogs out again. Then make a cup of coffee. Next we remember something we need to order on Amazon. Then with a flash of guilt, we realize we forgot to call an old friend back two days ago. We know she'll chat for ages, but get it out the way, and afterwards we'll have a clear morning for writing. Or what's left of the morning. Ooops, what's that van pulling up outside? Aha, the plumber! Have to go down and let him in, make him a cuppa, find some biscuits . . .

But at the end of the day there is no escaping that if we want to make a living as authors, then we need to write. A mantra that always spurs me on is *You cannot edit a blank page.* It's a sign that all of us should have on our desks. But that business of getting started in the morning is always hard. Graham Greene, one of my favourite authors, had a neat solution to this issue: he would always stop writing in the middle of a sentence. That way, his first task the next the morning was to finish the sentence – and it got him straight back into the flow.

It may not sound it, but I do actually love writing, although it took me years of perseverance before I could make a living from it, and during all that time I had to do a day job. My first three novels were never published (luckily, in retrospect!) My next three, not very good spy thrillers, were published but sold a negligible amount of copies – around 1,800 in hardback and 3,000 in paperback. But I kept going because I believed in myself. I changed direction, wrote two more novels, one a kidnap story and one a political assassination which were never published. Then, with my ninth novel *Possession,* a supernatural thriller, I struck lucky. Every major British publisher bid for the book and it was auctioned around the world, going into twenty-three languages. Finally, twenty-one years after I had sat down to type the first line of my first novel, I was able to actually make a living as an author.

Possession hit number two on the bestseller lists. But it was to be another fourteen novels and twenty years before I finally achieved my dream of hitting that coveted Sunday Times number one spot.

I'm seldom happier than when I'm hammering away at my keyboard and the story is flowing. I especially love the satisfaction of coming up with an inventive description for something, or a character I'm pleased with, or a plot twist that makes me punch the air with excitement. But it's not been easy and writing never is. The hours are long and often lonely, and when I've finished I'm a bag of nerves waiting for my agent and my editor's reactions – and then, much later, the reactions of my readers. Those nervous peeps at Amazon to see how the star ratings are going. Followed by an anxious wait for the first chart news . . . Plus the knowledge that I'm on a treadmill to turn out a new book every year – and my one golden rule is that with each new novel I want to raise the bar.

So, what is my motivation? Simple. First and foremost, it is the way I know best how to make a living. And that I want to do my best to try to please my loyal readers by making each book I write better than the last. I could list a dozen other factors, such as getting even with teachers at school who never thought I would amount to anything. Getting my revenge on the bullies who tormented me at school. A sense that I have something to say. A mission to try to understand human nature and why people do the things that they do. It is all of these and more. But at the end of the day my wife and I need food on our table and our animals need food in their bowls.

The late, odious film director Michael Winner was once asked by a precious actor, whom he had instructed to walk down a street, what exactly his motivation was in walking down the street. Displaying all his normal charm, Winner bellowed at him, 'You're walking down that street because I'm fucking paying you to walk down that street!'

Oscar Wilde, another writer whose work I love and admire, lamented on his deathbed, 'I've lived beyond my means so I suppose I will have to die beyond my means.' His drive to produce his great work was produced largely from his need to make money. He used his gruelling American lecture tours to help boost his sales there, and once famously said, 'Of course, if one had the money to go to America, one would not go.'

Helping his nation to win the Second World War did little to help Sir Winston Churchill's bank account. Having financially stretched himself buying his beloved country estate, Chartwell, much later he began writing the first of his six-volume opus, *The Second World War*, because he needed the money.

In 1974, scammed out of everything he had by a Ponzi scheme and left deeply in debt, Jeffery Archer penned *Not A Penny More, Not A Penny Less* in a last-ditch attempt to stave off bankruptcy. It worked, launching a career that would make him one of the richest novelists on the planet.

It is pretty simple. If you are a professional author, money is going to be pretty high up your motivation list. Over the years I've met a number of people who told me they have *writers' block*. But I cannot remember a single author who writes for a living ever telling me that. What other profession complains of block – other than perhaps plumbers? You don't hear of solicitors complaining they have *solicitors' block*, or taxi drivers saying they have *cab drivers' block*, or accountants having *accountants' block*.

I can't imagine any professional author I know saying to his or her family, 'Sorry everyone, I have writer's block, I'm afraid there's no food today.'

Sure, writing isn't easy – if it was, everyone would be doing it. As it is, a great number of people do, mistakenly, think it's a doddle. Margaret Atwood tells of the time she was at a cocktail party and had a *what-do-you-do-what-do-you-do* conversation with a rather pompous man. In response to her question he said, 'I'm a brain surgeon. What do you do?'

When she replied that she was an author, he immediately responded, somewhat arrogantly, 'Actually I'm planning to write a novel when I retire.'

'How very interesting,' Atwood retorted. 'Because when I retire, I'm planning to be a brain surgeon.'

I often wonder, did he ever write that novel? And if he did, was it published? I'm doubtful of both, for one simple reason: lack of motivation. As a successful brain surgeon he was

probably wealthy, living a nice lifestyle. In his mid-sixties, was
he seriously going to lock himself away in his study for months
and months of hard grind, trying to forge a whole new career,
then go on the road and engage in social media? And then
spend the next ten years writing more books to try to build
his name? I doubt it, because I just don't think he would have
had that crucial motivation.

Thirty-five novels on, I still get a huge buzz out of the page
proofs arriving. Out of seeing my publisher's first cover ideas.
It was a dream when I first began writing that one day I would
see a copy of my book on an airport bookshelf. Now that
dream comes true pretty much every time I enter an airport
bookstore. I know I've been lucky, but I also I know how easy
it is for an author's sales to slide if they don't keep up their
standards. I guess my biggest motivation of all today is to keep
that dream.

One question facing all writers is: how do I make a living? For
anyone who isn't independently wealthy, the challenge is to strike
a balance between time spent writing, often with little or no immediate financial reward, and working to put bread on the table.

Many people dream of becoming full-time writers. Research
undertaken in recent years, most notably by the Society of Authors,
is discouraging: authors' earnings seem, in broad general terms, to
be low and in steady decline. And even if giving up the day job
were feasible, would it be such a good idea?

Not according to Celia Fremlin, a Detection Club member who
coped with demanding domestic commitments while pursuing a
successful career as a writer. On her family website is a letter she
sent in 1984, in which she said, 'The first bit of advice I'd give to
anyone aspiring to be a writer is to start by deciding what *else*
he/she is going to be? It always saddens me to hear a talented
young person saying: "The only thing I want to do is to write"

– because this is virtually a guarantee that this is just the one thing they *won't* do.

'Writing (I'm talking here about fiction, of course – text-books and such are another matter) is, and must be, an off-shoot, an out-growth, of a full and interesting life, lived among all sorts of tiresome and uncongenial people, and beset by all the problems, difficulties, pressures and pre-occupations that real living involves. The best writing is, and always has been, squeezed out somehow from the turmoil of a demanding and absorbing life – happy or miserable, in sickness or in health, loved or hated – it doesn't matter, so long as you are right there, in the thick of it.

'Peace and quiet is fatal. Tuck yourself away in a country cottage, with a private income and freedom from all interruptions and distractions – and you've had it! Sorry, but you have!'

So how to get started? Janet Laurence is the author of, in addition to a variety of novels with contemporary and historical backgrounds, *Writing Crime Fiction*; in an introduction to the book, Val McDermid said it 'will teach you to flex your writing muscles . . .and offers guidance on developing your own voice so that you can tell the stories that clamour in your heart and your head.' Here are Janet's thoughts about how to get started.

Getting Started

Janet Laurence

You may have an investigative character or a fiendishly clever way of disposing of someone buzzing around your brain. If this is the case, what are you waiting for?

Maybe you enjoy reading crime novels and feel that you could write one as good if not better than the ones you have come across. That is how Colin Dexter started during a wet holiday in Wales. His chosen setting was Oxford, a city he knew very well. The outcome was *Last Bus to Woodstock*, which introduced Inspector Morse and Sergeant Lewis. The rest is history. All you need is the right idea.

Ideas are everywhere, you only need to open your mind to the possibilities. Read the newspapers, browse the library, listen to people talking, in the train, in the office, at social gatherings; there will be stories that can form the basis of a crime novel. Look for motives, methods, and how crimes are solved. Do beware, though, of opening yourself to being sued through not disguising the source of your plot and characters.

The best crime novels provide characters that grab the reader and drive the story. They need to have attractive qualities but also flaws. Think about your friends, what makes you like them enough to forgive their drawbacks? Who are the people you meet or read about in your daily life that you remember and why? We are not talking background or appearance here, but inbred qualities. You need characters who will behave in ways that will take your plot in interesting directions and that the reader will enjoy spending time with. The investigator you create, whether a member of the CID murder squad, a forensic pathologist, or someone unofficial, needs to be interested in the human psyche, someone who can explore questionable situations and puzzle out unexpected answers.

There must be suspects with a motive for murder, one of whom actually is the murderer and must occupy a reasonable space in the action. No bringing in the culprit just before the end. Finally you need the victim, or victims. Often there will need to be a second victim, or even a third. There may be one or two subplots which somehow link in with, or reflect in some way, the main plot.

The actual crime doesn't have to be complicated: it can be a blow to the skull with a blunt instrument; a hit-and-run with a car; a push off a balcony or through a window. Less simple will be poison; a gangland kidnap and torture before death; a fire that makes identification of the victim difficult; and so on. Your imagination can provide any number of other examples.

Every crime has a motive. What has driven someone to kill?

In your novel there should be several candidates who can have a motive for wishing the victim dead. They are the suspects. It is difficult to keep the reader guessing as to which one was responsible with fewer than four suspects, though Minette Walters has in one instance done an excellent job with only three. However, more than six suspects and the reader, sometimes even the writer, can get confused.

Alongside motivation your investigator has to consider the evidence surrounding the murder scene. These days the official investigation involves forensic teams minutely scanning both body and area and sending samples to a laboratory for analysis. Personally, I don't feel equipped to enter this world and these days much prefer to set my crime novels in the past, with three novels featuring the Italian artist Canaletto and two more set in the Edwardian era with Ursula Grandison as the lead character. I like to make my investigator use eyes, ears and brain to assess what the scene offers as evidence, rather than looking to science. It is possible, though, for a modern unofficial investigator to manage without the forensic science aspect.

Crime novels rose to popularity in the Twenties. Most relied on the puzzle element in their story to keep the reader engrossed. Some were fiendishly clever. In the Thirties, what is known as the Golden Age of crime writing, female authors such as Dorothy L. Sayers, Margery Allingham and Josephine Tey wrote detective novels with strong and memorable characters. Their investigators Lord Peter Wimsey, Albert Campion and Inspector Grant, have remained popular; new editions of their books are constantly being produced and their influence has continued into the present day.

Some element of puzzle, as superbly demonstrated by Agatha Christie, continues to have appeal. It is taken for granted that readers will look for clues to enable them to work out who 'did it' before the writer reveals the answer. There will be 'red herrings', clues that suggest the perpetrator is one of the other suspects, alongside subtle references that keep the reader in the dark until the denouement. There will usually be a number of 'twists', turning what has been suggested as the answer to the mystery on its head, maybe more than once, with a stunning 'revelation' providing the climax to the book. When I told P. D. James that I'd be hopeless at writing a crime novel as I could never sort out who 'did it' in any of the books I so enjoyed, she said, 'It's easier when you *know* who "did it".' This is true, though sometimes the writer will change their mind as to which suspect was the murderer. Ruth Rendell once said she had sometimes changed the perpetrator as she approached the end of a book: 'If I can fool myself, then I'll fool the reader as well.'

The setting and background to a crime novel can be anything that fires the writer's imagination; it can look at a social problem such as knife killing or forms of dementia, reveal how a cruise ship is run or a television programme put together, or consider the need for food banks. Readers love to learn while enjoying a good read.

Most good crime novels will involve a theme, usually subtly suggested rather than shouted out. Writers such as Philip Pullman and Val McDermid say that they discover their theme while they are writing the book.

The denouement of a crime novel has to offer a resolution, one that will satisfy the reader. Many of today's most successful crime novels work on a number of different levels but the ending has to bring the various strands together. Subplots should be settled before the final revelation. The main questions that have been raised need to be answered but there can be others left to the reader's imagination, or that may provide hooks for another crime novel that includes a character or two from your initial one. Many authors find the kernel of their next plot emerging as they get towards the end of writing the current book.

To sum up, you need an interesting setting for your story, a strong plot, believable characters and a resolution that surprises whilst it makes sense of everything that has gone before. Writing a crime novel is hard work – Ian Rankin once said that being a crime writer was absolutely great, apart from the actual writing. There will be times, though, when the characters come alive, the plot explodes with new ideas, when that elusive

ending is staring you in the face and you know that writing
crime novels is the best thing in the world.

'Ideas are everywhere', Janet Laurence points out. Patricia
Highsmith, who said in her fascinating book *Plotting and Writing
Suspense Fiction* that she was driven to creativity 'out of boredom
with reality', recommended writers to keep a notebook. You can jot
ideas down before they are forgotten. Highsmith also argued that
emotions, both positive and negative, could be a fertile source of
ideas. In her view, it is almost impossible to be out of ideas, and
the usual reason why writers sometimes feel bereft of inspiration
is that they are suffering from fatigue or external pressures.

One of the most successful writers during the Golden Age of
detective fiction between the wars was Freeman Wills Crofts. His
work suffered neglect for half a century following his death, but has
recently enjoyed a revival. Reprints of his novels have brought him
back into the public eye after a long absence from the shelves, and
his work has even been optioned for television. Resolutely traditionalist in approach, he outlines five types of ideas for crime stories.

Finding Ideas
Freeman Wills Crofts

If we're lucky we shall begin with a really good idea. This may
be one of five kinds. Firstly, it may be an idea for the opening
of our book: some dramatic situation or happening to excite
and hold the reader's interest. The standard way of finding a
body in the first chapter, if hackneyed, is hard to beat.

Secondly, our idea may be for the closing or climax of our book. This must also be dramatic. As an example I suggest the well-known situation in which Tom, who thinks Jack is dead and has impersonated him, is unexpectedly confronted with Jack in a police office or court of law.

Our idea, thirdly, may be for a good way of committing a crime, probably a murder. It should be novel and ingenious – but not too ingenious – and if possible concerned with things with which the man in the street is familiar. This is probably the most usual way of starting work on a book. Every detective fan will think of dozens of examples.

A fourth kind of idea on which to build a book is that we shall write about some definite crime, such as smuggling, gun-running, coining, arson, or frauds in high finance.

Lastly, our idea may be simply to place the action in a definite setting, such as a mining setting, or a golf or fishing setting, or to lay our scenes in a certain place: a bus or an office, an opium den or Canterbury Cathedral.

We may of course build our book on some idea which does not fall under one of these heads. For instance, Dr Austin Freeman's book, *The Red Thumb Mark*, was probably built on the idea that a fingerprint is not necessarily convincing evidence.

This then is the first stage in our work: getting the idea to start on. Our second stage is more difficult: we have to build up the plot on our idea.

We do this in a very simple, but very tedious way: we ask ourselves innumerable questions and think out the answers. One question invariably leads to another, and as we go on our plot gradually takes shape.

Nicholas Blake – the poet Cecil Day-Lewis – began writing ingenious Golden Age puzzles to earn some extra cash in the 1930s, but as time passed became increasingly ambitious as a detective novelist. Introducing an omnibus edition of his finest stories, he explained their diverse origins. Unluckily for him, one clever idea had already occurred to another crime writer, who later became a colleague in the Detection Club.

Sources of Inspiration

Nicholas Blake

Imagination at full stretch: emotional involvement . . . During the Thirties, I saw my little son narrowly missed by a road hog. Suppose he had been killed, and the police were unable to trace the hit-and-run driver? Such was the germ of *The Beast Must Die*. I tried to imagine myself into the mind of a man – a widower whose only child had been killed like this: how would he find the culprit, and how might he set about destroying him? Revenge, incidentally, seems to be the motive in quite a few of my detection novels, though I am not an overly vindictive person. Perhaps, if I had lived in the early seventeenth century, I would have turned out revenge dramas after the Jacobean pattern. But the point is that, if *The Beast Must Die* has a sharper edge than most of my thrillers, it is because it sprang from that initial involvement of my emotions, and because I was enabled thus to take the hero's plight at a more serious imaginative level. This book has the one first-rate plot I have ever invented – a plot, by the way, which was no great shakes till, halfway through the book, I suddenly saw how the hero could use his diary.

The plot of *A Tangled Web*, on the other hand, was given to me gratis – by 'The Case of the Hooded Man', as Sir Patrick Hastings called it in his Memoirs, the first case in which that celebrated KC led for the defence. At Eastbourne early this century a policeman was shot by a burglar – a clergyman's son who bore the most remarkable resemblance, in temperament and actions, to Hornung's 'Raffles'. Sir Patrick was chiefly concerned, in his book, with the legal aspects of the case. So I could exercise all my imagination in reconstructing the character of this young burglar, of his beautiful and innocent mistress, and of the 'friend' who proved to be their downfall – a man who, even through Sir Patrick's factual account, shines out luridly as the nearest thing to Iago I have ever heard about in real life. My emotions, even at the distance of 45 years, became thoroughly involved with the burglar's girl as I interpreted her. After the book was finished, inquiries among retired policemen who had taken part in the case discovered that several things I had imagined about the Iago character, though not mentioned at the trial, were in fact true.

The germ of *A Penknife in my Heart* was also given me. A friend suggested a story in which two men, previously unknown to each other and both needing to get rid of certain human encumbrances, meet by chance and decide to swap victims. Neither my friend nor I had read Patricia Highsmith's *Strangers on a Train*, or seen the film Hitchcock made of it. Later, I found that Miss Highsmith's treatment was entirely different from mine; but its starting-point was identical – and, horror of horrors, I had given two of my characters the same Christian names as she had used for two of hers. The plot of *A Penknife in my Heart* is the most 'fictional' of the three presented here, and the most diagrammatic. To put flesh on it, I had to work myself into the minds of two very different men – a coarse brute and a weaker, more sensitive character, plunge as deep as I could into their weird relationship, and *be* each of them as he made his murder-attempt (upon a complete stranger), and live with them through the aftermath. It needed a pretty strenuous stretching of the invention.

Even before the plot is constructed in detail (or not constructed, in
the case of authors like Eric Ambler, who regard writing a crime
story as a voyage of discovery) there comes another question. Which
type of crime fiction to choose? How to put it all together? Anthea
Fraser and Ann Granger, two highly experienced novelists who both
worked in other genres before specializing in crime fiction, describe
their personal approaches.

Making Choices
Anthea Fraser

Crime writing is a broad church, offering a choice of police
procedural, supernatural, hard-boiled, 'noir', psychological or
romantic suspense, espionage, thrillers or whodunits, though
sometimes the sub-genres can blur at the edges and overlap.
I came to crime writing myself by way of paranormal books,
which were enjoying a vogue at the time. When public interest
started to wane, my agent asked if I'd like to change genre,
and realizing there'd been a crime in each of the paranormals,
I found I'd already made my choice.

It's important to remember that although you'll be writing
over a period of months, the reader might take only a few days
to read the entire book, so the same 'tone of voice' should be
kept throughout. Sometimes I can tell where I've stopped for
the day by a very slight but noticeable change of style, so I
always begin by rereading (and heavily editing) what I wrote
the previous day to ensure it flows without a break.

The main aim, of course, is to grab the reader's attention
from page one, and there are various devices to achieve this.
You could start with a prologue covering an event that, unknown
to the characters, has already happened. Or begin with an
explosive incident that *hasn't* yet happened, but which the

reader is awaiting with trepidation until it occurs later in the book. Or you could have a catalytic event taking place in 'real time' which is the actual starting point of the story - such as the discovery of a dead body.

Conflict is, of course, a necessary component to a good story, whether between lovers, police colleagues or family members, and can pave the way to any number of situations, often resulting in murder. However the maxim 'Write about what you know' just isn't possible when you're dealing with murder, and anyway, what price imagination? I turn it round to 'Know about what you write', and try to make sure I check my facts – thoroughly – easy these days with the internet. When writing a police procedural, however, there really is no substitute for personal contact with a friendly officer who is prepared to answer any number of queries you might raise. What's more, they seem to enjoy it, and I used to send my contact a copy of each book to thank him for 'helping with my enquiries'!

If you're lucky, you might find your characters already waiting in the wings, fully formed and ready to go, but failing that it's useful to keep a 'Faces and Places' file containing photos torn out of magazines or newspapers of interesting faces (preferably not anyone well known) and the interiors of houses, or town or village streets along which you can imagine your characters walking. If any of these are applicable for the plot you have in mind, you can stick them up on a cork board in front of you. It's helpful to look at them and think, 'What would you do in this situation?'

Character names are extremely important and often people won't come to life if you choose the wrong name. Sometimes, as the characters develop, it might be necessary to change one halfway through – no problem with the Replace All key. Since names go in and out of fashion, consideration must be given to the age and social status of the character. I also try to avoid any that are unisex or begin with the same letter, which might cause confusion.

The setting you choose is crucial; personally I've found it gives me more freedom to use imaginary locations. I do, however, picture them in a particular part of the country, and try to ensure the made-up place names fit in with those in the appropriate locality. Then I draw town plans, filling in shops, police station, church, etc., so that I know in which direction a character will turn when he comes out of his gate and – important in establishing an alibi – how long it will take to get from A to B. I also do plans of the main house in the story, again with the aim of being able to 'see' the action taking place. The reader should feel completely at home there, able to follow the characters as they move from room to room.

A series might require the invention of a complete county, in which case I draw a map of it, positioning towns and villages at random and working out the travelling distance between them in both mileage and time. I can then choose the one that best fits the plot, and if there doesn't happen to be a town in a suitable place, I can always add a new one!

It can be quite a challenge to invent someone who'll mature and develop and whose personal life will progress through an indefinite number of books – someone, in short, whom you could live with. Your characters will, of course, age and develop as you go along. Relationships will be formed or ended, family members might die, couples divorce and children be born.

One problem with a series can be timing – how much has elapsed between the end of one book and the beginning of the next. My DCI Webb series lasted for sixteen books and it became increasingly difficult to keep track of children's ages and how long ago a certain event had taken place. So I invented my own time zone, in which the first book took place in year one and the second in the following year. The characters had met each other in year *minus* one or two. I could then check back in later books and life became easier.

After those sixteen books I wanted a rest from police procedure so wrote a stand-alone for the first time in years. And since I intended to limit police presence to the minimum, it had to involve a cold case that wouldn't tread on their toes, a past murder in the family that had never been solved. Families fascinate me, the dynamics between the different members, the tensions and unsuspected jealousies.

After this book I wrote another stand-alone, but when I embarked on what was intended to be a third, I began to miss the comfortable familiarity of a series and decided to expand it into a new one, which became the first of the Rona Parish books. I didn't want to return to police themes – in any case forensics had moved on in the past couple of years and I was out of date - but I wanted my protagonist to have a legitimate reason for repeatedly coming up against crime, so I made her a journalist and biographer. Both these seemingly harmless occupations led her, over the course of ten books, into considerable danger.

I have continued to slot stand-alones in between the series books. There's a sense of freedom in being able to visit an entirely different location with totally new characters who will obligingly tidy up their problems within the covers of that one book.

A perennial question every writer faces is 'Where do you get your ideas?' They can, of course, come from anywhere – a snippet in the newspaper, an overheard conversation – and don't discount dreams! I dreamed the idea for one novel and several short stories, so I keep a notebook and pen by my bed and make a quick note of any that might be useful before they fade.

If the title comes to mind first, that's a great advantage and points you in the right direction. There are various ways of choosing a suitable title. I occasionally use quotes – and was berated by no fewer than *three* fellow crime writers for choosing *A Necessary End*, when their own books, also under that title, were still at the proof stage.

The title of *Whistler's Lane*, one of the paranormal novels, actually evolved from looking at the portrait of Whistler's Mother, when I toyed with the fantasy that the whistler referred to was not a proper name. Ghostly figures in a dark countryside came to mind, and the plot developed from there. Another time I heard someone on the radio refer to a *Macbeth prophecy*, i.e. a self-fulfilling one, and filed it away for future use.

In terms of choosing titles, my easiest ride was with the Green Grow the Rushes series. The song itself has appeared in many forms in ancient and modern languages from Hebrew onwards, and the first time it was written down in English was in 1625. Whatever the original meaning of the verses – and they've become distorted over the years, like a game of Chinese Whispers – I've always thought they were most evocative. Who *were* the April Rainers, the Nine Bright Shiners, the Lily-White Boys?

I'd originally intended to use two at most, but as I wrote, more ideas offered, until I realized I'd have to use them all. They weren't written in order, but as ideas presented themselves. It was pure chance that the final three were Ten, Eleven and Twelve, and I have to admit *Eleven that Went Up to Heaven* was quite a challenge! Short of killing off an entire cricket side, it took me some time to come up with a hopefully convincing mass murder.

I used to plan my books meticulously, knowing how far the plot would progress in every chapter, though obviously changes were made as I went along. (In one case an old lady was due to be murdered, but I became fond of her so I spared her and killed someone else!) Then the time came when I was in such a hurry to start writing that I couldn't be bothered planning and jumped straight in, pushing the plot ahead of me chapter by chapter. It all worked out in the end, and that is basically the way I write now – a rough idea of what's going to happen, but letting the details emerge as I go along. Unlike most of my fellow writers, I never do drafts. I prefer to stick to the original, though since I can't read a page without making alterations, it will inevitably have changed considerably by the time I reach the end.

It has been said that writing is 10 per cent inspiration and 90 per cent perspiration, and certainly it's no good sitting back and waiting till you feel in the mood. If inspiration doesn't come, I write anything, however unsatisfactory, like working in a new biro. Then, when the flow is re-established, I go back and polish it. And I always try to stop for the day at an inter-esting point, which will give me the impetus to get going the following day.

Putting Murder on the Page
Ann Granger

'*How* do you write a book?' an earnest woman once asked me. I gave the usual reply: plots, characters, etc. A puzzled frown appeared on her brow. 'No,' she said, 'I meant, *how can you put it all together?*' She mimed writing with a pen.

I had been expecting the often-asked 'Where do you get your ideas from?' But she wasn't worried about that. I realized she thought of 'a book' as a sort of mental Meccano structure. Perhaps, in some ways, it is. But I confess that, at the time, I was stumped as to how to reply in a single sentence.

Writing crime fiction is a slippery subject to pin down. No two writers go about it in the same way. How can we? The books themselves vary so much. One of the attractions of writing mystery/crime has always been, for me, that it is an umbrella covering such a variety of topics, interests, historical periods, and so on.

So, once our thought processes start jogging along, what happens next? Our books are all different. We are all different. We work in different ways.

The only explanation that I can give as to how write a book is to say that it begins by growing in my mind. That does sound rather uncomfortable, if not downright dangerous. But what starts as a germ of a plot with its characters, theme, and so forth does finally threaten to take over and exclude all else. So discipline is very important. Be in charge of the book and don't let the book become your master.

I must add that writers tend to think a lot before they write anything. Some people might go for long walks, in order to be undisturbed when working out ideas or seeking the right turn of phrase. I've been told the poet Wordsworth (though not, of course, a crime writer) used this method, rushing back home to write down the resulting verse before he forgot it again. I've had some brilliant ideas in the middle of the night and forgotten them by morning. Or I've switched on the light and jotted them down, only to be disappointed when reading the scrawl by the cold light of day. Agatha Christie recommended doing the washing-up as a way of concentrating the mind. Or perhaps the creative activity takes place while staring into space – my own specialty.

There is no guarantee some brilliant idea will come to mind. But, like Mr Micawber, I hope something will turn up.

I have heard of writers who produce a minimum number of words each and every day, come rain or shine. If that is what works for them, excellent. It wouldn't work for me. I should probably begin each day by binning every word I'd written the previous one.

There are the meticulous planners, whom I admire greatly but couldn't emulate. There are others who sketch out a plot in general terms, perhaps under headings. Then there are those who know where the starting point is and can see the finishing post in the distance, but don't know exactly how they are going to get there and so scramble over the obstacles as they go along, in a sort of literary Grand National course.

I start by jotting down a few general notes. I have a location in mind and a set of characters. I work on the principle that if a development in the plot comes as a surprise to me, then, with any luck, it will surprise the reader. I do know the identity of the victim when I begin, and I know the identity of the murderer. If you have created distinctive characters they will helpfully make their own contribution to the mix. 'Distinctive' doesn't necessarily mean 'odd'. A few odd characters are nice, but a complete cast of oddities is confusing. Nor is it enough for a character simply to be eccentric. There has to be some form of reason at work, however bizarre.

It can help to make a few practical notes concerning the colour of a character's hair or eyes, and also about age. Write down his or her date of birth. Bear in mind, if possible, where your plot is in terms of the working week. Offices and some businesses tend to be closed at the weekend after Saturday lunchtime. If a suspect or a witness is at work, it is no use your detective going to his house during the day.

Setting is important, and I have spotted a few useful locations for scenes of crime while travelling on trains, gazing at the passing countryside. I think to myself, 'I could put a body there!'

Some years ago I went to the Chelsea Flower Show on a particularly wet day. Everyone there had crowded into the main marquee in a free-for-all. Who, in those circumstances, would be interested in a couple of strangers? Each person there was looking out for him or herself. I thought to myself that a murder could be committed there and no one would notice. The victim, mortally stricken, couldn't collapse on the ground at once, not in that press. He would slump, allowing the murderer to grasp him and propel him towards the exit, telling everyone who might show surprise that someone had fainted and 'needed some air'. The surrounding crowd would recognize an emergency and part just enough to allow assailant and victim through.

I went home and wrote a novel called *Flowers for His Funeral* in which the murder takes place very much in that way.

Make sure you have enough plot. This will probably mean at least one, even two, subplots. But be careful that minor characters don't become more interesting than the main ones.

I have learned to watch out for a few things over the years. A single page may prove to be a minefield strewn with repetitions and contradictions. Reading aloud is very helpful here. A repeated phrase, for example, may not leap out on the computer screen. But if you have used one, or given the same adjective more than once in a single passage, you will hear it at once if you listen when it's read aloud.

A section of dialogue can also benefit from being subjected

to this test. Speech patterns are important and all the characters should not sound the same.

In my early days I read whole chunks of the day's output into a tape recorder and played it back. Hearing your voice reciting chunks of your own prose comes as a bit of shock. I remember one of my offspring, on wandering into the room when the tape was running, saying unkindly that I sounded as if I am doing an impression of the Queen's Christmas speech. I don't record passages now, but I still read a page or two aloud, when it seems helpful.

When writing my early books, I found myself occasionally in danger of becoming addicted to a particular consonant, especially when thinking of names for characters. Possibly I am alone in that. I know I once wrote a whole chapter in which all the characters, including the corpse, had a name beginning with the same letter. Luckily, I realized in time but it was an alarm bell, and I still watch out for it.

Whether aloud or silently, always read through carefully more than once. Familiarity can be a trap here. You can find yourself skimming over whole pages, the text flashing by in a blur. So it helps to put the finished work aside and go away physically. Go on holiday, tackle the garden; just take yourself away from the work itself. Believe me, it's much easier to spot the mistakes or glitches after a break away from your creation.

Ronald Knox's 'Ten Commandments' for writing a detective novel date from the 1920s and offer limited assistance for the twenty-first century author. Natasha Cooper draws on experience as an editor and reviewer, as well as from her career as a novelist, in her ten practical tips for crime writers of today.

Intensity in Crime Writing
Natasha Cooper

The one thing – and the only thing – that a crime novel must not do is bore the reader. The old rules about what you may and may not include have gone. You can identify the villain in the first chapter if you want; you can have lots of blood or no blood; you can have any number of identical twins or secret passages; you don't even have to have a killer. But you must keep your reader interested.

As you plan your novel, you may find the following ten points helpful.

1. Know your characters
You will find it easier to write engaging fiction if your characters feel real to you. Get to know them before you start writing. Who are they? What do they like? What do they fear? What do they want? Who do they piss off? What do they look like? What do they eat? What music do they listen to? What films do they watch? Are they snowflakes? Are they bullies? What are their weaknesses? What are their private tragedies? For what would they kill?

You don't need to tell the reader everything, but you need to know it all. Some writers find that it helps to chat to their characters as they potter about, and no one looks weirdly at anyone talking in the street now because they assume everyone's on the phone.

2. Write in scenes
To keep your novel vivid, you need to set the scene for each piece of action or dialogue or introspection. So think, before you write a word, about where your character is, who else is there, what can they see, what can they hear and smell and taste and feel. Once again, you don't have to tell the reader everything, but you need to know it all so that you can select the most telling details to share with the reader.

3. Don't waste time

It is all too easy when writing a novel to prattle on without much point, especially if you've given yourself a daily word-count target. Don't. Think about why you are including the scene you're writing. Is it to establish a character? Is it to advance the plot? Is it to heighten the tension? Is it to give the reader necessary information?

If your scene does not do at least two of these things, consider binning it.

Giving information is one of the hardest aspects of crime writing. Some readers love innumerable details about weapons, or the stripping of bones by pathologists, or the operation of complex financial frauds. Others don't. They can, of course, skip anything that bores them, but you need to be judicious about the amount of information you give and the way in which you give it. Explanatory dialogue can be dangerous, and it often sounds impossibly artificial to the reader's internal ear. If you need your reader to know about the speed at which a Kalashnikov pumps out bullets, it is probably best to announce it straightforwardly rather than to have characters sitting over a beer in a pub, with one saying, 'I've always wondered how many bullets a Kalashnikov fires every second', the second replying, 'Well, it rather depends on the year it was made; some Kalashnikovs fire at . . .'

4. Realistic dialogue

If your characters sound like cyborgs, or DIY manuals, or pompous sermonizers, you will lose the reader. It is well worth speaking each piece of your dialogue aloud and possibly even recording some of it so that you can hear how it sounds.

Make sure that each character's idiom is distinct from the others. Ideally the reader should be able to work out who is speaking without your adding 'John joked jaggedly' or 'Maggie muttered murderously'.

Consider confining the relevant verbs to 'said' or possibly 'shouted' or 'whispered'. Synonyms for 'said' can seem absurd. One historical novel published in the 1950s included,

'"Honeycakes," Jenny ejaculated as she sat among the gilly-flowers.' A more modern infelicity is: '"I don't care," she deadpanned.' 'I don't care' is quite enough on its own.

Every group, whether social or professional, has its own private language, and using the relevant ones will add authenticity to your novel. If you have the time and resources to hang around your target group and listen, you will pick up the right words and phrases; but you may not have time and so it's worth finding a single individual – police officer, firefighter, lawyer, gang member – and asking how he or she would describe something specific. You don't have to write your whole scene in the relevant language, but adding a few unexpected but accurate words and phrases will always help to convince your readers that they are reading something real. If your novel is historical, it's well worth looking up letters and diaries of the period so that you can add an accurate sound to the dialogue.

5. Research

Don't do too much research too soon. The risk is that you will include much too much detail in your novel. Read around your subject and then write, leaving space within square brackets labelled something like [add scientific detail here]. Experts are remarkably helpful and will give just enough information in reply to a specific question to add authenticity to a novel without overloading it. You are more likely to be able to ask the right question once you have finished your first draft.

6. Tension

All novels need tension to persuade the reader to turn the pages, but crime needs a lot of it. The most straightforward way of generating tension in your fiction is by setting up a question and delaying the answer for as long as possible. Shakespeare's *Romeo & Juliet* provides a wonderful masterclass in how to do it. The Chorus tells the audience at the beginning that the play concerns 'a pair of star-crossed lovers', who 'with their death bury their parents' strife'. We know from the beginning that Romeo and Juliet will die but not how or when.

Throughout the play there are scenes in which one or other is likely to be killed, but again and again death is postponed. By the last scene the audience is in the state most of us know when waiting in for the plumber all day, leaping up at the sound of a van in the street or a knock at the door, perpetually thwarted and twitchy beyond belief. You need to generate that kind of edginess in your reader.

7. Emotional intensity

No one can live in a state of unremitting drama, and any novel that makes its characters do that will lose credibility. You need to vary the emotional intensity, interspersing action scenes with reflective ones. Never forget that one emotion intensifies its opposite. If you are about to plunge your readers into tragedy, think about softening them up with humour first.

8. Adverbs

Many writers are tempted to add colour to their narratives with adverbs, but it's a mistake. Adverbs diminish intensity. Don't write 'he ran breathlessly, hurriedly and clumsily to rescue the child from the fire'. Instead describe his headlong rush, perhaps showing how he trips and rips his skin on a piece of broken glass in the grass. Blood will drip unnoticed from the cuts as he forces himself on, panting and trying to control his banging heart. He can feel the heat of the flames on his face now and has to brush sparks off his clothes as he surges forward. The child's screams drill into his brain as he trips again, spraining his ankle. Limping, he makes it to the burning building just as the child falls from the open window, missing his outstretched hands by inches.

9. Naming characters

When you are considering what to call your characters, do think about the reader. Similar-looking – or similar-sounding – names can make it hard to keep each person distinct. You will know who they are, but for the reader Dave, Dan and Dick will merge into each other, as will Maeve, Steve and Niamh.

10. Moving characters around

Don't worry about getting your characters from room to room or even city to city. Use what filmmakers call the jump cut. In a novel this can be achieved by ending one scene in the attic bedroom of a flat in Rome and then beginning the next with a short comment about the new venue; for example, 'The Whispering Gallery of St Paul's Cathedral in London gave Jim an excellent view of his target.'

Above all, enjoy planning your novel and like your characters. Even the wicked ones.

Opening sentences matter. They don't come easily, and Frances Fyfield notes: 'You may have to relinquish the beginning. The best idea might be at the bottom of the page. Bring it up. And, if it is three a.m. in the morning, it's time for you and your characters to go to bed. To sleep and yet to dream.'

As John Harvey explains, good openings come in many different forms:

Openings

John Harvey

The opening sentences of Dashiell Hammett's first novel, *Red Harvest*, published in 1929, are these: 'I first heard Personville called Poisonville by a red-haired mucker named Hickey Dewey in the Big Ship in Butte. He also called his shirt a shoit.'

It's all there: the directness, the way it buttonholes you instantly, a hand taking hold of the lapel of your jacket while the voice speaks confidently, not overloudly, into your ear. And the poetry: the poetry of the vernacular, the rhythm of real speech.

The first sentence in his first novel. I wonder how many times he rolled the sheet of paper out of the typewriter, read it through, tossed it over his shoulder, lit another cigarette, set a fresh sheet in place and tried again? I wonder if he'd been testing it in his head at a little after four, four-thirty, those mornings it was impossible to get back to sleep? I wonder if he had it all pat from the start?

At the time of writing that first novel, Hammett was thirty-five years old. He'd been an operative for the Pinkerton National Detective Agency, a private detective working for an vast organization with government connections. He had twice enlisted in the army, world wars one and two, and it was during the first of these periods that he was diagnosed with the tuberculosis that would seriously affect his well-being for years. When he was no longer with the Pinkertons, realizing, perhaps, that henceforth he would be physically less active, he enrolled at a Business College and set about learning the business of writing.

Going back to the opening of *Red Harvest* made me think of the distinctive ways in which other crime books begin. Some, like the Hammett, are short and punchy, grabbing the attention at the same time as having a close-to-perfect satisfaction of their own. Others are longer, with a deliberately complex sentence that winds you along its length and so into both the style and the narrative. Others are paragraph-length and draw you in more carefully, and often then stay in the memory – sometimes after the book itself has been read, enjoyed and set aside.

Opening lines matter. Here is a selection of my favourite single sentence beginnings, some of which will be familiar, others perhaps less so.

They threw me off the hay truck about noon.
               James M. Cain, *The Postman Always Rings Twice*

Jackie Brown at twenty-six, with no expression on his face, said that he could get some guns.

George V. Higgins, *The Friends of Eddie Coyle*

When I finally caught up with Abraham Trahearne, he was drinking beer with an alcoholic bulldog named Fireball Roberts in a ramshackle joint just outside Sonoma, California, drinking the heart right out of a fine spring afternoon.

James Crumley, *The Last Good Kiss*

Much later, as he sat with his back against an inside wall of a Motel 6 just north of Phoenix, watching the pool of blood lap toward him, Driver would wonder whether he had made a terrible mistake.

James Sallis, *Drive*

When she was killed by three chest knife blows in a station car park, Megan Harpur had been on her way home to tell her husband that she was leaving him for another man.

Bill James, *Roses, Roses*

And here are two of my favourites of the longer variety, each humorous in its own way. The first is, of course, a well-known classic, the second by Brian Thompson, a writer whose forays into crime writing deserve to be better known and appreciated than I think they are.

It was about eleven o'clock in the morning, mid-October, with the sun not shining and a look of hard wet rain in the clearness of the foothills. I was wearing my powder-blue suit, with dark blue shirt, tie and display handkerchief, black brogues, black wool socks with dark blue clocks on them. I was neat, clean, shaved and sober, and I didn't care who knew it. I was everything the well-dressed private detective ought to be. I was calling on four million dollars.

Raymond Chandler, *The Big Sleep*

Mrs Evans was teaching me the tango. As it happened, I already knew the rudiments of this exciting dance, but never as interpreted by Mrs Evans, naked save for her high heels and some Mexican silver earrings – a present, she claimed, from Acapulco. The high heels were there to add grace and I suppose authenticity, but even with them on, the lady's head barely reached my chin. We swooped about the room, exceedingly drunk, to the most famous tango of them all, the Blue one. It was past two in the morning and the rain that had been forecast had arrived as grounded cloud, moping blindly about the streets, tearful and incoherent. But we were okay – we were up on the third floor, looking down on the damned cloud and having a whale of a time. Mrs Evans was warm to the touch and her make-up was beginning to melt. For some reason a piece of Sellotape was stuck to her quivering bottom, and as we danced I tried to solve this small but endearing mystery. It came to me at last; it was her sister's birthday and earlier in the evening she had parcelled up a head scarf, some knickers and a Joanna Trollope paperback.

Brian Thompson. Ladder of Angels

Over the years, some of the finest openings have appeared in novels written by members of the Detection Club. The Club's founder, Anthony Berkeley, changed his pen name to Francis Iles for his first novel of psychological suspense, *Malice Aforethought*, which began brilliantly:

It was not until several weeks after he had decided to murder his wife that Dr Bickleigh took any active steps in the matter. Murder is a serious business. The slightest slip may be disastrous. Dr Bickleigh had no intention of risking disaster.

The ironic tone is maintained throughout, and reflected in the outcome of the story. The next Francis Iles novel, *Before the Fact*, had an equally memorable beginning:

> Some women give birth to murderers, some go to bed with them, and some marry them. Lina Aysgarth had lived with her husband for nearly eight years before she realized that she was married to a murderer.

Almost half a century later, Ruth Rendell published *A Judgement in Stone* which begins:

> Eunice Parchman killed the Coverdale family because she could not read or write.

Peter Robinson describes this as the perfect narrative hook. An opening that hooks the reader's attention is invaluable, but by itself, it's not enough to guarantee a good book, let alone a novel to compare with those classics by Iles and Rendell. It may even, as Peter explains, be a mistake to worry too much about the opening if that leads to neglect of keeping the reader hooked throughout the whole narrative.

'Something Should Happen Now':
Narrative Hooks

Peter Robinson

I always get nervous when I'm asked to write about the craft of fiction. As I teach creative writing courses often, I have read a lot of books on the subject. You know the sort of thing: *5 Shortcuts to Perfect Plotting, 3 Techniques for Creating Award-winning Characters, 10 Simple Steps to Writing the Greatest Crime Novel Ever Written,* and so on. But when I write, I don't

think about these books; I just follow my gut instinct. As a jazz
pianist needs to practise scales before moving on to wild improvi-
sations, so a writer needs to become familiar with and internalize
the basics of his craft in order to set off on a flight of fancy.
For what is a novel, after all, but a flight of fancy? You may
have studied plotting, structure, dialogue, description, action
and character as separate strands of the writing process, and
done all the requisite exercises, but when you start working on
a book, they all tend to blur into one another, and when the
writing is going well most writers rarely stop to make sure they
have adhered to the three-, five- or seven-act structure, got
their plot points in the right places or put in enough narrative
hooks. When it comes right down to it, I can't really know what
will hook 'the reader', but I do know what hooks me. And I'm
a reader, too, so maybe I'm my own best audience?

What is a narrative hook? Perhaps the best way to think of
it is as anything that keeps a reader turning the pages. The
writer's least favourite question is 'Where do you get your
ideas?' Usually when people ask that, they mean the outlandish
overall concept for the book, such as a serial killer who skins
his victims, but when you get right down to it, a book isn't
made of one idea. Every sentence is an idea. And in the same
way, every page, or at least every scene or every chapter, needs
narrative hooks. Perhaps the first lesson, then, is that you
should always think of narrative hooks in the plural.

Beginnings are notoriously difficult; there's no way around
that. The main problem is that many writers, especially begin-
ners, tend to put too much exposition up front. Someone is
murdered in a particularly gruesome fashion in the first
sentence, then the writer spends two pages giving us the victim's
life story. There's very little narrative hook in that. Some more
cunning writers try to get around this problem by using a
startling prologue as their hook, often written in the present
tense and italicized. This prologue, though full of atmosphere,
mystery and menace, appears at first to have no relation whatsoever to the story that follows, and the reader is hooked on
wanting to know what the hell it is there for. Eventually, all is

revealed. The problem with this is that it has become a cliché. I should know; I've done it once or twice. In his ten rules for writing, Elmore Leonard advises us to avoid prologues. I wouldn't take this as an absolute rule, but perhaps it is better to avoid routinely including prologues.

Too much attention is also given to hooking your reader with the opening sentence. Yes, it is all well and good if you can come up with a real humdinger, but in most cases, you won't. By all means aspire to perfection, but remember, you can always come back to it later. What you really need to do is get the story moving. Becoming obsessed with the opening sentence is often a sure-fire way of procrastinating. If you're not careful, you'll end up like Camus's Joseph Grand in *La Peste*, who was such a perfectionist that he couldn't get beyond writing and rewriting the first sentence of his book.

Not all opening sentences hook the reader as strongly as Ruth Rendell's *A Judgement in Stone*, in which she not only names the murderer but supplies the motive. The entire opening scene of this book merits study for any writer, as Rendell continues to describe the crime and its outcome in a way that seems to be 'giving away' everything we expect to find out bit by bit in the course of the reading the whole novel. Instead of encouraging us to stop reading, however, this technique proves to be perfect narrative hook, perhaps because it leads us to become more interested in how it all unfolds rather than simply what happens and to whom. As we read, we find ourselves watching a car crash in slow motion.

The lesson here is to think beyond the first sentence to the whole opening scene, for that is where you must set your first hooks. Most readers are generous enough to allow a writer a couple of chapters before deciding whether to give up or carry on. That's where to concentrate your efforts. An agent or editor, should you be fortunate enough to come to the attention of one, will also read at least a few pages.

The first scene or chapter usually introduces the setting and the main character and kick-starts the plot, or sets the groundwork for it. It also sets the tone for what is to follow, and it must also raise a lot of questions we want answered or set up situations we want to see resolved. It gives you more than enough opportunities get your hooks into your readers. You need to give them a feel for the world they'll be spending the next few hours in. The books we enjoy most are the ones that envelop and absorb us the most completely, that give us a place, or places, to inhabit, interesting characters to love or hate, action and dialogue that we want to go back and spend time with day after day, a fully realized world that we can immerse ourselves in. When you finish a book like that you should be feeling both joy and sadness. Sadness that it's over, of course, but also joy because you had the experience, and you can have it again and again with more of that author's books. If you understand that as a reader, you will also understand it as a writer. It will be your task to create that world, to provide that experience for others. It doesn't matter whether you're planning a series or just a stand-alone; the more you give the reader that glorious sensation of immersion in the fictional world you have created, the more successful your books will be.

The opening scene is where you must set your first and most powerful hooks. Think of it as a seduction. They need to know what kind of world they will be entering and what sort of ride they may be in for. For the hook is all about creating a world. It's OK to be subtle, but make sure you set up possibilities, hints, whispers, a vivid setting, something that grabs the reader's attention and makes her want to keep reading. Make the reader fall in love with the story. It's as simple as that. And as difficult.

And after that? Don't let up. Keep the hooks coming. My first editor went over my first manuscript with me, page by page. There were yellow Post-it notes everywhere, and around page thirty or so I noticed that she had written in pencil at the top of the page: 'Something should happen now.' Something happened five pages later, but she had sensed that my pacing was off, that I had set up a hook that didn't pay off quickly enough, and I knew I needed to cut five pages from my first thirty to make something happen sooner. That was an important lesson to learn.

Of course, a hook may be greater or lesser in magnitude. There are big hooks, of which you will need fewer, and little hooks, of which you will need many. Yes, we may be hooked by the big concept – will the protagonist stop the serial killer before he kills and skins the young journalist we have come to like. But while all of that big stuff is important, and should always be in your mind, you should not lose track of the numerous little hooks you need to keep the story moving along. 'Something should happen now.' Maybe just a little thing. But something. Maybe in a subplot. One example is a relationship. The protagonist is having problems with his girlfriend, say, or his wife, or family. We should care about this and want things to be resolved. Or it could also be a health issue, the result of an X-ray, or a work problem – conflict with one's boss or partner, perhaps – but it is all grist for the hook mill. You have so many opportunities. Don't waste them. It's like the fairground plate-spinner or juggler. The more plates your protagonist has to keep spinning, or the more balls in the air, the faster your reader will turn the pages. And if once in a while he lets a plate fall and break or drops a ball, then it means he's only human, and the broken plate or dropped ball can work as a narrative hook itself, perhaps misdirecting us for a while.

A crime novel – by which I mean here a mystery, usually involving a murder, a police detective, private eye or talented amateur sleuth – is often more cerebral than action-filled, which can cause hook-related problems of its own. Raymond Chandler once wrote, 'When in doubt have a man come through a door with a gun in his hand.' He was describing the experience of writing for the pulps, but his words are often taken as advice about how to move on the action when you think the plot is in a bit of a slump and you need to re-hook the reader. It works. I know; I've done it! But you can only get away with it once, especially if your books are set in the UK, where guns are not so prevalent.

In a crime novel, you have a huge variety of possible hooks at your disposal, many things you can substitute for the man with the gun, either of greater or lesser intensity. Most obviously, you can place your protagonist in harm's way. Some of the most effective lesser hooks are information, a revelation of some sort, or secrets and lies. It is always a good idea to hint early on that someone has a secret or is lying about something and to delay the revelation of what this is. You control this revelation; you can use it when you want, when you feel 'something should happen now'.

There are numerous little questions raised in every chapter of every story, and each one of them is capable of becoming a narrative hook, so you need to exploit them to the best of your abilities and use both the question and its answer as a means of getting the most tension and best pacing out of your writing.

A good example in crime fiction is forensic information, all of which will eventually be pieced together to help form a solution to the puzzle (or a red herring, at least). First you get the crime scene sorted, the trace evidence packed away and sent off to the various lab departments. You've probably got fingerprints, possible DNA, hair, a footprint, a tyre track, a dodgy alibi, a mysterious stain, a witness or two to track down. The answers to all these questions can be spread out throughout your novel almost at will, and the information they provide can be used as and when you feel that 'something should happen now'. Revelation is also a kind of action, especially if it is not the answer you have led the reader to expect.

Crime writing isn't formulaic, as some critics would have us believe, but there are certain structural possibilities in the genre that may act as signposts along the road and help keep you travelling in the right direction. These will also offer opportunities for further narrative hooks. For a start, there will be the crime. It's usually murder because, as P. D. James most perceptively pointed out, the taking of another life is one thing that can't be undone. And it means the stakes are high. The victim is dead, and it's left to society, or its representative in the form of the investigator – private or official – to find out why and, if possible, restore some sort of balance and order. This kind of situation is intrinsic to a crime novel and is a gift in terms of narrative hooks. A good writer makes the reader want to take the journey with the detective and find out who and, perhaps more important, why this victim was killed in such a way. You don't have to do anything extra to get this hook – it's a gift of the genre.

P. D. James also pointed out that this restoration of order can never be complete and does not always include justice. It also doesn't preclude any of the devastation and heartbreak such a crime leaves behind in the community and the lives and psyches of those individuals involved. Catching the killer never brings back the victim; nor does it bring peace to those who, through being serious suspects at some point, may have lost their livelihoods, families and friends. Make readers care about these characters, however minor some of them may be, and you will have even more narrative hooks. It would be well to bear this is mind as you build up the characters and their relationships, along with the picture of a community under stress, as you will be setting hooks there that heighten expectations for something to happen later. Relationships will be altered, something will be lost, and perhaps something else will replace it. All these things you can prepare for by the judicious use of narrative hooks. Remember: 'Something should happen now.'

People

A crime novel – any novel – with dull characters is destined to fail. A strong plot and a fascinating setting are important, but unlikely to compensate for a failure to create interesting people. This is not to say that the characterization needs to be exceptionally sophisticated. Agatha Christie's murder suspects were usually drawn with a few brief strokes, and characterization was not her greatest strength; yet her people are recognizable human types, their presentation sometimes enlivened with touches of humour, for which she had an underestimated talent. This element of universality helps to explain the enduring popularity of Christie's work with people the world over, many of whom have never visited an English country house or met a butler or an elderly female amateur detective.

Skill at characterization is highly prized by writers, publishers, and readers alike. It doesn't matter so much if a character is not likeable or behaves badly. That's par for the course in a crime story. Readers can still care about the character's fate. The enduring appeal of Patricia Highsmith's amoral Tom Ripley illustrates the point; he's not so much a series detective as a series sociopath. But if readers aren't bothered about what Fate may have in store for a character, the wise writer will rethink.

Mark Billingham has explained on his website how he always envisaged that his most famous character, DI Tom Thorne, would develop book by book, and would never become predictable. He took the deliberate decision not to describe Thorne physically, and made sure that his detective carried with him the events that had shaped his life; he 'is someone who deals with violent death, with terrible grief, and it would be ludicrous, inhuman, if he remained untouched by such things'.

Character from Suspense
Mark Billingham

I have been asked many times over the years – at events or during creative writing workshops – how a crime writer goes about creating suspense. There was a period when, in answer to this question, I would talk about what I considered to be the tricks of the crime writing trade. I would bang on about the importance of the cliffhanger, the twist and the 'reveal'. Such devices remain hugely important, but I have come to realize that the answer actually lies in something far more basic, something that should be central to the writing of any piece of fiction: the creation of character.

All the techniques mentioned above are, of course, vital weapons in the mystery writer's armoury and, as such, components of the genre that readers of crime novels have come to expect. They are part of the package; the buttons that a writer has to push every so often. When a crime writer thinks up a delicious twist, it is certainly a good day at the office, even if the 'office' at that particular moment happens to be the shower, the car or the park in which you're walking the dog. Time to relax and take the rest of the day off.

I do think that it can be overdone, however.

There is a particular strain of crime and thriller writer who believes it is his or her duty to throw as many curveballs at the reader as possible. To twist and twist again. These are what I think of as the 'Chubby Checkers' of crime fiction and, while I admire the craft, I have come to believe that a super-fluity of such tricks and tics can actually work against the creation of genuine suspense. Put simply, I find it hard to engage with any book that is no more than a demonstration of technique. I am not *invested*. A character dies, but why should I give a hoot when I know this particular writer's stock in trade means that the character in question is almost certainly not dead at all? The cop or private detective or amateur sleuth has caught the killer, but is that the end of it? No, you can bet your boots it isn't, because there are still three chapters left and I don't have to be Hercule Poirot to work out that they have got the wrong man.

Make no mistake, this kind of intricate plotting can be hugely important and the success of writers who perennially give their readers a corkscrew ride is testament to its enduring popularity. But I don't believe that in terms of creating suspense, it is necessarily the only way to go.

The 'reveal' remains a very effective technique, and one with which I am very familiar from my time as a stand-up comedian. It may sound surprising, but, having made the move from stand-up comedy to crime writing, I quickly discovered that a joke and a crime novel work in very much the same way. The comedian leads their audience along the garden path. The audience allow themselves to be led, because they know what's coming, or at least they *think* they do, until they get hit from a direction they were not expecting.

My grandfather died recently. He just slipped away . . . sitting in his chair. He went very peacefully . . . unlike the passengers on his bus.

Or:

My wife and I have a very spontaneous love life. The other day we just took our clothes off and did it on top of a freezer! I don't think they'll let us back into Sainsbury's again.

Old gags such as these show exactly how comics *reveal* their punchlines. The readers of crime novels are an equally willing audience, who can just as easily be blind-sided.

The best example I can think of from the world of crime fiction is in the wonderful Thomas Harris novel, *The Silence of the Lambs*, the second outing for the iconic Hannibal Lecter. Towards the end of the book, a SWAT team have the killer cornered and are approaching his house. At the same time, Clarice Starling has been dispatched to a small town many miles away to tie up a few loose ends. A member of the SWAT teams ring the killer's doorbell. We 'cut' to the killer's ghastly cellar from where he hears the doorbell ring. This is the moment when the 'dummy' is sold and the reader buys it completely. The reader stays with the killer as he slowly climbs the stairs, butterflies flitting ominously around him in the semi-darkness. We know he has a gun . . . we know what he is capable of . . . He opens the door, and . . .

It's Clarice Starling! Boom-tish! The SWAT team are at the *wrong* house, she is at the *right* house and she doesn't know it. It's the perfect reveal and it is sublimely timed because it happens at the precise moment that the reader turns the page. The best crime fiction is full of heart-stopping moments such as this. They, too are punchlines, pure and simple, albeit rather darker than the ones you might hear trotted out at the Comedy Store.

But the reason that Harris's reveal works so wonderfully is not just because of its exquisite timing. It works, above all, because of the *character* of Clarice Starling: a young woman the reader has come to know well over the course of the novel; to care about and to empathize with.

Ultimately, *this* is where I believe that the key to genuine suspense is to be found.

This revelation happened a good many years ago when I was reading a novel called *The Turnaround* by the American writer George Pelecanos. Pelecanos is happy enough to call himself a 'crime writer', or 'mystery writer' as they are more commonly known in the US, but he is not one of those writers overly concerned with the sort of tricks already described.

There is usually an episode of shocking violence and there is
often an element of investigation in its aftermath, but his books
are not traditional mysteries by any means. What he does do,
however, as well as any writer I know, is create characters
who live and breathe on the page. As I read his novel, I realized I had come to know some of these people so well that the
idea something terrible was going to happen to them – and I
knew it most certainly would – had become almost unbearable.
I was turning each page with a sense of dread and it dawned
on me that *here* was the best and most satisfying way to create
suspense. That it had been staring me in the face all along.

These are crime novels, after all. The reader has seen the
jacket, read the blurb and knows very well what they are in
for. Yes, there may be redemption and resolution of a sort, but
there will also be suffering and pain, grief and dreadful loss.
You know it's coming, but not when or to whom.

The tension is real and terrible, because you *care*.

So, by all means throw in a thrilling twist every now and
again, but not so often that they lose their power to shock.
Time those 'reveals' to perfection to give your reader a punchline they will remember for a long time.

But above all, give your readers characters they can genuinely engage with, who have the power to move them, and you
will have genuine suspense from page one.

Mark Billingham's discussion of the comedian's 'reveal' leads to
consideration of the skilful use of humour, which can help flesh out
characters, whether or not they are on the right side of the law.
Bill James's novels illustrate the point time and again. As John
Harvey has shown, James has a flair for attention-grabbing openings, and these often employ humour, as in *The Lolita Man*, which
begins: 'Ruth Avery used to say that making love with Harpur was
like being in bed with all of E-Division'.

Cops and Criminals, Contrast and Comedy
Bill James

My criminals display good as well as bad qualities and my policemen (Detective Chief Superintendent Colin Harpur and Assistant Chief Constable Desmond Iles in particular) blur the boundaries between good and evil. This gives me more material to play around with. The contrasting qualities in character mean, I hope, that they're more interesting. It certainly makes them more interesting to me.

I'd like to think I have a comic view of society and mankind in general and that I sometimes get this across. Yes, sometimes the humour is meant to come from the sight of people struggling towards an objective, even an ideal, and, of course, making a muck of it.

I introduced Harpur and Iles in *You'd Better Believe It*, which I wrote as a one-off. There were quite a few rewrites and there was some difficulty in selling it at the beginning. I wasn't altogether confident about it. And it didn't get many notices at first. But I wrote another book about the same characters, *The Lolita Man*. And that got enormous coverage and reviews. And that, I suppose, then prompted me into thinking I must stick with this for a while, at least. And so then I went on and wrote *Halo Parade*, and the series grew from there. It's now been running for more than thirty novels, published at a rate of roughly one a year.

I think that it was Len Deighton who said that he likes to get something on every page that makes the reader smile or possibly laugh. It's a continual job. You've got to keep on making the book amusing page by page, not overall.

I like aggressive humour. The kind that quite often comes, on the police side, from upending order. And on the crooks' side, the humour springs from their aspirations to be businessmen: serious, sometimes even moral people. The way they talk is at variance with how really they are. The humour in that contrast usually works well and suggests what I'm always trying to suggest: that we're on the edge of chaos all the time.

Iles is the more complicated of the two lead characters. He's basically a good cop. But very basically. He never takes money; he's not bent in that sense. He's ruthless in what he does, and sometimes acts in the way the criminals act in order to catch the criminals. In some ways, he's also weak. He's unattractive to his wife, who has an affair both with Harpur and one of the other cops, Francis Garland. And Iles knows this and it drives him berserk.

Harpur represents the proper, nose-clean side of policing – most of the time, although he will take short cuts. Iles constantly mocks him for being too conventional and too timid. But quite often Harpur is the one who gets things put right, who actually runs the place behind Iles's back to some extent. He neutralises Iles. And he appears to work his own way, and sometimes actually does work his own way, and succeeds where Iles's methods might not.

Somebody asked me, in an interview in France, if I was Harpur. 'Oh, no!' I said. 'I'm Panicking Ralph!' I understand people who get scared, which he does. I understand people who have crazy kind of ambitions. He wants to turn his rather seedy club, The Monty, into something like the Athenaeum in London, which is preposterous. But, we all have those ambitions and they are in some ways poignant and in some ways comical, so that I can get a fair number of laughs out of Ralph and similarly out of the other big dealer, Mansel Shale, who pretends to a kind of social style.

The technique of the books is to give qualities to people that are a surprise in them. Harpur and Iles work, if they do work, as fiction characters because they are not sergeants and constables, they are extremely high-ranking cops who don't always play by the book. So there is kind of a shock element in that. Of course, I'm not the first or only crime writer to show a cop (or cops) with faults. Perhaps Iles drifts closer to the outrageous, though, and he is always beautifully dressed – uniform or civvies.

A key question for authors with police officers as protagonists concerns how much attention they devote to describing police procedure realistically. John Wainwright was a serving police officer for many years before becoming a prolific and successful crime writer and, from 1983, a member of the Detection Club. His inside knowledge of the lives and work of detectives gives his books a strong flavour of authenticity.

Conversely, Colin Dexter achieved global success with his books about Inspector Morse without troubling too much about the detail of police procedure. The millions of readers who love Ruth Rendell's books about Reg Wexford and P. D. James's series about Adam Dalgleish are not unduly concerned about technical minutiae. The strength of the characters, settings, and plots offer more than adequate compensation.

Similarly, Marjorie Eccles' prime focus is on telling a story about interesting people. In the course of a career lasting over thirty years, she has written a wide range of books; contemporary and historical crime series as well as stand-alones and many short stories. Like Mark Billingham, Bill James, Colin Dexter, Ruth Rendell, and P. D. James, she has seen her police detective brought to life on television.

Making Characters Believable

Marjorie Eccles

It is a truth universally acknowledged that a crime writer possessed of an idea for a novel must be in want of characters.

All right, so we have our basic idea. What has triggered it off? Where has it come from? That perennial question, often as unanswerable to writers as it is to the readers who invariably ask it. To which the response has to be, who knows? Anything could have given birth to it: an intriguing incident that's been squirrelled away for further use and suddenly raises its head with possibilities; the unexpected recall of an atmospheric place; a niggle that's been buzzing around in your subconscious. It may be a new, exciting snippet of news that's sparked off possibilities for a story; it may have lain dormant for a long time; but now the seed is there, ready to germinate.

And here too are the shadowy figures in the wings, waiting to put flesh and blood on the skeleton idea. No problem, one would imagine . . . it's relatively easy to put together a few random people to carry the story through, isn't it? Maybe, but the tricky bit lies in making them come alive enough for the reader to recognize and identify with, to care enough about.to want to turn the pages and reach the end of the book. They have to be realistic, recognizable and believable in an imaginary world in which chaos, crime and violence exist, or which will certainly intrude; a world most people will hopefully never encounter.

In an ideal situation, there would be a convenient recipe handy, a formula for creating such characters, but I've never been able to find it. In the end, I believe it has to be largely intuitive, relying on one's own experiences and observation of how people speak, think and act. Human nature doesn't change. The human race continues to possess the same propensities for good or evil, intelligence or ignorance, kindness or cruelty, love or hate, the same capacities for jealousy and revenge as it always has. But how readers will see the characters you have envisaged in the way you wish needs a good deal more thought.

How much does physical appearance matter? To begin with, readers need to be given a general but not necessarily lengthy picture of the sort of character you are envisaging when they are first introduced. Appearances being notoriously deceptive, something about them, the sort of first impression we get when we meet someone for the first time, is probably a better option than a detailed description at this point. We can leave it to the reader's imagination to do the rest, to build up their own impressions as the book progresses and more of the character's traits are revealed through their speech and actions.

It may be advice that's been given too often, but it's not a bad idea to try to get under the skin of one's characters. Look at how actors do this, stepping into the life of a role and *being* that person – and then look at how successfully they handle characters when they turn their hands to writing, be it novels or plays. Live, eat, breathe with these as-yet-imaginary people. Try to understand just how they will respond in any given circumstances (not least when they are under stress), learning everything about them, their idiosyncrasies, their habits, good or bad, as well as you know your own (some of which you might never have suspected you possessed). You can't help but bring them to life.

As writers, we should know far more about the characters we've brought into being than ever ends up on the printed page. Like an iceberg, the ninety per cent mass below the surface supports what shows above the water. It can be self-defeating to give too much chapter and verse, slowing the pace if the story is mainly one of action; or worse, boring the reader. Better to allow for some speculation about them and their role in the puzzle that is a detective novel: why they have acted in such a way, what has motivated them. The satisfaction of working it out for themselves is after all is one of the things readers of crime novels enjoy.

Having said that, it's worth remembering that if the book is not set in the present day. attitudes and opinions are bound to be influenced by the times in which people live. I have written crime fiction set in the past, ranging from the early Edwardian age to the 1930s, all in all a period of incredible social change. The holocaust of the First World War, beginning in 1914, turned the world upside down and afterwards, for most of the people who had lived through it, life was never the same again. Working men who had experienced the horrors of trench warfare and fought alongside those previously thought to be their betters had gained different attitudes towards social class. Women who had shown themselves capable of taking on men's jobs during the war now sought independence and careers of their own. A million young men were amongst the countless number who lost their lives, leaving behind a spinster generation: the maiden ladies who later turned up in so much post-war fiction. Writing today, we must beware of attributing modern mores to characters who lived fifty or a hundred years ago, or vice versa. How someone thought and behaved about racism in, say, the Twenties or Thirties might not – probably wouldn't – be how that same character would react today.

I am often asked if my characters ever take over and begin to take the story in another direction. Well, if such a thing should seem to be happening, I would take a good hard look to find where I've gone wrong. Maybe the character doesn't fit in and should be part of another story altogether, but it's more likely that they have stepped out of character in some way. They are not acting consistently with how they have been presented until then. It is sometimes necessary to ask readers to suspend disbelief, but not to overlook aberrations of character. As writers, we have to hover over our creations with a coldly critical eye. Consistency is vital, and unconvincing deviations jump off the page and take away any belief in the person you have so far created. If I find one of my characters persists in acting as they shouldn't, they have to be put firmly in their place, or summarily dispensed with.

That isn't always so easy. These people are your creations, your darlings, and you have learnt to like if not to love them . . . even the baddies – vices being more interesting than virtues.

Villains can be great fun to create and to read about. We may smile and admire their cheek while deploring what they've done. Conversely, someone who is too nice for their own good can be at best irritating or worse, dull. But in an effort not to bore the reader, it's sometimes too easy to fall into the trap of creating grotesques, caricatures rather than characters, or another Frankenstein monster . . . all best avoided, unless it happens to be your deliberate intention to feature such in your novel. I suppose, if we're being honest, most of us are rather dull in real life, but this is not to say your characters should be. Nor do they have to be larger than life, although they can be believable if you believe in them enough, and consistently show in credible ways that you do.

Of course, creating the principal character is always the main concern. When I wrote my first contemporary detective novel, I had no idea that Inspector Gil Mayo was to feature in another twelve. Crime fiction was a new venture for me and I had no way of knowing whether such a book would succeed or not. I knew from writing my previous books that my central character had to be not only someone whom the reader could recognize and identify with, care enough about to want to read to the last chapter; but also someone I strongly believed in. So, when Mayo finally became established in my mind, he was an expat Yorkshireman, living and working in the Midlands, on the edge of the Black Country. Plain-speaking, down-to-earth, shrewd, occasionally bloody-minded, but basically soft-hearted. The sort of person I was surrounded with as I grew up, and knew well.

Unless he was to be a cliché, a stage Yorkshireman, he had to have other qualities. I was naive enough at the time to have no idea that showing him as particularly unusual or quirky, even outrageous in some way, was considered a good thing. I settled for the man as he first appeared to me. He didn't carry any emotional baggage, he wasn't a loner though he was a widower with responsibilities for his teenage daughter. At that point his love life didn't exist, though that was soon to be remedied when he met Alex Jones, a fellow police officer. He enjoyed walking holidays in Scotland, his favourite tipple was a single malt and his passion was music, mostly classical. He was logical, persistent and a demon for work, and I did allow him a strong streak of perceptiveness, that indispensable gift to all fictional detectives, which must happily get them there in the end.

The so-called Golden Age of crime novels, where the focus of the story lay on the amateur detective, with the police a barely acknowledged presence, had by then long been left behind. With the detection of crime becoming more and more a matter of police officers working as a team, the police novel needed more than a detective inspector and his sergeant or sidekick to get to the heart of the mystery, solve the puzzle and apprehend the murderer. Inspector (later Superintendent) Mayo had to acquire assistants.

Detective Sergeant Martin Kite was younger than Mayo, impulsive and good-natured, a locally born, married man with a young family, willing to work hard but not ambitious enough for promotion if it meant moving his family away. The temperaments of the two men were not in any way alike but they worked well together. I have found that the influences of background and environment are useful tools for adding other dimensions to a character and I think it helped in this instance that Mayo and Kite had their roots in similar backgrounds, areas of historical significance in the Industrial Revolution. The tough character and typically dry, self-deprecating humour of the people of the Black Country is something very akin to that of people living in the north of England: an inheritance in both cases from the harsh times in which their forebears were forced to exist.

The possibilities of a career for an ambitious woman in the police was something which had interested me for some time. As the only woman so far in Mayo's team had been Jenny Platt, a young WDC, I felt the time had come for more balance. Hence the arrival of a new assistant for Mayo in the person of Sergeant Abigail Moon. Abigail was young, university-educated, a high-flyer who had been through the rapid promotion process.

She was everything the rest of the team, including Mayo, was not and therefore provided a good contrast and another dimension to spark off the other members of the team. She lived alone and was highly ambitious, and achieved inspector status before long.

What all this amounts to, of course, is that characters are only formed through the filter of the writer's mind; there can be no set rules to follow, except learning to develop an eagle eye for inconsistencies and a ruthlessness in correcting them.

Sitting alone all day, over-caffeinated, making up stories and lies about imaginary characters on a word processor in the hope that someone will have the courage to publish your efforts is a cross that writers have to bear. But if and when someone does . . . well, like childbirth, the agony of producing it is soon forgotten. And meanwhile, who is that new character, hovering in the wings?

Integrating characters and their relationships with the setting and storyline is a key skill for the crime writer. June Thomson's contemporary series, set in rural Essex and featuring two police detectives, reached 'an extraordinarily high level of achievement, standing perhaps second only to P. D. James . . . in the art of combining the puzzle story and the novel of character', according to H. R. F. Keating in *Whodunit?* He chose *To Make a Killing* for his list of the hundred best crime and mystery books, making the point that Inspector Finch enters the story 'only after more than eighty pages have gone by. June Thomson uses those pages to give us three fine character studies of people who come to seem as real as anyone we have known in the flesh.' Although she established her reputation with novels about investigations conducted by police officers, in recent years she has become a leading exponent of the Sherlock Holmes story, while continuing to take care to integrate people, place, and plot.

Characters, Relationships, and Settings

June Thomson

Whether reading or writing it, I admit I prefer crime fiction to any other form of literature.

Crimes take many very different forms. Theft? Espionage? Fraud? Blackmail? Manslaughter? Or Murder? It's a broad range, and that in itself is interesting, especially to us – people who on the whole are not guilty of any of these transgressions but are emotionally moved by reactions that are unfamiliar and therefore intriguing. We want to know more about these responses. In other words, their effect on us can be a new experience in itself, which we find tantalizing.

This can affect our attitude to the crime novel. As ordinary, normal people we are, in short, nosey, and we want to know what happened, in reality or imaginatively. The crime novel, at its best, can supply the answers to these questions.

For me, firstly and most importantly a crime story gives the opportunity to explore a small circle of characters and the relationships between them. Statistics prove that murder is most often committed in such an intimate group or family setting. The random homicide is relatively rare despite publicity given to such cases by the media. Most killers and their victims are known to each other.

This gives the crime writer a fascinating and challenging opportunity. The permutations of relationships within such a group, and also within the even more tightly closed circle of the family, offer the chance to examine a whole cross-section of emotions and motivations. Jealousy, fear, revenge, hate and greed – all reasons for murder – are the basic stuff of human interactions, which have fired the imagination of such classic writers as Shakespeare and Dostoevsky. And in order for murder to be committed, two other factors are implied. Firstly, the relationship is usually long-standing but has reached the point of irrevocable breakdown; a far more interesting state of affairs to write about, in my opinion, than a romantic love affair where the intimacy has only just begun. Secondly, in real life – or real death – murder knows no social barriers. It is committed within all sections of the community, and this also gives the crime writer the opportunity to choose characters from widely differing social and economic backgrounds.

For the reader's sake, the number of characters has to be limited. I usually try to keep mine to about eight at most. If there are more, I feel the reader can't get to know them as intimately as I would like.

Mine are chosen from the ordinary men and women whom the reader might already know in real life. Murderers are not, generally speaking, depraved monsters. They are husbands and wives, sons and lovers, friends and colleagues – people who, apart from this single aberration of murder, are often decent law-abiding citizens. I like to feel the old adage 'There but for the grace of God go I' applies to them.

In my contemporary novels, I choose my backgrounds from those I am also familiar with – the rural Essex communities where I grew up and which can still be found in that particular south-east corner of England. In these close-knit villages and small towns, the local people know one another intimately. It's here where tensions and jealousies can develop and where old resentments and bitternesses that have built up over the years may suddenly explode into violence.

At the end of the books, I aim to show the effect that murder can have on these communities. Even when my Detective Chief Inspector Finch (renamed Rudd in the UK to avoid any risk of confusion with Margaret Erskine's Inspector Finch) and his sergeant, Tom Boyce, have successfully solved the case, not all the threads are neatly tied off. In real life, people's lives are affected, sometimes shattered, by violence happening in their communities and nothing is ever the same again.

This rural background allows me describe the type of

countryside which I find particularly attractive. It is not spectacular; it contains no mountains or waterfalls. It is agricultural
land, worked by generations of farming families, and to the
casual observer could appear unromantic. But its small woods,
full of primroses and bluebells in the spring, its flat fields of
wheat and sugar-beet and its wide skies give it a low-keyed
beauty which has its own appeal.

As regards plotting, one important rule I always try to follow
is this: the writer must be fair to his or her reading public.
Although it's permissible to lay false trails and to keep the
reader guessing, I like to include in my books some small clue
– sometimes only a phrase or a comment made in the course
of a conversation – which can be picked up and used as a
pointer to the identity of the murderer. I prefer, when the
denouement is reached, that the reader doesn't feel cheated
and that the thread, which has been there the whole time, has
led through the book to its conclusion.

Writing a crime story gives the author a broad choice of
time and context. When did it happen? Who was involved?
You can, if you wish, make it a real murder case which took
place in the past, using the past as your material, making sure
that such details of the people and the events are correct. This
makes less of an imaginative demand upon the author. Both
the events and the people have been based on reality.

An alternative approach is the story based on your choice of
the when, why and who of the event. For example, do you take
on the personal 'I' role and describe the events from that point
of view? If this is your choice, you may wish to create a second
person who you can share the case with. This personalises the
story, but the second character needs a specific role to play.

This is a method used in many novels, the relationship
between the two characters making the plot material much
easier to use. It's one I've used in novels such as the Finch
and Boyce books. In recent years, I have moved away from
this approach because although you can fill in a great deal of
detail with discussion of the events, the demands of an official
police inquiry can complicate the construction of the plot.

In recent years I have written stories featuring that classic relationship: Sherlock Holmes and Dr Watson. I find that this allows me greater freedom with both the characters and the plot itself.

But whatever form you prefer, it is important to have a setting and a plot that will catch the attention of your readers. Descriptions are valuable, as long as they aren't overused. Too many adjectives can slow up the plot and spoil the excitement of the story, which should be puzzling to the characters and, most of all, to the reader. The aim is to give him or her the thrill of the final explanation – the 'of course' reaction which creates the perfect response to your story.

Places

Where should you set your crime story? Somewhere you know intimately? Or somewhere far distant that you know much less well but find fascinating? As usual with writing, there are few if any hard and fast rules.

The ideas for most of P. D. James' stories sprang from particular places, often parts of her beloved East Anglia. One evening on Dunwich beach, she pictured a small dinghy drifting, oarless, and bearing a neatly dressed corpse whose hands were severed at the wrists. This striking image was the genesis of her third novel, *Unnatural Causes*. Even in *Innocent Blood*, where for once the starting point was not a location, the London Underground, the streets of the capital, and 'the darkly numinous roof of Westminster Cathedral' are all integral to the narrative.

On the Suffolk Coast
P. D. James

I have used East Anglia as a setting for a number of my novels, the last example being *Devices and Desires*. The book had its genesis when I was exploring Suffolk with an elderly long-standing friend, Joyce Flack, who drove me in her ancient Mini. I stood for a few minutes alone on a deserted stretch of shingle and looked over the cold and dangerous North Sea. I remember that there were two wooden fishing boats scrunched into the shingle and some brown nets strung between poles, drying in the wind. Closing my eyes, I could hear nothing but the tinny rattle of the shingle drawn back by the waves and the low hissing of the wind, and I thought that I could have been standing on the self-same spot a thousand years ago, hearing the same sounds, looking out over the same sea. And then I opened my eyes and, looking south, saw the silent and stark outline of Sizewell nuclear power station dominating the coastline. I thought of all the lives that have been lived on this shore, of the windmills, once providers of power, now prosperous homes; of the ruined abbeys at Leiston and South Cove, which seemed like monuments to a decaying faith; of the detritus of my generation, the great lumps of concrete half embedded in the shingle, and the concrete pillboxes, part of the defences against the expected German invasion on this coast. And immediately I knew with an almost physical surge of excitement that I had a novel. The next book would be set on a lonely stretch of East Anglian coast under the shadow of a nuclear power station. The book, at present no more than a nebulous idea born of a moment in time and a specific place, might take more than a year to research and plan and the writing even longer, but already it has life.

Rural landscapes are a crucial ingredient of Ann Cleeves' fiction, and have provided vivid backdrops to successful television series based on her books, *Vera* and *Shetland*, as well as her new Two Rivers series, set in north Devon. Here she offers thought-provoking observations about the connections between people and place.

The Human Geography of Crime Fiction
Ann Cleeves

My daughter's an academic, a human geographer. She researches specific communities in some of the more deprived areas of North East England; her work has taken her to a women's group in Gateshead, into an old people's home to explore the attitude of the elderly residents to end of life care, and to talk to men who are suffering from cancer. She spends time with them and uses their words in her writing. The places where these people live – the streets where they grew up, formed friendships, met their partners, brought up their children – affect who they are and the way they see the world. This is human geography and I think it provides a model for the way crime writers work. Place is an indicator of educational background and financial status. It influences how healthy we are and how long we live. In many cases it defines class, and class is still potent in every genre of British fiction.

If characters are at the heart of the books that we write – and I believe that they are – then place is vital for authors too. The setting we choose for our novel plays a more important role than simply providing a pretty or atmospheric background to the action. It can explain the motive of the killer and the back story of the detective, the relationships between suspects and witnesses. It fixes the characters in our readers' minds and helps writers to consider them as concrete, rounded beings, with a credible history; they become solid, rooted in the land-scape, whether the landscape is real or fictitious, rural or urban. And place can influence plot.

In the very best contemporary crime fiction, place is intrinsic to the book, and provides the glue that holds all the different elements together. It would be impossible to imagine Chris Hammer's amazing debut novel *Scrublands*, for example, set anywhere else but Riverend, the fictitious drought-ridden small town, where a well-loved priest stepped out of his church to kill five people. The place explains everything about the book. Emma Flint's debut *Little Deaths*, set in Queens in New York in the 1960s, throbs with the energy of the city. Ruth, her central character, couldn't have come from anywhere else. In the same way Gillian Flynn's *Sharp Objects* grows out of the steamy, oppressive American South.

Because of the power of the setting, I know where a new novel will be based long before I know anything else about it, before even I have a sense of the general theme, tone or voice. Place is always the first decision I make. More recently, because I've been alternating between Vera Stanhope books set in Northumberland and Jimmy Perez books set in Shetland, the choice is inevitable, fixed in the contract with my publisher. There has been a joy in coming to the end of a book and thinking: 'Now I can go home again and spend some time in Northumberland.' Or to get excited about sending my imagi-nation back north to the Shetland Isles. Within those places, however, I still have to decide on the *kind* of community I want to use, and that can be random, triggered by a whim or a visit or a scrap of overheard conversation.

My backgrounds are generally rural; I've scarcely lived in a city and don't understand how they work. But there's a tremen-dous variety within the British countryside. A former pit village in south-east Northumberland is quite different from a village built around an almost feudal estate in the north of the same county. Often the community that's caught my interest will lead to the theme of the story. It might be an enclosed setting, like the writers' retreat in *The Glass Room* or the tiny island of

Fair Isle in *Blue Lightning*, for example. Other places are more open to outside influences, like the seaside town of Whitley Bay in *The Seagull*. Not every place ends up as real in the book – I feel free to invent, or to merge. But the human geography *is* always real and at the heart of the story.

The Seagull, a Vera Stanhope novel, grew out of a conversation with regulars in my local pub. They were talking about how my home town had changed over the years, from a thriving holiday town, packed by visiting families in the summer, to a party town, rather sleazy and depressed. Now it's regenerating again into somewhere a bit smarter and arty, with an independent cinema, a poetry festival and a thriving community garden. Still a bit scruffy, but definitely more alive. The theme of the book is about the possibility of change and growth, both for places and for individuals. That theme grew out of the place and the book would never have been written without it. In turn, I needed to find characters who had changed and developed too and that meant a plotline about digging into the past, an explanation of the protagonists' growth.

With the Shetland books, the scope is rather different and more limited. There are no big cities, not even any large towns. While the geology varies, the landscape experienced by people is similar: bleak, bare and beautiful. That's why I stopped writing about the place after eight books, and why the TV series has developed story-lines with wider themes, taking their characters away from the islands to Glasgow or Norway. However, the books are still entirely influenced by the place, and by the preoccupations of the people who live there: crofting, the decline of oil wealth, the importance of family and tradition. That's the element of human geography again. In a more direct way, how Shetland looks has a bearing on my writing. I love the contrast between the open landscape – there are few trees, so usually it's possible to see right to the horizon in all directions – and hidden secrets. The Shetland books are all about secrets and the kind of psychological archaeology that digs into the past to explain family rivalries and tensions.

So, that's how I work, but if you're a new writer trying to

decide on a setting for your book, what's the best way to go about it? Do you have to choose a place that you know well? I hesitate to give advice, because everyone has his or her own way of working. Famously, it's said that Harry Keating had never been to India before writing his Inspector Ghote books, and for me they conjure up perfectly the heat and the noise of the place. But I've never been to India either and someone born and brought up there might see things rather differently.

Of course, it's easier now with Google Maps and all the information at the click of a mouse to get a sense of a place. It's still possible to get things wrong, though, and locals can be unforgiving about a small mistake. A very fine writer set a book in Shetland without visiting. She did a lot of research and saw that the islands were famous for their seabirds and specifically for puffins. In one scene she had a puffin perching on a windowsill. Anyone familiar with the islands, or with natural history in general, knows that the puffin nests in rabbit holes on the tops of sea cliffs. They spend all their time over the ocean and never venture inland. Unfortunately, this one error clouded some people's judgement about what was otherwise a very scary and exciting book. That was all they remembered.

I might set a piece of short fiction in a place I've only visited briefly. That initial stunning response to a place can trigger an idea for a whole story. I've set work in Alaska, Tanzania and Finland on the basis of the first excitement, of feeling that I have an understanding for a place in a single moment. We're immediately aware of the difference, the smells, the sound, the sense of being an outsider, and that instant impression is invaluable. One never sees a place in exactly the same way again. Once we're used to it, the impact is gone. A novel is rather different, however. I think a novel needs a longer knowledge. The imagination needs time to simmer.

We come back to the *human* geography when we talk about researching a place that's new to us. Of course, drive around the area you have in mind for the setting of your book; take photographs and look at Ordnance Survey maps. Pick out small, interesting details in the landscape and the built environment that make the area special. As with character, it's the small specifics that bring a scene to life. But meet the people. Hang out in cafés and shops, lurk in the library, use the public transport. If you have questions, ask them. Most people will be fascinated to hear you're a writer and nearly everyone likes talking about their lives.

We think it's entirely natural to talk to experts about police procedure and forensics. When it comes to place, the experts are the people who live there, and they're easy to get to know with just a little effort. It's impossible to write with any authenticity if you don't understand a region's anxieties and preoccupations. In a village café in the Northumberland National Park, much of the conversation will be about sheep. In Shetland it might be about fish, or fiddle music, or the extortionate price of the ferry. In a city it might be school closures, or theft or vandalism. But you won't know until you listen. None of this detail might come into your book in a hard, indigestible chunk, but it will be there in the confidence with which you create your characters and in a greater ease when you're driving the plot.

Of course, the easiest thing is to set your work where you live or have lived for some years, and I've taken this route, which feels at times like cheating. This has its dangers too, though. We can make assumptions about the places we know well; a region can change and we can have an impression of it that might be stuck in the past. We don't approach it with the same clear-eyed vision that we do a place new to us. And we can be so close to a place that we blur the line between fact and fiction, introduce real people and real issues without quite realizing.

I make no apology that my fiction can be escapist. I love the fact that people can lose themselves in my stories and the world that I've created. We all need times of escape. I want there to be a certain authenticity, though. I want readers to believe in my characters, in the relationships I describe, the ways families might fracture or hold together, the communities

in which a murderer might grow. And in my opinion, I have
to understand place before I can attempt that kind of reality.

Writing in 1986, Robert Barnard, who had spent most of his adult
life lecturing in Australia and Norway, said that when he was writing
his early novels he felt so out of touch with his native Britain that
he eventually moved back home. He had felt that 'at least the British
people in my books would start talking as British people do today.
He believed that visits to a country, even your own, only allow you
to skim the surface of local life, and that 'package-tour mysteries
. . . are always less than satisfactory'. He gave examples of books
written by three Detection Club members, Agatha Christie (*A
Caribbean Mystery*), Ngaio Marsh (*When in Rome*), and Ruth Rendell
(*The Speaker of Mandarin*) and concluded in *Colloquium on Crime*:
'Better to invent your own country as in [Christianna] Brand's *Tour
de Force*.'

But you really do not have to be confined to your homeland or
to invent a country unless you wish to. Christie's personal experience
of archaeological digs in the Middle East, for instance, strengthens
books such as *Murder in Mesopotamia*. Ngaio Marsh was equally
at home writing whodunits set in Britain or her native New Zealand.
Many authors have shown that it is possible to write novels which
carry the flavour of authenticity despite being set in a country where
they have never lived. Michael Ridpath explains how it can be done.

Setting Stories in Unfamiliar Places
Michael Ridpath

The Icelanders have a saying: *'Glöggt er gests augað'*, which means: 'A guest's eye sees better.' It's an answer to two important questions. How can a writer write about a country in which he is not a native? And why should he?

To take the second question first. 'Write what you know' is good advice, especially for a writer writing her first book, but it is one of those rules of writing that is made to be broken. Novelists enjoy writing about worlds that are not theirs, just as readers enjoy reading about them. In theory, authors could just stick to their own areas of experience, their own backgrounds, people who are just like them. It is easier to write a novel in a setting with which you are intimately familiar. But why renounce enthusiasm for foreign people, countries and landscapes? Why not harness it? The same impulses that encourage an author to tackle a particular subject: curiosity, excitement, affection, even love, are exactly those ingredients that give a novel its heart, that make it stand out from the rest.

I started my career writing financial thrillers, many of which took place overseas in places like Brazil, South Africa and Wyoming. Each one of these locations required a massive amount of research, which was only useful for one novel. So when I was searching for a setting for a new detective series, I decided to pick a foreign country and stick with it over several books. In choosing Iceland I completely ignored the 'write what you know' rule. I had only visited the country once, on a book tour ten years before, but I had been fascinated. And I was still intrigued by the place.

Now we come to that first question: how can a writer write about a country he doesn't know?

The answer involves reading, talking, visiting and recording, mostly in that order.

I usually start with a couple of general books about a country.

In the case of Iceland, I read a wonderful memoir by Sally Magnusson about a trip to Iceland with her famous father Magnus. For my Brazil novel, I found an excellent book entitled *The Brazilians* by Joseph Page. Don't underestimate the benefits of a close reading of the 'Basics' and 'Contexts' sections of good guidebooks, like the Rough Guide and the Lonely Planet series. At this stage you are trying to get an overview of the country and a list of more books to read.

This list should include memoirs, biographies and novels. You want to get an idea of the society and culture of your chosen country. You want to meet its people and to understand them. You are not really looking for facts, but you *are* looking for details. When you eventually write your novel, it is these little details which will make the location come alive. This is so much more than descriptions of town or countryside. It is habits, speech patterns, etiquette, furniture, superstitions, seasonal traditions – anything that is different from your own country, especially if it elicits a spark of interest in you. It will probably elicit the same in your readers.

Here are some examples of the kind of details I mean. In Iceland, people always take off their shoes when entering someone's home; Icelanders refer to everyone by their first name – even the President; and there used to be no TV broadcast on Thursdays. And when an Icelander hits a bit of unexpected good luck, he exclaims 'beached whale!', because what could be luckier than a massive store of meat, oil and blubber showing up on your doorstep one morning? I love that. All this needs to be written down. You need to record the small stuff; the big stuff you will remember.

This is also where you will find the ingredients for the characters who will people your novel. You will absorb their attitudes and thought patterns, but write down their backgrounds, their education, their professional careers.

Personally, I like to read some of the literature of the society I am writing about. Literature is particularly important in Iceland: it replaces the historical architecture the country lacks. The sagas are medieval stories, many of them set in the settlement period of 874 to 1100, when Norsemen farmed and squabbled. *Independent People* by the Nobel laureate Halldór Laxness is a novel about a tough independent farmer named Bjartur at the beginning of the twentieth century. Both these sources inspired story ideas, and both helped me understand the Icelanders better. Many Icelanders are Bjartur at heart: if you understand him, you understand them.

Read crime fiction by local authors. Good crime fiction shines a light on society, and different crime novelists illuminate their own countries from different perspectives. Reading about crime, you learn about the police and investigation procedures. But there is a difficulty: you can become inhibited in planning your own novel by a fear of stealing plots from the locals.

Finally, you should consult more ephemeral written sources such as blogs and magazines in the English language, which are easily found on the internet. Seek out some you like, read them regularly and note down useful details. For information on Iceland, I regularly read a Facebook page by Alda Sigmundsdóttir, the *Reykjavík Grapevine* and the *Iceland Review*. Every country has its English-language media and bloggers.

Which brings us to language. It clearly helps if you are fluent in the language of the country you are writing about, but it is not absolutely necessary. If you speak English, there will always be plenty of information written in or translated into that language. Nevertheless, it is a good idea to teach yourself a smattering of the language. I have tried to teach myself Icelandic, and I even spent some time learning Portuguese when I was writing about Brazil. It makes research easier, it makes travelling around the country easier, and it brings you slightly closer to the country you are writing about.

Having read a lot, it's time to talk. You need to find natives of the country you are writing about, and you need to ask them questions. Finding these people is surprisingly easy. People love to talk to novelists: well over half the individuals I approach, most of whom don't know me from Adam, are happy to talk to me. When I started I only knew one Icelander – the publisher

of my first financial thriller – but that was enough. I asked him
who he knew that could help me. I asked my friends and
contacts in England if they knew any Icelanders. If I read about
an Icelander based in London (where I live), I got in touch out
of the blue. They were all willing to talk to me. Later, when I
travelled to Iceland on a research trip, I put together a list of
contacts of contacts to speak to.

You have to be very specific in these conversations. If you
are not careful, an hour can be frittered away discussing politics or economics or the merits of different airlines. A good
technique is to sketch out an idea of a character in the book
you are planning to write – a rural priest, say, or the son of
an Icelandic fishing captain – and ask what that person would
be like. This works especially well if the person you are speaking
to is from a similar background to your character. In this case,
by talking about an invented individual, your interviewee is
more likely to tell you about their own experiences or those of
their friends than if you asked them directly personal questions
about themselves.

Once again, you are looking for details, details, details, and
you have to write them down.

A police contact is important. It's possible to manage without:
many highly successful crime writers are happy to make up
police procedure as they go along. But if you are the kind of
person who likes to get details right, you need to know what
the country's investigating procedure is. Most countries do not
follow the same legal systems that we see and read about in
Britain and the US, which means that their police investigations
proceed very differently.

Finding a police contact is not as hard as it seems. You will
find that someone knows someone who knows a policeman.
Failing that, you can always wander into a police station and
ask. If you are brushed off, go to another police station and
try again. If police officers are bored, they will talk to you. I
have tried this in America, Scotland, Greenland and, of course,
Iceland, mostly with success. It's worth waiting until you have
a good idea of the crime you are writing about, so you can ask

your police contact specific questions about it. These you really do need to write down in as much detail as you can. From experience, when you are actually writing your novel, you are likely to wish you had asked just one more question about the procedures for arresting and interviewing a suspect.

Do you have to visit the place you are writing about? After all, it will cost money and take time, and many writers do not have much of either of these to spare. I nearly always travel to the places where I set a novel. But there is now so much information you can gather online – from Google image searches to Google Earth to YouTube videos – that it is perfectly possible to write a novel based in a foreign location without ever visiting it.

But it's much better to visit the place if you can, for a number of reasons. Most obviously, your description will be better, not just because you will see more of the location, but also because you will hear it, smell it and *feel* it. Secondly, you will have a much better chance to talk to locals and ask them specific, useful questions. But also it will make writing the novel so much more pleasurable, and as I said before, a writer who enjoys what she is writing is more likely to be writing good stuff. When I'm at my desk writing about my detective Magnus in Iceland, I feel that Magnus is there, that I am there, that I or we are moving through the landscape I have visited. I love it.

I have found the ideal time to visit is just after you have started writing your first draft. You probably know where most of the action takes place, and you also know the locations you still need to find for various events in the plot – where to hide a body, perhaps, or where to locate a showdown at the end of the book. Then you go where your characters go.

Researching the country itself is fun. Your senses are alive, your brain buzzing with how you can fit what you see in front of you into the book that you see in your imagination. There are a few things to keep an eye out for.

Note your first impression of a location. How does it *feel*. Write it down before it is overwhelmed by second impressions.

Look out for anything that *moves*: people, clouds, birds, vehicles, machinery, patterns of light. Portraying these, especially if you use imaginative verbs for the movement itself, will bring your description to life.

Look for *symbols* of the place you are visiting. This is my single most effective trick to encourage the reader to feel she is in the place you are describing. Find an obvious landmark or feature and mention it several times. That way, as the reader works her way through the book, she will begin to feel that the location is familiar. This works. Frankly, you don't even have to describe the landmark; repetition will do it. For Reykjavík, I usually use Mount Esja, which is a large rocky ridge to the north of the capital, or the big smooth concrete church on a hill in the middle.

And always talk to people.

You have read dozens of books, you have scoured the internet, you have spoken to people, you have visited your chosen country, and you have written it all down. You now have a *lot* of notes. It's time to organize them. This next step can take a week or two, but is time well spent. I create a monster file on my computer, which I label 'Research by Subject', which is broken up into dozens of headings. These might be general categories such as history, farms, superstition or birds. There will be different headings for each location or neighbourhood. And there will be sub-categories for descriptions of bars, restaurants, cafés, parks – anywhere characters might meet. Police, crime, lawyers and police procedures have their own sections. I then go through all the notes I have taken, copying and pasting paragraphs from the original notes into the new file under the relevant category.

This file can become quite large. My Icelandic file is now 420 pages. Even my file for one book, *Traitor's Gate*, which was set mostly in Berlin in 1938, is over 200 pages.

Organizing your research notes in this way is extremely helpful when you are actually writing the novel. Before you start on a scene set in a particular location you can quickly read over all your notes about it in one place, and you know exactly where to look when you need to find a detail as you write.

A few chapters of my novel *Amnesia* take place in Capri in the 1930s and '40s. Initially, I wrote them without visiting the island. But they didn't quite make sense to me, so I booked myself on an easyJet flight to Naples and spent two days there with notebook, voice recorder and camera. A couple of important scenes take place at the Villa Fersen, an abandoned mansion perched on the cliffs overlooking the Bay of Naples. It's hard to describe how I felt as I walked through those musty rooms where my characters had fought and loved, as I looked out over the sparkling blue water they had marvelled at. It was beautiful, yes. I had got some of the details right and some of them wrong in what I had already written. But at that moment I felt a kind of sublime elation, an awareness that my book and my characters were standing there with me, a sense of being at one with the world around me and the world inside my head.

That's why I write abroad.

M.O.

How do you set about writing your books? It's a question often asked when writers give talks. Inevitably, there is no single answer. Writers may be larks (P. D. James preferred to write in the early morning) or owls (Peter James favours working between 6 p.m. and 10 p.m., six days a week). Practical methods vary too; although most present-day novelists write straight onto a keyboard, Andrew Taylor sometimes dictates his stories. As usual, the question for any author is simply: what works best for you?

The *modus operandi* of crime writing involves far more than simply organizing your working day. A whole range of questions arise, many of them discussed in this section. And even after you've found methods that suit you, you may feel the urge to try something fresh.

Experimenting carries risks, but may also bring rewards. Mary Kelly abandoned her series character, a police detective, and promptly became the youngest author to win a CWA Gold Dagger with her next book, *The Spoilt Kill*. She told a Swedish interviewer, Jan Broberg, that she loved the discipline and order of crime writing: 'I should perhaps get lost in lack of form and all I want is a straight line . . . I want to grip people by the mystery and to have attention to the last page due to the unsolved secret . . . That is why I try sometimes something new. In *Due to a Death* I gave first a tantalizing view of the end without telling the secret. In *Write on Both Sides of the Paper* I gave flashbacks in order to indicate what sort

of happenings had undermined the security of my hero . . . I try
. . . to see how far I can go.'

You need to find your own voice. This involves expressing your
own experiences and personality through the rhythm and tone of
your writing. There are techniques that may help, such as making
use of all five physical senses in your writing and keeping in mind
that 'voice' is much more than just a matter of writing believable
dialogue.

There are no rules; you may have an instinct about how best to
tell your story, or you may find that success only comes through a
laborious process of trial and error. Val McDermid, who is not only
one of the leading crime writers of the modern era but also one of
the most versatile, puts her finger on the importance of finding the
right structure for the particular story you want to tell.

Let the Story Be the Driver

Val McDermid

More accidents happen in the home than anywhere else, which
may lend some much-needed plausibility to the overworked
genre of domestic suspense, or grip-lit as it's sometimes known.
About sixty debut novels cross my desk every year (I chair the
New Blood panel at the Theakston Old Peculier Crime Writing
Festival) and in recent years, the proportion of this sub-genre
has been rising.

That's not a problem in itself. If the books were original,
well-written or thought-provoking, nobody would be happier
than me. But sadly that's not generally been the case.

There have been notable exceptions, of course. Clever,
suspenseful reads such as Renee Knight's *Disclaimer* or Ben
McPherson's *A Line of Blood*. And then there are the mega-
sellers such as Gillian Flynn's *Gone Girl*, Paula Hawkins' *The*

Girl on the Train and S. J. Watson's *Before I Go to Sleep*, which all gave us interesting twists on the idea of the unreliable narrator.

These books need to deliver at least one shocking moment when the reader realizes that they've been looking at the picture the wrong way up. There must be a sudden twist in the direction of travel which takes us to an entirely unexpected destination. We readers journey hopefully, willing that moment to come.

There is, however, one fundamental problem for writers of such novels. To come up with one high-concept thriller with a genuine 'OMG' moment is a big ask but not an impossible one. To come up with a second, a third, a fourth – that's a lot harder. Structuring a whole novel round one twist that the reader cares about is hard to achieve.

One of the reasons for the popularity of crime fiction is its faithfulness to the idea of narrative. Crime novels provide their readers with stories that engage with their hearts and minds, but most of all, stories that make sense.

I'm often asked where my ideas come from, and my answer is that stories are everywhere. Once you train your antennae to hear them and see them, you can't avoid them. But a story is only the beginning of the process of producing a novel.

What's just as important as story is structure – how we tell that story. The stories that satisfy us have a beginning, a middle and an end. But they don't necessarily come in that order. Think of how you tell an anecdote in the pub or at work.

Sometimes you begin at the beginning. 'John picked me up to go fishing this morning.'

Sometimes you begin in the middle. 'So there we were, out in the middle of the loch, when John suddenly realized he'd left the back door open.'

And sometimes you begin at the end. 'You're probably wondering why I'm sitting here in the pub all wet and covered in fish scales.'

One of the questions that comes up again and again when I'm working with aspiring writers is, 'How do I know where to start?' The answer I usually give is simple. Imagine you're having a drink with your best friend. Where would you start telling them your story in a way that makes sense?

Over the years, the crime novel has proved itself to be extremely nimble when it comes to storytelling. Of course there's a place for the linear narrative that begins at the start of events and continues in a straight line to the end. But not all stories lend themselves to that sort of shape. And one of the toughest struggles we often face is trying to find the structure that allows us to tell the brilliant story niggling away at us.

I know from bitter experience that it can take years. Probably the longest I've struggled with a book before finally cracking it was the twelve years – yes, really, twelve years – it took me to figure out the structure of what became *Trick of the Dark*. The story sprang from a chance encounter in Oxford one sunny Saturday afternoon in August. By the end of the weekend, I knew who was dead, who had killed them and why. But I couldn't figure out a way to tell the story that preserved suspense and would induce a reader to persevere.

I wrote the first 10,000 words of that book and tore them up five times before I figured it out. The answer, when it finally came, arose from a change in circumstances in the world around me, not from anything smart that I came up with. It was an object lesson in patience.

Most structural problems are far less intransigent than that. And although the novel that emerges can seem complex, the route to reach that complexity is often as simple as working out how you'd summarise that story to someone else. For example, if you get a little way into it, then go, 'Oh. Wait a minute. Before this next bit makes sense, you have to know this,' then it's probably an indication that you need a prologue or a split time frame. The key thing is that the structure is ultimately organic; the shape is dictated by the story, not by a single moment where the world of the protagonist is turned upside down.

When I was working out the mechanics of *The Mermaids Singing*, I struggled with how to convey to the reader the events that had happened before my main multiple third-person narrative began. I could have had my police officers briefing Tony Hill, the psychological profiler. But I thought that lacked immediacy. It told the reader nothing about the impetus behind the killings and it felt very one-dimensional.

Then I hit on the idea of writing the killer's story from their point of view, in the form of a personal record that would be their own way of reliving what they'd done. It never occurred to me that it might be problematic to have two distinct time frames in the finished novel because it made perfect sense to me. The killer's first-person narrative begins some considerable time before the third-person narrative but they eventually converge. Many readers have spoken to me about *The Mermaids Singing*, but not one person has ever indicated they were confused by the timeline. I learned from that experience to trust that when a story made sense in summary, it would make sense when I'd written it.

The Mermaids Singing was the first time I struggled with finding a structure that bucked the traditional shape of the detective novel; but it was far from the last. One reviewer of its sequel, *The Wire in the Blood*, began by complaining it broke all the rules of the crime thriller – by page three, we know who the killer is; we know his target group and his motivations; and not all of the characters we're invested in make it out the other end. By the end of the review, the critic conceded he'd been completely won over.

Since then, I've played fast and loose with the narrative conventions in books such as *A Place of Execution*, *A Darker Domain* and *The Vanishing Point*. But I've done it because it was the only way I could imagine to tell the story, not because my goal was to reach a moment that made the reader gasp.

I'd learned a valuable lesson – let the story be the driver. Focusing on the shocking moment of the twist so often distorts a novel, bending it out of shape in a way that either frustrates or disappoints the reader. Of course there's a place on our shelves for the novel that relies on a sudden reversal of fortune. But it's a tough trick to pull off; it should be only one tool in the storyteller's kit. It's much more fun to play with the whole box of tricks!

Critics unsympathetic towards crime fiction have tended, especially in the past, to be patronising about the literary skills of crime writers. The truth is that many distinguished writers, from Edgar Allan Poe, Wilkie Collins, and Charles Dickens onwards, have worked in the crime genre from its earliest days, while there are many fine writers among today's bestsellers. Lindsey Davis speaks for many when she emphasizes the importance of literary technique, and she does so with her customary wit – and style.

Style
Lindsey Davis

I write historical novels. People are fascinated. But I complain that I am most often asked about how I handle the historical material yet I am almost never asked about style.

I started a sentence with 'But' there, because I needed to separate off a key point and a paragraph should have three sentences. Generally. A sentence should contain a verb, but I am writing this conversationally. If you break a rule, always understand why.

Variety is good. It keeps the reader interested. An ideal way to break things up is with a short paragraph.

Are you starting to see how I think about style all the time?

I am old enough to have been taught grammar. Baby boomers learned the parts of speech – verb, noun, adjective, adverb, preposition, conjunction – *at primary school*. In secondary school we were deconstructing sentences with in-depth parsing of clauses and phrases. By degree stage I actually liked 'gobbets', which were short examples of interesting usage for comment; I could knock off a gobbet while standing on my head in a bucket of water and singing a comic song, to use a phrase from Noel Streatfield. Do you want *your* work to be remembered fifty years later? Then you need style.

You can tell if you will enjoy a book from page one – and that will be because of how it is written. The mystery genre is wonderfully inclusive, in style as well as everything else. Agatha Christie supposedly wrote so simply that foreign students can use her for reading practice. Raymond Chandler's classical education made him the rich opposite: linguistic, muscular and witty. You need to find your own method. Mine is complex: educated working-to-middle class, Brummie, Oxford, BBC, both premillennial formal and whimsically maverick. I say this produces a versatile all-weather, multipurpose fabric, but I would say that. Like Chandler, I exaggerate my metaphors.

Times have changed, but any writer who was never taught grammar should learn it. (Research isn't only about guns or tides.) Emails and text may be degrading language, but once you know the basics, you have a choice. Know what rules you are breaking; then you can break them with panache. Boldly go. Start sentences with 'But' or 'And'. Use 'very' and nice'. I am hog-tied by 20th-century rules, so it gives me a thrill to use 'nice' very carefully or 'very' with nice precision. Older, old-fashioned people will appreciate this. Of course you want to write for the Young, but remember even the Young are impressed by good writing because the poor things can't believe anyone can express themselves so well so easily.

Regarding my repetition of 'so' there: 'rep' is a sin. Publishing rules have nothing to do with grammar, let alone style. Writers need to move with times they do not approve – or don't approve of. I recently learned that all 'is nots', 'would nots' and 'shall nots' etc. should be 'isn'ts', 'wouldn'ts' and 'shan'ts' nowadays, not only in dialogue but even in narrative. Well, I do write in a formal style, yet is not (isn't) the ideal to 'find your own voice'? ('It sounds like you, Lindsey!' Afraid so.) I wouldn't naturally say 'isn't' in a narrative sentence (unreliable narrator, or in-joke as we used to say). Nevertheless, because my novels usually bounce along in the first person, for pace or lightness, I do now consciously use contractions more often.

However, don't get me going on writing novels in the present tense.

A copy-editor or software checker will want to insert a comma at every opportunity. Commas are to indicate where to breathe or to clarify the sense, so don't be bullied. Prose splattered with commas like measles will drive readers mad.

While discussing punctuation, this reflects your personality. I use semicolons when two sentences are closely linked. One year my publishing house decided to have none – then the next year they wanted them everywhere . . . hey ho.

Hey ho? Ideally a writer/narrator should neither be visible nor show opinions. This chapter is non-fiction, by me, so I allow myself to sigh. In a novel, I would have a character do it, to illustrate and develop them. Of course in a whodunit any sigh may be fake or deliberately concealed, a useful subtlety. Mind you, with a historical, readers will tediously demand, 'Did the Romans sigh? Weren't they unemotional Stoics?' Hey ho again.

Equipped with general grammar and punctuation, you need your own tone. I am authoritarian. (Interesting that it starts with 'author'.) When wannabes flutter at me unsurely, I rage back. Never write a story unless you believe it deserves to be told. If you don't believe in it, why should anybody else? Don't ask readers to pay for your product unless your product has value. In your whodunit it's only the characters who should worry and be baffled. Give readers faith that despite the mystery, you do know where you are heading. Then you will be on your way – even while you still have no idea of the end. Style is partly bluff.

For me, this is like driving a car; you cannot mither, you alone must assume charge of the vehicle. Oddly, readers don't seem to mind bossiness; mine suppose I am somebody they like. Letters starting 'I've never written to an author before . . .' attest to it. This is a huge joke to friends, and surprising even to me. It shows what a wonderful tool style can be. For making you an admired personality it is so much better than wearing a big hat or a monocle.

Generally a whodunit is fast, clean and realistic. Historicals may be luscious and ludicrous, though dammit, they need not be. My Roman series involve touches of spoof, so I've had a gorgeous time mingling styles as much as I mingle content. Nothing beats variety, not only in plots but in word choice, sentence structure and length, paragraph length, narrative, and dialogue. This keeps people's attention. In outlining routine procedure you may even venture into forms, lists or sketches. I have occasionally used text boxes, Greek letters, fancy fonts to distinguish witness statements, ionic capitals for bullet points. Do this with a light hand though, because the story has to stride ahead without irritating people.

Words are a passion with me. Len Tyler writes wisely about this elsewhere in *Howdunit*. I strive for a wide vocabulary and am even allowed to invent, though it's rationed. The key is to be understood in context. I was proud when Australian fans tried to get 'nicknackeroony trays' accepted into general use for fancy comports for finger food at functions. I see some terms as pretentious; personally I would not use 'plangent' or 'mordant'. But I've learned to love 'louche'.

Meaning is only the start. I make conscious contrasts between monosyllables and polysyllables, words of Anglo-Saxon origin (concrete/domestic) or Latinate ones (abstract/intellectual). I love technical terms and they have a point: showing characters in different walks of life becomes easy if your accountants make accountancy jokes and use accountancy terms. Your thugs, of course, will have limited language skills. Thugs grunt, don't they? Well, they do until you create that even more interesting one, a thug who devises fiendish word puzzles . . .

It's a truism (posh phrase for true) that a single telling detail is better than lashings of banality. 'The cat sat on the mat' or 'the white Persian sat on the blue Axminster'? A warning though. One school of narrative stolidly tacks an adjective or adverb to every noun and verb: 'The tall man carefully entered the seedy bar. His icy gaze quietly noticed the peeling paint and the tired waitress . . .' Used throughout a book, I find this stompy. Much better to have no adjective sometimes, then enrich with several. Piling on colour with a list is particularly good when your much-abused protagonist finally snaps: 'Oh shut up. You're a foul, lying, ferrety, degenerate pest!'

I myself would punch in a contrast: 'With fleas,' I added.

Your own style may be plainer, but heck, such flash feels good. With age, I grow more daring. 'Only Davis could somehow ace the insertion of the anachronistic expression "pimping his ride" into a narrative about the splendors of ancient times' (*Booklist*). Actually, I discussed with my editors whether this was acceptable for that gorgeous jalopy, the emperor's triumphal chariot, and if so should we opt for 'pimp' or 'primp'? Incidentally, *Booklist*, top marks for 'ace'.

I do Humour. I have no space to talk about humour here. All I can say is be careful. Historical novelists are seen as woolly stereotypes and funny ones as even worse. You might prefer to be known for gritty realism.

In fact, I do Grit. Blood is fun. Perversions rock. My streets are mean, my villains vile, commerce stinks, politics are depraved and family life is dire. My smells are legendary (in description, use all five senses) . . . I try to do my grit properly. For instance, no poison victim is found lying serenely on their bed as if in a TV drama. I tackle the pain, diarrhoea and vomit. But style, or taste, comes in here, so I may show horror and cruelty not with sickening details of what occurred, but through reactions of witnesses, especially my investigator.

The whodunit is a helpful genre. *Who? Where? How? Why? With what?* and their lively derivatives, *However the hell?* and *Whatever was that for?* will give you structure and characterization as well as juicy content. How you handle them lets your style blossom. The necessary questions will handily fill up your manuscript, too, because you must include answers – wrong, misleading and impossible-to-find ones – before the right ones. This helps any obsessive author who keeps a word-count spreadsheet (who, me?), thus encouraging happiness, which is vital for a relaxed style.

I think rhythm is vital. We post-war babies hear our work like a radio play rather than envisaging it on a screen. If a book reads aloud well, this helps your audiobook readers and you, when you give public readings; I do think silent readers find a good rhythm pleasant too. The *Times* leader column was previously reputed to be in poetic iambs – thanks, Shakespeare. People once requested to use a Falco sentence they really liked: 'Being formally civil to idiots and wastrels was not my idea of a festive day.' Did they spot it was mainly dactyls? (tiddy-tum, tiddy-tum.) I had not planned it; that would be weird.

I keep coming back to variety. Sections where investigators mentally wrestle with problems don't only move the plot forward and show their professional intelligence; you can introduce reflection on wider issues like problems in society, quirks of law or public order, theories of investigation or interview techniques. In such passages your writing may be quite leisurely, extended with clauses as thoughts develop. Action scenes are different. I used to be nervous of action, but I learned to do two kinds. One is comic, therefore stuffed with vivid movement such as overturning vegetable stalls. The other is scary and tense. Then I strip down to heavy reliance on verbs, using short words and simple sentences. 'I ran. He came after me. I fell; he jumped on me. I kneed him where pain would take over then I fled . . .' This packs even more punch as a contrast to more elaborate sections.

I hope I've given you some ideas, and that they won't include copying me. Your style is central to your craft and must be personal. Don't let anyone muck it about. Enjoy it. Develop it. Make it serve your purpose.

When I began this piece, I may have been wrong to complain. Perhaps the best style is frequently invisible. It's a vital tool, yet however skilled your writing technique, what matters is your subject. You want your readers to notice what you have to say, not how you say it.

The importance of theme in a crime story is often underestimated. Thematic concerns are certainly not the exclusive province of authors of so-called 'literary' novels. The thriller writer Desmond Bagley argued in an article in *The Writer* in 1973 that the theme is the core of a book: 'It is what you want to say.' He gave examples from his own bestsellers: 'The theme of *Running Blind* was the sheer damned stupidity of international espionage, the theme of *Landslide* was the search for personal identity; that of *The Vivero Letter* was of the danger of using vanity to cure a punctured ego.'

Choice of theme may also enable a writer to address specific aspects of the broad questions about the moral reach of crime fiction, considered earlier by James Runcie and Frances Fyfield. Kate Charles, one of the Detection Club's American-born members, writes detective novels that are very different from Desmond Bagley's work, but she places similar emphasis on the question of theme.

Choosing a Theme

Kate Charles

People write crime novels – any novels, really – for all sorts of reasons. Some writers insist that they write to entertain, and anything else is superfluous. Others just like to tell stories – the more page-turning, the better. Some novels are plot-driven while others are character-driven. High-concept 'hooks' excite some writers; others are inspired by locations.

Perhaps it has something to do with all of the English literature courses I took at school and university, but I've always
found that my novels develop around distinct themes. This isn't
always something I plan from the beginning, but it usually
becomes evident by the time I'm in the middle of a novel.
Something has niggled at the back of my mind and is somehow
translated into the thoughts and actions of my characters.

I'm not altogether comfortable with using my own writing
as examples, though in this case I see no other way to do it.
I might infer the intentions of other writers as they develop
themes in their novels, as I was taught to do in all of those
English literature courses, but can speak with any degree of
certainty only about my own.

Utilizing themes is part of the privilege for a novelist, as I
see it, of having a 'bully pulpit'. My books are largely set against
the background of the Church of England, and often explore
issues which confront the Church in the modern world. I'm
sometimes asked by people within the Church why I never
sought to be ordained, and I tell them that my calling as a
writer gives me far greater scope to put across my own opinions and concerns than preaching sermons – to a few people,
in a specific place – ever could. I take a situation or issue that
I feel strongly about and wrap it in a story – a story about
people that I make the reader care about, and without them
knowing that they've done it, they've absorbed the point I'm
trying to make.

One of the ways I do this is through the use of a unifying
theme (or two or three) in a novel. For example, my first novel,
A Drink of Deadly Wine, explored the theme of choice: every
day, throughout life, everyone is confronted with choices to
make, large and small, whether they like it or not, and these
choices have consequences that influence and impact upon the
future. In this book I also tackled the relationship of the past
to the present, and secrecy versus openness and honesty.

In my second novel, *The Snares of Death*, I deliberately took
on a big theme: extremism. I wanted to look at the whole
spectrum of adherence to a cause or a point of view, and try

to identify at what point commitment (which most people would agree is a good thing) crosses the line to become single-minded fanaticism. This seems particularly relevant now, more than twenty-five years on. So this book features religious extremism, of course, but the theme is echoed in other ways – for instance, there is a linked subplot involving animal rights activists. A second big theme in this novel is 'change': good thing or bad thing? And to what extent is change possible in a world of black-and-white loyalties and alliances?

Sometimes my themes are actually reflected in the novel's title, as in *False Tongues* or *Cruel Habitations*. Others are perhaps further under the surface. The title *Deep Waters* is more metaphorical, exploring as this novel does the weird world of the cult of celebrity. Why, I asked myself, is the virtual worship of celebrity acceptable in a society which has largely turned its back on the worship of an actual deity? Again, this seems more rather than less relevant with every passing day.

Other themes which have engaged me in various novels include ambition and greed, hypocrisy, sacrifice, appearance versus reality, forgiveness, the potential costliness of love, and the meaning of 'family'.

My Callie Anson series, featuring a Church of England curate, is particularly reliant on themes. I didn't want to make Callie a clichéd crime-solving cleric, so the novels typically have two parallel story lines, one with Callie carrying out her church-related duties – in the course of which she engages with various parishioners and their problems – and the other in which the police investigate murders. What ties these two strands together is the theme or themes, so that one echoes the other thematically. In *False Tongues*, for instance, the police are dealing with a death linked to cyberbullying, while Callie contends with untrue and destructive gossip: two different manifestations of 'false tongues'.

Many words have been written about genre fiction – arguing that it is either overvalued or undervalued, that it is (or isn't) inferior to 'literary' fiction. Much has been made of crime novels that somehow straddle the boundaries between the genre ghetto and 'real' novels, citing such writers as P. D.

James and her successors. I would argue that it is the layers
of meaning imparted by themes that erase those boundaries
and transform what might have been an exercise in storytelling
– albeit a skilful one – into a full-fledged novel.

Pace matters in writing, as several contributors to *Howdunit* emphasize. In *Writing Crime Fiction*, Harry Keating suggested that, just
as there is a right speed for every stretch of road when driving, so
there is a right pace for each scene in a book; it's unwise to dwell
on the trivial, and a mistake to rush a denouement. More specifically,
he quoted advice once passed on to him by Margery Allingham,
who suggested getting a surprise into the story every ten pages and
a shock every twenty. But he acknowledged that this was nothing
more than a crude rule of thumb, not to be taken too literally.

How to pace a story is inevitably a personal question for each
writer, but pace is as important a component of a historical mystery,
for instance, as it is of an espionage novel or adventure story.
Michael Jecks is best known as an author of medieval mysteries,
but he has also written short stories set in the present day and a
contemporary spy thriller, *Act of Vengeance*. Here he offers practical
insight into the techniques he employs.

Pace

Michael Jecks

One of the hardest aspects of writing is getting the pace right.

All authors know that first pages are absolutely crucial. Those
initial paragraphs can set the scene, the tone, for the whole

book. They are vital for grabbing the readers' attention and persuading them to embark on the story's journey with you. It's why it takes as long to write the initial lines as it does to write entire chapters later, when the basic character traits and themes are already developed.

But the author also has to sort out how to put the information on the page for the rest of the story. There are action scenes, but you don't want to have them all clumped together in an indigestible bolus halfway through the book; you have some humour, but it all occurs in the beginning, and there's nothing in the second half . . . and then you see that the section you define as character development is actually a tedious roadblock to the main thrust of the story itself. There is no pace, only a series of scenes with some form of linking between them.

As an author, how do you get around this?

When I started out, I had little idea of pace. I wrote for the joy of writing, and after reading a lot of books, I had a natural appreciation for aspects of storytelling that have stood me in good stead. When I outlined my first plot, I had no concept of planning for pace, other than a vague ambition to have gradually increasing tension through the book. It was pretty much a flow chart, since I had come to writing from the computer industry, and considered the crime story to be effectively a problem that could be set out logically.

However, after writing my first two books, I was suddenly struck with the problem of pace. I had good characters, I knew the direction of travel of the story itself, but the plot just didn't feel quite right. It wasn't strong enough in places. I was deeply dissatisfied, and somewhat confused. I had no idea how to analyse my own work.

So I took a rough draft of a previous book printed on A4 paper and tore it into eight strips. On each strip I wrote a heading for a scene and a brief synopsis of the scene (including what I wanted the reader to take away from it), and I put in a coloured blob.

Each of these strips was stuck to a block of shelves in my

office directly in front of my desk, where I could see it at all times while typing.

What was the purpose?

Well, first I wanted to be able to glance up and see at any time exactly how the story was progressing. From the synopsis, I could make sure that all the basic clues had been incorporated, and I could see how the story was developing as my scene descriptions grew. But the coloured blob was essential, because that was my pace marker, for want of a better description.

At first, I set out an ambitious range of colours, from deepest red for action, to purple for psychological thrills, to green for humour and – well, you get the idea. Very quickly I realized that the three most important were the ones I really needed: physical action, tension, and humour. And soon I learned that the main characteristic that I needed was action and conflict (psychological or physical, in other words). The humour was good to have, but I tend to find that I put in more so that it is marbled through the entire story. It would be more relevant to put in a marker where I had forgotten to put it in.

My own rule of thumb was to have a red marker for about every five scenes. That meant that there was a degree of tension in the story – a row between my two leading characters, marital issues, the effect of violence on other people, how the victim's death affected friends and family, or how the killer was impacted personally in the aftermath. These were more mental issues. Then I would try to ensure that there was a strong element of physical danger or action every ten to twenty scenes. Hopefully these would be much more impactful, and by using both, I would draw the reader on into the story.

So that is all very well, but how does it look when you have the strips of paper on the wall? Well, I took the decision to have the action/conflict set out with a large red circle on the scene. From sitting at my desk, I could easily see whether there was a preponderance of blobs clustered together or not. From that it was easy to see where the plot needed radical first aid. Similarly, if the sections are showing long periods without any

tension or action, you will see that at a glance and can plan
to balance the story more for pace.

For example, think of a four-scene chapter in which every
scene has a strong action element, but then the following
chapter has a bunch of scenes which are much milder – perhaps
the aftermath of the action. Or perhaps it's the scenes leading
up to the violence that slow the progress of the story. Either
way, it takes little effort to break up the flow of scenes by
perhaps using the action in flashback: use the post-action point
of view of a key character looking back at a fight; move from
their perspective to the initiation of the fight itself; back to the
present with the protagonist making a cup of coffee while
considering the argument or fight, and how someone looked
surprised; back to the fight and describing what actually
happened to the man – and so on. By breaking up the scene
the writer can make it more digestible.

With my approach, by having a title and synopsis with a
tension marker, the flow and pace of the story can be easily
understood at a glance. When necessary, my strips of paper
can be pulled from the wall and reordered (I used Blu Tack to
fix them to the bookshelves). After writing an entire book,
sitting back and considering it all was easy, and the only work
was rewriting scenes where their position in the story had
altered significantly, mainly to ensure that the timeline was
still effective – for example, making sure that I hadn't introduced a clue or weapon that hadn't yet appeared in the story.

I find this leads to a story that is better paced.

In recent years I have moved on from tearing up old drafts
of my work. When I moved to my current house, I invested in
a pair of enormous whiteboards, and rather than writing scenes
on paper, I began writing onto the board, using blue or black
ink for the majority of scenes, and red ink for those in which
there was conflict.

I have to admit, I stopped using this approach some years
ago. The simple fact is, it was so much easier to pull off one
scene and insert it in a new location. If one scene was too
long and needed to be split into two, it threw out the whole

of the rest of the book, necessarily meaning that I had to wipe the board clean and rewrite all the scenes. At least with strips of paper all I had to do was add two new strips and reorder all the other ones, with no need for rewriting them all.

Of course, in recent years software has been developed to make writing an easier process. I personally use the excellent Scrivener, which allows writers to break up their work into chapters, scenes, or any other series of useful sections. Each can be titled, together with a brief synopsis, and colour-coordinated. These can all be viewed as record cards sitting on a corkboard, which is wonderfully helpful. And yet I am returning to my old approach with my latest book. Why? Simply because I find it is easier to get an overall feel for the format and progression of the novel when I can see the whole story set out on a wall in front of me. I can get a better impression of the flow and pace at a glance. Scrivener is excellent, but seeing only some twelve cards at a time is limiting. I prefer to see the entire story.

There is another aspect of pacing which I would like to talk about briefly.

Some years ago I was employed by the Royal Literary Fund to help students at Exeter University with their written work. The RLF provides essential support to all levels of student, no matter what their discipline, by suggesting different approaches to dealing with problems.

One of the most common issues, I found, was students attempting to write to a perceived 'academic' standard. This would often involve the use of convoluted language and lengthy, largely incomprehensible sentences. I was determined to help them write with greater simplicity and clarity.

Here's one example. Often I would find a paragraph that was difficult to understand – usually because a sentence was so long that all meaning was lost. I would ask the student to copy and paste the paragraph into a new document. Then I would ask them to put in two carriage returns after each full stop. This meant that the paragraph would be presented as a series of sentences, more or less like bullet points down the page.

This has several advantages:

1. Rather than being embedded so they distract the eye and confuse the reader, each sentence can be viewed separately and individually;
2. The length of each sentence can be viewed relative to the ones before and after it;
3. The logical flow of the text through the paragraph can be seen with greater clarity.

Understanding each sentence without the confusion of surrounding text is essential. All too often when reading a sentence, the eye will see what it wants to see, and skip on to the next sentence. By breaking each out into a separate block of text, the writer can concentrate on it with ease. This is also helped if – as is always the case when editing – the words are read out aloud. The act of reading aloud forces a higher degree of concentration than merely reading silently.

Getting the sentences to be of similar length is more important in academic writing than in creative writing, but it is still vital that the author has a clear view of the relative lengths of the text. If writing action scenes, for example, you are likely to want to use shorter sentences that are more direct and pull the reader with you. It gives more of a sense of breathlessness and urgency. But if you have a series of short, snappy sentences, and then one that drags on for five lines, you can lose the pace of the scene. So in certain scenes, it can help to have more consistency of sentence length within the paragraph.

And finally, when the long sentences have been broken up into their constituent themes and concepts, it is easier to change the pace within the paragraph. It allows the author to increase the pace, beginning with longer (relatively) sentences, and gradually moving to shorter and shorter ones which pull the reader into the scene.

Are these hard and fast rules? No! These are merely

guidelines. There are some writers who will use such mechanisms (and who are very successful) – but that does not mean you have to be bound by them. After all, as any author will tell you, the most important rule of all the rules of writing is that there really aren't any rules. Only hints, tips and guidelines.

It's really up to the author to pick and choose the methods that appeal the most.

The obvious way to write a novel, you may think, is to start at the beginning and proceed from there to the end. Not everyone finds that approach suits them. P. D. James adopted what she called a 'jigsaw method of creation'; she visualized a book as a series of scenes, and the order in which she put them down on paper depended on her mood at the time.

The way in which a scene is written is crucial to the extent to which it fires the reader's imagination. It may even be helpful to write key scenes that don't actually appear in the final version of the book (for instance, the scene in which the murderer commits the crime) so as to be sure that what exactly happened is clear in your own mind.

The way in which individual scenes are integrated into the story as a whole is a key test of an author's skill. To take just one example, a small incident near the beginning of a book may foreshadow subsequent developments. Harry Keating called this 'planting', that is 'slipping in as mere hints at an early stage things that will later bulk large'. William Ryan, who like many other contributors to this book has lectured on aspects of creative writing, explores the detailed practicalities of constructing a scene.

Writing Scenes

William Ryan

Crime novels are made up of a series of scenes, designed to tell the story in the best way possible. That said, each scene is necessarily different, from a storytelling perspective, and will have its own needs.

You'll have noticed that I'm talking about scenes rather than chapters; and that's because they are different. A chapter is whatever passage of writing the author (or editor) says it is. Probably the best description of a scene is an episode in a novel where something *happens,* generally in the same place, often defined by a continuous time period and usually with the same characters involved. The scene ends when there is a shift in time, or a shift in location, or a shift in the characters that are the focus of the scene. That's probably more complicated than it needs to be and, in some cases, completely wrong. Fortunately, you're an intelligent reader, so probably have a good idea of what is and isn't a scene already.

So, let's get down to business.

Purpose
The starting point when writing a scene is to know its purpose within the overall story. Most likely, a scene will do one of three things in a crime novel – it will reveal a key piece of information about the crime or the investigation, present a challenge or danger to the investigator, or tell the reader something about the investigator or another of the significant characters (who isn't related to the crime). Sometimes, it will do all three things and very occasionally it will do none of them at all. What it must do is take the story forward, in some way or another, and if you know what the purpose of the scene is when you sit down to write it, you know that it has a place in the story. It also means you know what *has* to be in the scene and what you can do without. In addition, if your scene

is focused on a specific purpose, it has momentum both on its own and within the story.

Where should I start?

This is a tricky one but, in general, the sooner your scene gets to its purpose the better, particularly with scenes that are mainly made up of dialogue. If, for example, you are writing a conversation between a detective and a witness in which a key piece of information will be told, it's tempting to start almost at the point of the revelation. Obviously there has to be some lead in, but try to ensure that is done as efficiently as possible. This accelerated beginning doesn't work for every scene, of course. If the scene is about atmosphere or the setting, that's something you probably want to take time creating. Likewise, where the reader is aware that a key event will happen in the scene, possibly involving risk, delaying getting to it will create anticipation and tension. To an extent the approach you take is determined by the purpose of the scene and your desire to convey the purpose both efficiently and entertainingly.

Who is telling the scene?

Many novels are told entirely from one point of view, but if your crime story is told by multiple narrators, it's worth exploring the decision as to which perspective to use for a particular scene.

Even though there are no rules, if your investigator is present in a scene you will probably avail yourself of their point of view because the novel is, after all, their story. However, the character 'telling' the scene can generally only record for the reader their own inner thoughts and what their senses tell them. This means they can't know what other characters are thinking and nor can they see themselves, unless in a mirror. If your investigator is to be visible in a scene, then you may want to use a different character's point of view in order to show them to the reader. Likewise, if you want to be inside another character's head, for example to reveal that they are lying, then you might want to use that character to 'tell' the scene.

Another reason to shift to an alternative storytelling perspective is where you want to give information to the reader that the investigator doesn't yet have. This can be useful to create tension and anticipation. If, for example, the investigator is unaware that a colleague is in love with them, but you allow the reader to know about the attraction early on in the novel, hopefully you've created an ongoing tension that can colour the interactions of the two. This technique, of putting the reader ahead of the investigator, can also be used to foreshadow danger, crucial revelations and so on. In each case, the reader is engaging with the novel by wondering what will happen when the investigator uncovers the reality of their situation.

One last point on who is telling a scene. If a dramatic or exciting event occurs at which your investigator is not present, it's seldom a good idea to tell the investigator (and therefore the reader) about it through dialogue. Rewrite the scene, if you're able to, from the perspective of someone who is present at the dramatic event, who can then tell your investigator about it in abbreviated form. Mystery novels often have lots of dialogue, by their nature – so if you can show rather then tell something dramatic, it probably makes sense.

How should you start?
It's always a good idea to begin a scene by informing the reader which character's point of view you're using, where it is taking place, which other characters are present or soon will be, and any other crucial information (such as if someone is pointing a gun at someone else). This can all be done in one or two sentences. You may also want to remind the reader of any previously discovered information that is going to be relevant to the scene. Are there exceptions? Sometimes withholding or obscuring information is essential to building tension or creating questions in the reader's mind. For example, if you are writing a scene from the killer's perspective, you probably want to obscure quite a lot of information – but, at the same time, give

the reader some clues to get them thinking. If the reader is trying to work things out, they're engaging with the story and that is very much a good thing.

Conflict, risk, obstacles and subtext

There's a lot of overlap between these but if your scene is feeling a bit flat, you may want to consider adding some extra ingredients.

Conflict is ingredient number one. Nearly all crime novels revolve around an investigator who is at odds with most of the other characters and, likely as not, the environment they find themselves in. On top of which, the likelihood is the other characters won't be on good terms with each other either. This is just as well as a mystery novel would probably end very quickly if this weren't the case. For a start, no one would have a motive to kill the victim so there would be no murder, murderer or possible suspects; and even if we managed to overcome that minor problem, we'd have all the characters doing their best to help the investigator to solve the crime – which would mean honesty, cooperation, support, a lack of misinformation, no hidden agendas and quite a lot of very easily obtained truth. You don't need your characters to be shouting at your investigator on every page, but you do need them to make life difficult and to force the investigator into finding ways to overcome those challenges. It's worth identifying, therefore, possible points of conflict in a scene. If, for example, you are planning a scene in which your investigator will uncover a certain piece of information from a witness, you may want to consider why the witness might not want to tell the truth, and how this will manifest itself. Likewise, anything you can do to create difference of opinion on how to manage an investigation between colleagues will be useful, and any opportunity to create awkwardness of any kind for your investigator should at least be considered.

Risk, or danger, is also a nice thing to have, particularly in the second half of the book where you are generally looking to escalate drama and tension. The risk doesn't necessarily need to be physical; it can also be emotional – something that will cause the investigator mental concern or stress – or status-related, where the risk can be to the investigator's economic or social wellbeing. The risk can be either to the investigator or someone they care about – a lover or child, for example – and it doesn't necessarily have to be significant. It can be just a fear of embarrassment, making a mistake or risking rejection from a member of the opposite sex – although physical danger definitely works. Risk is not something you want to introduce in every scene, but it can certainly add a little flavour if you do.

Obstacles are another ingredient that can help a scene, and indeed your story as a whole. The more challenging you can make the investigator's progress towards the final objective, the better; and you can add a useful obstacle to almost any scene. Obstacles can be minor, such as a phone that doesn't work or a missed appointment, or more substantial, like a serious injury or a lost piece of evidence. While a more substantial obstacle will have significance for the entire novel, sometimes it can work solely within the scene. For example, if your investigator needs to extract a piece of information from a witness, making that witness deaf or unable to speak the same language is going make your investigator have to work that little bit harder, which is good.

It's also worth thinking about what might be going on underneath the surface of a scene. Overall, having a subtext to the novel may lead to a twist or a reveal which undermines or even contradicts everything the reader has understood up to that point. In scene terms, introducing a hidden element may just make the scene more interesting. If you have a straightforward information-gathering scene, where your investigator is perhaps interviewing a suspect of the opposite sex, introducing a strong attraction between them or, even better, a strong but hidden antipathy will alter how the scene develops. If one of the characters is unaware of the emotion on the other side, it's going to change the shape of the scene still further.

When to end a scene

Each scene in your novel will have at least one narrative purpose and if it doesn't, it probably should. The good news is that if you have worked out that narrative purpose, the scene should probably end pretty soon after you have achieved it. If you do continue past an obvious connection with the purpose, you need to have a good reason to do so.

How to end a scene

When you're ending a scene, you need to think about where you're going next. Momentum in a crime novel comes, at least partially, from regularly engaging the reader's interest, often by posing them a question. If a scene has delivered an interesting revelation, it is often worth summarising it and musing on its implications. 'What does this piece of information mean for the investigation?', 'What is going to happen next?' or 'How will the investigator get out of this very difficult situation?' might be questions you want the reader to consider; and implicit in each such question is the promise that it will be answered by reading on.

Even when you don't necessarily have a hook-like question, you still want to encourage the reader to look forward to the next scene. Even something as simple as telling the reader where it is set can help build a sense of anticipation. However, you can also give or withhold information that leads to the next scene. For example, once a scene's purpose has been achieved you may add something on – perhaps the presence of a mysterious man. If the scene is told from the investigator's point of view, you might want to withhold the man's identity but indicate that his presence is very interesting, thereby drawing the reader onward to find out who they are. If, however, the same scene is told from a different character's point of view, it might be interesting to give the mysterious man's identity, so the reader knows something that will be of considerable interest to the investigator and possible importance to the plot.

Enjoy yourself

This is perhaps the most important point. Crime writing should be imaginative, tricky, witty, frightening and a host of other good things. Be relaxed and embrace the unlikely and the impossible. If you're relishing the writing of a scene, then the likelihood is the reader will be reading it with relish as well.

Dialogue is a crucial ingredient of most crime stories. Special considerations arise with dialogue in historical novels, and these are discussed later in this book. In a nutshell, the key functions of dialogue in a story include revealing character and advancing the story. Dialogue can also set the tone of a story right from the start.

Margery Allingham demonstrated the force of this last point more than once. Her flair for dialogue and for striking openings was evident early in her career. *Mystery Mile*, published in 1930, when she was just twenty-five, begins:

'I'll bet you fifty dollars, even money,' said the American who was sitting nearest the door in the opulent lounge of the homeward-bound *Elephantine*, 'that that man over there is murdered within a fortnight. I'd say six weeks, only I don't like to rob you.'

Even better known is the first sentence of her most famous novel, *The Tiger in the Smoke*:

'It may only be blackmail,' said the man in the taxi hopefully.

Dialogue, Rhythm, and Keeping to the Point

Margery Allingham

Good dialogue is easier to read than anything else and its very shape upon the page invites the lazy eye, but even more valuable still from a crime author's point of view is its virtue as a space saver. A character can be revealed out of his own mouth more quickly than in any other way and the action of the story is not held up – or rather, it does not seem to be held up – while it is done.

It is a fact that most readers of mystery stories read for plot but are held by, and afterward remember a tale for, the characters in it. Generations of obliging writers have found that the best way of giving their clients both what they want and what they think they want is by an intelligent use of dialogue in which both needs are catered for simultaneously.

Some authors write dialogue with astounding ease. Once the character is clear in their minds, they say, they sit back and 'let him talk'. But while this is obviously true, it is also pretty clear to the rest of us that a very complicated process is taking place in their subconscious minds while they sit around.

Mere reportage is of no use to the would-be writer of dialogue whose character remains obstinately dumb or when induced to speak shows a stilted address and a terrifying tendency to begin every sentence with 'Well . . .'. No one who has ever taken the trouble to record living conversation can have failed to notice that when it comes to ordinary talk, very few of us succeed in saying what we mean at the first attempt and that most of us make a prodigious number of them. All but the few exhibit an affection for the same half-dozen words and seldom do our remarks follow logically upon those of anybody else.

Perhaps it would be true to say that good written dialogue which aims at the natural rather than the scintillating is an idealized form of the real talk which would have taken place in the scene presented. It is idealized in the sense that each character knows what he has in mind and has no difficulty in expressing it. He listens intelligently to his opposite number, his reply refers accurately to what has been previously said, and by his choice of words he does not break the essential rhythm which alone creates the illusion of sound in the reader's mind.

Probably it is this rhythm to which those authors who 'hear' their characters speak are referring. The English language when spoken fluently has a clear 'tock-tick-tick, tock-tick-tick' rhythm which is so familiar to us that we recognize it as sound as soon as our eye meets it on the page. Heaven forbid that I should suggest that the young crime writer put his dialogue into blank verse, but I have noticed that one can achieve quite a remarkable degree of smoothness in one's dialogue by keeping the tune in one's mind.

As to the place of dialogue in the crime story, I should say whenever possible, but always with the proviso that no character should be allowed to talk just because he can. A character in a detective story must do what no one in real life ever seems able to do, and that is *keep to the point*.

As Margery Allingham's writing career neared its end in the late Fifties, Patricia Moyes's was beginning. Moyes explained in an article for *The Writer* in 1970 that she was an avid reader of classic detective fiction who 'liked a puzzle, neatly plotted and with fair-play clues'. When she broke her foot at the start of a skiing holiday in Italy and was 'immobile and with no reading matter' she watched 'the chair-lift gliding inexorably up and down between the pine trees' and came up with an idea that became the core of her debut novel, *Dead Men Don't Ski*.

Patricia Moyes makes the case for listening as the key to developing a facility with writing dialogue. She wrote occasionally about the craft of writing detective fiction and liked to emphasize the advice given to her by Peter Ustinov, for whom she had once worked.

It's a good credo for any writer: 'Above all, make your own mistakes, and not other people's.'

Listening and Dialogue

Patricia Moyes

However well you may come to know your characters, it will do no good unless you have developed a technique for communicating your knowledge to your reader through the medium of the printed page. In my view, this is best achieved by dialogue.

Many excellent prose writers go all to pieces when they try their hands at dialogue. I think this comes about because writing dialogue takes a special discipline which they have never taken the time to study. There is a world of difference between words intended to be read, and words intended to be spoken, and, whether in a play or a book, all dialogue falls into the latter class. The writing of it is a technique, and it must be learned.

I wish I could simply recommend that every writer have the good luck I had – the chance to spend years working in the theatre before I ever came to novel writing. Of course, that's not possible, but there is a lot you can do.

See as much professional theatre as you possibly can. Don't just sit there and enjoy yourself; bring out your analytical faculties. Read the play both before and after you see it. Learn to distinguish among the various contributions which go to make up the production – those of the writer, the actor and the director. Remember that as a novelist your job will be even tougher than the dramatist's, for you will not have the benefit of a talented interpreter – a really good actor can make magic and touch his audience with the most banal of lines. Your dialogue will have to be good enough and punchy enough to make direct contact with your readers. If possible, join an amateur dramatic group and start looking at lines from the actor's viewpoint. You will very soon discover that there is a world of difference between dialogue that reads impressively and dialogue that plays well. A critic once said about *The Taming of the Shrew*, 'It's really a terrible play. The trouble is that it plays so superbly.' Read your Shakespeare again, not as great literature, but as an actor's script. *He* knew all about dialogue.

Listen to people. Listen to everyone you meet, and take time to analyse your reactions. You will find that a great many of the opinions you form of people speaking are based not on what they say, but on how they say it.

For instance, that man in the railway train the other day. You classified him at once as fussy, self-centred, and a bit of an old woman. Why? He wanted the window closed. Well, there was nothing so strange about that; you were thinking of closing it yourself. All right, think back. He was reading a newspaper, and you noticed that instead of flapping the pages around like most people, he had folded it neatly into quarters in order to read his chosen piece. Then, he was already on his feet and closing the window before he spoke, and he certainly did not request your opinion. He said, 'You don't mind if we have the window closed? I'm extremely prone to chills at this time of year.'

One mannerism, one short sentence – and you had made up your mind as to the sort of man he was. You'll notice that it is not necessary to describe his appearance at all. Your readers will fill in the blanks for themselves.

How very different was that woman at the cocktail party.

'I'm Amanda Bickersteth. I've been *dying* to meet you. I've read *all* your books.'

'I'm so—'

'Now, you must tell me exactly how you think up all those *marvellous* plots.'

'Well, as a matter of—'

'That one set on the tropical island . . . you must know the Caribbean *inside out*. Come on now, do tell – which island was it really?'

'I don't—'

'Dwight and I go to St Thomas every winter. Oh, I know *just* what you're going to say – it *is* crowded, but we just love it. Oh, dear, there's Dwight now. I'm afraid I must rush. It's been *so* interesting talking to you, I really feel I've learned *a lot* about writing . . .'

You get the idea? One day, both those people will find a niche in one of your books.

Among present day crime writers, Cynthia Harrod-Eagles has regularly been praised for the quality and wit of the dialogue in her novels. She is also a persuasive advocate as regards the importance of dialogue in fiction.

Writing Dialogue
Cynthia Harrod-Eagles

One of my duties, when I was president of an amateur writers' circle, was to read and criticize the members' work. Generally the weakest area in their creative – rather than technical – skill was in the matter of dialogue. Almost universally, they failed to see the point of it. When there was direct speech, there was no difference between one speaker and another: it was simply the continuation of narrative, in the author's own voice. Its main use seemed to be to fill the pages and make the work look more substantial – five pages rather than four.

As a professional author, you will know that dialogue uses up more space than prose. You can gallop through your day's writing quota and get to the gin and tonic early by having loads of:

> 'Who's that?'
> 'Where?'
> 'Over there.'
> 'I can't see anyone.'
> 'Are you blind? Behind that woman in the hat.'
> 'I don't know who you mean. What woman?'

And so on to the end of the page.

But leaving aside page-filling, I tried again and again to convince my Circle strivers that they were missing a very important trick. Dialogue can lift and enliven and add colour as perhaps nothing else can. A beautiful descriptive passage can be moving, but how often can you get the same punch from it? Whereas clever, witty or passionate dialogue will get you every time. When Cathy says, '*I am Heathcliff* – he's *always, always in my mind* – *not* as a pleasure, any more than I am *always* a pleasure to myself – but as my own being,' it's more effective than any amount of exposition.

We tend to think that the plot is the most important thing in a crime novel, and indeed it probably is, but what is it that makes you return again and again to a story when you already know how it turns out? Not the puzzle, which is only a puzzle once, but the characters and the dialogue – and for our purposes, they are pretty much the same thing. Because you can *tell* the reader what a character is like, but it's so much more effective to *show* them through direct speech.

Compare:

> He was plainly a man who liked to play with words, and was always ready with a quick, and sometimes saucy, riposte.

With this:

> 'Procreation is the thief of time,' he said.
> 'Come again?' she said doubtfully.
> He grinned. 'I wish you'd said that last night."

Consider how much information is imparted about both characters in this exchange from Dorothy L. Sayers' *Busman's Honeymoon*, and how much prose you'd need to explain the same thing.

> 'Shall I put them peas on, Mrs Bunter?'
> '*I* will see to the peas at the proper time, Mrs Ruddle. His lordship is very particular about peas.'
> 'Is he now? That's jest like my Bert. "Ma," he allus says, "I 'ates peas 'ard." Funny 'ow often they *is* 'ard. Or biled right away outer their shells. One or the other.'

You may think that humour is out of place in a crime novel, but the police themselves, like the Tommies in World War One, use humour all the time to relieve the tension of facing horrible sights and situations. And from the author's point of view, relieving the tension allows it to have extra force when it returns. Unrelenting blackness can have a numbing effect.

Speech is different from prose. Listen to people on buses, trains, in pubs, in restaurants, in shops. When we talk to each other, we rarely explain things, because the person we're talking to probably knows them already. So explanation needs to be reserved to the prose section, or the dialogue will not sound natural. And when talking we employ contractions, elisions, caesuras, fractured syntax, mispronunciations, slang, argot. People almost never say 'do not' rather than 'don't'. The more grammatically deviant the speech, the merrier, from the author's point of view. The only purpose, really, of a person with perfect diction is to be a contrast to the teeming others. The judge may say, 'I cannot and will not have this sort of disturbance in my court,' and you will know what he sounds like simply from the lack of contractions. While the felon may well have put it: 'I can't be doin' with that.'

Pinter's observation of the working class was that they often spoke in uncompleted sentences, or in the form of questions that weren't meant to be answered. 'What's your game? What's wrong with that? I did, didn't I? What d'you want me to do – stop breathing?' Of course, he grew up before and during the war, and he wasn't strictly working class himself, so there's a bit of Ealing Studios, Celia Johnson in *This Happy Breed* about it, but a certain amount of truth as well. Think of EastEnders or Corrie and remember how often a character puts their hands on their hips and says, 'What's that supposed to mean?' and how little they want or expect an answer.

When it comes to reproducing accent, less is definitely more. Larding dialogue with colloquialisms makes it tedious to read. The difference between authenticity and ridicule is a narrow one. With Yorkshire talk, for instance, if you slip in a few pointers like Ah for I, summat for something, and the occasional tha, a lot can be taken on trust. The reader will always do a lot of the work for you. James Herriot – himself a Scot, as it happens – does Yorkshire to perfection.

> 'Now, afore ye go, young man, I'm going to tell thee summat nobody knows but me. Ah could've made a lot o' money out o' this. Folks 'ave been after me for years to tell 'em, but I never 'ave. All you have to do is rub on this salve of mine and the 'oss walks away sound. He's better by that!"

It doesn't matter that he uses both *I* and *Ah* and *'ave* and *have* and *ye* and *you* in the same passage. Editors, sadly, often alter your precious work for consistency, but speech does not follow editors' rules. And you don't have to reproduce every single diversion from the norm to create the effect: once you have the accent established, the reader will supply it in his head.

The alternative, rendering everything phonetically, results in an agonizing trek through the literary equivalent of knee-deep mud. A literary Passchendaele. Who can forget Joseph in *Wuthering Heights*?

'Aw woonder hagh yah can faishon tuh stand thear i' idleness un war, when all on 'em's goan aght! But yah're a nowt, and it's noa use talking – yah'll niver mend uh yer ill ways; bud goa raight tuh t'divil, like yer mother afore ye!"

The only puzzle is why Emily B wrote *like* instead of *laike*, and *mother* instead of *mither* when she had the chance. She shows little compassion elsewhere to the reader. There's reams of this stuff.

It's also worth noticing that too many apostrophes make the page look untidy. It's off-putting.

There is another problem with rendering an accent phonetically, which is that the way you hear in your head what you've written may not be how the reader hears it. I still remember my desperate confusion when first reading *Lady Chatterley's Lover* and, during some distressingly anatomical pillow-talk, Mellors suddenly said, 'Arena Ah.' What sporting venue was he referring to? And why mention it at all? The Ah sounded a bit oriental. Could he possibly – I wondered with a shudder – be referring to Constance's private parts as a Japanese stadium? Only years later did I come to realize that what Lawrence heard in his head was the Yorkshire version of 'aren't I'. It's always worth reading your dialogue aloud, not only to avoid this sort of thing, but to see if it trips off the tongue. If you stumble saying it, probably your character wouldn't have said it.

There has been one notable unintended consequence of the phonetic rendering of speech in fiction. I think most of us have done it – certain the late, great Terry Pratchett did. It concerns the phrase 'bored with'. Noting that the common man pronounced with as 'wiv', and elided it to 'bored'v', Terry – and I've done it myself – rendered it in prose as 'bored of'. It was just a piece of fun. Unfortunately, not everyone realized that, and the phrase smartly reversed direction and re-entered public speech as its unironic self, so now we have the hideous 'bored of' proliferating everywhere, even in the Daily Telegraph – even on the BBC, for goodness sake! In Downton Abbey, Lady Mary said, 'I'm really bored of this,' and a little piece of England died.

On the subject of Downton Abbey, it's worth mentioning that it's easy for anachronism to slip in, and easy to avoid it if you actually want to. When a character in Downton says, 'I'm on a steep learning curve,' one winces, but the moment dissipates. The effect is worse in a book, because the words are there in solid black and white, to be reread and groaned over for ever. The complete *Oxford English Dictionary* is invaluable because it gives the first known printed example of words and phrases, so you can be sure you're right.

One final observation: when talking to each other, people do not constantly say each other's names. Nothing marks out bad dialogue more quickly than this sort of thing:

> 'Honestly, John, I wish you wouldn't do that.'
> 'Sorry, Mary. I try not to.'
> 'Well, try harder, John. It's annoying.'
> 'Well, I must say, Mary, your attitude doesn't help."

Really, please don't do it.

Perspectives

The choices a writer makes about viewpoint are crucial. This truth isn't immediately obvious, as Aline Templeton explains, but it's inescapable. The first significant analysis of viewpoint in a crime novel came in Dorothy L. Sayers' groundbreaking and highly influential introduction to her first anthology of crime short stories, mentioned earlier by James Runcie.

Sayers pointed out that Agatha Christie's early books borrowed the 'Watson viewpoint' method (with the feats of a great detective narrated by an admiring and much less brilliant friend) introduced by Edgar Allan Poe and refined by Arthur Conan Doyle. An early bestseller of the 1920s was *The Red House Mystery*, written by A. A. Milne, best remembered as creator of Winnie-the-Pooh but also a founder member of the Detection Club. Sayers described Milne's approach as 'a mixed method. Mr Milne begins by telling his tale from the position of a detached spectator; later on, we found that he has shifted round': he makes use of a 'Watson' figure before allowing the reader to see events through the eyes of his amateur detective.

Sayers applauded the ingenuity with which Agatha Christie used the first person viewpoint for purposes of the plot of *The Murder of Roger Ackroyd*, and examined in detail the subtle shifts in viewpoint employed in *Trent's Last Case*, by E. C. Bentley, who became the second President of the Detection Club. *Trent's Last Case* was in effect the catalyst for the Golden Age of detective fiction, with its focus on 'playing fair' with the reader. Sayers regarded this as a 'revolution', but also a turning back to Wilkie Collins' method in *The Moonstone*, in which the events are recounted by multiple narrators, a device which in capable hands can enrich the quality of a novel as well as its plot. Sayers herself experimented with this 'casebook' method in *The Documents in the Case*, a novel whose construction is explored later in this book.

A comparable approach is often used today. Paula Hawkins' follow-up to her global bestseller *The Girl on the Train* (in which we see events from the perspective of three women) was *Into the Water*, a novel which boasts no fewer than eleven different viewpoints. However, such an ambitious approach is not for the beginner or the faint-hearted. As Val McDermid said when reviewing *Into the Water* for the *Guardian*: 'To differentiate 11 separate voices within a single story is a fiendishly difficult thing.'

Patricia Highsmith usually opted to use two viewpoints, to allow for changes of mood and pace, as in her first novel, *Strangers on a Train*. In another of her masterpieces, *The Talented Mr Ripley*, she opted for a single viewpoint, seeing everything from the perspective of the eponymous killer. This can help to increase the story's emotional intensity. An inexperienced novelist may find it easier to adopt the viewpoint of a character whom, in emotional terms at least, he or she resembles. But this isn't essential, and may not even be desirable. The key to success when writing about detectives, suspects, and murderers unlocks the door to a richly imagined world.

Aline Templeton suggests that to tell a story from the viewpoint of a wholly credible character, it's vital to understand him or her. As Liza Cody puts it, the writer's aim is to know what it is like to *be* that person. Achieving that calls for curiosity, experience, imagination, and humanity.

Getting a Perspective

Aline Templeton

When I started writing, there was no such thing as the internet, with its 5,180,000,000 results to answer the question, 'How to Write a Book'. There was no such thing as *Writing for Dummies*, either. The only rules I had come across were Monsignor Ronald Knox's Ten Commandments, and since I didn't envisage using identical twins or Chinamen, they didn't seem terribly relevant.

I had the naive idea that when you wanted to write a book, you just sat down – with, of course, a typewriter, carbon paper and Tippex – and wrote on until the story was finished. And as a matter of fact, it worked, sort of. Eventually. Sadly I didn't keep the rejection slips before the blessed acceptance came in, which would have let me paper the smallest room.

I had never heard of flow, three-act structure and the narrative arc. When, after the first book had been published, I did and realized that actually those were features of what I had written, I was as astonished and gratified as Molière's *bourgeois gentilhomme* who discovered to his delight and surprise that he had been speaking prose all his life without knowing it.

In fact, I'm still not entirely convinced about these special rules for structure. Perhaps they do provide the scaffolding for the building, but how do you know where to erect it before you know what the house is going to be like?

So I blundered along happily, a child of nature. And then I went to a workshop. These were not as popular then as they are now and the idea was something of a novelty. I think I probably went along in a sceptical mood, expecting that it would have the same sort of effect as buying an issue of one of the new writers' magazines: I would be briefly buoyed up, convinced that big success was just around the corner if I followed some clever piece of advice, only for the confidence to wear off when I tried it.

I certainly didn't realize that this workshop would change

my writing life. The subject was points of view and here I pay tribute to the lecturer: Dianne Doubtfire – genuinely her married name, she assured us.

One image she used has always stuck with me. Someone reading a scene between two people where the author has not worked out the point-of-view technique, she said, was like a spectator sitting at the side watching a tennis match, turning his head first this way then that as the ball bounces from one player to the other. Trying to occupy the heads of two characters simultaneously had a similar effect. When I reread my own work, I couldn't believe that I hadn't noticed how distracting, how amateurish this was. (This is the book I refuse to let anyone reprint.)

With that perspective, I started looking closely at everything I read and it began to leap out at me. All the good writers were operating a point-of-view system, but confusingly, they were applying it in several different ways. I found out later these are usually categorised as: First Person, the story told as if by the protagonist; Second Person, the reader being involved directly as 'you'; Third Person Omniscient, the author has access to the thoughts and actions of all the characters; Third Person Limited, the author confines the viewpoint to one character; Third Person Multiple, the author sees the story through the eyes of several different characters.

Or, since I'm not a great believer in laid-down rules, it can even be a mixture of all or any. There are, they say, no rules in a knife fight; and writing's a bit like that. You do whatever you think it takes to get the result you want.

I had to make some decisions before I started again. Second Person was the first to be eliminated. Yes, I know that both Jay McEnery and William Faulkner had used it with great success, but I know my limitations.

First Person? Though I did rather like the idea of choosing an unreliable narrator, like Agatha Christie in *The Murder of Roger Ackroyd*, or breaking through the fourth wall like Charlotte Bronte in *Jane Eyre* ('Reader, I married him.') I felt it would be like being a horse in blinkers. What discouraged me too was the contortions that have to be imposed on the plot when there is no way to explain what is happening outside that personal experience. One book I read had the narrator saying, 'I don't know what they did but I imagine it was like this. He took her by the shoulders, then his hands tightened round her neck . . .' The writer lost me at that point.

Third Person Limited, where the action is seen through the eyes of only one character, has some of the same practical drawbacks.

With options narrowed, I was looking at Omniscient, with full access to all the thoughts and experiences of all the characters; or Multiple, where there are a number of perspective characters.

Omniscient is probably the most straightforward and one that we are familiar with from classical writers, but somehow it didn't appeal to me. All-knowing felt a bit too head-prefectish for my style of writing, and it has the risk too of being categorised as what Ogden Nash memorably described as the HIBK school – when the veil is lifted to give the reader a sneaky peek at the future: 'Had I (or he) But Known what grim secret lurked . . .' He ends the poem, 'I wouldn't have bought it had I but known it was impregnated with Had I But Knowns.' After reading that, Omniscient was out.

I like getting involved, feeling I'm right there with my characters. When I write a major scene, there will be one character whose eyes I look through. I then can't know what another character is thinking or feeling unless there is visible evidence. I could write, 'She gasped and put a hand over her mouth,' but I couldn't say, 'gasped in horror' because my point of view character couldn't know that.

Conversely, there can be no external description of the point-of-view character since he can't see outside himself – 'He was very scared and he looked as if he'd seen a ghost.'

Language comes into it too. If my point-of-view character is young, I would have to make sure that the style of the scene reflects that, even when it isn't direct speech. For instance, 'she would have to keep the home fires burning' isn't something a teenager would think. If the point-of-view character is elderly, the expression 'getting down with the kids' wouldn't be in his head.

One thing I have discovered is that when a scene isn't working, when it all grinds to a halt and you can't think how to move it on, it's nearly always because you've chosen the wrong point of view. Change it round and it often just falls into place.

You do need to be a bit choosy, though, I think. If there are too many point-of-view characters, it's easy to dilute the impact of the main characters who you want the reader to identify with, and it can become confusing. It's certainly vital that you make it clear when the point of view changes and the action has moved into another scene, with a clear space or even a marker like ******.

There's a sort of hierarchy too. By and large, I would say it doesn't work very well to have a main character viewed through the eyes of a subordinate character. Generally if my detective is interviewing a suspect, I'll be recording his thoughts and observations rather than the other way round because I think he is of more interest to the reader.

Sometimes I break this though; rules are made to be broken and for a rounded picture, I need to have him viewed by other people, otherwise I couldn't show what he looked like at all. (I always smile at the 'mirror scene' in First Person/Third Person Limited narratives; 'I/She looked in the looking-glass on her dressing-table and saw a round, dimpled face with big blue eyes.')

It's not always easy to get the tone right with new viewpoint characters. It can take time to get to know them and, as many authors will tell you, characters can develop a will of their own and defy you. It probably comes about when the conscious mind and the subconscious are out of sync and I've always found it pays not to try to overrule the subconscious.

In a series you can come to understand your regular viewpoint characters so well that they more or less do the job for you. I have a character called Tam MacNee, a wee Glaswegian

DS, and when I sit down to write a scene looking through his eyes, I find myself looking forward to finding out what he's going to say.

Multiple points of view can add greatly to the texture and depth of the writing. They draw readers into intimacy with the main protagonists and ideally will sweep them along so they barely notice how the scenery of the plot changes as it is viewed through different eyes, leaving an impression of a richly characterized novel. It's worth all the effort when readers say they feel they actually know your characters as if they were real people.

I'm still have a certain ambivalence about rules, even these. Yes, some techniques do seem to work better than others to achieve the sort of book a publisher will want, but for every rule there's a brilliant writer who's written a brilliant book that determinedly pays no attention to it. I cherish Raymond Chandler's roar of rage when an editor corrected his solecism in splitting an infinitive: 'When I split an infinitive, God damn it, I split it so that it stays split!'

So if you like, pay no attention to what I've said. Just write what you believe you need to write and if you want to break the rules, don't do it apologetically. Do it with panache, and your reader will be right there cheering you on from the sidelines.

What On Earth Is It Like to Be You?
Liza Cody

When you *read* a book, you need to have interest, curiosity or excitement enough to turn the page and find out what happens next. If you don't have them, the book will be put aside. Simple as that.

Writing a book is very similar. If the writer isn't as curious as a reader to find out what happens next, he or she might as well stop and start something else. Or donate the laptop to the nearest charity shop.

Everyone has an interest or obsession – it might be rococo plots, history, love of place, the law, cops or private investigators. For me, what gets my brain ticking and my blood running faster is character. Whether I'm a reader or a writer I can't become truly engaged in what's happening until I begin to engage with who it's happening to.

I started writing in the late Seventies and I picked genre writing because the giants in the US hardboiled field, like Chandler, Hammett, and Cain, were such good writers and so funny and exciting. So good in fact that I was almost tempted to let the extraordinary misogyny and sexism slide. But not quite. I'd always reach a point where I'd address the author in silent fury saying, 'Do you actually *know* any women? Have you ever wondered what it's like to be a woman? Have you even tried to understand the women you see around you? Probably not, because if you had you wouldn't be writing (beautifully, to be sure) this trash about, for instance, Carmen Sternwood (my favourite *bête noire*, from *The Big Sleep*.)'

Eventually, I came to write my own first book, but before I started I knew that if I was going to redress the balance somewhat I would have to write about a female private eye. So I had to ask myself what sort of woman would end up doing a job like that.

It seems obvious now, of course, but back then I didn't have any role models. I had to ask and answer my own questions. Then, one day at a bus stop, I found myself watching a woman police constable trying to look after two lost, screaming toddlers while her male colleague went off to locate the responsible adults. There was just a flick of her eyes as she watched him walk away, hands free, to search for the parents that made me wonder if she was thinking, 'And here *I* am – left holding the babies again. Why?' A question which can be just as relevant today as it was then. She was young, obviously had no children of her own, was daunted by the responsibility for calming the toddlers' distress and trying her best to stop them running off again.

Ironic, I thought, she probably joined the force looking for adventure and independence. I wonder what on earth it's like to be her. I wonder what her family life's like, that she needs adventure. Or, does she come from a police family? Does she actually like the uniform and those ugly shoes? Does she have to be a team person? How does she cope with on-the-job sexism? Why, yes, why is she the one left holding the babies?

Questions like these, which occurred to me while watching a very ordinary young woman, led to the way I wrote my first book, *Dupe*, about an ex-police officer, now a junior member of a firm of PIs. Her name was Anna Lee. She wasn't particularly tough. She couldn't have any cleverer powers of deduction than I do. When she got beaten up she passed out and lost a tooth. Men did not fall over themselves trying to attract her attention. Being noticeable was not part of her job. What she had was the edge a woman acquires when she has to pull her weight and try to excel in a man's world.

She interested me. And if I can't interest myself in a character, how can I hope to interest a reader?

It's true, though, that I wrote Anna partially as an antidote to Philip Marlowe, Sam Spade and, especially, Dashiell Hammett's Continental Op. I wanted readers to find an ordinary woman in difficult circumstances as interesting as I found her. I wanted to be able to describe small, banal violences as having the enormous impact they have on ordinary people in real life. I did not want to indulge in the escalating pornography of violence that I'd read in books or seen on TV or in the movies. In order to do that, I needed a reader to care about Anna Lee. Which meant I had to care about her. And I did.

Partly, I suppose, that approach was engendered by the times I'd been brought up in. It wasn't just male writers I was infuriated by, it was the expectations and constraints my culture had made so suffocating while I was growing up. Even as an adult, in the Sixties I was not allowed to obtain a mortgage or be prescribed birth control without a man to co-sign or give permission.

Culture changes, slowly, and so do women's problems – well, certainly some of them. And so must I and my characters.

After a series of six books about Anna, I found my character stereotyped as a 'good deed in a naughty world.' Which she isn't. And I found that whenever anyone wanted a story from me, they insisted on 'a strong female protagonist'.

It was around then that I saw a poster advertising wrestling. Along with the usual display pictures of men-mountains was a photograph of a snarling, feral-looking woman. She was no oil painting and obviously not eager to please – not the sort of woman, visible for her beauty and placatory qualities, who I was used to seeing on posters. In fact, right next to the wrestling poster was one for Revlon which showed a flawless blonde displaying utterly ravishing cosmetics. 'Love me, admire me, buy what makes me look so lovely,' her expression said.

That was how I first saw Klondyke Kate. Quite unlike the cosmetic model, KK's expression said, 'Fuck with me and I'll suck your eyes right out of your face.'

Well, I thought, no one in his right mind could call *her* 'a good deed in a naughty world.' But from the look of those shoulders, she's definitely a strong woman.

There she was, advertising herself in a culture where it's only women of beauty who show their faces on posters while the imperfect ones are supposed to make themselves invisible. Expectations are such that even minor faults are corrected by cosmetic surgery, mousy hair is coloured, and even young women routinely expect a boob job for their eighteenth birthdays.

Yet Klondyke Kate was making a living because her *defects* allowed her to play the villain in a pantomime world of heroes, villains and (not always) faux violence.

What on earth can it be like to be you? I thought, staring at her unlovely face. Surely she has the same need for love and approval that we all do.

So of course I had to go to the wrestling and discovered the upside-down world of the wrestling villain. KK measured her success and approval by the number of people who booed, spat at, and hated her. If people behaved to her in a way that would make the rest of us want to cry and hide in a cupboard, she'd had a good night.

And I thought long and hard about someone who is, by reason of genetics, born outside the oppressive, fascistic cultural expectation of what a woman is supposed to look like. In wrestling, as well as other showbiz contexts, what is left to her is to be the brutal, cheating bully who beats up the blonde, pretty-in-pink heroine. That gave me Eva Wylie and the Bucket Nut trilogy.

But in thinking about someone who, through no fault of her own, lives well below the cultural norm in the way of looks, I began thinking about the pressure exerted on the women who occupy the stratosphere above it. This gave me what I think of as MTV's Guide to Gorgeousness and the media exposure it subjects them to. Every young girl's dream, you think? Well no – not if you know the first thing about it.

So I thought about the most beautiful women of my youth – the ones I'd wanted to be like. And, you've guessed it, what was it like to be Marianne Faithfull then? What was it like to be her thirty years later? Of course Faithfull was just the example I began with before finding my own ex-rock-chick, musician and conwoman Birdie Walker in *Gimme More*.

Because whoever you, as a writer, might use as a paradigm, you are not painting a portrait of an existing woman. That would make you a biographer, or just plain lazy. You have to use your own imagination and experience. You have to breathe your own breath into her lungs to bring her alive.

Lately my curiosity has centred on a rough sleeper called Lady Bag, and her dog, Electra. Lady Bag has shown me once more how much someone who is a reject of society can teach you about your own culture and your own humanity

So if I were to be rash or brash enough to give anyone advice about writing a character – woman or man – I'd say curiosity is your first tool. After that comes your own experience, imagination and humanity. A long hard look at your own culture and what you would like to change about it is a big help too. And lastly I'd say that once you've found your character, be true to her. Don't squeeze her out of shape to suit your plot. Change your plot plans to accommodate her. Writing is way more interesting if, instead of trying to control her, you let your character take the lead and show you what a weird country you might end up in.

Plots

Aspiring writers (and plenty of established writers too) are apt to be intimidated by the challenge of constructing a plot for a crime story. Almost a century ago, in *Aspects of the Novel*, E.M. Forster defined plot as 'a narrative of events, the emphasis falling on causality'. Forster believed that 'mystery is essential to a plot', but cautioned that: 'Sometimes a plot triumphs too completely. The characters have to suspend their natures at every turn, or else are so swept away by the course of Fate that our sense of their reality is weakened.'

There is nothing new about suspicions that too intense a focus on plot may damage the quality of a novel. Anthony Trollope famously damned Wilkie Collins' fiction with faint praise, saying, 'The construction is most minute and most wonderful. But I can never lose the taste of the construction'.

Light has been cast on the techniques of Agatha Christie, the supreme exponent of the intricate whodunit plot, by the private journals in which she jotted down story ideas; they are discussed in detail by John Curran in *Agatha Christie's Complete Secret Notebooks*. Her usual method involved a gradual accretion of ideas. *The ABC Murders*, for instance – one of her most brilliant achievements – concerns a series of murder victims who are killed in alphabetical sequence. Yet although the focus on the alphabet seems integral to the mystery, she doesn't seem to have contemplated it when the genesis of the story first sprang into her mind. The harder she worked at the initial story idea, the more she was inspired to elaborate upon it.

Plots

Agatha Christie

Plots come to me at such odd moments: when I am walking along a street, or examining a hat-shop with particular interest, suddenly a splendid idea comes into my head, and I think, 'Now that would be a neat way of covering up the crime so that nobody would see the point.' Of course, all the practical details are still to be worked out, and the people have to creep slowly into my consciousness, but I jot down my splendid idea in an exercise book.

So far so good – but what I invariably do is lose the exercise book. I usually have about half a dozen on hand, and I used to make notes in them of ideas that had struck me, or about some poison or drug, or a clever little bit of swindling that I had read about in the paper. Of course, if I kept all these things neatly sorted and filed and labelled it would save me a lot of trouble. However, it is a pleasure sometimes, when looking vaguely through a pile of old note-books, to find something scribbled down, as: *Possible plot – do it yourself – Girl and not really sister – August –* with a kind of sketch of a plot. What it's all about I can't remember now; but it often stimulates me, if not to write that identical plot, at least to write something else.

Then there are the plots that tease my mind, that I like to think about and play with, knowing that one day I am going to write them. Roger Ackroyd played about in my mind for a long time before I could get the details fixed. I had another idea that came to me after going to a performance by Ruth

Draper. I thought how clever she was and how good her imper-
sonations were; the wonderful way she could transform herself
from a nagging wife to a peasant girl kneeling in a cathedral.
Thinking about her led me to the book *Lord Edgware Dies*.

*An extract from Agatha Christie's notebooks featuring
a story idea based on the Detection Club.*

Many gifted crime novelists have questioned the importance of plot.
Raymond Chandler drew a distinction between 'the people who can
plot but can't write' and 'the people who can write and, all too often
can't plot'; and he undoubtedly belonged to the latter group. Julian
Symons, fifth President of the Detection Club, confessed in an autobiographical note to 'a lack of interest in constructing a tight and
watertight plot' and was scornful of 'the Humdrum school of

detective novelists' who 'had some skill in constructing puzzles, nothing more'. When talking about Humdrum writers, he had in mind the likes of Freeman Wills Crofts, John Rhode, and J. J. Connington, three early stalwarts of the Club. But as the contributors to this book have demonstrated innumerable times, skill at plotting can be married to writing of distinction.

The academic Peter Brook has defined plot broadly as 'the design and intention of narrative, what shapes a story and gives it a certain direction or intent of meaning'. In the Seventies, another academic, Tzvetan Todorov, emphasized the duality of the typical whodunit, which 'contains not one but two stories: the story of the crime and the story of the investigation'. Thirty years earlier, Connington (a distinguished professor of chemistry who in his spare time became a successful exponent of 'fair play' whodunits) spoke for traditionalist detective authors when, in *Alias J. J. Connington*, he described his method of constructing his mysteries.

Logic and Working Backwards

J. J. Connington

My publishers have asked me if there is any connection between my work as a scientific investigator on the one hand and my detective-story writing on the other. There is not the slightest parallelism between these two lines, except that in both a logical mind is required.

In scientific research, the inquirer plays the part of a detective in real life. It is his business to seek for relevant clues; to push red herrings off the scent; to free himself from any preconceived ideas about the solution, if they conflict with the facts which he is collecting, often at the cost of wearisome labour; and, finally, to present a mass of detailed evidence in such a way that it will carry conviction.

On the other hand, the author of a detective story begins with the solution already in his pocket, and his initial task is to invent a 'chain of evidence' which leads inevitably to that solution and to no other. But this, in itself, is hardly sufficient, for the good detective story is really a duplex affair. Superficially, it presents a series of events as seen by Dr Watson or his deputy; below that lies concealed the tale of what actually happened; and the skill of the author is to be gauged from the manner in which he can blend these two themes in such a way that the reader, after perusing the story, can go back and start afresh, punctuating the second reading with the ejaculation: 'What a fool I was not to have noticed that point the first time!' Any well-contrived detective story should admit of at least two perusals if its full interest is to be extracted from it. When, in addition to this, the author is able to make the plot appear to arise from the characters – as Mr A. E. W. Mason did in *At the Villa Rose* – then his work touches the high-water mark of detective-story writing and constitutes a rarely achieved feat which fills less skilful authors with mingled admiration and envy.

Evidently, then, there is no resemblance between the scientific investigator, working from details towards a solution, and the detective-story writer, starting from his preconceived solution and working back to the details of his plot. To find an analogy, we must seek elsewhere, in another field of art.

The closest likeness to the writing of a detective story is to be found in the composition of a chess-problem. In both cases, the constructor begins at the end and works backward. The chess expert, having hit upon his checkmate position, has then to devise moves leading up to it, and has to place on the board a pawn here or a piece on some other square, in order to block certain moves which might otherwise be made. In the same way, the writer of a detective story has to invent various characters and episodes which limit the possibilities in his imagined course of events leading up to his solution. In both fields, it is permissible to introduce in moderation a supply of red herrings which serve merely to distract attention and play no essential part in the puzzle. And in both chess-problem and detective story there is a 'key-move' or a key-episode, which must be fixed upon by the would-be solver if he is to get immediately upon the track of the solution.

The approach that Connington describes elaborates on the method of Arthur Conan Doyle, who was approached by Anthony Berkeley, shortly prior to his death, to become first President of the Detection Club, but was unable to accept. Talking about the construction of the Sherlock Holmes stories in *Memories and Adventures*, he said: 'One could not possibly steer a course if one did not know one's destination. The first thing is to get your idea. Having got that key idea one's next task is to conceal it and lay emphasis upon everything which can make for a different explanation. Holmes, however, can see all the fallacies of the alternatives, and arrives more or less dramatically at the true solution by steps which he can describe and justify.'

An incisive analysis of Agatha Christie's methods is to be found in 'Strategies of Deception', a chapter in Robert Barnard's study *A Talent to Deceive*. He explains how Christie often bamboozles the reader into excluding a character from suspicion because events are seen from their point of view. This may be achieved by employing an unreliable narrator, as in one of her most famous novels (a trick which she ingeniously repeated towards the end of her career) or by presenting an individual subject to apparent threat who is in fact the culprit. Interestingly, given that Christie's skills at characterization have often been criticized, Barnard points out that in many of the books where she adopts this technique of fooling the reader, the depiction of the murderer is 'significantly superior to the norm . . . either they are marked by strongly individual personalities or else they engage the sympathy of the reader by the pathos and interest of their situation'. Conversely, some of her characters seem to be so stereotypical (a bluff major, an elderly spinster, a naive young girl) that readers assume they cannot be guilty. But they are mistaken; time and again, Christie manipulates conventional assumptions to create surprise solutions.

Since the heyday of writers such as J. J. Connington, the typical novel of crime and detection has become something much more than a literary chess problem or crossword puzzle, although it's interesting to note that both Barnard and Colin Dexter, the creator of Inspector Morse, were champion composers and solvers of crossword puzzles.

Sayers, Berkeley, and other early members of the Detection Club (including A. E. W. Mason) led the way in raising standards. Today, books matching – or indeed surpassing – the quality of *At the Villa Rose* are far from uncommon. There is simply no logical reason why a facility for plot should be incompatible with skill at evoking people or place.

A Detection Club member whose work bridged the gap between the Golden Age writers and today's crime novelists was Mary Kelly, who emerged as a writer of distinction in the second half of the 1950s and later served as the Club's Secretary. She won the Gold Dagger for her fourth novel, *The Spoilt Kill*, a private eye story which blends a whodunit mystery with incisive characterization and an unfashionable but well-realized setting, a pottery works in Stoke-on-Trent. Her writing was unorthodox and so were some of her methods, but even a novelist for whom plot isn't the prime focus, and who wants to reflect the untidiness of real life, may start a book with a clear idea of the shape of the whole story. Here she discusses the novel that was her own personal favourite among her books.

All Will be Revealed

Mary Kelly

Write on Both Sides of the Paper concerns a robbery at a paper mill, attempted forgery, and death. There are frequent switches from first- to third-person viewpoint. The characters are tools in a larger plot, which they don't know about; they simply carry out instructions. I quite deliberately didn't say what the plan was. My characters find out a certain amount, and thereafter it's just their guess as to what's happening . . . The story has two main streams converging on one another, and mine was the problem of bringing all the people concerned together in one place. When I came to tackle it, this method of a series of short pieces seemed to suit it best.

Although the action goes to and fro, it isn't random. I did it deliberately and meant every part to be exactly where it is. Writing's nothing but a great big fraud anyway, isn't it?

What I had in mind for this book wasn't so much crime as people's feelings of threat and self-doubt. Sometimes, people are pushed and pressed so much that they become antisocial and behave in a delinquent manner. Things happen in the book without explanations being given, just as they do in ordinary life. What I'm asking you to do is to read for the *moment* and to suspend wanting to know the 'why?' All will be revealed in the fullness of time!

I like to tantalize – to tell a little and make you wait for the rest . . . I put in a crime to give shape or focus, but I really write for pleasure, and although I put in clues I don't write for plots or because I'm interested in real-life crimes. I seem to imagine the whole of the book in outline, and I always know the end I'm working towards.

When constructing a story, it helps to think about its structure, a point emphasized by Val McDermid earlier in this book. A flexible mindset is desirable. As Kate Ellis, a contemporary novelist who works broadly in the Christie tradition (and also keeps jotting down ideas in notebooks) explains, a writer who plans a complicated story in detail may even find a flow chart helpful to keep track of developments.

Structuring a Plot
Kate Ellis

The structure of a crime novel can vary according to the author's taste. I tend to begin with a murder but the great Agatha Christie often takes time to set the scene and show the relationship between the victim and the various suspects before the first corpse is discovered.

Some crime novels use flashbacks or sections written from the murderer's point of view. Some even identify the killer at the beginning and the reader is invited to follow the detective's investigation to find out how the guilty party is eventually brought to justice. The structure of the novel is something a writer has to decide on at the start, like the use of the first person or third, and whether the story is told in the past or present tense.

My Wesley Peterson series is set firmly in the present day but there is always a parallel historical case running through the narrative reflecting, or perhaps connected with, the main contemporary plot. This secondary narrative often derives from the investigations of Wesley's old university friend, archaeologist Neil Watson. The use of archaeology to reflect the police investigation was inspired by the observation that inside every archaeologist there's a detective trying to get out; and Wesley's enquiries and Neil's do indeed have a lot in common.

As for plot, my personal preference has always been for the satisfying and intricate. I became addicted to the works of Agatha Christie at an early age and I must confess I always adore a good twist at the end. Later on, I also became hooked on Glenn Chandler's wonderful *Taggart* series on TV (starring the late Mark McManus) which was full of twists and turns in the plot and usually had a breathtakingly unexpected conclusion. It was these two early addictions that led me to follow the same path in my own books.

Character, of course, is vitally important. Without strong characters, the reader's interest in the story would flag and the whole book would feel flat and lifeless. But it is still an intriguing story that hooks many readers every time, and in my own books my ultimate aim is to create an 'I never saw that coming' moment at the end.

All of my books have both strong, twisting plots (with lots of added red herrings) and strong characters; but I find that it is the plotting that takes the most planning and thought.

With my Wesley Peterson series, I tend to go through a similar ritual with each book before I even type a word on my trusty laptop. I keep lots of notebooks scattered around the house and whenever an idea strikes me (as it can any time) I try to jot it down. There's nothing so annoying as having a brilliant idea for a book and then forgetting what it was an hour later (and this inevitably happens if it's not written down at once).

Before I start on a new book I usually have a vague notion of the crime that's been committed; or perhaps it can just be a character or a situation – or even an intriguing title. But when it's time for me to start work in earnest, I need to gather these nebulous thoughts and get them into some sort of order. That's when I collect my notebooks together (along with the press cuttings about crimes and possible plot ideas I've collected over the years) and dip into them for ideas that will fit well with the book I have in mind. This stage can take a week or two before the mist starts to clear and a plot begins to form itself in my mind.

As well as plotting Wesley's modern day case, the historical and archaeological investigation has to be thought out too. Each of Neil's investigations covers a different period in history, or a different aspect of archaeology, which means I have a lot of research to do. Having said that, this is one of my favourite parts of the writing process.

Once I've been through my notebooks and cuttings and finished my historical research, I have a brainstorming session, jotting down any appealing ideas that I might include in the forthcoming book. Then I look through this list of possibilities, cross half of them out and have yet another think. Once I'm fairly happy, I make a flow chart on a large sheet of paper. I place the main crime at the centre with all the clues and events leading up to it branching off (and if a clue is a red herring I might add a little picture of a fish). Down one side of the paper I do the same with the historical case, so I can see everything at a glance.

I find that I rarely stick to this chart religiously, because things change and better ideas occur to me as the book progresses. For instance, it might occur to me halfway through the manuscript that if I stick to my original course, the element of surprise for the reader may be less than I'd anticipated – and having got to know my characters, I am by that time much better placed to devise a fresh twist or two. However, the flow chart is a useful guide and it certainly helps to focus my thoughts at the beginning of the writing process.

I tend to plan in detail about three chapters in advance (using sticky labels that I can change around as I go). Making a timeline is also useful as it helps to pinpoint what happened on certain days and in what order. It also stops me forgetting what I've already written – I think I must have the worst memory in the Detection Club!

However, in spite of all this apparent planning I suppose I'm an instinctive writer; and during the long writing process I find that invariably I have fresh ideas to increase suspense, make the story more exciting or believable, or supply an unexpected turn of fate.

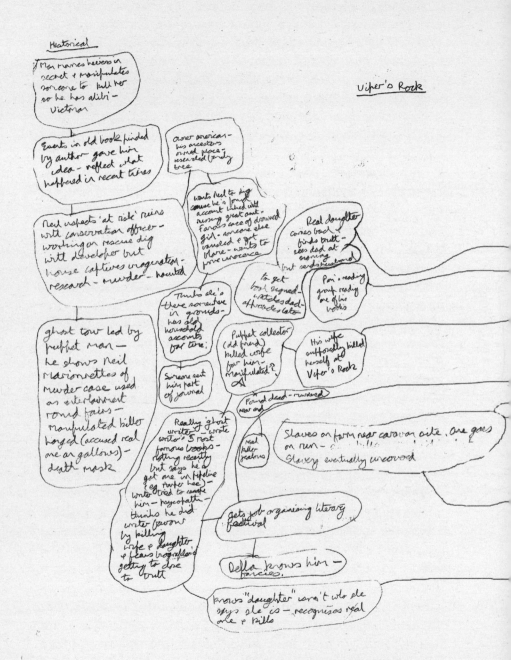

An example of a flow chart for one of Kate Ellis's novels.

I'm always prepared to change or abandon my original ideas. Sometimes it isn't until I've written several drafts that everything finally falls into place; and I've even been known to change my murderer or the motive if it will create a better story. My recent novel *The Burial Club* is an example: although my initial concept satisfied me at first, I came up with a fresh idea that excited me even more. I've never been able to write a full synopsis before I begin work on a book, because I feel it would restrict me too much. That elusive factor which adds an extra sparkle to a story rarely makes itself known at the early planning stage.

Different series require different approaches. My Albert Lincoln trilogy, set in the aftermath of the First World War, consists of whodunits in the classic tradition, but I've varied the points of view from which the events unfold. The majority of the story is seen from Albert's viewpoint (in the third person) but in addition I use another character's first-person viewpoint in each book. The first book in the trilogy, for instance, includes important scenes from the viewpoint of a doctor's daughter, while the subsequent books employ the viewpoints, respectively, of a boy and the wife of an abusive husband.

The Albert Lincoln series, incidentally, was sparked by writing a short story for a Crime Writers' Association anthology set in 1919. The research into the period fascinated me, and I wondered how communities came to terms with the loss of so many of their men. My interest was also personal. After my mother's death, I came across two letters among her possessions, handwritten on fragile paper and dated 1916. They were from the matron of a military hospital in France, telling my mother's grandmother that her son was gravely ill and not expected to live. Fortunately that young soldier survived to become my grandfather, but those letters stuck in my mind. I became interested in the treatment of the war-wounded, and the way in which large houses converted into military hospitals provided sanctuary from the trenches. A chance conversation with a friend taught me that masks were created for soldiers with horrific facial injuries. This was wonderful, pioneering work and gave disfigured men their lives and confidence back – yet to a crime writer, a mask can hide identities as well as hideous wounds. And so the book that became *A High Mortality of Doves* was born.

Ernest Hemingway said 'the only kind of writing is rewriting' and I would agree with this wholeheartedly. Working on each draft is like a sculptor chiselling away at a block of stone, roughly at first then more finely as the finished product emerges from the chaos.

Reading through a manuscript again and again and working on it helps you to identify the places where the story loses momentum and needs an injection of tension. Crime novels need pace; they need to keep the reader wanting to find out what happens next. Cliffhangers (either major or minor) at the ends of chapters can help with this, and over my writing career I've found that short chapters help to maintain pace and suspense.

I like to write at least two thousand words a day, which means I can get a first draft done pretty quickly. However, my first drafts are so rough that anybody could blackmail me if they got hold of them! It's after this stage that the serious work begins and I always like to do at least five drafts before I consider a book is fit for human consumption. By this time, hopefully, I'll have sorted out all the baffling twists and turns and perfected the conclusion.

So even a writer who designs the mystery with care and the use of a flow chart may, in the course of writing the novel, relish the freedom to make major changes to the original plan. Crime novelists who don't specialize in whodunits may also use visual aids: Patricia Highsmith once used a diagram to help her with the construction of a story. Kate Ellis captures the appeal for readers

of the traditional whodunit when she describes that 'I never saw
that coming' moment at the end. Some authors, even those as
distinguished as the late Eric Ambler, author of the classic *The Mask
of Dimitrios*, and the first out-and-out thriller writer to be elected
to the Detection Club, don't see the end coming until a late stage.

Voyages of Discovery
Eric Ambler

For me, writing a book is a voyage of discovery. The metaphor,
I know, is neither new nor particularly felicitous, but I can
think of no better way of describing the process.

It begins, of course, with an idea. This may take many forms.
The heart of it may be a character, either seen whole in real
life or assembled from fragmentary observations made of
different persons at different times in different places. The idea
may have grown from some seed such as an unusual piece of
information or anecdote. On occasion, though rarely, the idea
has come from the experience of an unfamiliar danger like,
say, a desert brushfire. More often it is the product of unusual
conversations in strange surroundings . . .

The fun begins – and in the beginning stages it is all fun –
when I start to work the thing out on paper. There will be
many false starts and long pauses for reflection . . . Generally,
the pauses can be measured in days. And all the time I am
gradually discovering what the story I have embarked upon is
about. However, I am not yet committed. I can still scrap the
fifty or sixty pages of writing and rewriting that may have by
then accumulated and turn to something else. I have no set
plan for the book, only an idea and the loom of a possible
story somewhere in the murk ahead.

This method of composing by discovery, of letting the

material go its own way and then seeing what happens, is not unusual, though writers who always think their stories through completely and plan before they set pen to paper tend to dismiss it as an impossible way of working. I have been accused of being a secret planner and told that the very complexity of some of my plots proves that I must plan in advance. The only thing those complexities prove, I think, is that, if they work, I must rewrite carefully and often.

All the same, I do understand the planners' feelings. When working as a screenwriter I have always held that the 'step-outline' – that is the breakdown of the film into a bleak series of numbered paragraphs describing the basic story content by sequences – is an essential first stage in the preparation of an effective screenplay. But for me that is only to underline the differences between two writing disciplines. The planners could argue, I suppose, that all the rewriting I do on a book proves their case and that my early drafts add up to a kind of planning. I would say that they were quibbling.

Obviously, however one chooses to describe it, my way of working is slow. It can be wasteful too. I spoke casually of scrapping fifty or sixty pages. That was to look on the brighter side. Not so long ago I scrapped a book when the fourth attempt to make sense of it had reached page 170. It had taken me almost a year to realize that none of it was ever going to work and that the idea had been congenitally defective. Odd as it may seem, the moment of decision was more exhilarating than painful. I was relieved, no doubt, to find that I had not been tempted to ignore the inner warnings and finish a book knowing it to be substandard . . .

I have been trying to think of some advantages of the voyage-of-discovery multiple-draft approach to the writing of thrillers. One is that you can clean up the worst litter of such things as faulty syntax, bad spelling and too many adverbs as you go. A more substantial advantage perhaps is the psychological one. Because you have not planned it all, you will not always know what is coming next. So, you will start work each day with hope in your heart and a sense of anticipation. That means that you will not easily be diverted from your true purpose by the outside world.

Have I any advice for would-be thriller writers? Yes, one piece.

Story ideas are fragile things. Never talk about them. Not, I hasten to add, because they may be stolen. Ideas that can be stolen and used by thieves are rarely worth having. No, it is simply that, in my experience, a story idea discussed, or even vaguely described, is an idea lost. Ideas should be written down but not spoken about. To explain or begin to describe a story aloud is to be trapped into developing it aloud. Once that act of communication has been performed the story is done for, it has gone. There is no point in trying to retrieve it. It has been told, so forget it. It will have forgotten you.

This may be a personal idiosyncracy. I have just realized that what I was describing there was the scar tissue of old wounds suffered at movie producers' story conferences. But let it stand. Some highly successful writers are quite capable of talking about a story, then writing it as a novel and then going on to write a screenplay based on the novel. I am not of that company. The only time I tried to write a screenplay based on a book of my own, I failed because I became bored. The producer complained that I had ruined a good book. I had sense enough left to agree with him.

The danger with a voyage of discovery, as Eric Ambler recognized, is that it may end with a shipwreck. Fortunately, there are ways of managing the risks, as Andrew Taylor explains. He mentions *Caroline Minuscule*, an award-winning first novel with a delightful example of the arresting opening:

Typical, William Dougal thought, how bloody inconvenient.

He was standing just inside the door of his supervisor's room in the History Department. Three yards away a corpulent, tweed-covered shape sprawled on the oatmeal carpet, to the right of the desk. The eyes and the tongue protruded from its bloated face towards Dougal in the doorway.

How to Change Your Murderer
Andrew Taylor

Writing, Simenon remarked, is a vocation for unhappiness. He was probably agonizing over the plot of his current novel at the time. You would think that crime writers of all people would have the knack of it, if anyone could. But plot is a bugbear for many of us, and a common source of writer's block. Characterization, theme, setting and dialogue flow naturally and often enjoyably. Plot is where the process gets painful.

After 45 novels and counting, I have begun to suspect that there isn't a simple remedy – it's one thing to write a wonderful opening to a story, but to continue it and bring it to a satisfying ending we need to be able to plot. A story needs a plot as a body needs a skeleton.

Memorable plots tend to have elements of surprise and originality. Once you've read Flann O'Brien's brilliantly surreal *The Third Policeman*, you are unlikely to forget how it ends. Or *The Murder of Roger Ackroyd*. Or *Gone Girl*. Readers like books whose stories come at them from unexpected angles. As John Le Carré once put it, 'The cat sat on the mat is not a story. The cat sat on the other cat's mat is a story.' A predictable plot is dull, however well constructed, which poses a particular problem for those of us who write genre fiction.

Some writers plan their plots in detail before they start writing. This is the logical way to do it, after all, and it can certainly save time in the writing of a book. But there's a danger: if you cling too tightly to your plan, you don't leave space for the plot to grow on the page, when you are immersed in your narrative. This can lead to a bland and flavourless story.

Others, however – and I'm one of them – allow their plot to unfold as they are writing their narrative. They tell themselves a story as well as their readers. It took me a long time – getting on for ten years – to realize that this is a perfectly viable way to write fiction.

In the end, it was panic that saved me. I was in my late twenties and on the verge of abandoning my ambition to become a novelist. Again and again, I had tried to plan a story before I wrote it, and my brain simply refused to cooperate. So, in desperation, and in the knowledge that I had nothing left to lose and that this was my last chance, I began to write without any plan at all.

All I had was a title, a garrotted corpse in a setting I knew well, and a protagonist who was a bit like me but, I hoped, of lower moral fibre than I was. In the two paragraphs, I made my protagonist discover the corpse. Then I decided he might sneak off, for trivial and purely private reasons, and let someone else be the official finder of the body.

What might happen next, I wondered? By 'next' I meant in the next paragraph or so, not in the rest of the chapter, let alone in the rest of the book. 'What if?' I asked myself, and filled the next paragraph with a possible answer. 'What if?' I asked again, and carried on with the next paragraph. Rarely looking much further ahead, I blundered on in this way for six or seven months until, much to my surprise, I reached an ending.

More by luck than judgement, I had stumbled on a variant of what I now think of as the E. L. Doctorow approach: 'Writing a novel is like driving a car at night,' he wrote. 'You can only see as far as your headlights, but you can make the whole trip that way.'

At the end of this first draft, though, the book was a complete mess. But it was also a complete book. I rewrote it. This time, knowing what it was about, knowing my characters, I began consciously to shape the plot and to make it less incoherent than it was the first time around.

I was aware that I was using a different part of my brain for this: I wasn't telling myself a story any more: I was editing one that was already written. During the first draft, I was watching it unfold as I wrote it; at any one point, I knew a little more about what might happen next than the reader did, but not necessarily a great deal more. During the second draft, however, I knew almost everything about the story. I saw it as a whole.

I sent the result to a publisher, Livia Gollancz, who made me rewrite the book all over again. 'First-time novelists,' Livia said, 'almost always put in about three times more material than they need. Then they find they've nothing left for the next book.'

The consequence of that moment of panic was a slim crime novel called *Caroline Minuscule*. As first books go, it did quite well, and it's still earning modest royalties nearly forty years after publication. It also launched me into a career as a full-time novelist, which is what I've been ever since.

My method (if I can call it that) of developing a plot hasn't changed a great deal since *Caroline Minuscule*. What has changed is that I understand the process better.

It begins with the ideas. The nature of these varies from writer to writer, but for me the setting – in time and place – is often one of the first things I know about a story. I've learned not to be too critical of ideas – my own or anyone else's. Ideas are tender plants that shrivel rapidly at a hint of disapproval. You can recognize them by the sensation that accompanies them. And it's generally just that – a sensation, a tingle of excitement, a tantalizing glimpse of potential.

The next stage in the process is when the ideas begin to dance and breed among themselves. Again, this isn't a process which requires me to play much of an active role – I'm more of a facilitator, I suppose, an archivist of their social and indeed copulatory manoeuvres. Two examples may clarify this resolutely murky process.

An Air That Kills, the first novel in my Lydmouth series, began for me with a uncomfortably vivid mental picture of an old man in a tweed jacket lying dead on a carpet, with Remembrance Day poppies scattered around him. Five or six years later, a friend suggested I write a crime series in the area where I live. I knew, instantly and mysteriously, that the series would be set in the 1950s. At the time I happened to be reading Housman's poems, and potential titles leapt out of almost every page. The elements mingled, and began to grow in my mind. That's when the hard work started – trying to shape them into something that might eventually turn into a novel.

Another book, *The American Boy,* started with the discovery that as a boy Edgar Allan Poe had walked the streets of Regency London. But it was only years later that this combined with a title and with the idea of a murder mystery set in the early nineteenth century, with Poe as a sort of ghost in his own childhood on the periphery of it all.

Almost at once, ideas like these tell you something about the plot framework that a novel will require. First, and perhaps most importantly, it gives you the setting, both in time and place. We humans are creatures of context – not just in terms of the clothes we wear or the dentistry in our mouths, but in terms of our beliefs about the world and our place in it, and how we express them in our language and our thoughts. Setting can suggest a great deal about your characters, their motivation and the general shape of the plot.

Ideas can also suggest themes, and a theme can provide a compass for a novel's plot. The dead man among the poppies led me to the idea that the story would be about remembrance in some way, which brought me to the Housman quotation, which in turn led me to the notion of nostalgia, and the way it can twist the past into something it wasn't and poison the present. This led me to think of characters and episodes that would allow me to explore these ideas.

Similarly, research – both beforehand and during the writing

– can feed into the plotting by suggesting settings of scenes, or events that might happen with them, or surprises that could be sprung on the reader.

I now know that there need be nothing unchangeable about any of this. There is no preliminary fixed plan, in the sense that a builder works from a plan. The process is organic and provisional. The planning continues when I start writing, and it carries on, constantly modifying itself, to the end of the final draft.

For me at least, the writing itself helps to generate elements of the plot that might lie ahead. I will often visualize a scene or a character – or even just a single ingredient of one – and put it in the messy heap of possibilities I call my notes. My narrative may reach it or it may not. Writing a story is about finding a path through a tangle of possibilities.

Where to start? If there seems to be an obvious place – like my hero finding his garrotted tutor – I go for that. Sometimes there isn't an obvious beginning, so I start anywhere and hope I will find somewhere to go. I often change my opening chapter when I start to glimpse the overall shape of the story or when I revise the whole book. Nothing in a novel is written in stone until I sign off on the proofs and send it out into the world. The important thing for every storyteller is to start: to take that terrifying leap into an unknown narrative; then, and come what may, to carry on.

I've learned to trust myself. The story will come with the writing. It may take time and effort, it may take constant revision. I find it useful sometimes to alternate how I look at the story I'm writing: usually I am in the middle of it, following the narrative from the inside, from the character viewpoint; but sometimes it pays to step back and consider what I've already written in relation to my shadowy conception of the whole book. I think of plot as a combination of the two – the underlying sequence of events together with how it's filtered to your reader.

There are techniques in plotting crime fiction, and I consciously apply them. Some of them are obvious. They may

seem mechanical but, done well, they won't to the reader. Begin
with something that draws the reader in, usually by arousing
their curiosity. A little dialogue on the first page will also attract
their eyes: they will follow it automatically, just as it's almost
impossible not to follow the ball if there's a tennis match on
the screen. End a section or a chapter with something that
makes the reader want to turn the page and move on. Vary
the tempo: a narrative feels monotonous and mechanistic if
every chapter ends with someone bursting through the door
with a gun in their hand.

A plot needn't necessarily be plausible but it does need to
aim for internal consistency, especially if we are writing for a
print medium. (You can afford to be a little more slapdash if
you're writing for film or TV because it's much harder for the
viewer to pause to analyse what's happening.) If your story
turns on a shatteringly implausible coincidence, slip it into the
narrative as early as possible, before your readers have time
to realize, in terms of your story, what's a coincidence and
what's not (more good advice from Livia).

In crime fiction, timing and misdirection are both crucial,
just as they are for stand-up comedy and conjuring. It's about
second-guessing your readers: think of what they are expecting
to happen next and do something else instead. As a rule,
though, a surprise you spring on your readers should not be
arbitrary: instead, it should make them think 'Ah, I should
have thought of that possibility.' By some quirk of human
nature, we find this sort of surprise – the one whose existence
we should have foreseen – to be intensely pleasurable.

The best Golden Age crime fiction excels at this technique.
The surprise often takes the form of a clue. The late H. R. F.
Keating, a distinguished crime novelist and a former President
of the Detection Club, had some practical advice about how to
insert information that will later prove vital without the reader
noticing. I've shamelessly appropriated and adapted it for my
own books.

- Sometimes you want to seed something early in the narrative without the reader noticing it. Conceal it in a long and rather boring list of items, for example your investigator listing what she finds when she's searching a suspect's suitcase.
- Or break up the piece of information into two parts and insert in widely separated parts of the story. The significance only becomes obvious later, when a character links the parts together.
- Insert the information and then have something dramatic happen. The reader, distracted by the man coming through the door with a sledgehammer, won't remember what happened immediately before.
- Similarly, drop in the information while your character is doing something urgent – for example, driving fast to catch a train. The reader's attention is on whether he will catch the train, so the clue doesn't really register.
- Rely on your reader's stock responses. Say there's mention of someone in the past called Kay. Until the last chapter, your other characters and your reader assume that this is a girl from the context in which the character is mentioned. But maybe she's a he. (This is one from Agatha Christie.)

The late and much lamented Reginald Hill, author of the intricately plotted Dalziel and Pascoe novels, once said that the plot is something he puts in afterwards, during the hacking and tweaking and shaping of the second draft. If it worked for him, who am I to quibble?

I rarely know how a book will end until I get there. It happens surprisingly often that I have an idea of the murderer's identity for much of the first draft, only to discover in the final chapter that it was someone else.

In the end, there are no hard-and-fast rules, only guidelines, opinions and suggestions. We read Chandler for his language, not his convoluted and improbable stories. A good publisher's editor would savage the plot construction of *Wuthering Heights*.

Genius can get away with anything, even technical incompetence. The rest of us need an effective plot. Some fine writers can construct a detailed chapter-by-chapter outline before they write a word of the narrative; for them, perhaps, the outline functions as a skeletal first draft. Others, however, discover our story as we write it, by fits and starts – and then we tidy up the loose ends afterwards.

Trust yourself and your imagination. If all else fails, change your murderer.

Detectives

A detective is usually a key protagonist in a crime story, even if it's not a conventional whodunit. Many of fiction's most popular characters are series detectives, memorable individuals to whom readers find themselves drawn irresistibly, even if they cannot remember the name of the writer who created the much-loved character. Because readers love series, so do many publishers.

Apart from any other consideration, a series gives a writer the chance to build a readership over the course of time. Contributors to this book such as Ian Rankin, Val McDermid, Peter Robinson, and Ann Cleeves would be the first to say that their early ventures in crime writing did not result in overnight celebrity. It took time for the quality of their work to reap its full reward; all four have now seen their books become international bestsellers and achieve huge popularity when adapted for television.

Not all crime writers enjoy creating a series. Julian Symons, fifth President of the Detection Club, created a handful of recurrent characters, but detested the constraints (as he perceived them) of a series. His forte was the stand-alone novel and some of his books were filmed or televised, but he never became a household name like a younger Detection Club member, Colin Dexter, the creator of Inspector Morse. Possibly his reluctance to write a long-running series helps to explain this.

Series may come about unexpectedly. A writer who creates a memorable protagonist in a novel intended as a one-off may face a demand from the publisher or readers to keep the character alive. Edith Pargeter, a Detection Club member better known as Ellis Peters, intended her novel *A Morbid Taste for Bones*, about the medieval monk Brother Cadfael, to be a stand-alone. She was in her mid-sixties, and at first Cadfael made little impression. But another idea for a Cadfael story occurred to her, and ultimately the Cadfael Chronicles became an international phenomenon, with the monk portrayed in a popular television series by Sir Derek Jacobi.

A long-running series can become wearisome for a writer, even if (sometimes, especially if) the detective becomes an iconic figure. Arthur Conan Doyle famously killed off Sherlock Holmes at the Reichenbach Falls before succumbing to public pressure (and handsome financial inducement) to resurrect the sage of Baker Street. Agatha Christie had her fictional alter ego, the writer Ariadne Oliver, tire of her Finnish detective, just as Christie herself became frustrated with Hercule Poirot. Dorothy L. Sayers' series about Lord Peter Wimsey ran out of steam after about fifteen years and she abandoned one Wimsey novel, only for it to be completed more than half a century later by Jill Paton Walsh, who proceeded to continue the Wimsey chronicles.

Reginald Hill's method of avoiding staleness or boredom was to alternate books about Dalziel and Pascoe with other novels. If one has the stamina and ability to manage this approach, it has a good deal of merit. A variant technique is to write a short story or two in between one's series novels. This can yield unexpected dividends; Reg Hill introduced Joe Sixsmith in a short story and later wrote five books about him.

When creating a detective character, it's worth considering what might happen if the series continues for years. Ruth Rendell came to regret making Inspector Reginald Wexford a man in his fifties, although it did not prevent the Kingsmarkham cop's fictional career lasting for close on five decades, much as Hercule Poirot's did after he came over to England as a refugee during the war, having already retired from the Belgian police.

James Melville, writing thirty years ago in a booklet associated with the Philadelphia Bouchercon festival, pointed out that from Edgar Allan Poe onwards (an American whose series investigator was a French aristocrat based in Paris), crime writers have tried to add piquancy to their mysteries through the use of exotic settings and characters. Melville, whose real name was Peter Martin and whose principal series featured a Japanese superintendent, Tetsuo Otani, argued that 'ethnic' detectives are at their best when acting as 'a kind of cultural ambassador, one who helps to counter ignorance and bigotry and to encourage tolerance and understanding' of unfamiliar cultures.

So who should be your detective? Police officer, private investigator, a professional whose work brings them into contact with crime? Or an amateur who just happens to stumble upon mysterious murders? Priscilla Masters explains how she has chosen different types of investigator for different series.

Amateur Detective or Professional?

Priscilla Masters

It only occurred to me as I was thinking about this contribution how my three serial protagonists: Dr Claire Roget, a forensic psychiatrist, DI Joanna Piercy and coroner Martha Gunn, would look at the same case from very different angles.

Each would hold certain advantages while also posing separate challenges, constrained by rules and the confines of their role and the various restrictions imposed on them.

As a forensic psychiatrist, Dr Claire Roget has a skill that borders on clairvoyance. She diagnoses various psychiatric disorders, focusing on behaviour likely to cause serious problems in the future, such as violent aggression, morbid jealousy, extreme paranoia, personality disorders, previously challenging behaviour, substance abuse leading to violence. She picks out those most likely to commit a crime in the future, treats them and if necessary restrains them under a section of the Mental Health Act. If a crime has already been committed, she might focus on possible causes, look at the subject's past history and search for clues which would make the perpetrator more or less likely to reoffend in the future. The release of a psychiatric patient back into the community will depend on her diagnosis and opinion. Part of her interview might be a delve into the past, looking into family history and previous tendencies, trying to anticipate if the patient is likely to be an ongoing danger to themselves, the general public or one person in particular – for example a jilted boyfriend or a sibling or spouse they have a grievance against, real or imagined. This might result in a restraining order and hopefully prevent another crime. A psychiatrist who is aware that a patient is likely to commit a crime has a duty to safeguard the public. Failure to alert the authorities could result in the psychiatrist being prosecuted. To commit a person to a secure unit would involve invoking a section of the Mental Health Act and the opinion of a second psychiatrist. And these sectionings are reviewed at intervals. Some conditions are lifelong. Others, such as narcissistic personality disorders, meliorate with age. And many patients with other psychiatric disorders, such as schizophrenia, may be perfectly well controlled with the correct medication and are less of a danger to society than society is to them. The tortuous maze of Dr Claire Roget's role is the unpredictability of mental illness and sometimes a deliberate attempt by the subject to deceive and minimize the severity of their condition.

The obvious constraints of using a forensic psychiatrist as one's main character are the very constraints Claire works under: a shortage of mental health beds, the rigid rules surrounding the incarceration of a subject, and the difficulty in being precise over likely future behaviour.

Detective Inspector Joanna Piercy is presented with a crime already committed and it is her job to find the perpetrator and bring them to justice. Her role too has its benefits as well as its restraints. She has the power of the law behind her, access to a mound of information – mobile phone records, CCTV, bank accounts and the mountain of information stored on the HOLMES police computer – as well as a team of trained colleagues and forensic investigators working towards a safe investigation and conviction.

But strict law governs police investigations, preservation of crime scenes, preserving and documenting trace evidence – including avoidance of contamination – as well as the treatment of suspects and witnesses, recording of interviews and cautioning, questioning and arresting. If these rigid rules are not adhered to, however thorough a police investigation has been, the case may collapse when brought to court. Anyone who has asked the police about crime scenes or watched some of the plethora of television dramas or documentaries will know that there can be a huge body of evidence, sometimes running into hundreds or even thousands of items to sift through. And the collection, supervision and custody of each of these pieces is vitally important in case it is the one link between the suspect and the victim. Any forensic examination has to be justified as there are financial constraints and a constant stream of other crimes to be investigated. The police are often asked to focus on various target areas such as knife crime, stop and search, or county lines, either because of public concern or under the direction of the government. In real life these can divert resources from local problems. In a work of fiction, this would introduce a subplot which would in turn slow the pace of a novel.

So to Martha Gunn, coroner, who never knows the people whose inquests she is conducting. Another challenge for an author. Everything Martha learns is gleaned from family and friends, teachers, medical staff and anyone else who has had meaningful contact with the dead person, whether positive or maybe negative. Her remit might be limited; her job is simply to ascertain who has died, where they died, when they died and how. Unlike Claire Roget or DI Piercy, Martha does not have the luxury of long interviews with the victim; neither does she have a police investigation to focus on. But the verdict rests on her shoulders. Martha's power, social platform and influence over social change cannot be underestimated in matters such as exposure to asbestos or the wearing of seat belts in cars. She can (and does) suggest lines of enquiry the police might focus on and she does make the final decision. Recently the powers of a coroner have been extended to hold inquests over stillbirths to indicate whether there was any preventable cause for this tragedy.

One of the early lessons junior doctors learn is which deaths should be reported to the coroner, including those that occurred within twenty-four hours of a medical procedure or hospital admission, that are the result of neglect or alcoholism, that are drug related, and so forth. Martha has a variety of verdicts at her fingertips: homicide, suicide, accidental or even an unexplained death. She can't magic up evidence that is simply not there. Her job is not to point the finger towards a suspect, but she can direct police enquiries and appeal for social change. Of my three series characters, perhaps she is the one with the most potential for working 'off script', as the police and the medical profession are ruled by tightly drawn edicts.

To lighten the narrative, my characters have their sidekicks and little helpers.

Claire Roget has a boyfriend, Grant, and can bounce ideas off him as well as her medical colleagues at Greatbach Secure Psychiatric. She can use the opinion of trained psychologists and psychiatric nurses. Patients under her care may be the focus of multidisciplinary meetings to decide the outcome that is best for the patient and safest for the general public. With her team and with limited resources, she must do the best she can – bearing in mind she is answerable both to the law and to the General Medical Council if she fails in her duty.

DI Piercy has a secret weapon: her boyfriend (later husband) Matthew is a forensic pathologist always willing to explain cases and terminology. She also has the ever-loyal stalwart Detective Sergeant Mike Korpanski, physically an intimidating presence, but to Joanna a capable, loyal and comforting sidekick. As the series progresses, other officers are introduced. Some are promoted, some focused on, and others discarded.

Investigating a homicide can involve a huge army of professionals. Too many for a novel. And it's not always clear at the start which officers will feature in only one title and which become ongoing secondary characters

Though Martha Gunn is a widow, she does have two interesting children, twins Sukey and Sam. And she has her coroner's officer, an almost Dickensian character named Jericho Palfreyman, whose interest in her cases borders on ghoulish; as well as a friend in the police force, Detective Inspector Alex Randall, an intelligent officer well able to match her wit.

There is a wealth of information (and misinformation) out there which pins you to the real world. However, this is fiction, and the story can be compromised by sticking too tightly to the so-called rules – such as the one that a subplot should bear some relevance to the main plot. Martha has no power to investigate her cases, though she's not above donning a wig and sunglasses and hanging around outside the school gates – something which in real life would definitely put her on the front page of the tabloids if recognized.

Fans of crime fiction are generally well informed and expect to be entertained and intrigued – something which we authors are only too well aware of. Mark Twain once advised that we should never let the truth get in the way of a good story. It's a dilemma facing many authors. We walk a tightrope of sticking to known and credible procedures and presenting our readers with a good, exciting and intriguing story that doesn't flag or divert too far into a subplot. How closely should we stick to the fact that provincial police stations are closing, that much police work is centred around a computer screen, that more than 90 per cent of police work has nothing to do with the crime under investigation? That, according to a police inspector friend of mine, at least 46 per cent of police work has more to do with mental health problems and domestic concerns than crime? How to pull out the facts that are relevant to the case they are investigating when a simple mobile phone might contain three thousand text messages? How to select which trace evidence we follow down the rabbit hole and analyse, when the number of forensic laboratories is dwindling along with their budget? Which items are stored and which discarded, bearing in mind that cold cases can sometime be solved thanks to advances in science like DNA profiling? These are the real problems facing the police force but they don't necessarily make for an entertaining story. So the trick we play is to pretend, to leak enough facts to convince our readers that this is a real story. Every time we get it wrong, we ask our readers to suspend their incredulity.

The amazing thing is that sometimes we get away with it.

The obvious challenge for a writer creating a series detective who is an amateur sleuth rather than a professional police officer is to find a way of making it credible that the protagonist should keep stumbling upon murder mysteries. It's a daunting challenge, but not insuperable. A writer of talent can persuade readers to suspend disbelief: after all, two of the most popular police detectives of the past thirty years have been Inspector Morse and DCI Reg Wexford, and the homicide rate in Colin Dexter's Oxford and Ruth Rendell's Kingsmarkham was truly extraordinary.

And there are advantages to writing about non-professional detectives. It's possible to skip the tedious realities of police procedure and to concentrate on an attractive character and milieu. An example is Simon Brett's actor Charles Paris, who has now appeared in twenty detective novels as well as occasional short stories. As well as his novels about Inspector Ghote, H. R. F. Keating's series detectives included a cleaning lady and a Victorian governess, while his first novel, *Death and the Visiting Fireman*, saw the sleuthing undertaken by a schoolmaster (the profession of Keating's father). As Keating said: 'You can write about the sort of person you know well, or even are.'

Susan Moody has written three distinct series about amateur

detectives, although Alex(andra) Quick, who first appeared in *Quick and the Dead* in 2016, was formerly a police officer. How best to bring such individuals to life?

Believable Amateurs
Susan Moody

From Aristotle on down, storytellers have always argued about which is the primary staple of a crime novel : believable plot or convincing characters?

For many readers, it's a chicken-and-egg question. Which should come first? For me, until you have a credible character the other aspects of a novel are inconsequential. Without a realistic protagonist, you might as well not bother to write. It's the duty of the author (female for the purposes of this essay) to engage her readers in the story, and that can't be done without a leading character they can connect, engage, and empathize with. Drawing from life is the surest way to ensure this occurs. Someone who, if not exactly like the readers, is at least recognizable as a plausible human being, with all the faults and flaws that entails – plus of course, other positive attributes. At this stage, observation counts for more than description. We don't need a passport photo of height, weight, hair colour and so on. A physical idiosyncrasy can be more telling than a long list of attributes shared by the majority of humankind. A limp, a squint, an accent, the tip of an earlobe missing, is enough – as long as it is not overdone. And it can be useful if your protagonist always wears a red tie, or co-respondent shoes. But it isn't necessary to create a full dossier on him, though I know many writers who do. On the other hand, the writer has to beware of giving her protagonists too many quirks and foibles. Idiosyncrasies do not define a character: they must be mentioned but not dwelt on.

Nobody, fictional or not, is all good, or all bad. Producing a character who is one or the other is an instant turn-off. Writing an all-good character is difficult enough; much easier to produce a bad one. And where better to find an engaging and memorable fictional creation than Thackeray's *Vanity Fair?* Becky Sharp is immoral, heartless, selfish, she is nonetheless the heart and soul of the (long) book. The reader recognizes her at once, and identifies with her. Especially when compared to her antithesis . . . timid little brown sparrow, Amelia Sedley. Good *people* are admirable; good *characters* can end up being insipid, mawkish, and ultimately tedious. Of course there are exceptions. Look at Chesterton's lovable Father Brown, virtuous through and through.

Some people would disagree with the statement that while we all admire a hero, we don't have to love him. No one could call Sir Harry Paget Flashman VC, KCB, KCIE a hero in the classic sense of the word. A self-confessed snivelling coward, a careless bully, an insatiable but well-endowed lecher – in one book he calculates that he has enjoyed 478 sexual encounters (and that is not including return engagements!) – Flashman is a stimulating anti-hero. He's the male equivalent of Becky. Over the course of George Macdonald Fraser's *oeuvre*, he is not in the least embarrassed to detail his pusillanimous behaviour in the face of danger. Macdonald Fraser has taken over Thomas Hughes's character and made him someone both vigorous and exciting, yet like Becky Sharp, both callous and depraved. Neither of them is so much *real*, as plausible.

But to augment your character (male for the purposes of this essay), however ingeniously constructed he is, you must have conflict. Conflict will widen our view of him as we note his reactions to dealing with adversity, and thus can only enrich him in the reader's eyes. Conflict will show us how he copes with disaster and mayhem when everyone around him is crumbling; and will thus enlarge him, make him more *real*. Never hesitate to copy from life. Unless you are particularly specific, most people would not recognize themselves on the printed page.

My amateur sleuth, Penny Wanawake, sprang more or less fully formed into my head. Her genesis came about because many years ago, one of the national newspapers complained that there were very few contemporary crime novels featuring memorable female protagonists. The situation has changed enormously since then, but at the time Miss Jane Marple, the elderly spinster of St Mary Mead, was almost the only well-known representative of the species. At the same time, I had recently returned home to England after several years of living in Tennessee, where racial discrimination was rife. Non-white people had to live in enclaves out of town. They weren't allowed to use the same public swimming pool as the white folk, nor live in the same area, nor eat at the same self-service restaurant, though they could act as 'waiters', wearing white gloves and carrying the trays of food we had self-selected, to our table. I came from a liberal Oxford background and my blood boiled at hearing young (white) kids shouting 'Hey, boy!' at some black adult when they wanted more salt or water. We joined the NAACP; demonstrated against prejudice; held secret meetings with other members, the black ones making their way silently through the woods at the end of our garden; had a cross burned on our lawn; and saw the Klan come into town. Once an open jeep screeched to a halt beside me and when I turned to look, there were four backwoods rednecks grinning inanely, all pointing shotguns at me.

Those were frightening and disturbing times. So when, safely back in England, I came to produce a contemporary female detective, waiting in the wings was Bovril-black Penny Wanawake, who had no truck with racial prejudice and strode confidently into the pantheon of female protagonists. Her partner is a modern-day Robin Hood, literally stealing from the rich to feed the poor.

So where did Cassandra Swann come from; professional bridge expert and my second amateur sleuth? Was she based on anyone? No one specific. Only on the millions of women who constantly worry about their weight. Cassie sometimes goes so far as to cut her toenails before stepping onto the scales in the hope of reducing the figure displayed. Cassie is an orphan who grew up with her vicar uncle and his exasperatingly slender daughters, whose slimness is a constant reproach to her.

What I was aiming for in both these characters was to produce a recognizable somebody, not a head-to-toe physical laundry list. And the better you know your characters, the more realistic they become. Realistically rounded characters are the backbone of any crime novel. The reader has to care about them before he is going to want to get involved in your ingenious plot, enjoy your well-crafted settings or your scintillating dialogue. In other words, engage your reader's attention. And never forget that the Prodigal Son will always be more fascinating than the dutiful elder brother.

For a writer who seeks an alternative to writing about police detectives, but prefers to avoid an out-and-out amateur, the obvious choice is a private detective. Liza Cody has already described her creation of Anna Lee, and P. D. James and Val McDermid among others have also written about female private investigators. One of the Club's American-born members, Mike Lewin, enjoyed success with a long-running series about Albert Samson, a gumshoe from Indianapolis who narrates his cases in the classic fashion made famous by the likes of Raymond Chandler and Ross Macdonald. After moving to Bath, he created the Lunghis, whose detective agency is run as a family business.

Private Eyes

Michael Z. Lewin

So, you're interested in writing about private detectives . . . One question: Why?

I'm not trying to put you off, but the question needs to be answered if that's what you're thinking of writing. After all, there's already a very large amount of published PI fiction out there . . .

So, what's your particular interest? You like reading stories in the PI genre? You don't find enough of the stories and books 'out there' that you really enjoy? Someone you know has heard you explain what's wrong with the PI stories you're reading and has challenged you write one better, just to shut you up?

Whatever your motive, you do have to think about what you're trying to bring to the form. Are you looking to make it modern and tech-literate? Do you want to satirize it? Have you got an idea for a story that no professional non-police detective has ever explored before? Or an idea for a setting that hasn't been used before? Or a little-explored time in history you know a lot about? Or would you be offering the first PI who came to earth from Alpha Centauri?

Truly, I am not trying to diminish what you're thinking about. I was there once myself.

I was introduced to PI fiction more than fifty years ago when my (then) wife introduced me to Raymond Chandler. I went on to read Ross Macdonald; and with both authors I enjoyed their literate writing and the complexity of their stories. I also began to see that in a work of fiction, private detectives were more than just characters: they were literary devices.

A fictional professional detective is allowed to intrude in other characters' business and private lives in a way normal people (even fictional ones) can't, credibly. They're on a case; they're following leads; they have to follow wherever the facts direct them. That's the way the form works.

If I were to write a story about my neighbours upstairs,

trying to pin down why they're making such a god-awful racket
day after day, what excuse could I give for watching who comes
and goes, talking to their friends, trying to unearth their criminal and financial histories? 'I was curious?' No, no. Ordinary
people don't do that. But private detectives do. And that means
that in a story the PI character can pursue a very wide range
of enquiries.

When I sat down to start my first PI story in 1969, what
constituted a fictional 'private detective' was pretty well defined.
He – always a 'he' – was a tough guy available for hire to
investigate problems for strangers. He didn't shy away from
getting physical or taking chances. He lived and worked alone
and was beholden to nobody. All the women he met fancied
him. He had problems with authority and, perhaps, commitment. He believed that truth and justice were important, more
important than details of the law or the personal idiosyncrasies
of the people who enforced the law. He would find some way
for justice to be done. And fiction's early American PIs most
often worked in southern California or New York.

So, from my reading I knew all that, but before I considered
writing my own PI story, I did something that I later learned
is common to most people who write mysteries. I took a book
I liked and analysed it.

Could all the twists and turns *really* fit together the way the
author claimed at the end they did? They were certainly more
twisty and turny than I could keep together in my reader's
head.

I analysed a Ross Macdonald novel. And, ignorant of the
professionalism good writers apply to their plotting, I was
surprised to discover that the story did indeed hold together.
The only possible weakness I found was having a woman who
was five months pregnant appear in a bathing suit and not be
spotted as being with child. Yeah, just about OK.

Chandler once wrote about having analysed Erle Stanley
Gardner stories – even recommending to an aspirant that he
not only analyse a story but then take the story elements and
rewrite it again for himself.

Another writer I know analysed a movie (*Klute*) the same way. I'm not going to try to list what you might get from such an analysis of whatever form you're attracted to, but the process has certainly helped a lot of mystery writers I know get a first grip on what was required for their various forms.

Mine – and yours – is PI fiction. Having analysed the Macdonald book, I decided to write my own PI story. In retrospect what interests me is which of the PI stereotypes I retained and which I replaced with something (then) unconventional. What did I think *I* was going to bring to a PI story? Which bits of the conventional form appealed to me, and which didn't?

Some resonated easily for me, like difficulty dealing with authority. I'd never liked being told how to do things. I was also comfortable with the idea of a character who sometimes made his own justice. And I liked the idea that my story might include a philosophical thought or two, the occasional word of more than four syllables, and that character could be developed through sharp dialogue. I decided to have my PI work alone, and tell his story in the first person, recounting directly his travels and travails. I never considered a narrator who wasn't a bloke.

So what didn't I adopt? Although he was American – as I was – he was not a tough guy: he didn't own a gun. He also worked the mean streets of Indianapolis (which, for the world at large, even now often elicits the question, 'Where?') His PI business was not financially successful. He had a steady girl-friend he was faithful to. He was into Mom and apple pie (OK, his mom owned a luncheonette and served him the apple pie). And he thought he was funny so he spoke (and wrote) with a wry turn of phrase.

As well, something essential to all PI stories: he did not accept things he was told at face value. Reinterpreting information a character has been given is at the heart of plot-building.

I once had a reader who took me aside at a library show. He told me that my books 'had gotten him through the time when his son was missing'. How? Because they showed him 'that things did not have to be the way they seemed'.

PIs must look at facts and address what they *might* mean. Not the worst thing in the world to do when talking with anyone.

There are other things to say about PI fiction now. In the fifty years since I first set pen to paper (as the process was then) PI writers have answered the question I put to you in a wide variety of ways.

For instance, my decision to locate my guy in Indianapolis was unusual, even groundbreaking (I've been told). My '69 story was published as a novel in 1971. Robert B. Parker launched Spenser in Boston in 1973 and nowadays 'regional' detectives feature at just about every crossroads of the US. And, importantly, elsewhere. To be fair, by no means all of them are professional detectives. Or even human.

I haven't seen many in the US who don't own guns – or don't have pals with guns who are also happy to do violence which the squeamish hero PI eschews.

Another element of the stereotype that no longer applies is that the PI must be male. Fans of Chandler in particular began to ask themselves just why the hell a woman couldn't be the centre (or center) of a PI novel. And, indeed, to feel outrage at the way women were treated and described in his and similar novels. The first female properly professional private detective was Liza Cody's Anna Lee, who appeared in 1980 and worked not alone but in a London detective agency. Within a couple of years two subsequently famous women PI's appeared in the US: Sara Paretsky's VI Warshawski and Sue Grafton's Kinsey Millhone. Women PIs and women PI writers are no longer remotely rare. Their novels have changed many conventions that were common when I began. These include adopting a more realistic treatment of violence – if they get hit they carry bruises – and abandoning much of the early PI's casual and not so casual misogyny, racism and anti-Semitism.

So . . . what's going to make your PI story different? Will your character (someone like you or a complete opposite) live and work in a unique place? Will your detective have unusual physical characteristics? (There are PIs with a wide range of disabilities now.) Will your PI have specialist knowledge? Unusual ethnicity? Be of a different species? *Why* are you writing a PI story?

Which brings me to my work. Regionalism hasn't been my only (then) unconventional offering to PI fiction. I've also written about a detective agency run as a family business (talk about not being a loner . . .) I have murder mysteries with no murders. (Well, other people do that nowadays too.) I've written about a dog who solves problems for other dogs (OK – not as a licensed private eye, nose and tail.) And my latest book about my licensed PI – whose name by the way is Albert Samson – has a series *client*. The book is called *Alien Quartet*. Available via all good computers near you.

Research

'Write what you know' is one of the clichés of writing lore. It's advice that shouldn't be taken too literally. There is really no need to commit murder before writing a crime novel. Nor do you have to been professionally involved with the world of crime as a police officer, lawyer, forensic psychologist or trial reporter. A work of fiction is a work of the imagination.

Some authors keep their research to a minimum. In his essay 'Growing Up to Crime', Robert Barnard said: 'The critic whose praise I have cherished above all others is the American one who said of *Death on the High C's* that "Mr Barnard obviously knows the world of backstage opera from A to Z." God bless America . . . but it must be said that I have never set toe backstage of an opera house. Nor, for that matter, have I ever been inside a working monastery – the setting for *Blood Brotherhood*.'

That said, most crime novels benefit from a sense of authenticity, and the reader's willingness to suspend disbelief can be destroyed if the story contains obvious errors. So research can be very important, even in a traditional whodunit whose main purpose is light entertainment.

Research, like writing, can be hard work. It can also take many different forms. Some authors with artistic skills draw illustrations to help them with their researches. R. Austin Freeman, a talented amateur artist, made sketches of (among other things) intriguing inscriptions on old gravestones; one of these, ornamented with a skull, found its way into his novel *Dr Thorndyke Intervenes*. Decades later, Len Deighton, an accomplished graphic designer, produced a drawing sitting in the students' gallery of an operating theatre at Guy's Hospital, for reference while working on a book. Ultimately he abandoned the book, but the detail and care with which he made the drawing illustrate that infinite capacity for taking pains with his research that is one of the secrets of his success.

Len Deighton's own reference drawing done in
an operating theatre for an abandoned book.

Fortunately, research is often enjoyable. You can even find yourself undertaking valuable research by accident, a point illustrated by Catherine Aird in an anecdote for an article for *The Writer* in 1969. She was working on her first novel, *The Religious Body*, and the body in question was a nun: 'I was delighted when reading an otherwise exceedingly dull report on the wool trade to come across a note to the effect that the wool from black sheep was used to make the cloth for nun's veiling. I don't think any writer exists who couldn't make ironic use of that fact.'

Some Golden Age authors researched as assiduously as any

modern writer – and without the benefit of Google searches. John
Curran's history of Collins Crime Club, *The Hooded Gunman*, includes
an editor's rueful account of Freeman Wills Crofts' response to a
query about *The Ponson Case*, which involved the timing of the
discovery of a body washed up from the river. The author 'arrived
with a suitcase for discussion. He produced three large Ordnance
Survey maps showing the course of the river, a very full County
History, two reports on flooding in the county, one report on the
effect of the current on the river banks and lastly a batch of correspondence with a medical officer of Health showing how to tell how
long a body had been in the water.' Crofts' diligence may seem over
the top, but it paid off. In his day, he was a bestseller whose fans
included T. S. Eliot.

Among the Golden Age writers who strove for accuracy of detail
was Ngaio Marsh. Several of her books had a theatrical background,
drawing on her experience as a leading director, but in the course
of a long career as a novelist she needed to vary her settings and
storylines. *The Nursing Home Murder*, which she published in 1935,
was co-written with a surgeon, Henry Jellett, who helped her to
ensure that the medical details of the plot were accurate. In the
mid-1950s, while living in her native New Zealand and working on
Off with His Head, set in an English country village, she trawled
through reference books in her library in Christchurch to check
details of folk dances and ancient customs relevant to the plot. Her
serial killer whodunit *Singing in the Shrouds* draws on her personal
experience of travelling on a small cargo ship, and she also studied
real-life cases about psychopathic murderers such as 'the Blackout
Ripper'. But as this anecdote illustrates, however hard you try to
get details right, you can't satisfy everyone.

Getting It Right

Ngaio Marsh

A large number of the reading public for crime fiction are
professional men and women; the very people, of course, who
are best equipped to catch you out if you make a blunder –
doctors, lawyers, soldiers, sailors, academics, all read these
books and strangely enough, or so I am credibly informed, so
do policemen – these latter perhaps because they enjoy a
complete change from reality.

You might say the writer of a detective story is in much the
same situation as a barrister whose practice is largely in crimes
of violence. One gets up the case and in the process often has
to do a lot of research in a number of fields: medical jurispru-
dence, police law, poisons, the drug racket, the arts, ballistics,
or the laws of evidence. I have amassed a large collection of
reference books and often am obliged to fag through one or
another of them in search of some technical detail to which I
will refer in a single sentence. No matter how plain sailing and
simplistic you may consider the plot you've chosen, sooner or
later you'll find yourself involved with technical concerns.

Suppose you decide that the crime is simply this: one man
hits another man on the head with a half-brick in a dirty sock
and leaves the body in a dark alley. Plain sailing you think?
In no time your detective, and therefore you, are involved with
the component parts of brick-dust, the various types of wool
from which socks are woven or knitted and the places of origin
of such microscopic traces of dirt as cling to the sock in question. Once the book is concluded you forget all this stuff and
I'm told barristers who so confidently expound their expert
knowledge to juries do exactly the same thing. The information
has served its purpose: away with it.

Sometimes, however, things turn out oddly. One of the rare
occasions when I began with a plot rather than with people
was in writing *Scales of Justice*. A friend who was a member
of the Royal Society and an authority on trout, told me that

the scales of trout are unique in as much as those of one trout never have corresponded and never can correspond exactly with those of another. In this they resemble human fingerprints.

This, of course, immediately suggested a title and pleasing subject matter for a book. So I wrote *Scales of Justice* and in due course typescripts were sent off to my English and American publishers. To my astonishment the American script-reader wrote crisply in the margin 'Trout do not have scales.' I can only suppose she was thinking of eels.

Research is important even for writers who don't plan their books. Desmond Bagley insisted that in day-to-day writing, he never knew what he was going to put on paper next. He began his career as an author of action thrillers in 1963. Ten years later, he explained in an article for *The Writer* how he set about researching one of his most admired books, *Running Blind*. He visited and researched Iceland and the storyline 'came directly from the terrain and the peculiar social institutions of Iceland . . . I do not think that specific plot could have been set in any other country.' Careful research was the hallmark of his writing, and his quest for authenticity paid off: he was a bestseller throughout his career, and four of his books were filmed.

Keeping Up to Date

Desmond Bagley

We live in a world in which science and its more directly active partner, technology, have an increasingly greater impact upon the lives of all of us . . . This leads to problems for the writer, and the main problem is this: How can the writer – who is, himself, not a scientist or technologist – describe adequately the impact of these advances upon the lives of his characters? Some – I believe most – writers merely ignore the problem, but this can lead to anachronisms that give an old-fashioned look to the writing . . . your characters must live in the real world and interact with an environment that is becoming more complex year by year, and to write accurately about the people you must also know the environment.

For myself, I regard this as a challenge. I tend to use the environment as a character in its own right, and, since most of my books are science or technology oriented, I have to know exactly what I am doing or I will make a damn fool of myself in print. There is no one so quick on the draw with a pen as the science-oriented reader who catches out the writer in an error of fact . . . Recently I came across a letter to my publisher, in which I stated that I was going to write a novel about an avalanche. The novel, *The Snow Tiger*, was written in 1974 and published in 1975. The point is that the letter was written in December 1963, so what happened in the intervening ten years?

The short answer is that when I wrote that letter I knew absolutely nothing about avalanches. Preliminary studies into the nature of snow and ice led to my next book, *High Citadel*, set in the Andes, where the subject was treated in a more-or-less superficial way, but I was no nearer my avalanche.

The years went by.

In 1968 I was fortunate enough to be invited to go to the Antarctic – McMurdo Sound and points south – by the US State Department, and in due course I found myself standing on top of 10,000 feet of ice at the geographical South Pole. It was in the Antarctic that I met the snow-and-ice scientists, in this case those working for the Cold Regions Research and Engineering Laboratory of the US Army. Friendships were made, letters and books exchanged, and I learned a lot about snow and ice. This was augmented by visits to the Scott Polar Research Institute in Cambridge, England, where I talked to more experts.

Ask the experts

And so we have Lesson Number One: If you want to know about a subject, ask the experts. Don't be afraid that they'll be snooty or jabber technical jargon that is way over your head; they are human beings, too. There is nothing that a man likes more than to talk about his own job, and if you drop in the occasional question that is semi-intelligent and not too half-witted, the expert will talk until your ears fall off. If you are a good listener you'll learn something.

Lesson Number Two is a corollary of Number One: don't go to any old expert; go to the man at the top of his profession. For one thing, he is the best source of information, and for another, he has the latest information. Before writing *The Spoilers*, I needed to know about the manufacture, use, and abuse of heroin. A doctor friend put me in touch with the President of the Royal Pharmaceutical Society who provided a team of botanists, pharmacists, police officers and forensic scientists, and I was told of everything from the planting of the poppy seed in Thailand, to the distribution of heroin in the streets of London.

Similarly, before writing *The Enemy*, I needed to know more about genetic engineering. I started with the President of the Royal College of Physicians, himself a geneticist. Because I'm British, most of my sources are in England, but there are analogous American institutions. If the man at the top cannot help you in your particular line of questioning, he is sure to know of someone who can, and invariably he will provide you with a personal introduction that can be most valuable.

Professional men are only too delighted to help a writer get his facts right, and in no group of men is this more noticeable than the police, who are sick to their collective stomach of being caricatured in detective stories and on television. If you have police procedural difficulties, ask the Chief of Police in the town in which you live. He will offer you every facility, from giving you copies of the inevitable bureaucratic forms to letting you witness a post-mortem examination – if you have the stomach for it. I'm no stranger to Scotland Yard, myself.

Background reading

Before you consult your expert, it is advisable for you to do some background reading on your subject . . . Very often, after consulting these books, you will not need an expert at all, but if you do, then he will be favourably impressed by your unexpected layman's knowledge, and he will know that you are not there to waste his time.

Cultivate the habit of buying books you think you may need in the future. Second-hand bookshops are a source of often unanticipated treasures. I have not yet had a character who had to abandon ship at sea, but if I have this problem then there, ready and waiting on my technical shelf, is a book entitled *How to Abandon Ship*, which I picked up for twenty cents in Los Angeles a few years ago.

Experts, too, often come in strange guises. I wrote *The Snow Tiger* in a small English town of 6,000 population. I was delighted to find that the owner of a local second-hand bookshop had been a mountain guide in the Mount Cook area of the South Island of New Zealand, quite close to where I had put my hypothetical disaster. He was the source of much valuable information, tending more to improve the atmospheric feel of the book than to hard fact.

In your community there are at least three people you ought to cultivate and, if possible, to make into personal friends – a lawyer, a doctor and a policeman. These three professions cover ninety per cent of the human condition, and to have minor matters of fact cleared up in an informal manner is very useful. It goes without saying that when your book is published, anyone contributing information should receive an autographed copy. He will be delighted and regard it as reward enough.

The entertainment factor

And now we come to Lesson Number Three, the most important of all. Here you are, stuffed to the eyebrows with esoteric information, and your first impulse is to regurgitate it, thus sullying several hundred pages of virgin paper. This is disastrous – death to your novel.

Hemingway once remarked that what you leave out of a novel is more important than what you put into it. In this context, I take Hemingway very seriously. For instance, while not being an expert on avalanches, I can enter the shop talk of snow physicists without making a downright idiot of myself. And yet, I estimate that only one per cent of my avalanche knowledge went into *The Snow Tiger*. The point is that to put that one per cent into the book I had to know the other ninety-nine per cent.

When you write a novel you are not writing a text book on avalanches, genetic engineering, heroin or whatever technical subject your book hinges on. You are writing an entertainment, and any novelist who forgets this is doomed to the deepest pit in Dante's *Inferno*. Your readers are not naturally technically minded people; they buy your book to be entertained, and no matter what your reasons are for writing the book, entertained they must be. The crunch comes at the end of the first page – if a reader doesn't care enough to turn that page, then your book is dead. And the same applies to the second, third and on to the penultimate page.

The cardinal rule is this: you select only such bits of your newfound knowledge that will advance the story. A novel is about people, their interactions with each other and with the world in which they live. So you do not incorporate slabs of undigested fact; rather, you consider carefully the minimum you will need to get your points across, and then insert it as unobtrusively as possible. Generally, dialogue is a better vehicle than narrative, but always the style of presentation must be oblique rather than direct, and it is best to adopt a 'throw away' manner, as though your carefully garnered information is a mere matter of common knowledge.

If you cannot do it in this way, then you may like the reverse switch on the Holmes–Watson relationship. In the Sherlock Holmes stories, Holmes was the expert and Doyle introduced the somewhat half-witted Watson as a foil, so that Holmes could make his points in dialogue rather than by the stilted method of directly addressing the reader – a good technique in its day.

These days very few of our main characters are as expert as Holmes. That convention has died, but a reasonable technique is to make your Watson, a secondary character, into the expert. In *The Snow Tiger*, the main character had a friend, McGill, who was an unabashed expert, a snow physicist giving professional evidence at an inquiry into a natural disaster.

After having written books by these methods for a number of years you will have received better than a college education. Your friends – and enemies – will be impressed and alarmed by your knowledge of such subjects as clay mineralogy, Mayan architecture, the aerodynamics of aircraft of the 1930s, the metabolism of the camel, the route of the Spanish Armada, all of which I have studied for one book or another . . .

And so you write your book and may then receive one of the greatest rewards authorship can offer: the approval of a work of fiction by the experts whose brains you have picked . . .

The need to research a cutting-edge contemporary thriller is clear. But even a story in the traditional mould benefits from that touch of assurance derived from the careful use and checking of detail. Agatha Christie's storylines, for instance, often required relatively little research, but she made excellent use of her knowledge of poisons, gained while working in a pharmacy during the First World

War, and of the Middle East, from working on digs with her archaeologist husband. As John Malcolm shows, careful research can help
to give a story featuring an amateur detective that valuable ingredient
of plausibility.

Amateurs and Expertise
John Malcolm

'According to the enlarged edition of his *oeuvre* catalogue,
Corot painted over 2000 pictures. Of these, more than 5000
are in the United States.'

Frank Arnau thus prefaced his 1959 book, *3000 Years of
Deception in Art and Antiques*, highlighting the immense scope
for criminal activity that art and antiques provided. Long pages
of copy could be used to describe and classify things as forgeries
or fortunes. But when Arnau wrote, many of today's forensic
methods of analysis were not available. Neither were the information sources of the internet. Vast amounts of readily
accessible data did not exist. Painstaking research had to be
done clerically, making the frauds to which many valuables
were prone much easier to carry out. The specialist hero or
heroine in a given field, who provided an alternative to the
worthy policeman as main protagonist in a crime novel, had
to slog for the solution in gloomy library and original source
locations across a wide geographical area. Gerald Reitlinger's
1961 volume on *The Economics of Taste*, which traced the
rollercoaster prices of famous painters over at least a century,
had to draw on auction records stored on thousands of catalogue pages. To resolve a mystery, an art expert-hero would
have to thumb his or her way through yards of shelved documents and books whilst fending off villainous attacks from the

Bad Guy or Guys, refuting incredulous disbelief from the Good Guys, and galloping off at tangents in response to bibliographical temptation.

The attraction of the crime novel or mystery that is not a police procedural, with its discipline-conscious policemen and women obliged to follow credible legal routines and to defer to bosses with attitudes shaped by dogged experience, is that the central character can be of almost any background that will spark the interest of the reader. His or her specialist knowledge has been acquired uniquely from practice and performance in the field chosen by the author. It does not matter whether the hero/heroine of the story is an expert in art, orchids, cookery, photography, Renaissance furniture or horse racing. What does matter is that this expertise is a prominent element in the resolution of a mystery that brings character, personality, relationships and motivation to engage the reader's attention before its arresting conclusion. As such, it needs to be imparted with ease, so that it does not clog the narrative nor resemble a lecture of worthy content.

The important thing to bear in mind when setting out to write a crime novel or mystery in which an artefact or skill is a prominent feature of the story, shaping events and influencing decisions, is whether the thrill of the treasure hunt to find the said artefact is the most important part of the story or whether it is merely incidental. In his 1989 book on the detective in fiction, *Murder Will Out*, T. J. Binyon groups art and antiques sleuths in the Miscellaneous Male Amateur category and suggests that writers like Jonathan Gash and yours truly have departed from the usual form of the detective story in that the object at the centre of events is in the end 'more important than the mystery, the deductions and the solution'. This may be so in some cases, where a treasure trail is followed, but it is not a rigid form. The object and the scrambled treasure hunt can be just a background to a broader and more traditional story. In both cases there are certain principles to be observed.

The choice of a non-police detective or specialist central character is deliberately made to avoid the very precise expertise and established operational routines required of police officers. A credible knowledge of police procedures and the organizational structure of the force is happily accepted as necessary by many writers who are prepared to make sure their research establishes the genuine format of police work. Readers are surprisingly knowledgeable about the way the law operates and will spot any errors quickly. Outside a police procedural novel the author can more easily play games with the sequence of events and the behaviour of the central character. He or she can be as eccentric or conventional as the author wants. It is usually due to chance that the central character becomes involved in the crime and has to find the solution to it, or perhaps becomes a suspect interviewed by the police and has to clear his or her name. The events that draw the hero/heroine into the mystery provide the drama and attraction of the tale; they can be used to heighten the sense of danger as well as to provide the reader with interesting facts about a particular industry, trade or commerce. But therein lie the traps that the author must avoid.

It is almost always true that the research necessary to place the specialist central character in context has a fascination of its own. It provides a great deal of the pleasure in planning the book and its plot structure. What is more it adds additional spurs and branches to the story by providing the author with new and hitherto unknown facts which themselves add to the mystery and sequence of events. Dick Francis and his wife said that the horse-racing thrillers he wrote provided them with delightful journeys of research round different racecourses and foreign locations that yielded beguiling information. I found much the same when researching artists' lives and works. The increased depth that the research gave me broadened my liking for the subject. The problem of how much information to impart is one that is difficult to resolve, however, especially if you are not writing the equivalent of Michael Frayn's book *Headlong*, which has to delve deep into the work of Brueghel in pursuit of a missing masterpiece. The research has used up resources; all those notes and facts assembled with effort and perception;

the photographs of the *mis-en-scène*: surely they can be used
when the author, back at his or her keyboard, is hammering
out the book? The fact can easily be overlooked that diversions
to inform the reader very often clog the narrative and slow
down the action.

An author's display of expertise can bore the reader very
quickly. In one of my crime novels the businessman villain sets
up a factory in Wales using government funds in a fraudulent
scam. The factory uses dry-forming technology to make tissue
paper in a new process that is key to the plot. In an otherwise
kind and laudatory review for the *TLS*, Marghanita Laski wrote
that 'we learn far too much about tissue paper production',
which she found boring. Alarmed, I checked and found that
in a 200-page story I had devoted about a page to describing
the process. But industry is industry and technical processes,
traditionally, are Boring with a capital B. That page, even
though relevant to part of the development of the plot, taxed
the kind reviewer's patience unduly.

So the author should be aware that the fascination provided
by a specialist setting can become too much of a diversion.
The crime novel concerns a drama. The art, antiques, orchids,
cookery, horse racing, photography, whatever, is the pulsating
background to that drama, the scenery in front of which the
characters play out their roles. They have to blend in with it
and allow deeper detail to develop with events. There is also
a risk that the newly acquired knowledge can lead to a somewhat didactic approach, a sermon that comes over as
condescending or tedious, qualifying the book for admission
to Insomniacs' Corner. The facts have to be corralled with
caution and fed into the dialogue as well as the narrative so
that their intake does not cause receptive indigestion. Too much
explanation and history in chunks will disrupt the flow of the
story; the facts should be eased out in digestible quantities
sometimes as part of the action, sometimes in dialogue. Even
so, it is difficult to please everyone. If, for instance, stories
concern the interaction of high finance and art, one reader
may be fascinated yet another may start to yawn.

Allowing specialist material to run away with plot is an easy error to make, especially when the subject itself provides further machinations to the story. The research material needs control. The reader does not want to be lectured nor educated; a crime novel is a story written for entertainment. It is a pleasant bonus to find that one's knowledge has been enhanced whilst the central character dodges fatal attacks. One of the ploys I adopted to help smooth the flow of information was the invention of Mr Goodston, the Praed Street antiquarian book dealer, a fat man of great erudition from whom the hero Tim regularly buys books that contain biographical details of the artists he researches for White's Art Fund. Mr Goodston specializes in 'sporting, military and thespian volumes' and has pithy but accurate remarks to make about the protagonists occupying their pages. But he also has a weakness for placing bets on slow horses. His debts bring bookies' thugs to his bookshop to extract money from him by rough methods. From time to time Tim has to deal faithfully with these professional heavy men, something his rugby career as a front row forward has made him good at. He and Mr Goodston can then exchange biographical detail whilst sipping Celebration Cream sherry; Mr Goodston keeps a bottle in his desk drawer. Their post-violence conversation can then range over some part of the investigation Tim is pursuing, bringing a pause in the action whilst casting light and cross-references over the subjects in hand. In some cases the villain of the story goes after Mr Goodston himself in pursuit of additional information, adding tension to the research activity.

Another means of adding to the information from a different perspective comes from the smoothly pinstriped Bond Street auctioneer Charles Massenaux, a friend of Tim's as knowledgeable about modern British art as Tim's girlfriend and subsequent wife, Sue, who is a curator at the Tate Gallery. They deplore his propensity to become involved in violence whilst he follows his quests, but they add to his knowledge in short bursts from their own different viewpoints. No matter what the specialization, there are always associated occupations that can provide other opinions to build up the scene.

Other sources Tim visits are art dealers and auctioneers, some of them friendly, some competitive and hostile. Charles Massenaux and Mr Goodston are present in several of the adventures and Sue is nearly always present. In a series like this the specialist detective should retain the salient attractions and background expertise from book to book, but everything else should be changed as much as possible, making each story an individual case history. Above all, the author too should enjoy the environment and revelations about the different but sometimes overlapping elements in the special subject. The book should be fun to write. If it isn't and the author doesn't enjoy the creation, the readers won't either.

Detection

The traditional detective story reached a peak of popularity around the time that the Detection Club was founded in 1930 and maintained its preeminence in Britain until the Golden Age of detective fiction drew to a close with the return of global conflict. Traditional detective stories written by Agatha Christie, Margery Allingham, Ngaio Marsh, John Dickson Carr, and others continued to enjoy success but critical favour tended, from the 1950s onwards, to be bestowed on crime novels that seemed more closely in tune with the post-war world, such as those written by the new generation of Detection Club members, the likes of Julian Symons, John Bingham, and Patricia Highsmith.

Some leading Club members, like Nicholas Blake (the pen name of Cecil Day Lewis, the only author of crime fiction to have become Poet Laureate) strove to adapt their writing to the changed times. Others, like Michael Innes (in real life the Oxford don J. I. M. Stewart), Cyril Hare (the barrister and judge A. A. Gordon Clark), Edmund Crispin (the film soundtrack composer Bruce Montgomery), Christianna Brand, and – a little later – Patricia Moyes preferred to concentrate on the traditional whodunit, sometimes giving it an unorthodox or more sophisticated flavour.

Shortly before his death at the age of fifty-seven, Hare wrote a long essay, 'The Classic Form', for the anthology *Crime in Good Company*, edited by a fellow lawyer, the solicitor Michael Gilbert. Hare emphasized his view that the detective novel's sole aim is to

entertain the reader. For him, the detective story was 'no more a
picture of real life than *Hamlet* is a picture of how people really
talked and behaved at the court of Denmark in the Middle Ages'.
Hare felt that the need for plot twists and a surprise solution made
the detective story the antithesis of the 'straight' novel, where the
aim was to reveal rather than to conceal. Even so, he recognized
the importance of credible characterization, and demonstrated it in
novels such as *Tragedy at Law*. He despaired when people asked
him if he wrote the last chapter of each book first: how could he,
when he didn't yet know what the people in it were like?

Today's detective novelists often entertain greater literary ambitions. A new generation of writers is developing new types of clue,
innovative forms of plot twist, taking the genre to fresh heights. Yet
there is still something to be learned about the tricks of the trade
from leading exponents of Golden Age detection such as Crispin,
Carr, Brand, and Innes.

Detective Stories and Virtuosity
Edmund Crispin

What it boils down to is this: that the fully evolved detective story
is technically by far the trickiest form of fiction humanity has so
far devised. For we have come to demand of it not only a mystery
with a plausible solution, but over and above that a mystery with
a surprise solution; and over and above *that*, a mystery with a
surprise solution which by rights we ought not to have been
surprised at all.

I am not, of course, to be understood as implying that because
orthodox detective fiction is inordinately difficult to do well, it
is therefore, *ipso facto*, inordinately well worth doing. Walking
across Niagara Falls on a tight-rope is inordinately difficult to
do; but we do not for that reason cherish Niagara Falls

2

hotel bar at Belmouth, and whose touched-up photograph, issued

by the police, he had seen in that morning's papers, Super-

intendent Best heaved a sigh of relief.

"That's something, sir, anyway," he said.   "It gives us

a starting-point, at least -- and there's things in that ~~talk~~ conversation

you had with him that'll narrow it down quite a lot.   So if

you wouldn't mind coming back to the Station straight away,

and making a formal statement...."

Fen nodded assent.   "No other reaction so far?   To the

photograph, I mean?"

"Not yet.   There's almost always a bit of a time-lag, you

know."

"Ah," said Fen affirmatively; ~~and~~ and his eyes strayed to the

~~second table~~ shrouded occupant of the further table. "Who's that?" he ~~asked~~ demanded.

~~second of the two shrouded who were dead in that little room~~

~~and the other?"~~

Drowning case

"Chap called Edgar Foley. ~~a bit of a brute, by all accounts~~

~~.... What we feel is,"~~ said Best, ~~all at once expansive, "that~~

~~although we've got a nice up-to-date scientific place here,~~

~~still, people coming in to identify relatives and so forth~~

~~don't like seeing 'em pushed in and out of refirgerated~~

~~compartments like a load of fish.   So when there's visitors~~

~~for 'em, they're moved in here where it's a bit more human."~~

~~"Quite right, too.   And how did this Foley die?"~~

~~"Drowning.~~   They picked him out of the ~~river~~ water yesterday,

and his widow's coming along this morning to have a look at him."

Best consulted his watch.   "And talking of that, I think it'd

An extract from the manuscript of Edmund Crispin's short story
'The Drowning of Edgar Foley'.

tight-rope walkers above all other men. No, the case for
orthodox detective fiction depends on the fact that most of us
get great satisfaction out of contemplating, now and again, a
piece of virtuoso literary *contrivance*. Why this should be so I
have no idea. None the less, it is so. And far from repining,
we addicts ought to be grateful that the gods have given us
minds eclectic enough to accommodate this specialized variety
of literary pleasure along with all the others.

Rules and Prejudices

John Dickson Carr

Your craftsman knows, as Dr R. Austin Freeman long ago pointed out, that it is not at all necessary to mislead the reader. Merely state your evidence, and the reader will mislead himself. Therefore, the craftsman will do more than mention his clues: he will stress them, dangle them like a watch in front of a baby, and turn them over lovingly in his hands. He will give not only the clue physical, but the clue psychological and the clue atmospheric.

No speech in the book is included just because it sounds mysterious, or because it makes a given character look guilty, or because the author doesn't know what the devil his character does mean and simply throws in the words to fill up space. Not at all. In turning over the pages afterwards, the reader can see for himself – how rare it is! – just what each character was *thinking* at any moment.

And the result?

That is why the story pulses with vitality all the way through, and springs into living vividness at the end. The veil is twitched away; the masks are removed. Human beings walk here, and no sawdust dolls, because the author has described voice inflections, shades of feeling, as well as Inspector Hogarth's discovery of the blunted thumbtack under the sofa. He has not forgotten to study his characters merely because he is writing about them in reverse. That turn of the eyes – of course! That momentary hesitation, when Betty puts her hand on the window ledge as though to steady herself – naturally!

Each small detail glitters now with an effectiveness it should have had, and would have had, if the story had been written straightforwardly. It is in the mood, in the tempo, an arrow whang in the gold. And when, in addition to this, we find ourselves flumdiddled by some master stroke of ingenuity which has turned our suspicions legitimately in the wrong direction, we can only salute the author and close the book with a kind of admiring curse.

There, good friends, *is* a detective story.

But who writes such stories nowadays?

Those who nail a manifesto to the wall, saying, 'The beginner will do this, and must under no circumstances do that', are in many cases quoting not rules but prejudices. That is the danger. It is a prejudice, like my own prejudice against having the murder turn out to be a suicide; and should freely be indicated as such. With all due respect and admiration for those who have compiled lists, it would not be difficult to show that they were often giving dubious advice and sometimes talking arrant nonsense.

Here, then, is my own list of Dos and Don'ts: compiled partly from those of the writers quoted above and partly from my own heart's blood.

1. The criminal shall never turn out to be the detective, or any servant, or any character whose thoughts we have been allowed to share.

2. The criminal shall never at any time be under serious suspicion until the unmasking. If you haven't the ingenuity to keep his identity a secret until the end, at least pretend you have. Even if the reader outguesses you, and your thunderbolt ending doesn't come off, the effect is far more satisfying than if you apologize for your murderer by 'clearing' him in an early chapter.

3. The crime shall be the work of one person. While the murderer in some instances may be allowed to have a confederate, you will ruin your story if two or three or four people are dragged in as accomplices. The essence of a detective story is that the one guilty man shall fool the seven innocent; not that the one innocent shall be fooled by the seven guilty.

4. The crime shall be clean-cut. If a character disappears and is assumed to be murdered, state frankly what has happened to him. If he hasn't been murdered it's a pity; but the reader has a right to a clear stating of the problem.

Those are four golden maxims. In each one I believe. And each one you will find shattered – shattered admirably, shattered to bits, shattered by a mighty hammer – in the 'best' detective novels, while the reader wishes to do nothing but applaud. Because they are not really rules; they are only prejudices.

Classic Ingredients
Christianna Brand

Having chosen your form, decide upon your dominant detective and his more shadowy cast, or vice versa. Have a care with him, though. The day of the amateur is dying out, I think, as this form grows ever more realistic in treatment: but if you place an official investigator in an inland county, you may have a job getting him to the scene of a seaside crime! The safest bet is probably to place him at Scotland Yard . . .

Six or seven suspects are as many as can be dealt with comfortably. It is preferable to present them *all* early on in the book. Incidental characters should be firmly cleared of suspicion. My own simple method is to give a list of suspects at the beginning, saying, 'the murderer was one of these'.

A detective story needs at least one central pin, a new or odd motive or method, or some psychological quirk: not just a jumble of clues for the detective to unravel, eliminating suspects as he goes. For example – one reads in a text book that a man, fatally wounded and having died instantaneously, may yet walk several yards before he falls. A whole book could be written round this single fact: but one such piece of grit at least is necessary for your oyster to work upon.

How to go about writing a detective story, I honestly don't know: I only wish I did. The whole thing is so interdependent. Literally every sentence is a reference to something that has happened or is going to happen. Perhaps you have seen workers making 'pillow lace'? They arrange a pattern of pins, as you might rough out the main points of your plot: and, with threads of many colours, weave an intricate design. Starting a detective story is like embarking upon a piece of lace with only the pins to give you the barest outline of what your design is to be. My own laborious method is to work and unpick, work and unpick, and rewind my threads as my pattern develops and changes. As a general rule the outline will be diamond-shaped, or rather kite-shaped – broadening out to about two thirds of the book when the story is fully developed. After this point there will be no further progress of plot. Only a juggling with what has now been told, and of course such incident as results from what has gone before.

A second murder comes in handy. It is hard work keeping up the interest of the reader through seventy thousand words without further incident. A great effort should be made to have as little as possible 'explanation' after the denouement in which the criminal is unmasked. Try to explain away everything except the major clues which would actually give the murderer away. Your (impossible) aim should be to expose him on the very last page. But I must not say impossible, for Ellery Queen once contrived a book in which the last word, *and* it came as a surprise, was the name of the murderer.

Clues

Michael Innes

Clues, if they are to be acceptable, must not be recondite: the last reaction to be desired in the reader is an indignant 'But I never knew that!' Thus a polymathic detective may prove a liability, and here Conan Doyle's initial conception of his hero

was insufficiently considered. Holmes, it is true, is declared
(absurdly) to be ignorant of Copernican astronomy, but he has
a 'profound' knowledge of chemistry and has written a monograph discriminating the ashes of 140 varieties of tobacco. In
A Study in Scarlet he knows that somebody has been smoking
a Trichinopoly cigar, but since we have not read his monograph
there is no possibility of our making the same identification
and reasoning from it. Frequently Holmes has to explain to
Watson the significance of matters which Watson, like ourselves,
is not specialist enough to know anything about. Thus, in the
same story, Holmes detects that a cab and not a private carriage
has at one point been involved because of 'the narrow gauge
of the wheels'. We are regularly and justly impressed by Holmes'
powers of observation and inference. But there is no contest
between ourselves and the detective, just as there seems to be
none recorded between Holmes's prototype, Dr Joseph Bell,
and his pupils in Edinburgh (or, indeed, between that *Ur*-Holmes,
Voltaire's Zadig, and the authorities of Babylon in the mystery
of the sacred horse of the king and the queen's respectable
dog).

Clues, then, if they are to be fair, must fall within the area
of common knowledge the validity of which a judge in court
feels free to take into judicial notice: things so generally known
to be true that evidence need not be led to validate them. So
the writer becomes involved in matters of social tact, endeav-
ouring to estimate the likely extent of his readers' acquirements.
A great many people know that dentists commonly wear white
jackets; a smaller but still substantial section of society has
had the opportunity of observing that stewards on passenger
aircraft are (or at one time were) similarly attired. Almost
anybody of sufficient education to find the word 'haemophilia'
even vaguely informative is aware that the blood of sufferers
from the disease does not readily clot; and may even be able
to recall, and grasp as relevant to the plot he is following, the
fact that individuals descended from a particular European
dynasty are, at least marginally, more likely to suffer from
haemophilia than are the common run of us.

In the years since the publication of *A Study in Scarlet* the detective story has developed a great deal, and notably in the ingeniously unobtrusive presentation of clues. The height of virtuosity here is achieved, I suppose, by the writer who gets such a clue into the title of a book, as does Agatha Christie in *Why Didn't They Ask Evans?*, or into the very first word of it (as I believe I have myself twice managed). It is Agatha Christie, too, who regularly contrives that just as the clue is dropped a distracting incidcnt occurs. Here we are close to the art of the stage conjurer.

Again, over this long period of time the clue tends steadily to refine and even attenuate itself in consonance with the enhanced acuity of readers. It is no longer at all likely to be the imprint of a boot in the clayey soil. It may be no more than a nuance of speech. And here once more – rather surprisingly – Christie is supreme.

Even in the twenty-first century, the traditional detective novel retains widespread appeal, to authors as well as to readers. In 2015, the crime genre's highest honour, the CWA Diamond Dagger, was awarded to Catherine Aird, in recognition of a long and distinguished career as an exponent of the classic form. Her contribution develops some of the points made by Michael Innes a generation ago.

Snakes and Ladders

Catherine Aird

The presence of both genuine clues and red herrings differen-
tiates the detective novel from the more conventional work of
fiction. In the latter, 'facts' can normally be relied upon. This
is by no means the case in detective fiction, where a great deal
is purposely not what it seems. In my opinion there are just
two sorts of clue admissible in the detective genre and I think
it's a great mistake to try to invent any other variety. It's an
even greater mistake to try to blur the distinctions between
the two types.

In the first instance there are the perfectly straightforward
clues that are designed to be logical steps eventually leading
towards the solving of the crime by the reader – although of
course ostensibly put there for the benefit of the fictional detective (who is naturally as capable of being misled as everyone
else in the story). Hence we can think of them as ladders.
(These clues aren't ever perfectly straightforward of course but
we'll come to that later.)

And then there are what are known as red herrings – which
might be described as sheep in wolves' clothing. These are
made up of simulated information intended to be read as clues
to the crime but are no such thing. Their entire purpose in the
story is to confuse both the reader and (in the first instance,
anyway) the detective, too. They are otherwise to be thought
of as snakes, leading one and all astray and therefore well
away from the risk of solving the classic 'whodunit' too soon.

It is especially important that both varieties of clue are
entirely plausible and that the red herrings have quite separate
roles from both each other and from the genuine one within
the narrative. The genuine clues must be of a sufficiency for
the reader never to feel cheated when they are revealed and
should be of a quality and quantity that will enable the solution
to be reached by noting them. Integrity is not too strong a
word in this connection: cheating is to be frowned upon. Care

should be taken that the clues don't require abstruse background knowledge on the part of the reader: arcane learning
should have no part in the story, indeed, the simpler the clue
the better: better still if it depends on a well-known fact.

A good instance of this type of clue derives from the fact
that it is widely known that 'all sons are taller than their
mothers'. If he isn't, then (other than in very rare cases) the
son is not the child of his putative mother – which, in a detective story, could have some very important implications indeed:
it is a good example of how to turn biological fact into a clue.

There is no crime writer better to study than Agatha Christie
for learning about ingenious plot and clue. Try taking an old
paperback of one of her murder mysteries and underlining all
the clues that you come across. Then read it again and spot
those you – and perhaps other readers – missed the first time
you read it. She seldom used coincidences when plotting her
stories, and neither should you. Nor should you use already
overworked clues, especially those relying on the left- or
right-handedness of the murderer. Other clues long past their
sell-by dates concern clocks put forward or back with the
intention to deceive, and anything at all to do with mirrors.
Needless for you to write, too, is the whodunit with the body
in the library, murdered by the butler. It, too, has also had its
day. Forensic clues should be handled with care – remember
that these days scientists are always more up-to-date than the
detective writer can possibly be and what they discover is not
always available to the layman. Their scene changes very
rapidly as the laboratory makes more and more fresh discov-
eries, and thus fiction dependent on it can be very dated quite
soon.

The snakes – those pseudo-clues designed only to mislead
– should have two quite unconnected sources and must appear
in the narrative as often as the genuine ones. One way of
making sure of this is to plait three different-coloured strands
of wool together. Two of these colours should relate to two
quite separate red herrings and another to the real thing.
Looking at this will quickly show up any unevenness and

whether the appearances of both the snakes and the ladders are on the same scale. This should confuse everybody nicely and demonstrate quite clearly the fact that their even spread throughout the tale makes identifying the real one of the three even more difficult. What is of prime importance is the principle that both the clues and their treatment remain fair. This is as paramount in the world of detective fiction as it is in the setting of crossword puzzles, and if this isn't kept well in mind, I can assure you someone will very soon be calling out 'Foul!'

Remember, though, that while the genuine clue itself might be straightforward, its position in the narrative can easily be arranged to be deliberately misleading. An astute author will cause these clues to appear in the wrong order and thus of a significance that will only become apparent later when the story has moved on. A good instance of sleight of hand is to slip an important clue either fore or aft of some seemingly very significant paragraphs. Thus unstressed, it can easily be overlooked, which is the aim of many a crime writing author. Another little trick is to set it just before the cliffhanger end of a chapter about something different in the narrative, when hopefully the mind of the reader will have already turned over to the next page. And when it comes to the unravelling of the crime, remember that the same principle applies to the unveiling of clues. It doesn't have to be done in a logical sequence.

There is a subset of the genuine clue which I think of as 'double-barrelled' and should not be overlooked. This is where, to begin with, even the detective is misled by a clue that is not what it seems at first. Dorothy L. Sayers used this subtle approach in *Busman's Honeymoon*, where Lord Peter Wimsey misinterprets a suspect's statement – the village policeman who declares he had known the time of his arrival at the victim's house because he could see the clock through the sitting-room window. Because the face of the clock was normally obscured by a large cactus in a brass bowl hanging in front of it, Lord Peter assumed that the policeman was lying and that he couldn't have seen the clock-face. This had misleading consequences all round until much later when – as it is said – all was revealed.

Another 'double-barrelled' clue guaranteed to mystify the reader was included in one of Agatha Christie's books in the 1930s. It was deceptively simple: time was of the essence in the narrative and the elderly butler was invited by the redoubtable Hercule Poirot to confirm the time of the murder. The old man tottered forward pointing towards the clock until he could see it, and then duly said his piece about the time. But it wasn't the time that was of the essence. What Poirot was checking was the man's poor eyesight. That was what actually mattered.

A good source of clues is to be found in the construction of dialogue. This is where they can appear quite casually and are more likely to be overlooked or even dismissed as mere gossip. Remember that speech in detective fiction will always be there for a reason and the experienced reader will look out for what it is. There are no rules about the probity of information conveyed by the speech of the characters; the reader and the detective should both remember this. What the narrator writes is fact, but what one character in the story writes about another – or, indeed, about anything else – might very well not be, and it should always be suspect. A possible platform, too, for giving some – but not all – the game away can be in the title. *Green for Danger* is a very good example by Christianna Brand.

Every crime writer must keep a tight rein on who, within the story, knows what about the clues – ladder or snake. A character may behave quite differently after finding something out that hitherto hadn't been known to them. This is an important variety of clue, sometimes missed, and can have fatal consequences (in literature, anyway).

I have heard tell that an astute reader ought to be able to work out the identity of the murderer from the first three chapters, six at the outside; after which no really significant material or character should be introduced. I am still studying this interesting thought. It sounds like a counsel of perfection, but then nobody said that writing clues is easy, did they?

The techniques of plotting – clueing, foreshadowing, and misdirecting the reader – are fundamental to the traditional detective story. They help to make the 'twist ending' work and to satisfy the craving that many readers have for 'fair play' in detection. Acquiring a mastery of these methods can also be valuable for authors of other types of crime fiction. Ruth Rendell wrote traditional but sophisticated detective novels featuring her series police detective Reginald Wexford, as well as non-series novels, under her own name and as Barbara Vine, which pushed the genre's boundaries and rank with the finest crime fiction ever written. A current member of the Detection Club, the poet and novelist Sophie Hannah, has said that in Rendell's early novel *The Secret House of Death*, 'the murder itself is the twist . . . The last line, which underscores how profoundly the reader has been fooled, sent a shiver down my spine.'

Sophie Hannah bridges the gap between the contemporary best-selling novel of psychological suspense and the classic detective story, writing authorized continuation novels about Hercule Poirot, as well as her Waterhouse and Zailer series and stand-alone stories. She has demonstrated that the traditional methods of the detective novelist can be adapted and developed to meet the demands of a modern readership, familiar with the classic ploys but still yearning for a satisfying surprise.

Optimal Subterfuge

Sophie Hannah

In 2017, I wrote an article for *The Guardian* in which I picked my top ten twists of all time. One was in P. D. James's *Innocent Blood*. Ever since then, I've been receiving occasional emails – roughly every two months – saying, 'Hang on a minute – I've just read that book and I don't know what twist you're referring to.' I answer with an explanation, and most of those people then reply with, 'Oh, yes, *that*. That was brilliant.' They'd all noticed it, but it hadn't occurred to them to think of it as a twist because it was a revelation that had more to do with character than with plot, and it appeared in the middle of the novel rather than at the end.

We normally understand the word twist to mean something like 'You thought X was the murderer? No, it was Y.' But twists can be any kind of reversal of what we thought we knew. It is widely accepted that the job of a crime writer is to mislead or misdirect readers (while always playing completely fair, of course) and then show them at the last minute that the truth is something quite different. This is a highly effective strategy that has served crime fiction well, but I believe there's an even better one.

One can actively mislead a reader with great elegance and skill by writing this or that ambiguous paragraph which might be interpreted in two ways. But it's even more satisfying to mislead and misdirect in the most passive way of all: by writing nothing specifically designed to make the reader more likely to believe X when the truth is Y, safe in the knowledge that you don't need to go to any such lengths because the reader will mislead herself. P. D. James does this brilliantly in *Innocent Blood*. At the beginning of the book, we are given the bare bones of a situation, and from those bare bones, we immediately leap to a conclusion. At no point does James put any effort into steering us towards this conclusion. She simply knows that we will, unguided by her, and based purely upon our past experiences and our own beliefs about how the world works. She spends not one word nudging us towards making the assumption we make. However, she is 100 per cent certain that we will all assume that very thing – and then find out that we're completely wrong.

Creating a situation in which we know for sure that the reader will mislead and misdirect himself is a fantastic skill that all crime writers should learn. I always look for opportunities to do this, by asking myself each time I create a plot, 'What will the readers assume must be the case that, in fact, could just as easily not be the case?' In one of my novels, I did this in a context that involved passport photos. Everybody, without fail, thinks they look hideous in their passport photo. I knew that if I described something very similar to this well-known phenomenon, something that could oh-so-easily be mistaken for it, readers would automatically think, 'Oh, yeah, this is nothing noteworthy; this is that thing that always happens: people believing they look awful in their passport photos. This is obviously the thing that's going on here because I've seen this happen so many times and it's so familiar.'

Most readers (and most human beings) unquestioningly believe what they think must be true because it nearly always is in their personal experience, even when the evidence that it is true and the evidence that it isn't are equally substantial – and often even when the evidence against is more persuasive. Why? Because our primitive brains massively prefer all the beliefs we've got already, the ones we're so good at believing because we've had so much practice, to the new and different beliefs that would require effort and change if we were to install them.

There's another reason, too, why doing nothing more than allowing readers to mislead themselves is so much more effective than actively misleading them, and it works in crime fiction just as it does in real life. When someone takes steps to make us think or believe something, we might be convinced to a certain extent – maybe even completely – but we're not going to have as much ingrained loyalty to that belief as we would if we'd come up with it ourselves, based on our own observations and experience of life. And any novel written by a writer counts squarely as 'steps taken to make us think something'. So, when we read a thriller or a mystery, we encounter two distinct phenomena:

1. Thoughts/beliefs in our brains created by this novel in particular;
2. Thoughts/beliefs in our brains that were there already, long before we started to read this particular novel, of which we are now reminded *by* the novel.

When beliefs of the first type are overturned – by a twist – it's going to feel less deeply surprising and shocking to us than when beliefs of the second type are revealed as untrue, because we're only being asked to reverse something we believed about this one book, all made up by just one writer, and not something we believed about the world as a result of our extensive experience. The shock, therefore, affects us less powerfully.

Crime writers can use all of this to their advantage by thinking, in relation to their various story elements and plot points, 'What is this going to look like, quite unambiguously, to most people? And what might it be instead which is just as possible and likely – but which will occur to nobody?'

Suspense

Patricia Highsmith's *Plotting and Writing Suspense Fiction*, originally published in 1966, remains valuable for its insights into the working methods of a gifted author. So what is suspense fiction? Opinions and definitions vary. Highsmith said it was a story 'with a threat of violent physical action and danger, or the danger and action itself' while Alfred Hitchcock argued that the prime difference between a whodunit and a suspense story is that the former engages the intellect, while the latter engages the emotions. Another popular way of expressing the distinction is that in a detective story, the question is: 'What has happened?' In a suspense story, the question is: 'What will happen next?' Robert Goddard, a modern master of suspense fiction, explores techniques for building tension and making sure that readers want to keep turning the page.

Suspense

Robert Goddard

The year is 1972. And it hasn't started well, with a miners' strike causing rota power cuts. The teenage me is unimpressed, to put it mildly, when the all-will-be-revealed final episode of one of his favourite TV thriller series coincides with a blackout. His brother, a dab hand in such matters, manages to pick up the TV broadcast on his short-wave transistor radio. The family, swaddled in sweaters, gathers by candlelight to follow the episode in sound only. There are many long, unexplained silences, occasionally interrupted by thumps, groans and sighs. And the dialogue features frustrating lines such as a gasped, 'My God, it was you all along!' Who were they talking to? It remains a mystery to this day.

Well, obviously it wasn't a satisfactory way to follow a story. Everything was swathed in layers of uncertainty. But, goodness me, it was suspenseful if it was nothing else. And – not just because of that long-ago experience – I believe that suspense in fiction writing is really all about uncertainty.

For the reader, this uncertainty brings pleasure, agreeably tinged with pain, to the reading experience. What *is* going to happen? Some awful discovery is looming, some dark secret itching to reveal itself, as in *Rebecca,* for instance, where only Daphne du Maurier knows what it is until the moment of revelation. It's one of the most compelling – and enjoyable – features of reading the sort of fiction that deploys it. But what's really going on, behind the scenes, in the writer's head?

With any luck, I've already created a small amount of suspense in the last paragraph. I hope you want to know the answer to the question I've posed. We're going to edge towards it, taking care not to startle our prey, until . . . Well, let's not give the game away. Not just yet. And maybe . . .

You see? I can't help myself. I love this kind of writing. It was always what I wanted to do. I remember reading Wilkie Collins' *The Woman in White* for the first time (oh, happy day) and thinking how wonderful it would be to engage with stories like that from the inside, to shape and craft them to *my* satisfaction as well as the reader's.

The Woman in White never quite works on TV because one of its most gratifying surprises is the realization that Marion Halcombe's diary isn't just a narrative device but an actual physical diary (which of course we knew but somehow forgot) and arch-villain Count Fosco has been secretly reading it along with us. This simply can't be effectively managed on screen, so is often ditched altogether, to the story's great detriment. Read the book to get the full measure of Collins' genius!

It was genius in particular because back in 1860, when the novel was published, Collins was a pioneer of this sort of writing. He was one of the very first to explore its possibilities. Ever since, readers have relished the use of suspense in fiction. The techniques that lie behind it have received surprisingly little critical attention, perhaps because, if they work properly, they seem to arise naturally – effortlessly if you like – from the story. But there's no effortlessness about it. True, they can be difficult to grasp, almost more difficult to grasp than to use, in fact. But nonetheless it's time to do some grasping.

Let's go back for a moment to *The Woman in White*. Aside from the central question – who is the woman in white, what is she? – Collins gives us two villains for the price of one: Fosco *plus* the odious Sir Percival Glyde. Now, the point here is that they're not always working to the same end. They both have problems, constraints and objectives of their own. There's conflict between them, and also between them and Collins' wonderfully resourceful heroine, Marion Halcombe. That immediately complicates the unfolding of the story and multiplies the possibilities for wrong-footing the reader. Moreover, Fosco genuinely admires Marion. And to some degree she admires him. So, we have mixed motives *and* mixed feelings. There's nothing straightforward about their actions. But then there's nothing straightforward about their relationships.

This is only as it should be. The finest form of suspense-writing joins plot and character seamlessly, so the plot serves the characters and vice versa. That, after all, is how the world is. When we meet people for the first time – and often the second and third – we don't know much if anything at all about their backgrounds, their childhoods, their aspirations, their difficulties, their preoccupations. But we'd need to in order to predict how they'd behave in any given situation. The writer does know all this about their characters, of course, whereas the reader generally doesn't, at least to begin with. As a result, many developments that surprise the reader are, to the writer, merely the natural, indeed inevitable, outcome of the circumstances in which the characters find themselves.

You might say the writer has full control over those circumstances and therefore has an unfair advantage: the game is rigged. Actually, however, it's less rigged than you might think. The writer *doesn't* have full control. This is because suspense-writing is art as well as craft. If the characters are faithfully portrayed, then their actions arise as much *from* those characters as they do from the writer's imagination. The writer has to learn to surrender control at vital moments. It's probably the hardest lesson of all for a writer. Surely one small compensation for those solitary antisocial hours in front of the keyboard is that at least you get to tell people – your characters – what to do. Not so. You merely walked past the door of the room they'd been confined to and opened it. Now they're out, on the loose, and not in the least inclined to take orders from you.

That said, they can't stop you tossing problems into their path. And the greatest satisfaction for the writer is to observe and describe the consequences of the collision between the characters and the plot. In other words, there's suspense for the writer as well as the reader. I know what's coming, which neither the reader nor my characters do. But I don't exactly know how it's going to turn out.

Can that really be true? Can a densely plotted story really be properly managed if the writer isn't in complete control of it? I would say yes. In fact, I'd say incompleteness of control is absolutely essential to the writing process. That's not obvious to the aspiring writer. It certainly wasn't obvious to me when

I planned my first novel, assembling beforehand a detailed timeline and blow-by-blow summary of the action. I hadn't appreciated the fact that, just as the Duke of Wellington said his battle plans never survived first contact with the enemy, so synopses for suspense novels always come off worst in conflicts with the characters.

Even so, the Iron Duke probably wouldn't have slept well on the eve of battle if he hadn't done any planning at all. And so it is with the writer. Preparation is vital, even if it transpires you didn't quite know what you were preparing *for*. Creating a story is, as much as anything, about *discovering* that story. In a sense, it was there before you started writing it. But discovering it takes a lot of work.

In my latest novel, *One False Move,* there's a moment, about a third of the way in, when the story performs a somersault. It's not so much a twist as a turn, albeit a sharp and dramatic one. It's the point at which so much that was initially hidden begins to reveal itself. I didn't know, when I began writing the book, exactly when that moment would come or precisely what would happen when it did. I had to let the characters find the moment for themselves.

So, this is what suspense comes down to: uncertainty, not just about what's going to happen, but about what it is that's really happening. Obviously, this can't be achieved with an *I'll just start and see how it goes* approach to writing. The story is an iceberg, with most of its substance invisible beneath the surface, until, suddenly, unexpectedly, unforeseeably . . . you hit it. There aren't any twists as such in the story. There are just layers, depths that are waiting to be explored but won't wait for ever. That exploration is what the characters have let themselves in for. And they can't opt out.

One way to look at this is to recognize that we're all stories in our own right. Our biographies determine our actions. For all the characters in my books there's a biography, containing material that mostly won't get anywhere near the page. But, if and when the time comes, it's there to inform what happens. I don't always know which major characters will lose significance and which apparently minor ones will gain it. It's up to them. Again, there's the uncertainty. When they start jostling for primacy within the confines of the plot, who will come to the fore? And what will happen as a result?

In the same way that the characters' lives bring extra material to the story, plotting also has to incorporate an abundance of material to ensure that the unexpected is always there to be called upon in the service of suspense. Suspense *can* be achieved with limited plot material, but to sustain a story over the span of a full-length novel, to deliver a tantalizing opening, a constantly surprising middle, and a fulfilling ending, what's needed is depth. In short, lots of plot. Inspiration versus perspiration: it's the old creative conundrum; and the truth is that the more work that's put into the plot, the more inspiration it will deliver. But inspired or not, the writer has an obligation to play fair with the reader.

Suspense depends on trust, trust that the revelation, when delivered, will be plausible *and* satisfying. It can't work any other way. We've all read books where the resolution of the mystery isn't a resolution at all and looks suspiciously like something retro-engineered to fit a plot in which there were some basic design flaws right from the start. It might get the central character off the hook. But not the writer.

I've always felt that suspense is inevitably undercut by the use of a serial central character – classically, the detective figure, whether private eye or police officer. We know, barring a series-ending shock (though let's not forget what happened to Sherlock Holmes after he went over the Reichenbach Falls), that our hero, our guide and companion in the story, will survive. There is suspense in such stories, of course – often plenty of it – and the serial character has the advantage of being instantly familiar to the reader. But it seems to me the purest form of suspense writing requires *all* the characters to be at equal risk, with a personal stake in the story and everything to lose. That's why I've generally preferred to write stand-alone novels. They come with no guarantees.

Logically, this should make stories set in the past

problematic as far as suspense is concerned, especially those featuring real historical figures. We know what happened to those figures, after all. But there's plenty we don't know about them as well. And there are exceptions to every rule. Somehow, by some sleight of hand, Frederick Forsyth manages in *The Day of the Jackal* to make it seem possible that President de Gaulle really will fall victim to an assassin's bullet in 1963, seven years before he actually died.

Many suspense bestsellers make use of an unreliable narrator to keep the reader off balance, uncertain – there's that word again – about who and what to believe. Gillian Flynn's *Gone Girl* and Paula Hawkins' *The Girl on the Train* are recent, hugely successful, examples. The device is very effective. But it shouldn't be overused. We have to believe in something and, ultimately, someone. We have to be able to trust the writer even if we can't trust the narrator. In the end, that's what counts. And when that trust is fulfilled, the result is page-turning magic.

Suspense writing has an undeniably addictive element, for the writer as well as the reader. We speak, quite accurately, of being *hooked* on a story. The writer doesn't want to stop writing it; the reader doesn't want to stop reading it. Suspense has to be, I think, the fiction genre of which that's most true. Just as well, then, that this is one addiction that's essentially harmless. Apart from lost sleep and missed stops on the Tube, that is. But they're a small price to pay, surely, for such rich entertainment.

Julian Symons, who succeeded Agatha Christie as President of the Detection Club, was a prominent member of the new wave of crime writers that emerged after the Second World War. His crime fiction included whodunits in the classic vein, an international thriller, Sherlockian pastiches, and historical mysteries; but his most notable storylines concerned the behaviour of people under acute stress. Writing here in 1950s, and expressing views that were influential and ahead of their time, he remained for the rest of his life a powerful advocate for the literary merits of the novel of psychological suspense.

The Face in the Mirror
Julian Symons

A man sits down at his desk to write a book in which a crime of violence has been committed, and in which one or more of the characters is opposed to society and its laws. The theme is ancient, and respectable. The figures of the scapegoat, the law-giver, and the law-breaker are common to all myth and literature.

And in these days the moral attitudes involved in crimes of violence have a special significance. The devotion to an ideally peaceful and well-ordered society typified in Montezuma's human sacrifices on the altar of Huitzilopochtli was not greater than the devotion to peace and order shown by the decision to drop atomic bombs on Hiroshima and Nagasaki. What shifts of individual morality relating to violent action are implied in such fateful decisions, and in the very general acceptance of a greater wrath to come?

Seriousness of treatment is the first requisite of a crime novel. The second, closely linked to it, is a regard for realism. This is easily misunderstood: the sort of realism I mean refers to the treatment of relations between human beings, and not to an exact description of people and places, or to a scrupulous regard for the details of police procedure. These, too, can have their place: but it is unfortunate that most of the people who have an intimate knowledge of police work are either uncommonly bad writers, or else are so close to the work that they feel unable to use it except mechanically, as a kind of joke. (Thus, in an English detective story, the solution may depend on an intricate and faintly comic point of law, in an American one upon the lawyer-hero's ability to pull out some trick in the courtroom.)

The sort of realism I mean begins with the acknowledgement that violent crime is almost always the result of a deep strain or deficiency in human relations. If the crime novelist can show the nature and cause of that deficiency, he will add a great deal of depth to his work.

The crime novel has a symbolic interest and value for our time. I come back to the point made in my first paragraph: that the moral attitudes involved in crimes of violence have today a quite special significance. The licence to kill that has always been granted to soldiers in war, the right to exterminate inferior beings assumed by the Nazis, the necessity to kill civilians involved in large-scale air raids, and the elaborate justification of this necessity at Hiroshima and Nagasaki with the plea that the bombs dropped were really economical in ending the war and thus saving human lives: all these things, as we have absorbed them into our knowledge and emotional understanding, have imposed a strain on the fabric of our lives.

It is for this reason, I think, that such a book as Meyer Levin's *Compulsion* produces such an extraordinary effect. Mr Levin has taken the case of Leopold and Loeb, the two rich youths who some thirty years ago killed a younger boy as a gesture exemplifying their theories of being Nietzschean supermen, and has made a novel of it. Mr Levin is an admirable writer, and his interpretations of the two youths are subtle and convincing: but the book seems to have a symbolic value beyond itself, and beyond Mr Levin's conscious intentions. The homosexual relationship between the boys, the fact that they were both Jewish and that they killed to prove a natural superiority over their victim (who was Jewish too), the whole deliberate rejection of orthodox social morality in the book in favour of the killers' own 'higher' personal morality,

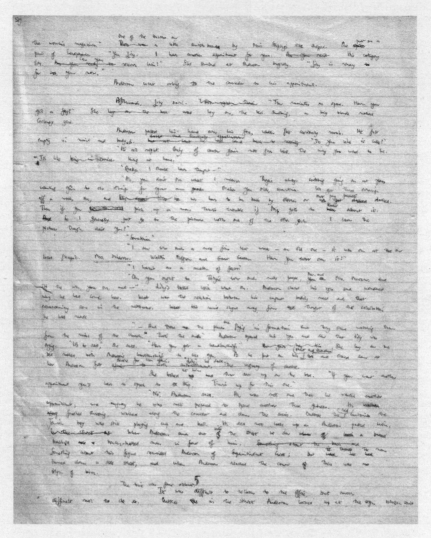

An extract from Julian Symons' novel The Thirty-First of February.
*Inscribing one copy to a friend, he described this, his fourth crime
novel, as 'the first piece of fiction I'm prepared to acknowledge'.
Like many writers, he continued to tinker with his manuscript.
In the published novel, for instance, the word 'naked', absent from
the original manuscript, is added to his description of Lily in bed.*

all this involves the most appalling of post-war moral problems: the individual's right to assert the validity of his conscience against the nation-state (the right that was asserted by the atomic physicists and spies Nunn May and Fuchs), and the state's right to take action affecting the lives of all individuals (the right to hold H-bomb tests). The fact that, as far as we know, these are problems only for the West does not make them less real.

We are a long way from the body in the library and the murders committed by a trapeze artist using soluble darts shot from a papier mâché blowpipe held between the toes. And that is as it should be. Puzzles pure and complex will no doubt continue to be written while the criminal form – in this parlour-game sense – retains public interest. I have been trying to show that the crime novel at its best is something more serious and more interesting than a parlour game. It may deal openly with social corruption like *The Glass Key* or with material that seems at times to come straight from a psychoanalyst's case book, like *Compulsion*; it may investigate the curious recesses of the personality, like John Franklin Bardin's *Devil Take the Blue Tail Fly* or Margaret Millar's *Beast in View*; it may be set as firmly in the world of tennis parties and small talk as Francis Iles's masterly *Malice Aforethought*: but its author's business will always be to investigate, with all the freedom that the medium permits him, the springs of violence. At its best the crime novel is a modern version of an old morality play, or a sort of mirror which when we look in it shows us a face naked with lust and greed, avarice and violence. We recoil from the face of this terrible stranger; and then a second glance shows, to our relief, our own warm harmless human features.

Julian Symons mentions Francis Iles, who wrote with devastating irony about the nature of justice and the imperfections of the legal system, and he utilized the novel of psychological suspense to address similar concerns in the Gold Dagger-winning *The Colour of Murder*, and the Edgar-winning *The Progress of a Crime*, with a storyline inspired by a real life miscarriage of justice.

Over time, his strategies as a novelist changed. As he said in a note in John J. Walsdorf's bibliography of his work, 'There is a moment when one realizes that the old kind of plotting won't do, that the order which had seemed to serve well over a number of books no longer satisfies.' As a result he wrote three 'Man Who' books which set out to show the social ironies of urban life. The first, *The Man Who Killed Himself* is in some respects a witty and clever updating of Iles' *Malice Aforethought*. *The Man Whose Dreams Came True* is equally ingenious and enjoyable, but in the third book, *The Man Who Lost His Wife*, social satire perhaps predominated at the expense of plot. Having worked out that vein, Symons continued to explore the possibilities of the novel of suspense in books such as *The Players and the Game*, a gripping story with origins in the horror of the real-life Moors Murders.

Towards the end of his career, Symons took the bold step of introducing himself as a character in one of his suspense novels, the intriguing and underestimated *Death's Darkest Face*. This is probably an approach that inexperienced writers should avoid. However, Jessica Mann – like Symons, an incisive reviewer and commentator on the genre as well as a novelist of high calibre – followed his example, giving herself a role in one of her last suspense novels, *The Mystery Writer*. In a prefatory note, she observed that the book 'contains some truths and some untruths. In literature, as in life, it is not always obvious which is which.'

Jessica Mann's novels put resourceful female characters to the fore, and her fiction contains many elements that are directly or indirectly autobiographical. Although she often wrote stand-alones, she created some recurring characters such as the child psychiatrist, Dr Fidelis Berlin, who appeared in the Gold Dagger-shortlisted *A Private Inquiry*. In *The Voice from the Grave*, Fidelis is diagnosed with Parkinson's disease, just as her creator had been a little while earlier.

The Suspense Novel
Jessica Mann

Suspense novels are not necessarily, though they may be, detective novels. That is, they are not stories whose main purpose is to answer the question 'Who did it?' or 'How did he do it?' Dorothy L. Sayers wrote that 'The detective story does not, and by hypothesis, never can, attain the loftiest level of literary achievement. Though it deals with the most desperate effects of rage, jealousy and revenge it rarely touches upon the heights and depths of human passion. It presents us only with the *fait accompli*, and looks upon death and mutilation with a dispassionate eye.' The writer of a suspense novel casts his dispassionate eye as much upon the passion, as upon the deed it produced. He refuses to accept the limitation upon his power to cause cathartic emotion, and while he may not always manage it, hopes to give his reader something more than a pleasantly intellectual stimulation. Yet this distinction is becoming increasingly blurred. Many modern writers of novels whose plots can be expressed purely as detective stories hope to touch the heights and depths of human passion as well. Many of P. D. James's books are examples of this.

Suspense novels are not, though they may be, thrillers. That is, they need not recount a succession of dramatic events, nor need they conform to Stanley Ellin's distinction between mysteries and thrillers, when he pointed out that in the mystery the crime takes place at the beginning, whereas in the thriller, if there is a crime at all, it is more likely to take place at the

end. Yet many a dramatically exciting book could be described
as a suspense novel or as a thriller. Stanley Ellin's own; or
Anthony Price's; or Eric Ambler's books, which he calls thrillers
himself; his own definition for the thriller is 'an extension of
the fairy tale; it is melodrama so embellished as to create the
illusion that the story being told, however unlikely, could be
true'. Not all thrillers are 'suspense novels', then; but many
suspense novels are thrillers.

Suspense novels are not, though they may be, mysteries; for
often the reader learns very early in the story who did what,
and how, and even why, so that the tension results from the
manner in which an expected conclusion is achieved. Francis
Iles, who first pointed out in 1930 that the detective story was
likely to become a puzzle of character, rather than a puzzle of
time, place, motive and opportunity, wrote an early example
of this type of book in *Malice Aforethought*, whose first paragraph tells us that Dr Bickleigh will murder his wife.

Suspense novels are not even necessarily about crime,
whether committed or contemplated, though it is true that most
include some form of law-breaking or misdeed. But the English
Celia Fremlin, for instance, or the American Ursula Curtiss,
frequently write about menaces that are undefined, and unre-
alized.

How then can we distinguish 'suspense novels' from any
other fiction? For there can be few novels of any kind that are
successful if not suspenseful, whether the uncertainty to be
resolved is 'Will the boy get the girl?' or 'Will he end up
President?' I think the difference resides in the intention of the
author and the expectation of the reader. The suspense novelist's aim is to engage both the intellectual curiosity provoked
by a detective story, and the emotional involvement achieved
by a novel. The additional pleasure of the actual story, the
procession of events each consequential upon the last, is something that 'novels' do not always share with good suspense
fiction. The novelist and critic Arnold Bennett believed that few
books improved as they proceeded; most became progressively
more boring. He was contrasting novels with adventure stories,

in which it was the story, and what happened at the end, that was interesting. If that was true in the 1920s, it is not true now. In Eric Ambler's words: 'Few thrillers depend now for their interest on mere narrative. What holds you in a good thriller is what holds you in any other good novel, the originality and interestingness of the author's mind and vision. Not to read through any novel once you have started it is proof that it has failed with you.'

In Arnold Bennett's era, critics drew a distinction between a novel and a 'tale'. The tale was about events and appealed only to the intellect, as though it were a crossword puzzle or a word game. To enjoy such books was regarded by literary pundits as deplorable if not actually vicious. The novel concentrated on psychological and social reality, and its object was to touch the emotions and enlighten the imagination. If such a distinction did really exist, the contemporary suspense novelist is determined to destroy it.

When Wilkie Collins wrote what T. S. Eliot called the first, longest and best detective story, *The Moonstone*, he did not suppose himself to be writing something that differed in kind from his own earlier work, or from the books of his contemporaries. The classification and sub-division into categories has come much later, and it is a pastime of critics, not writers. Modern writers of what we loosely call suspense novels probably seldom consciously differentiate their work either from mystery fiction, or from mainstream fiction, except in trying to achieve the vivacity, verisimilitude and enthralment that Wilkie Collins was aiming for in 1868. It is the publisher, not the writer, who decrees that Patricia Highsmith's work is called 'suspense fiction' in the United States, and treated as, simply, fiction in France. It is the publisher and literary editor who decide that novels with crime as their theme shall be published and reviewed in crime lists, unless they are by Graham Greene.

But whether or not they assent to such categorization of their work, authors of what we have come to call suspense fiction do share an interest in the dangerous limits of human experience, endurance, excess, and perhaps above all, in the extent of human duplicity. As Julian Symons says, 'If you want to show the violence that lives behind the bland faces most of us present to the world, what better vehicle can you have than the crime novel?'

Most of Julian Symons' own crime novels have had detective plots, but all have revealed an individual, sardonic eye focused on the emptiness as well as the violence behind his characters' bland faces. He strips them naked; and this is another feature of the best suspense novels. Their characters are shown as fully rounded people, their motives revealed not simply for their crimes, but for their whole lives.

There are critics who resent what they see as amateur attempts at psychological understanding. 'It cannot improve a genre to drain out its essence, fill the void with second-hand soul searching and arty verbal tricks, and pretend that the result is at once the classic article and something loftier,' complains Jacques Barzun, the historian and co-author of *A Catalogue of Crime*; there has been an abandonment of science and reason. For enthusiasts the injection of realism, and of psychological understanding, has been one of the enriching features of the modern crime and suspense novel, even though it means that there is now a pervasive pessimism about suspense fiction that is very different from the cheerful conclusion implicit in the traditional crime story, that everything can somehow, eventually, be put right. Right, that is, by the standards of an ordered society whose members accept its values.

The well-known authors in 'the golden age' of crime fiction, between the two world wars, had no doubt that it was desirable for society's rules to be observed, and this conservatism is implicit in all they wrote. The best contemporary suspense writers give a completely different impression. Neither law nor law-enforcers are necessarily admirable, and a general disobedience of laws and regulations seems to be common among both criminals and authority; indeed, those in authority are frequently criminals, without any value judgement being made of their behaviour. In crime stories, the police are often corrupt;

in spy stories, there is no perceptible moral distinction to be drawn between the behaviour of the 'good guys' and the bad ones. Even the psychological, domestic dramas are often now about anarchy, about people who seem to be part of society while inhabiting the psyches of outlaws. A writer like Simenon at least uses the framework of conventional society – Maigret is a policeman, after all. But Maigret, like his author, refrains from judging others. For Patricia Highsmith, the anarchist is presented without even the channel of Maigret's worldly view-point. She explores not so much guilt, as lack of guilt. This is particularly evident in the four books she has written about Tom Ripley, a free spirit untrammelled by any altruistic scru-ples. Commentators often describe him as a psychopath, that is, a person suffering from mental illness. But the fascination of Ripley both to his creator and to his readers, is that he is not mad, unless it is mad to be totally self-centred. Tom Ripley's own good is his only good.

Highsmith believes that only criminals are free; but also that we are all criminals, to a greater or lesser extent. It is much more common, though, for criminals in suspense novels to be demonstrably deranged. Those of Ruth Rendell, for example, have their peculiarities traced in approved psychological style, to childhood experiences and deprivations, and often their misdeeds are sparked off when a precarious equilibrium is accidentally destroyed. In *A Demon in My View*, Arthur Johnson has learnt to control his murderous urges by strangling a dressmaker's dummy, and only when the dummy is burnt as the guy on a Guy Fawkes Night bonfire is he unable to resist human necks. Ruth Rendell casts a coldly observant eye on the life of contemporary middle-class England. Half her books are detective stories with a recurring pair of policemen, the others novels in which the development of the characters is as inter-esting as the crimes; and the causes of the crimes in society and in the individual are of as much concern as their detection. Julian Symons spoke of the violence behind the bland face. In Ruth Rendell's books, the bland faces mask obsession and neurosis.

Suspense novels often have an undertone of unease, of nebulous threats. This is perhaps especially common in those about domestic life, by such writers as Ruth Rendell herself, or Celia Fremlin. The effect of such atmospheric writing can be powerful, though it is easy for books of this kind to be little more than what Jacques Barzun called a mongrel form, 'stories of anxiety which cater for the contemporary wish to feel vaguely disturbed'. But at its best this atmosphere of menace immensely enhances a story, as can be seen in the novels of Margaret Millar, most of whose books are set in California, in particularly well realized surroundings.

The late P. M. Hubbard was a writer regarded by many critics as supreme in conveying threats through atmosphere. His books are often as much love stories as murder stories, and the suspense lies in the development of the personal relationships against a subtly drawn background that is at once beautiful and sinister. But it is easy to fail in the attempt to write a novel in which the fear is ever present but undefined. Too many books are nothing but lists of vague fears and frustrated passions, and the term 'suspense novel' falls into disrepute when it is used for them. In such stories, the action centres on someone (usually a female character) the reader can imagine being, with whose fears he (or usually she) can identify. Other writers aim to 'give the reader fear', as Geoffrey Household once said, but it is fear for another, for a hunted hero quite unlike most readers. Household's heroes, like those in another kind of suspense novel by Dick Francis, are loners driven by peculiar and personal obsessions.

Jessica Mann refers to fellow Detection Club members Ruth Rendell and Celia Fremlin, two leading exponents of psychological suspense in the second half of the twentieth century. In June 1981, Rendell was one of several authors asked by the *Times Literary Supplement*

to nominate a writer or book which they felt had been underrated or unjustly neglected. She chose Fremlin, whose fiction concentrates on 'people leading lives of quiet or vociferous desperation in suburban backwaters. She enjoys creating characters the way Trollope did, with restrained gusto, and her conversation isn't dialogue, it's the way people talk.' Rendell heaped praise on books such as *Seven Lean Years* and *Uncle Paul*, as well as on Fremlin's debut, which won the Edgar Award given by the Mystery Writers of America for best novel of the year.

That book was *The Hours Before Dawn*, first published in 1958. Introducing a recent reprint, Laura Wilson writes: 'Tightly plotted and admirably concise, Fremlin's fiction is characterized by precise observation and the inclusion of small, telling details . . . which ensures that all of her characters, including the children, are fully formed and pitch-perfect. More surprising, perhaps, as well as wholly delightful, is the wit – effortless, acerbic, and just enough of it – that gives her work its distinctive and memorable pungency. ' For an earlier reissue of the novel, Fremlin herself wrote a prefatory note giving context to her unsettling story of domestic suspense.

The Hours Before Dawn

Celia Fremlin

The original inspiration for this book was my second baby. She was one of those babies who, perfectly content and happy all day, simply don't sleep through the night. Soon after midnight she would wake; and again at half past two; and again at four. With other people in the house, and a husband trying to study for exams, it was impossible to let her 'cry it out' as the professionals advised. As the months went by, I found myself quite distracted by lack of sleep; my eyes would fall shut while I peeled the potatoes or ironed shirts (that smooth to and fro of the iron, even while I was on my feet, was alarmingly soporific); I began to fear that in my dazed state I might find myself doing something so grossly careless as to cause disastrous damage; and the advice I received from all quarters – good in its way, I don't doubt – proved in our case absolutely useless.

I remember one night sitting on the bottom step of the stairs, my baby wide awake and lively in my arms, but all ready to burst out crying again the moment I put her back in the cot – and it suddenly dawned on me: this is a major human experience, why hasn't someone written about it? Written about it seriously, that is – there have been plenty of jokey references, of course, to being woken by the baby – but actually it *isn't* a joke at all. It is an experience as gruelling as anyone is likely to encounter, and it seemed to me that a serious novel should be written with this experience at its centre. I didn't know of any such novel: and it then occurred to me – why don't *I* write one?

And so I did. Not straight away – I was far too busy and too tired – but a few years later, when the problem (for me) was at an end.

Since then, I have been taken to task at various times over the years about the husband in this story. He must have been a monster, some people say, to have left the problems entirely to his wife. Any normal husband, I have been assured, would take his turn at these nightly vigils.

My answer to this is – yes, many normal husbands would; and many equally normal husbands wouldn't, especially when, as in this case, the wife doesn't even expect him to. The idea that the breadwinner, who has a full-time job to do, is entitled to his night's sleep, certainly would not have been regarded as unreasonable by most of us thirty years ago (which is when the book was written); and though I am assured by some that nowadays everything is quite different, and that modern young couples share and share alike when it comes to child-raising problems, I am not convinced. My own observation tells me that there are still many, many couples who believe, and certainly act, as if the babies and young children are the mother's responsibility entirely.

Be that as it may, I'd like to assure readers that I did *not* mean the husband to be any kind of a 'monster'. In fact, although this is a crime story, I did not intend *any* of my characters to be seen as monsters of iniquity. Rather, they are ordinary, well-intentioned people caught in a dilemma that is too big for them.

Action

At first sight, the story of action, adventure or espionage seems very different from the whodunit or the novel of psychological suspense. The stakes are often higher; sometimes the question is not so much whether a particular villain can be caught as whether our hero can save the world as we know it. Even so, the methods of thriller writers and novelists of crime, detection, and suspense have a great deal in common, as is demonstrated by the work of many writers of action stories who have been Detection Club members. Action is a crucial element in all commercial fiction, even in cerebral whodunits of the kind written by Colin Dexter among others.

Good writing usually has an inherent quality of movement, a focus on verbs rather than adjectives or adverbs, and on the active voice rather than the passive. The action that crime writers hope for from their readers is, of course, the constant turning of the pages. And even in thrillers, as in other forms of fiction, it often helps to find ways of deferring the reader's gratification for just a little longer, bearing in mind Charles Reade's injunction (sometimes attributed to Wilkie Collins): 'Make 'em laugh, make 'em weep, make 'em wait.'

Desmond Bagley, a bestselling thriller writer from the 1960s onwards, argued that his books belonged to the mainstream of a storytelling tradition going back thousands of years, and concerned the eternal battle between good and evil. In an article for *The Writer* in 1973, he said it was no accident that the classic drama was structured in three acts. In a nutshell, the first act introduces the characters and the situation; the second develops and complicates that situation; and the third resolves those complications. The effect is psychologically satisfying.

Bagley said that an action novel, like any other, stands or falls by its characterization, a view shared by his successors in the present day. He devoted just as much care to the evocation of place. In *Running Blind*, for instance, he treated the Icelandic setting as a character: 'This tends to give the story a free-flowing spontaneity that is hard to achieve otherwise.'

Theme was also central to his writing: 'The theme of *Landslide* was the search for personal identity, that of *The Vivero Letter* was of the danger of using vanity to cure a punctured ego.' For Bagley, the plot came 'out of the interaction of the characters, the environment, and the theme'. He didn't plan his books in advance because he prized unpredictability in the action thriller. What mattered to him, as to many crime writers, was not whether the events he recounted were probable, but whether they were plausible.

A Detection Club member working at roughly the same time, Gavin Lyall moved during the course of his career from writing aviation thrillers to spy stories and then historical adventures. He was interested in the idea of taking responsibility for one's actions, and writing in *Twentieth Century Crime and Mystery Writers*, he said: 'I seem to go in for heroes who have to take positive decisions – even perhaps moral ones – which change the course of the story.' For the adventure writer, this is often a useful method.

Lionel Davidson was far from prolific, publishing a mere eight thrillers between 1960 and 1994. He was not a quick worker, but three of those books won the Gold Daggers for the best crime novel of the year, an astonishing rate of success which rewarded his infinite capacity for taking pains.

Inspiration, Perspiration, Realization
Lionel Davidson

Ideas for books are another thing. Those I think about hard and long I never seem to do. The ones I do come about largely by accident. The second, for instance, surfaced abruptly during a winter walk in Kew Gardens. A thaw had started and I saw something pop suddenly out of a mound of melting snow. On closer inspection it proved to be an ear; a dog's, dead. For some reason this dead dog in the snow instantly transformed itself in my mind into a bear. I took a bus to the library for a book on bears. On the way in there was a display of books on Tibet – I don't know why, perhaps some fad of the librarian's. The library was thin on bear books but I took a couple of those on Tibet and was still reading them in bed that night. Next morning I woke up with practically the whole plot of a new book, and for the next two years, including research, sweated on *The Rose of Tibet*. Such, in my case, is the orderly process of inspiration, perspiration, realization. (The bear padded slowly into the book about three quarters of the way through.)

The perspiration, at any rate, is a constant factor. Because it never seems to me that I have enough plot, I research titanically to try and find more. This research always goes wild, the typewritten notes several times the length of the finished book . . . Hardly any of it proves necessary – at least in its plot-providing function. In the very first flash I usually have far more plot than I can conceivably handle. The snag is, I don't know it; or rather, since it has happened every time, I *forget* it.

Tom Harper's literary career was kick-started by success in the CWA's Debut Dagger competition for new writers – an excellent illustration of the potential value of entering such contests. In 2001,

The Blighted Cliffs was a runner-up for the Debut Dagger and he soon found an agent and a publisher. The novel, a historical adventure story set during the Napoleonic wars, was subsequently published (under his real name, Edwin Thomas) two years later, and became the first of a series.

Not content with this, he adopted the Harper name for a new series which began with *The Mosaic of Shadows* in 2004, and has been widely translated. More recently, he has again hit the bestseller lists with books written in collaboration with Wilbur Smith. He said in an article for the *Shots* ezine in 2010 that most of his novels 'deal, one way or another, with the constant dialogue between past and present'. His understanding of history enables him to retain a clear perspective on the present day. *The Lazarus Vault*, written in the wake of a global financial crash, dealt with villainous bankers, but as he said: 'So is this novel an earnest critique of modern capitalism? An indictment of a failing economic model? In a word, no. It's an adventure story and a thriller.'

Adventure Fiction

Tom Harper

Adventure is the oldest story in the book. Rewind to the dawn of written fiction, the *Odyssey* and the *Epic of Gilgamesh*, and what you find are adventure stories: heroes leaving the safety of their homes, embarking on doubtful quests to dangerous places. In his novel *The Killing Gene*, Ed Davey suggests it goes further back than that. He posits that the Gilgamesh epic is actually the written-down remnant of a folk memory that records *Homo sapiens'* evolutionary victory over Neanderthals. On that reading, adventure stories are actually hard-wired into our DNA.

And yet it's remarkably hard to locate the genre in the

modern publishing landscape. There are no shelves dedicated to adventure fiction in bookshops; while the great crime writers' mantelpieces groan with dozens of international prizes, there is only one award for adventure writing, and that relatively recently minted. A look at the shortlists for the Wilbur Smith Adventure Writing Prize shows how elastic the genre is. A Costa-winning literary writer rubs shoulders with mainline thriller writers; ancient Roman legionaries mix with international people smugglers. Adventures can happen anywhere, any time, to anyone. So how do you define the genre?

There's a saying that crime fiction is about solving something that's happened, while thrillers are about preventing something that's going to happen. Adventure writing might include elements of either or both, but fundamentally it's neither of these. An adventure novel is about setting out on a journey and taking the characters (and the reader) somewhere they never expected. It's not about what *has* happened or is *going to* happen. It's what *does* happen along the way.

As to where the journey takes you – it's a staple of the genre that it should be somewhere exotic and dangerous. There are many books where the setting becomes a character in its own right: think the Los Angeles of Philip Marlowe, or the Edinburgh of Inspector Rebus. This is even more true in the adventure novel. A big part of the appeal to the reader is being taken somewhere wild and different, whether it's the Arctic wastes of Alistair MacLean, the African savannahs of Wilbur Smith, or the ocean depths of Clive Cussler. But this is not just sightseeing. In an adventure novel, the scenery is an active part of the story. Almost certainly, it's trying to kill you. It lurks in the background of every chapter, waiting to pounce, ready to make the most innocuous task a potentially lethal ordeal. Whatever the dangers the protagonists in the story face (and there are probably a *lot*), a big part of them will come from the environment they find themselves in.

I had a small taste of this firsthand when I visited the Arctic island of Svalbard while researching *Zodiac Station*. We were out in the wilderness on a snowmobile expedition, fifty kilometres from anywhere. Inside the snowmobile helmet, my glasses kept fogging up. Cleaning them required taking off my glove so I could unzip my coat and extract the end of my scarf to wipe the lenses. So simple, back home you wouldn't even think about it. But at minus 30°C, in the time it took to clean my glasses my bare hand went white and numb. It was shaking so hard, I couldn't get my glove back on.

Luckily, I had a guide with me who spotted my distress. He put tea into me, made me do jumping jacks, and warmed my hand until it had feeling again. With hindsight, it seems so trivial. But if I had been alone, it's reasonable to think that I might never have got the glove back on, never managed to restart the snowmobile, never made it back. In the landscapes of adventure fiction, those are the fine margins – a dropped glove, a broken zip, one wrong step – that can make the difference between life and death.

The story also illustrates another critical aspect of the genre. It's not enough to write about a particular place or landscape: you have to be able to persuade your readers they are really there, sweating in the heat, touching the vegetation, tasting the air. If the setting doesn't feel completely real, the story won't work. This places certain obligations on the author. Either you write from extraordinary life experience like the adventure authors of the old school. Or you put in some legwork. Or you do a lot of reading.

Any of these can work. Research for my novels has taken me all over the world, to some spectacular places; but it's also taken me to a lot of libraries. We place primacy on first-hand experience, but Stef Penney famously wrote *The Tenderness of Wolves*, set in the frozen remoteness of Canada, without leaving London. For one globetrotting novel I wrote, I had to combine places I had actually been to with places (for reasons of time and budget) I had only read about. Reviews praised the authenticity of my exotic locales, the you-are-there quality I'd conjured up – but focused much more on the places I hadn't been than those I had. There's a reason it's called fiction.

How you do your research is up to you. But however you

do it, it's vitally important you know the world your hero will inhabit, and the natural obstacles they'll be up against.

Your hero may cope in different ways. Broadly speaking, the protagonists of adventure stories fall into two camps. There are the out-of-their depth amateurs; and there are the super-competent action heroes. For the latter, think of someone like Allan Quatermain in *King Solomon's Mines*; or Johnny Porter in Lionel Davidson's *Kolymsky Heights*. Porter is a Canadian who can pass as a native of Siberia, build a car out of spare parts in a snow cave, break into an impenetrable hidden base, and make his escape across hundreds of miles of frozen tundra while avoiding the Russian authorities. The joy with him, and others of his type, is seeing how these implausibly competent people use their particular skill sets to overcome challenges that to most of us would be insurmountable.

At the other end of the spectrum is the everyman or everywoman dropped into a situation where they're perilously out of their depth. Here, the dangers of the location are turbocharged by the hero's inexperience: demonstrated in Jack London's short story 'To Build a Fire', where the unnamed protagonist underestimates the Yukon cold, and makes a series of elementary missteps which lead to his doom. More often, the pleasures of this kind of story come from seeing a character get to grips with their environment and learn, through often painful experience, how to master it. We bond with the characters over the most primitive desire of all, the need to survive; we identify with them because we know that in those situations we would struggle too.

A person and a place can be all you need for an adventure story. Character + hostile location = drama: the environment serves as setting, antagonist, and – by virtue of its particular challenges – a series of well defined plot points. But often the author will want to add more by way of plot. Many novels revolve around a quest for something lost: the wreck of the Titanic; a fabled city; a legendary cache of treasure; safety; home. It doesn't really matter what. The main purpose is to set the journey in motion, raise the stakes for the hero, and perhaps motivate a human rival or opponent who stands in the way.

Because in an adventure novel, the plot usually isn't the point. If a thriller starts with a plot to kill the President, it will probably end with an assassination attempt. If a crime novel opens with a body in the billiard room, then you will be disappointed if it doesn't conclude with the detective revealing the culprit to the suspects assembled in the library. But an adventure story doesn't have such fixed rules. The plotting can be looser, more kinetic. What matters is that at every stage, the hero knows what they are trying to achieve; and that their actions and choices serve to bring on the next stage of the adventure. Wilbur Smith's *Monsoon* starts with captain Sir Hal Courtney commissioned to hunt down a dangerous pirate who has been terrorizing English shipping in the Indian Ocean. The reader's natural assumption is that the story will lead to a climactic showdown between Courtney's ship and the pirate's. Nine hundred pages later, through a series of extraordinary twists of fate (spoiler alert), one of Hal's sons has become an Arabian prince; the other is a nomadic big game hunter in Africa, and the pirate is far in the rear-view mirror, having served his purpose to set the story in motion. With an adventure novel, much more so than in other genres, you're free to go where the story takes you.

Is there a future for adventure writing? In the age of satellite surveillance and Google Street View, the world is losing its mysteries. When I was researching my novel *Black River*, I read a lot about the explorer Percy Fawcett, who disappeared in the uncharted wilderness of the Amazon jungle in 1925 and became one of the most famous missing people of the twentieth century, on a par with Amelia Earhart or Lord Lucan. The area where he vanished is now soya fields; a highway runs through it. On a research trip through the most remote parts of the Peruvian rainforest, my travelling companion discovered that he had better mobile phone signal there than he did at home in Yorkshire. As the wild places of the world shrink, so too does the scope for real adventure. But imaginative authors find ways of expanding the genre. Sarah Lotz's *The White Road* combined mountaineering on Mount Everest with the supernatural: chilling in every respect. Tad Williams adapted many of the tropes of the genre in his *Otherland* series, with the twist that most of the adventures took place in an online virtual-reality world. Cormac McCarthy's *The Road* put a post-apocalyptic spin on things. Space has been the final frontier for adventuring – the ultimate hostile environment – since at least the days of Edgar Rice Burroughs' Barsoom series.

Where the genre will go next? Who knows. The best way to find out is to set off on the journey, and see where it takes you.

Dick and Felix Francis are unique among members of the Detection Club as a father and son whose thriller writing became a family business. Following a career as a famous steeplechase jockey, Dick published his first novel in 1962. Julian Symons, a stern judge, said in his history of the genre, *Bloody Murder*, that Dick's 'rare and enviable ability to drive a narrative along, combined with thoroughness of research in a given subject, are what makes readers keep wanting to turn the pages'.

H. R. F. Keating, who was elected to the Detection Club at the same time as Dick Francis, said in *Writing Crime Fiction*: 'With all the sense of timing learnt as a champion jockey, he creates situation after situation of rising suspense to hold readers . . . glued to the battle of wits between hero and villains that he has devised.' In the twenty-first century, Felix carries on the tradition, and is the ideal person to explain in more detail how these effects are achieved.

Writing Action Scenes
Felix Francis

There is no magic formula for writing action scenes, but what is most important is creating a picture through words that the reader can flesh out in their own thinking; not giving too much detail that might confuse, but just the right amount to convey the tension.

We are all so familiar with watching exciting action scenes in both film and on television that those created through words alone may initially seem to be second best. But the written word has so much more to offer in depth and perception.

As my father Dick Francis did before me, I always write my novels as first-person narratives and, as such, we are able to communicate the feelings and emotions of the protagonist along with the description of the action itself. In this way we can express the terror and dread that such action can create, especially when it places our characters in mortal danger – something quite common in a crime story.

Dick Francis was the master at writing action scenes, as the following (slightly edited) extract from his fourth novel, *Odds Against*, clearly shows. Sid Halley, ex-jockey turned private detective, has been trying to work out who is *Leo*, the nickname of the culprit behind a string of unfortunate 'accidents' that have almost brought Seabury racecourse to its knees financially. Needless to say, *Odds Against* was written long before the invention of the mobile phone, and Seabury racecourse doesn't really exist, now or ever, except in the reader's mind's eye – and slightly differently in each person.

> I walked across to the press room to see if the security men had anything to report.
>
> They hadn't.
>
> All four of them were fast asleep.
>
> Stupid fools, I thought. Ex-policemen letting themselves be put to sleep like infants. One of the first rules of guard work

is to take your own food and drink and not accept sweets from strangers.

I picked up the press telephones to call for reinforcements, but all the lines were dead.

I walked out of the press room and, in the light from the door, I saw a dim figure walking towards me.

'Who's that?' he called imperiously, and I recognized his voice. Captain Oxon, the racecourse manager.

'It's only me, Sid Halley,' I shouted back. 'Come and look at this.'

He came with me back into the press room.

'What's the matter with them?' Captain Oxon said.

'Sleeping pills. And the phones don't work to call for help.' I shook my head in disgust. 'I hope they have terrible headaches when they wake up, and serve them right.'

'I can understand you being annoyed . . .' he began, but I was no longer really listening. Over the back of a chair occupied by one of the sleeping security men was hanging a brown leather binoculars case, and on its lid were stamped three black initials L.E.O. Leo. Leo!

'Something the matter?' asked Oxon.

'No.' I smiled at him and touched the strap of the binoculars. 'Are these yours?'

'Yes. The men asked if they could borrow them.' He smiled back. 'Let's go to my flat. You can make a call from there.'

'Right,' I said. But I had absolutely no intention of walking into his flat.

We went out of the press-room door.

A familiar voice, loaded with satisfaction, spoke from barely a yard away. 'So you've got him, Oxon,' Howard Kraye said. 'Good.'

'He was coming—' began Oxon in anxious anger, knowing that 'got him' was an exaggeration.

'No,' I said, and turned and ran for my car.

When I was barely ten yards from it, someone turned on its lights. The headlights of my own Mercedes. I stopped dead.

Behind me one of the men shouted and I heard their

footsteps running. I swerved off right towards the gate. Three steps in that direction, and the headlights of another car turning in caught me straight in the eyes.

There were more shouts, much closer, from Oxon and Kraye. I turned, half-dazzled, and saw them closing in. Behind me now the incoming car rolled forward and the engine of my Mercedes purred separately into life.

I ran for the dark. The two cars, moving, caught me again in their beams. Kraye and Oxon ran where they pointed.

I was driven across and back towards the grandstand like a coursed hare, the two cars inexorably finding me with their lights and the two men running with reaching, clutching hands. Like a nightmare game of 'It', I thought wildly, with far worse than a child's forfeit if I were caught.

Across the parade ring, under the rails for the unsaddling enclosure, inside the owners' and trainers' lunch room and through there without stopping into the large kitchens. Weaving on from there into the members' restaurant, round acres of tables with upturned chairs, through the far door into the wide passage, which cut like a tunnel along the length of the huge building.

The pursuit was left behind.

I went up a steep stone staircase to the open steps of the grandstand and sank down in the shadows, gasping.

At the bottom of the steps lay the large expanse of the members' lawn stretching to a metal mesh fence, chest high, and beyond that the whole expanse of the racecourse. Half a mile to the London Road with yet another barrier, the boundary fence, to negotiate.

It was too far.

Looking at it straight: if I ran, I had to be successful.

My kingdom for a horse, I thought. I had a hundred-and-fifty-mile-an-hour white Mercedes, and someone else was sitting in it.

To run and be caught running would achieve nothing and be utterly pointless.

The security patrol hadn't been drugged for nothing. Kraye

wasn't at Seabury for his health. Some more damage had been planned for this night. Might already have been done. But there was just a chance that, if I stayed to look, I could find out what it was. Before they found me – naturally.

If I ever have children, they won't get me playing hide-and-seek.

Half an hour later, the grim game was still in progress. My own car was now parked on the racecourse side of the stands, where the bookmakers would stand for the following day's racing – that is if there was any. The car faced the stands with the headlights full on. Every inch of the steps was lit by them and hence I was not able to hide on that side of the building.

The other car was similarly parked with its headlights illuminating the weighing room, bars, dining rooms and offices on the other side.

Presuming that each car had a watching occupant, that left only Kraye and Oxon to run me to ground: but I gradually became aware that there were three, not two, after me in the stands. Perhaps one of the cars was empty. But which? And would the keys be in the ignition?

Bit by bit I covered the whole enormous block. I didn't know what I was looking for, that was the trouble. It could have been anything from a bomb downwards, but if past form was anything to go by, it was something which could appear accidental. A jinx. Open, recognizable sabotage would be ruinous to their scheme.

I went cautiously, carefully, every nerve-racking step of the way, peering round corners, easing through doors, fearing that, at any moment, one of them would pounce on me from behind.

I was in the passage, creeping along from the men's lavatories to the members' bar when Kraye appeared at the far end, and began walking my way. He hadn't seen me. One stride took me across the passage, one jump and a wriggle into the only cover available, behind a stack of stored outdoor chairs and sun umbrellas.

Kraye's footsteps scraped hollowly as he trod towards my

ineffective hiding place. He stopped twice, opening doors and looking into storerooms. They were dead ends and no good for me: if I was found in one of them, I couldn't get out.

The door of the bar I had been making for suddenly opened, spilling light into the passage between me and Kraye.

'He can't have got away,' Oxon said anxiously.

'Of course not,' said Kraye furiously, his voice bouncing up and down the passage. 'We're not getting anywhere with all this dodging about. We'll start methodically from this end and work down.'

The two men began to walk away leaving the bar door open, which still lit up the passage. I didn't like it. If anyone came in at the other end, he would see me for sure.

I started to crawl along the wall for better concealment, and one of the sun umbrellas clattered off the side of the stack with an echoing noise like a dozen demented machine guns.

'There he is. Get him.'

I stood up and ran, past the gents and through the last possible door, that of a long, bare, dirty room smelling of beer, the public bar. I nearly fell over a bucket full of crinkled metal bottle tops that someone had carelessly left in the way, and then wasted precious seconds to dart back to put the bucket just inside the door.

Kraye and Oxon were running. I snapped off the lights and, with no time to get clear through the far door out into the paddock, I scrambled down behind the bar counter.

The door jerked open. There was a clatter of the bucket and a yell, and the sound of somebody falling. Then the light snapped on again, showing me just how tiny my hiding place really was. Two bottle tops rolled across the floor into my sight. If it hadn't been so dangerous, it would have been funny.

'For God's sake,' yelled Kraye in anger. 'Get up, you fool.'

He charged down the room, the board floor bouncing slightly under his weight. He yanked open the outside door and yelled across to the stationary car to ask where I'd gone.

I felt rather than saw Oxon run down the room after him.

I crawled round the end of the counter, sprinted for the door, flipped off the lights, slammed the door shut and ran back up the passage.

In this extract, as in all first-person narratives, the action is only witnessed and described from one point of view but that, in itself, can simply add to the suspense as neither the reader nor the character know what the other side is up to. And, while the chase is going on, the underlying storyline of looking for potential damage continues, giving the whole episode important meaning and structure.

In 1968 the film *Bullitt*, staring Steve McQueen as Lieutenant Frank Bullitt of the San Francisco Police Department, laid down a new benchmark for on-screen car chases as McQueen pursues the bad guys up and down the steep streets of San Francisco at speeds up to a hundred and ten miles per hour. The scene lasts for less than ten minutes of film-time, but took three whole weeks to shoot. Full on and without much subtlety, the sequence rightly won the Oscar for best film editing.

Chase scenes portrayed in the written word, by their very nature, tend to be more measured, as in the extract from *Odds Against* above, or in the following from my novel *Gamble*. It doesn't mean they are any less exciting.

As I walked down Lichfield Grove I could see that there was a man standing outside my house with his finger on the doorbell. I was about to call out to him when he turned his head slightly, as if looking over his shoulder.

In spite of telling the police that I hadn't seen Herb Kovak's killer at Aintree, I knew him instantly. Here he was standing outside my front door in Finchley, and I didn't think he was visiting to enquire after my health.

My heartbeat at once jumped to stratospheric proportions and I stifled the shout that was already rising in my throat. I started to turn away from him but not before our eyes had made contact, and I had glimpsed the long black shape in his right hand: his trusty gun, complete with silencer.

Bugger, I thought.

I turned and ran as fast as I could back up Lichfield Grove towards Regent's Park Road.

Lichfield Grove may have been used as a busy short-cut during the rush hour but it was sleepy and deserted at four o'clock in the afternoon with not even any schoolchildren on their way home.

Safety, I thought, would be where there were lots of people. Surely he wouldn't kill me with witnesses. But he had killed Herb with over sixty thousand of them.

I chanced a glance back. It was a mistake.

The gunman was still behind me, only about thirty yards away, running hard and lifting his right arm to aim.

I heard a bullet whizz past me on my left.

I ran harder and also I started shouting.

'Help! Help!' I shouted as loudly as my heaving lungs would allow. 'Call the police!'

No one shouted back, and I needed the air for my aching leg muscles. Oh to be as fit as I once was as a jockey.

I thought I heard another bullet fly past me and zing off the pavement ahead as a ricochet, but I wasn't stopping to check.

I made it unharmed to Regent's Park Road and went left round the corner. Without breaking stride I went straight into Mr Patel's newsagents, pushed past the startled owner and crouched down under his counter, gasping for air.

Of course, not all action scenes are due to conflict with other characters. Sometimes they are simply man against machine, circumstances or, indeed, the elements.

I remember as a teenager reading Alistair MacLean's wonderful *Ice Station Zebra* while in the desert in Bahrain.

Despite the forty-degree heat in which I was sitting, I positively shivered with cold as I devoured the account of Dr Carpenter and two US submarine crewmen making the near impossible trek across the frozen Arctic.

The ability to conjure up such intensity, emotion and excitement from just the written word is what made MacLean one of the greatest storytellers of the last century. And this ability was not just down to his magnificent writing, it was also a result of the depth of his research, not least from his time in the Royal Navy on wartime Arctic convoys, a setting he also utilized in his debut novel, *HMS Ulysses*, capturing superbly the bitter cold and crew hardship that MacLean himself had suffered on trips to Murmansk.

Researching and knowing your subject will give your writing greater depth in all aspects, not just in the action scenes. This is demonstrated in the opening paragraphs of *Dead Cert*, the very first of the 39 novels by Dick Francis, where he used his experiences as a champion steeplechase jockey to evoke a true sense of 'being there' in the reader.

The mingled smells of hot horse and cold river mist filled my nostrils. I could hear only the swish and thud of galloping hooves and the occasional sharp click of horse-shoes striking against each other. Behind me, strung out, rode a group of ten men dressed like myself in white breeches and harlequin jerseys, and in front, his body vividly red and green against the pale curtain of fog, one solitary rider steadied his horse to jump the birch fence stretching blackly across his path.

All, in fact, was going as expected. Bill Davidson was about to win his ninety-seventh steeplechase. Admiral, his chestnut horse, was amply proving he was still the best hunter 'chaser in the kingdom, and I, as often before, had been admiring their combined back view for several minutes.

Ahead of me the powerful chestnut hindquarters bunched, tensed, sprang: Admiral cleared the fence with the effortlessness of the really great performer. And he'd gained another two lengths, I saw, as I followed him over. We were down at the far end of Maidenhead racecourse with more than half a mile to go to the winning post. I hadn't a hope of catching him.

The February fog was getting denser. It was now impossible to see much farther than from one fence to the next, and the silent surrounding whiteness seemed to shut us, an isolated string of riders, into the private limbo. Speed was the only reality. Winning post, crowds, stands and stewards, left behind in the mist, lay again invisibly ahead, but on the long deserted mile and a half circuit it was quite difficult to believe they were really there.

It was an eerie, severed world in which anything could happen.

And something did.

The use by my father of the sentence 'And something did' acts as a pre-marker and heightens the anticipation for the reader, forcing the imagination to run wild. It is a technique I occasionally use myself , often at the end of a chapter to keep the reader guessing. Here is the end of chapter 12 in my latest novel, *Guilty Not Guilty*:

Maybe I could try telling the police to bugger off, but they probably wouldn't take any notice.

And they didn't.

It sets up the next chapter and, I hope, keeps the reader turning over the pages rather than turning out the light and going to sleep. Even if it took the best part of a year to write a book, there is nothing that gives us, as authors, greater pleasure than our devoted readers spending a sleepless night as they eagerly consume our words and rush to the end in one sitting.

Michael Gilbert was a versatile author whose bibliography encompasses classic whodunits, an 'impossible crime' puzzle set in an Italian POW camp, police procedurals, historical mysteries, international thrillers, spy fiction, and adventure stories. For decades he combined a demanding role as a partner in a prestigious law firm (he was a friend and trusted adviser of Raymond Chandler) with his literary career, writing his books on the train journey into work.

In 1959, he edited on behalf of the Crime Writers' Association *Crime in Good Company*, a book of essays about the genre by authors including Julian Symons, Cyril Hare, Roy Vickers, Eric Ambler, and Chandler. His own contribution, 'The Moment of Violence', raised a few eyebrows with its argument that 'a thriller is more difficult to write than a detective story'. But as a good lawyer, he advanced a persuasive case. The following paragraphs are taken from that essay.

Filling the Gaps

Michael Gilbert

One of the real problems of a thriller writer is to fill in the ninety-five per cent of the book when no actual violence is taking place. If, by the way, you doubt these proportions you may be interested in analysing Raymond Chandler's story *The Lady in the Lake*. No blow of any sort is struck, you will find, until page 123, when the hero gets his face slapped, twice, by a policeman. Fifteen pages later he runs into more serious police trouble. (Two pages of action here.) On page 169: 'The scene exploded into fire and darkness. I didn't even remember being slugged.' On the last page of the book the villain is shot and his car plunges a hundred feet down a canyon; and that is that. It is true that we are in the top grade here. Lower down the line the quantum of physical violence increases. But I doubt if it ever exceeds a measured twentieth of the whole.

Reverting, then, to the argument. There is a good deal of space to be filled up. How to fill it?

First, and I will deal with this now in order to put it on one side, you can cheat. You can introduce great slabs of unnecessary love-making, or detailed physical brutality. Or both. Sex and sadism walk quite comfortably hand in hand.

Do not misunderstand me. I am not suggesting that a thriller should be conceived, either in style or content, as a supplement to the Parish Magazine. Its form is such that almost anything can be accepted in it which contributes, functionally, to the whole. But there comes a moment – and it is curiously easy to detect – when one perceives that an author is simply being beastly for the sake of being beastly. It may be an essential part of the story – it often is – for the villain to torture the hero. But as soon as the writer says to himself, in effect, 'Why waste a good opportunity? With a little care and manipulation we can fill up a couple of chapters here. After the red-hot poker, the whips; after the whips, the iced water; after the iced water, *fetch on the tarantulas*' – he is not only bringing his craft into disrepute, he is running an even graver risk. And that is that the whole of his carefully constructed edifice of suspense and terror may explode into guffaws of unfeeling laughter.

Let us assume, however, that you do not cheat. The descriptive and narrative parts of your story are planned, not only to connect, but to assist and develop its moments of violence. The character of the hero at once becomes a matter of paramount importance. After all, you are going to be with the chap most of the time. Not just close behind him, where you would be in the way of his gun arm, but actually inside him, seeing things with his eyes, assessing things with his judgement. If he be a bore, the prospect is dismal. If he be a real and entertaining person, then the smallest detail, of architecture or of dress, of food, and drink, of irrelevant conversation, of unimportant passers-by, becomes, as he describes it, a true and lively part of our common experience.

A lot lies, of course, in the tone of voice.

I.   PROLOGUE WITH VIOLENCE
a thin streak of grey across the darkness.
The complete stillness of suspended animation. The stillness of held breath. The stillness of checked movement; and round it the darkness.

It was a cold, blackness, but dusty, and Rod was plagued with the fear that he might break into the father & mother of all sneezes. He was watching the thin grey streak, as he had been watching it now for the past five minutes.

It seemed like hours. The streak was vertical, not horizontal, and it represented the edge of a door standing a few inches ajar. The door was at the top of a flight of stairs which ran down from the first floor to the half landing. And the greyness was all that was left, at that distance and infiltration, of the electric light in the basement room where the caretaker sat.

A glow-worm came and went ten feet away, and Rod guessed that "Joiner" was using his pencil-torch with discretion. There followed an interminable period of scratching. (Lock picking was all very well, he reflected, when done in the comfort and security of the back room, with friends to applaud prize and applaud. Even when you were blindfolded and had nothing to work by guess she got with a stop watch against you.)

"A loud scrat — the Lifter had slipped again."
His thoughts ran on.
This was It. This was the real thing. This was a job. Which made things both easier & more difficult. More interesting, certainly. In the sixteen years of his life had never known anything

*The opening page of the manuscript of Michael Gilbert's
second book, the thriller* They Never Looked Inside.

Since Eric Ambler's election, the Detection Club has welcomed into membership numerous spy writers of distinction. Several members (perhaps rather more than we realize) have had first-hand experience of top-level intelligence work. One example is J. C. Masterman, who presided over the Double Cross counter-espionage operation that played a vital role during the Second World War. Another is John Bingham (later Lord Clanmorris), who worked in MI5 for many years. The majority of his books were crime novels rather than spy stories, and although *The Double Agent* won the CWA Silver Dagger in 1966, it has recently been revealed that he wrote a novel called *Fugitive from Perfection*, dealing with fascism and a Whitehall cover-up, which has never been published, possibly for security reasons.

Michael Hartland worked in government service and also for the International Atomic Energy Agency prior to publishing his first novel in 1982. A former Secretary of the Detection Club, he remains an expert guide to the mysteries that abound in the murky world of international double-dealing.

Constructing a Thriller

Michael Hartland

Every writer will approach planning a book in their own way. Remember, you may be writing your first thriller, but no doubt you have read quite a few – and so will all your readers. In this genre – as in all fiction – a freshness and originality will mark out a book, but there will also be some basic expectations. A thriller is expected to be pacey and *exciting*.

Characters
Your characters are the living heart of the story. They need to be tangible, empathic, engaging – so think carefully about them, especially the key figures. Before you put them into action you

need to know a lot about them. I usually write a short character sketch of each main character – maybe six or seven – describing their background, personality, appearance, motivation. They all need a hinterland which makes them a real person, but crafted to fit their role in the book. Ask why do you need them there – and make sure their character will fill the dramatic part you have in mind. Really evil characters can be more engaging, especially if they have a sense of black humour (like some of Ian Fleming's villains), so your hero or heroine must be equally interesting, tough, no-nonsense, but with an attractive side too. And, of course, both plot and characters always develop as you write.

Douglas Hurd and Andrew Osmond's iconic thriller, *The Smile on the Face of the Tiger*, published in 1970, shows that a character can also be morally ambiguous – and all the more interesting for it. It starts with Lawrence Pershing serving as an officer with the Gurkhas in the Malayan jungle, 1957. The enemy are communist terrorists (CTs) and his section are to attack a CT camp and capture a leader who wants to surrender and be deported to newly communist China. But in the fighting, in a fit of panic, Pershing empties his carbine into a young woman CT, who wants to surrender but instead is stretchered for miles screaming and bleeding, because their morphine ampoules are all smashed. At base camp, she dies.

The girl's brother, Chiang Li-shih, is the leader who surrenders and goes to Beijing to become a senior figure in the new government. Fourteen years later he encounters Pershing, now a British diplomat. They are both at a conference chaired by the UK and the Soviet Union, in Phnomh Penh, to seek peace in Vietnam, Laos and Cambodia. When they both visit the temples at Angkor Wat, Chiang contrives to confront Pershing alone, accuses him of cowardice and murdering his nineteen-year-old sister. Chiang threatens to reveal the truth of what happened, Pershing has another panic attack and spills out the American strategy, which is to accept defeat in Vietnam but organize a right-wing coup to neutralise Cambodia. The rest, Pol Pot and the killing fields, are history.

Pershing is flaky, a coward with a marriage that is a sham. But by 1976 he is a Conservative MP and a junior minister in the Foreign Office, when he is blackmailed again – this time when China demands the immediate return of Hong Kong, to avoid a bloody invasion by the Peoples' Liberation Army. It's getting serious, and there is a lot more to this sinuous drama, but Pershing was always an unwilling traitor and suddenly finds the courage he's lacked all his life. The reader is on his side as he prepares to sacrifice his career, save Hong Kong but go to gaol.

To take a couple of more straightforward examples, in my own spy series David Nairn is very much a creature of his background. From a poor family in Paisley, after some manual work he makes his way in his twenties to Oxford, joins MI6 and turns out to be a natural, both in the field and as a spymaster. Dangerous threats – mainly from Moscow and Beijing – are seen off in a series of separate novels. But his private life is a mess.

He struggles with the contradictions of working among people who he feels are 'posher' than he is, while in fact respected by them for his intellect and courage on the ground. There is an on-off relationship with a colleague, Ruth, who at the end of *Down among the Dead Men*, ends up married to a more exciting Chinese spymaster and settled in Hong Kong (where she pops up again in the last book of the series). Then suddenly, in the middle of tracking down the 'Fifth Man', he bumps into an attractive middle-aged foster mother, with no interest in spies or class, but blown away by a kind man when she needs one – as he is with her. They end up living together in Chiswick in his first real home, a comfortable flat by the river. Despite a brilliant mind, Nairn has no personal ambition – at one level he is glad just to have a job – so when he is suddenly summoned to the Cabinet Office and asked to be Chief of the service, she says of course he must do it. When he is knighted, he goes to work in the morning, they call in at Buckingham Palace, then go to Waitrose together and pick up a takeaway on the way home.

His main antagonist in the first book – and subsequently from a distance – is a woman who has risen close to the top of the GRU, Soviet military intelligence. Nadia Alexandrovna Kirova joined the Red Army as a teenager in 1943 during the siege of Leningrad. Conditions in the city were dreadful for three years, with bombing, thousands of dead and injured, starvation, disease and failing medical supplies. Like most other young people, she wanted to fight the Germans. She has risen from girl tommy-gunner to colonel and in the end major-general. She has an uneasy relationship with Marxism, but is locked into the system and fighting to keep her place as the only woman at the top of a male-dominated organization. She is as ambivalent about her links with those around her as Nairn is, but she has become ruthless and has to be tougher than him in a world where the price of failure is still a bullet in the back of the head.

She has had men in her life, including a dangerous love with a brilliant writer, Anatoly Levshin, who fell foul of the system and ended up bitter in a labour camp. In *Frontier of Fear,* he has been released and is begging on the streets, when he turns up at her smart apartment on the Lenin Hills and she gives him a bath, a meal and a bed. He in turn has picked up gossip at the Writers' Union that Gorbachev is about to be overthrown and has come to warn her because he knows she is vulnerable.

If things were different, Kirova and Nairn would probably get along quite well, but history has made them deadly adversaries. After books one and two, they are not (usually) the man and woman at the sharp end – the characters with whom readers can really empathize and root for. In each book, the story develops from the interaction between a particular cast of personalities (friends and enemies, old and new) and circumstances. Nairn and Kirova may appear often or seldom, but their influence as puppet masters is always in the ether.

They are just three examples, so you will need to decide on the nature of your own front-line hero or heroine: civilian who stumbles into a story, professional intelligence officer, long-term sleeper, blackmail victim, undercover agent in a terrorist cell?

What are they trying to achieve, what is threatening them? Your reader will need to empathize with them, then engage more and more emotionally as the plot unfolds.

And remember that you might want to use that hero or heroine again in a sequel or a series.

Dialogue

The dialogue spoken between characters is a key tool for conveying their background, motivation and, most importantly, emotions. It can also add to direct description of their surroundings. All sorts of people will crop up in a good spy story and if you are not familiar with their speech you'll need to do some research. Ones that I recall needing work are Chinese and Japanese men and women – their distinctive sound (in English or their own language), accent and use of English. The same goes for anyone whose first language is different from yours.

You'll have been hearing and learning dialogue all your life and it should come fairly naturally, but for special categories like foreign diplomats, Russian oligarchs, the armed forces (and from which country?) it needs to be authentic. If you don't meet Russian oligarchs in your branch of Tesco, then iconic thrillers, TV and radio drama, documentaries, films and your own travel are all potential sources. In the Far East, I sometimes made almost phonetic notes of what I was hearing, whether in English, Japanese or Chinese, as a guide to use later.

Your cast may include people working in particular structures – men and women in MI6, Chinese or Russian intelligence and embassies, the armed services, police, whether British or another nationality. It's important to get the detail right. For instance, British civil servants such as a minister's private secretary will always address the boss as 'Minister' or 'Secretary of State', not 'sir' or 'ma'am' (even quite distinguished writers often get this wrong). But the minister will probably use the official's first name. It's probably still the same in the United States, for example, but you can check. These days MI5 and MI6 (and GCHQ) are all open-plan offices and first names. With

Naval officers, whether on Trident submarines carrying enough
warheads to destroy a continent, or a minesweeper on the
surface, it's a mix of 'sir', 'ma'am' to someone more senior
and, today, mostly first names the other way. Surnames are
usually used for ratings.

That's just a matter of nuts and bolts. More importantly,
your dialogue is a main tool for carrying forward your storyline.
It can explain what is happening, show relationships between
characters (respect, contempt, love, hate, irritation?) and reflect
background. Speech can help to indicate the landscape and
surroundings (such as sun, a harbour, yachts, bars if on the
Mediterranean) or to explain the politics and oppression of a
government, fear of secret police and so on. Speech can often
be more effective than straight description.

In a similar way, dramatic events like threats, blackmail,
indecision, conflict, murder can be heightened when partly
described in dialogue. For example –

'Hi, darling,' she gave a welcoming smile. 'You're early, we
can have a drink before we go out.' Then she saw the knife
in his hand.

Plotting – background and threat

There needs to be a mystery (of course), which is significant
and may not be resolved until your last pages – much as in a
good crime novel. But the empathic and colourful characters
you have crafted also need to go into situations of danger, with
a developing background of menace and fear – and if that
danger threatens from the start or soon after, so much the
better.

So where do you set your story? How do you contrive it?
The real drama will lie in conflict between your characters,
leading to suspicion, betrayal, fear and perhaps physical danger
of torture or death. But a menacing background helps to set
the scene and the emotional response you need. The Cold War
had a built-in chill factor for more than forty years – because
everyone in the Soviet Union, United States, East and West

Europe was fully aware of the danger of nuclear attack. They were also aware that spies were based in foreign embassies and, more insidiously, might be long-term 'sleepers' just down the street, whether in Ruislip or a Moscow suburb.

That was a strong canvas to draw on, but the Cold War is over. Even so, espionage novels set in the Cold War are still popular and there seems to be a second Cold War developing between China and Trump's America. The possible antagonists have changed around from time to time, but undercurrents of menace and personal threat go back to the Great Game of British and Russian agents facing down each other in 19th Century Afghanistan or India. The same, almost tribal, currents are still swirling around – and no doubt always will.

A century ago, Buchan's *The Thirty-Nine Steps* was a good example of an ordinary young man stumbling on the murder by German spies of a British agent, who gives him a vital notebook to deliver to MI5. Suddenly pursued for the murder himself, he flees from both the British police and gun-toting Germans. It's a great man-on-the-run yarn. Despite a touch of Keystone Kops, it's made more exciting by the growing fear and confusion in Richard Hannay's mind – and more convincing because when published in 1915 there was a strong background of real-life fear about German spies.

Second World War stories are also still going strong. The last two centuries were a powerful time of totalitarian states cultivating terror as a means of enforcing the will of the government on a population at home – and sometimes on those who have fled as refugees abroad. Good examples are the Soviet Union and Putin's regime today, from Stalin's agents pursuing Trotsky to Mexico City – and putting an ice-axe in his brain – to recent events with Novichok in Salisbury. Traitors and spies usually faced, and often still face, torture and death. Put a well-crafted character, man or woman, into one of the past or current totalitarian states as a spy and they will immediately face great personal danger, surrounded by a whole population living in daily fear of betrayal and the midnight knock on the door. Think of Iran.

The threat of extremist Islamic terrorism has been common currency since the destruction of the Twin Towers and creates a miasma of fear throughout the West, in Russia and all over the Middle East. It's a strong backdrop, but you'll need to study Wahabi Islam, at least enough to understand the rhetoric. Also the plight of Palestinians living in the West Bank and Gaza – and how it relates to the politics of Iran, Hezbollah and Hamas. And, of course, the catastrophic results of the wars in Iraq and Syria. It's a complicated pattern, but every Friday afternoon or evening, after prayers at the mosque, in well-off developed countries, groups of young men and women are meeting in their homes to debate all these issues. They are probably hard-working, sober and well brought-up. They may fall in love with each other, but also collect money for fellow Muslims, bombed-out and homeless, the displaced and starving – and sometimes for the Taliban in Pakistan or Afghanistan. This can happen in Hackney, Bradford, Birmingham, anywhere.

Sometimes one or two of those young people feel they must do more; and there are plenty of inspiring preachers who will join their gatherings and be encouraging. This can lead on into radical venues and maybe networks that will help the young recruits go to training camps or, most recently, to travel to join ISIS in Syria. This has been going on progressively for decades and there are strong, moving and exciting tales here – of young people with high ideals in danger of exploitation; plus other young MI5 agents sent undercover, in real danger, to penetrate their most secret cells. The routes to active terrorism change all the time, but they do not go away.

Somewhere in the mix are Guantanamo Bay and everything linked to it, especially waterboarding and 'extraordinary rendition' by ghost planes operated by the CIA, delivering captives to prisons in countries where torture is normal – trying to gather intelligence to avoid attacks and hunt down terrorist leaders. Then death can be delivered by special forces like US Navy Seals or from a drone flying across Syria but controlled from a safe bunker in Nevada.

In addition to state or non-state threats, don't forget

mafia-style organized crime. Drugs are so common as to be old hat, but people-trafficking is strong material if you take the time to research it. One of my first pieces of research, years ago, was into the story of a group of twenty wealthy refugees from the civil wars in the Congo, who paid to be taken by a small merchant ship to Britain. After their valuables had been stowed safely and they had parted with $20,000 each, and once the ship was a hundred miles from land, they were hustled on deck in groups and tossed over the side to drown. The ship had done this before, plying the war-torn coasts of Africa for ten years. I never had the heart to use it then, but news from the Mediterranean in the last few years has revealed unbelievable courage, desperation, exploitation, and tragedy.

Action and pace

I've dwelt on choosing a sufficiently murky background, and making sure you know your main characters, because if these are right your story has a good chance of being credible and tangible, as if it is really happening.

Characters and background should also come together to suggest possible storylines, to add to your own ingenuity and observation to sketch out your plot. Whatever period and background you've chosen, your characters will need to face a challenge or threat which is hopefully in a strong menacing background, but also immediate and personal – and the sooner the better. Some writers start from just characters and work towards a plot, but I've always preferred a two-pronged attack. I guess different approaches suit different writers.

Whatever the challenge or threat, there will be many twists and turns before they are safe; and sadly some won't make it. Unless you start with a foreign agent blackmailing – or, more likely befriending – your hero or heroine, the enemy may be well hidden (and sometimes far away). It's up to you how soon you bring the opposition and its mind into play. We may see a single individual, not knowing what strength of threat they represent, or become aware of the organization

behind them. Build in suspense and tension by placing characters in danger or keeping information secret until it suits
the drama to reveal it.

Make the action fast, with a reasonable body count, and
every now and again ask what should logically happen next
– then do the reverse. Remember that fast action and scenes
becoming closer together will help to build up pace, but so
should the fears and emotion felt by your characters (and
between them). That will be giving you a genuine thriller.

Spy stories or international thrillers are apt to date even faster than
other books as the geopolitical landscape keeps shifting. Thrillers
need to thrill, but the best action novels also tell us something about
human nature, showing people's behaviour under extreme pressure.
Writers need to respond to the changes going on around them, and
further afield, but whatever happens in the outside world, opportunities for gripping stories abound.

At one time some people suggested that the fall of the Berlin Wall
and the end (or apparent end) of the Cold War sounded the death
knell for contemporary novels about espionage. Far from it. The
success of Mick Herron, who has won or been nominated for more
than twenty awards over the past decade or so, illustrates the
immense potential of spy fiction in the twenty-first century.

The Cold War, Then & Now
Mick Herron

A year or two ago I came across a fascinating book called *Oxford: Mapping the City*, by Daniel MacCannell. As the title suggests, it's a collection of different versions of Oxford down the ages, the earliest dating back to 1568. Of all the images on offer, the one that most captured my imagination was a Soviet map of the city, compiled in 1972, for use during a military invasion. Apparently there were many such maps, created 'in anticipation of a street-by-street conquest of the United Kingdom', and this one, which renders all of Oxford's street names into Russian, shows key industrial targets – chief among them the Cowley Motor Works, which was of far greater significance, of course, than the University.

Having said that, one of the other key targets – and we can tell this by the colour-coding used – was University College. MacCannell's theory is that the college's importance, relative to all the other colleges, was overestimated, because of what it's called – University College. The clue's in the name.

Such errors aren't uncommon. Not long after that map was compiled on the other side of the Iron Curtain, my reading habits had expanded to include the works of Alastair MacLean, at the time the world's most successful writer of thrillers, whose depiction of the conflict between East and West was largely unhampered by nuance, but who was responsible for a major part of my own understanding of global events. For example, *Ice Station Zebra* – a classic of the genre – provided me with a cast-iron explanation as to why the Cold War was so called. It was because it was being fought in freezing places, surrounded by icebergs, with any prospect of a thaw seeming massively unlikely.

I should emphasize, I was about twelve when I read *Ice Station Zebra*.

The Cold War was the backdrop of the world I grew up in: it informed my childhood, and haunted my teenage years. Many of the thrillers of the time, *Ice Station Zebra* among them, took that landscape for granted, and rather than interrogate the reasons for its existence, simply used it as a backdrop for struggles between right and wrong, good and evil. Shades of grey were available too, of course, in novels written by subtler hands – Len Deighton, John Le Carré – but the stakes, in general, remained the same. Novels feed off the atmosphere of their times, and the Seventies were a paranoid era.

Like many who reached their teens in that decade, I had recurring dreams of nuclear war. They lasted well into my twenties. They were usually literal, involving images of missiles being launched (though never of their landing); occasionally figurative – I would dream of floods, huge tidal waves. If I were having such dreams today, I'd ascribe them to more contemporary fears, a different variety of man-made apocalypse; back then, I was dreaming that the Cold War had heated up. That was a constant possibility; it hovered at the back of the mind, always. You could die without realizing any of your ambitions. You could die before you'd finished reading the book you'd started yesterday. Which didn't prevent me from embarking on some pretty long novels, but it did colour my general outlook.

And perhaps this has persisted. I hope not, but I wonder if it has. The background we grow up against can seem the natural state of affairs; when it alters, for good or bad, at some level we expect it to change back again eventually. We wait for the other shoe to fall. Sometimes this happens very slowly.

The Seventies were the decade, too, of the conspiracy thriller. The Cold War had a lot to do with that, obviously, but there were other factors, not least Watergate, to use the familiar shorthand. Which is not to say that the genre blossomed out of nowhere. A generation of novelists had long been engaged with what Leo Braudy, in *The New York Times Book Review*, called 'the style of paranoid surrealism'. Its practitioners included Norman Mailer, Thomas Pynchon, Joseph Heller, William Burroughs, and Ken Kesey; Margaret Atwood and Don DeLillo were to be among the heirs to that tradition. And key thrillers in the genre had appeared earlier. Indeed, Richard Condon's *The Manchurian Candidate* – perhaps the epitome of the conspiracy thriller – was published in 1959.

But Watergate helped shift the paranoid – or conspiracy – thriller into the cultural mainstream, not least because it validated the sense of paranoia already taking root, other contributing factors being the assassinations of John F. Kennedy, Robert Kennedy and Dr Martin Luther King, and the then ongoing Vietnam War. Watergate was a government conspiracy – a cover-up, secret tapes – which left people more susceptible to believing in other government conspiracies. Polls carried out in its wake indicated, for example, an increase in the number of people who believed that the moon landings had been faked. Lack of trust in major institutions was leading to a situation in which people were ever more ready to accept as fact what they'd read in fiction, and correspondingly unprepared to admit as real what was actually happening in the world – or on its moon.

And the fact that the events which were undermining faith in those institutions were taking place against the backdrop of the Cold War only added to the hall-of-mirrors effect. Pay attention, said the conspiracy thriller, to the man behind the iron curtain. Because he's the one pulling the strings.

Now, despite my chosen genre, I'm not much of a one for conspiracy theories. As a character in one of my early books put it, 'I think most conspiracy theories are invented by the government, to spread paranoia and uncertainty among the masses.' But it's hard not to be aware how closely intertwined these two worlds – the Cold War conspiracy thriller and what we like to think of as real life – can be. The genre feeds into reality as much as it feeds off it, and one of its key features is the way it blurs the lines between fact and fiction, leading the reader – and sometimes the author – into an infinity of mirrors.

Take Malcolm, the CIA analyst from James Grady's 1974 novel *Six Days of the Condor*. Malcolm is an office worker, in an anonymous three-storey townhouse on Capitol Hill in Washington DC, and he spends his days reading mystery novels. He's also a spook, whose most daring venture has been to paint his office wall red in protest at being made to wear a suit and tie. Occasionally it's his turn to step out and collect lunch, and – happily – this is what he's doing when a hit squad turns up and wipes out his colleagues.

Because fiction can be dangerous. As Malcolm explains in the movie version: 'I'm not a spy. I just read books. We read everything published in the world, and we feed the plots into a computer, and the computer checks against actual CIA plans and operations. I look for leaks, I look for new ideas.'

In a preface to a reissue of the novel in 2011, author James Grady revealed that, according to *Washington Post* journalist Pete Earley in his book *Comrade J: The Untold Secrets of Russia's Master Spy in America After the End of the Cold War*, the KGB, alarmed by the apparent existence of such an intelligence-gathering unit – which they discovered in 1975 by the dastardly means of watching the Robert Redford movie based on Grady's novel – established their own version, the so-called 'All-Union Scientific Research Institute of Systems Analysis'. It apparently employed 2,000 Soviet citizens.

As if authors don't have enough to worry about, the possibility of writing something that reality will plagiarize is a very real danger. Set against that, job creation is a positive achievement.

The world has changed since then, of course. And the Cold
War too has altered. Its primary iteration came to an end on
9 November 1989, with the dismantling of the Berlin Wall, or
on 3 October 1990, with the reunification of Germany, or on
26 December 1991, with the formal dissolution of the Soviet
Union . . . Other dates are available. Unlike fiction, history can
be imprecise and woolly.

But some things remain. Secret histories, as evidenced by
that Soviet map of Oxford, still exert fascination for thriller
writers: the stuff going on behind the scenes; the events that
never actually happened, but nevertheless left their scars on
the landscape; the abandoned nuclear shelters which might
still have their covert uses.

Because it could all kick off again, given the right – or wrong
– circumstances; given a particular kind – or lack – of leader-
ship. Here in 2020, all those years after the Wall went down,
none of us have to look far in either direction, east or west,
to find evidence of untrustworthy, and quite possibly mad,
world leaders. If yesterday's despots have morphed, in the
intervening years, into gangsters, more driven by greed, narcis-
sism, lust for power and fanaticism than ideology, that doesn't
dilute the dangers they represent. And as we grow increasingly
doubtful about who controls our media, our technology and
our democracy, familiar spectres of the past grow substantial
once more.

It was often said, in the Nineties in particular, that the age
of the spy thriller was over; that the demise of the Cold War
meant that the genre had seen its time, and that those who
practised in its paranoid corridors would need new stamping
grounds. The part of me that tries to be a good citizen, of
nation and planet, wishes that it were so. But the truth is, the
Cold War – or at least, the fears and terrible possibilities that
the Cold War embodied – didn't end, it merely put on different

colours. We might need different maps to read it now, and the names might have been altered, but underneath it all we're occupying the same territory: somewhere between borders, where it's always murky, and we're always out in the cold. Which, secretly, is where spy writers prefer to be.

History

Historical mysteries are so popular that it comes as a surprise to realize that, prior to the 1970s, they were much less common than they are today. Agatha Christie's 1944 novel *Death Comes as the End*, set in Ancient Egypt, was more the exception than the rule, although John Dickson Carr published numerous historical detective stories in the later part of his career.

Peter Lovesey's novels about the Victorian policeman Sergeant Cribb began in 1970, and led to two television series, while Ellis Peters' Brother Cadfael books appeared from 1977 onwards. The Cadfael Chronicles benefited from Peters' insistence on accuracy in historical detail, coupled with vivid characterization and an admirable sense of place. Peters, a native of Shropshire, located her series in Shrewsbury and the borderlands between England and Wales, which she knew intimately.

Despite her familiarity with the setting, Peters was writing about a world that seems very remote from the present, but her biographer Margaret Lewis quotes her as saying, 'I've tried to write the books from the viewpoint of someone who was there and found all these things quite normal.'

Lindsey Davis says in *Falco: The Official Companion*, 'I had always wanted to write, and knew that I wanted to write historicals.' Nowadays there are plenty of specialists in historical crime fiction, but other crime writers, well known for contemporary novels, from time to time delve into the past. Many successful examples are to be found in the bibliographies of Detection Club members, including Jean Stubbs' *Dear Laura*, Gwendoline Butler's *A Coffin for Pandora* and Julian Symons' *The Blackheath Poisonings*, *The Detling Murders*, and *Sweet Adelaide* (all set in the Victorian era). Harry Keating's *The Murder of the Maharajah* is set in the Raj of the 1930s, while Colin Dexter's *The Wench is Dead* saw Inspector Morse investigating a 150-year-old cold case from his hospital bed and Anthony Price's novels blended military history with contemporary espionage. Peter Lovesey described Price as 'a writer who demonstrates brilliantly . . . that the past is often the key to learning about the present – which is surely the best justification for learning about history.'

Occasionally, as Michael Pearce's experience illustrates, an incident from one's own past may, perhaps indirectly, supply inspiration for a historical novelist.

A Laying On of Hands

Michael Pearce

I grew up in what was then Anglo-Egyptian Sudan. One day I heard chanting in the distance. The chanters came into view. There were lots of them, nearly two thousand, at least. To this day I can hear their words: 'Sayid Ali, Sayid Ali, Sayid Ah.' Sayid Ali was the name of a political leader, and they all marched along with vigour. The singers were students from Khartoum University. I was not a member of the university. My father, who worked in nearby Khartoum, had asked if I could go along with them and, good-naturedly, they had said yes.

The rally was political. What Sayid Ali was leading them towards, God knows. But it was exciting, uplifting, marching with them and singing with them: 'Sayid Ali, Sayid Ah.' I was too young to be a student. But my friends were all students. It was a time when all the campuses were stirring. I became one with the chanting. As we marched, the students, brushing past me, looked at me questioningly. One came up to me. His eyes were red and weeping. Many of the people in the Sudan suffered from bilharzia. It was a water-borne disease, the product of the Nile which affected almost everyone in Egypt. I didn't like the way this man looked at me, but ignored it. A small stone skittered around my feet. My friends brushed past the thrower and hurried on. I forgot about it and gradually succumbed to the whole atmosphere: the pad of feet on the sand, the rhythmic chanting, the press of dark faces. The stones were more frequent now. My friends exchanged glances and we began to veer away from the procession. I did not wish to show fear – I was a true son of the Raj – but all the same a feeling of uneasiness was creeping over me.

My friends now broke away distinctly from the procession. I was not frightened however. I was drawn into the torchlight, the pad of feet and the warmth of the evening. The cries became more rhythmic: 'Sayid Ali, Sayid Ah.' 'Time to go home,' my friends said. But I was still excited, carried away, rapt you might say. Everything was humming. This rhythmic shouting, on and on, drew me in, and exalted me.

The next day things were quiet. I learned later, however, that the Chief of Police, wandering about in the press of people, had been stabbed during the night. We had known him. McGuigan was his name, Hugh McGuigan. My mother was not pleased when she heard of my exploits, but my father shrugged his shoulders. All the excitement died down. But afterwards, when I began to write, I knew that something had happened to me. I had been touched by something, and it was not stones.

One advantage of historical crime fiction is that the writer does not need to keep up to date with developments in technology and changes in the minutiae of police procedure. Scientific progress has killed off plenty of plot devices that were once beloved of writers, such as the corpse which (in the days before DNA testing) was misidentified as someone who turns out to have been alive all the time, and may even be the murderer. The ubiquity of mobile phones and the ready availability of information about almost everything on the internet present further challenges for the writer aiming to mystify and build suspense.

Yet resorting to historical fiction is not an easy way out. History mysteries need to give an impression of authenticity, for instance as regards period detail and dialogue. This demands not only research but also careful thought, given that authenticity is not the same as total accuracy. Imogen Robertson and Len Tyler, whose historical fiction has achieved success in recent years, discuss questions about research and dialogue in the context of history mysteries.

The Christmas Tree Theory of Historical Research

Imogen Robertson

In the days before Audible was available for long car journeys, my family had my mum. When we were towing the caravan to Scotland or the south of France, or when we had finished our dinner and were playing Patience on the Formica table under a hissing gas light, she was our Netflix. She chose what to read to us, and as she had to keep my older brothers, Dad, and me all happy during the long summer evenings she often chose Dorothy L. Sayers, Margery Allingham, Dickens, Austen and a lot of Georgette Heyer. When people ask me why I write historical crime fiction, I tend to point to Mum, browsing the shelves at home for a few things to keep us entertained.

I didn't study history, but have always been fascinated by the past. I love the onion-skin layers of mystery, the forgotten stories, and the light that the past sheds on us now as we compare and contrast periods, attitudes, ways of life. Crime fiction I've always loved for its form. A body is discovered and a promise is made to the reader. I, the writer, promise you that you are going to find out how and why this person died and who did it. On the way to solving that mystery, you, dear reader, are going to discover a new world. In modern crime novels that world might be the criminal underbelly of a city or a village, the luxurious corruptions of the rich, or the mechanics of a modern crime investigation. In a historical novel that world is a different time, one that you can inhabit alongside the characters for 120,000 words, give or take, and in doing so acquire a rich sense of what it is to walk through places and with people who no longer exist, or only exist as ghosts in the architecture and archives. In both cases, modern or historical, your job as a writer is the same. Take the reader somewhere new, and make them feel what it is like to be there. What does this place look like, feel like, sound like, smell like? What are the people like? How do they speak? What do they value? What do they fear? What do they want? Why?

So how do you create this new world? Easy. You build it with specific, concrete details that will conjure a place and a character in your reader's mind. Now all you need to do is work out what those details are. It will take research, whatever setting or period you choose, and I hope I can sketch out something about the form that research might take, for a historical novelist at least.

I don't think you need to be a trained historian to be a writer of historical fiction. The concerns of the professional historian are often very different to those of a professional fiction writer. The historian wants to know about political change, shifting social currents; often they are continuing decade-long debates with other historians. Those debates and long-term changes can be fascinating, but are of not much practical use to me as a writer. I want to know specifics of what it was like to be this particular person, on this particular day in this particular place. That said, increased interest in social history and material culture, and in the less-recorded lives of women and the working classes in particular, has given the historical novelist a lot more to work with in the secondary sources these days in comparison to thirty years ago. I am massively grateful to historians from Asa Briggs to Amanda Vickery for opening up the archives and sharing and illuminating the lives they found there. They are digging up the raw material for us to fashion into fiction.

Before I take you through how I manage the research, though, a word of warning about how to handle what you find. The biggest danger with historical fiction, crime or otherwise, is what I've often heard described as 'info dump'. It's a harsh term, but often bandied about. It describes the habit of sharing a great splurge of research on the page, paragraph after paragraph that tell the reader all about the social and political background of a scene, rather than letting it emerge out of the drama of the story. It can be very tempting, when we are immersed in a period that we find exciting, to share everything we know with the reader, but whenever we feel the temptation to do so, we have to draw back and see if we can dramatize the information in some way. It's important to make it part of the fabric of the story, rather than shoehorn it in.

The best way I know of avoiding the info dump is to stay in character. When you are setting a scene, think about all your senses, of course; but also think carefully about what would attract the attention of your point-of-view character. Say your character is a country girl just arrived in the big city, what would stand out? Probably the same things someone coming in from the countryside would notice today. The noise. The traffic. The people. So what are the specific, concrete details you are after? The noise today might be someone's car stereo. In 18th-century London it might have been the cacophony of street cries. What street cries? Milk? Herrings?

Be specific. The smells? Food maybe, roasted chestnuts, or the stink of the sewers. The traffic? Carts, carriages, sedan chairs. Be specific again. Tell the reader a cart is going by, and they'll have a vague idea. Tell them it's full of apples and they'll see something more concrete. If your character loves fine clothes, let them notice what people are wearing. If they are afraid of crime, let them pick out for special notice the beggars, or someone pursuing a pickpocket along the street. That way, you are telling us something about the character as well as the scene they are observing. And if you need to let the reader know war with France has just been declared and why? Perhaps two businessmen are discussing the effect on trade as your character steps back from the mud of the road, or a trader is reading out a newspaper article to his illiterate friend as your character pauses to buy something they want.

Sometimes you need to let readers know something more than a headline about the political environment or events of the day. Let your characters discuss what is happening between themselves then. Every time a character opens their mouths, you'll learn something about their background and preoccupations, and in their reactions and arguments you'll be able to tell readers the basic facts of current events at the same time. Does that feel awkward? Can't think of a reason your character would get into a fight about this? Well, if your main characters aren't thinking about these events, aren't talking about them, that might suggest they don't have a place in your story at all.

But how does this work in practice? How do you find the details which will bring scenes alive, and decide on what events and facts of day-to-day life do matter? I always think of research for a novel as being something like a child's drawing of a Christmas tree. That initial bit of trunk is your first inspiration, the fragment of story idea you think you can build a novel round. For *The Paris Winter*, for example, my first idea was that an English woman of modest but respectable background, who was studying art in Paris, might get pulled into a criminal conspiracy. Also, I'd just read that Paris had been badly flooded in 1910 and I thought that would make a brilliant backdrop, so I had my date, my location and a rough idea of a character.

So research phase one begins. This is that longest horizontal line, the base of your Christmas tree coming off the trunk, where your research should be general, unfocused and range widely. Keeping *The Paris Winter* as an example, I read general histories of the period, studies on the flood or the art world, and also biographies of some of the artists of the period. I flicked through the copies of the newspapers and magazines of the time, read diaries and travel books that focused on Paris, bought guidebooks and searched YouTube for archive footage or documentaries on the Dreyfus Case, art history and women's rights in France during the Belle Époque. This stage of research is about getting a feel for the period, but also picking up on potential incidents, locations and characters. Embrace serendipity and chance. I was looking for a report in *The Times* about the floods, when I came across an advert on the front page which ended up as a major plot point. Do look at contemporary travel writing – a foreigner in London or Paris writing for a home audience is doing the same job you are trying to do now, bringing an unfamiliar world to life, so you'll often find they'll pick up on the specific colourful and telling details that diarists or writers living in London might miss. To quote Quentin Tarantino's *Pulp Fiction*, this is the 'Royale with Cheese' secret of historical fiction writing.

Now, the danger is that this stage can go on forever. It's very easy to convince yourself you need to read everything in existence before you get on with the annoying work of actually plotting and writing a book. Don't do that. This stage is about deciding which things you will need to know about in more detail later. I manage to stop by setting myself a time limit, and that's dictated by when I have to deliver a book so I can pay my bills; but as a rule of thumb I'd say don't spend more than a month of working time on this stage. Now you have to narrow your focus, drawing your first set of diagonal lines sloping towards each other on the Christmas tree picture, and you do that by making decisions about your character and the

plot. In *Paris Winter*, I decided that my character was studying
to be an artist in a fictional version of the Académie Julian;
that she would find herself on the edge of destitution and end
up employed as a companion by a woman with an opium
addiction.

OK. New research stage. This time it's much more specific,
so my horizontal line is shorter. This is also usually the time
I find it's a good idea to leave the library occasionally and go
and talk to people. I found a contemporary artist who was
trained in the same way my character would have been, and
hung out in her studio, watching her work. I also brought her
pictures of artworks which I thought were bad, and some I
thought were brilliant, and asked her to talk about them. That
gave me a sense of the language my character might use and
how her artistic training would affect how she saw the world
and, crucially, what details she might pick up on as she walked
the Parisian streets. It's also the time to use your own imagination and experience too. Doing twelve-hour shifts in December
in Borough Market is a great way to discover what being very
cold and hungry feels like, should you ever need to do so. On
a happier note, I also went to Paris, but at this point I had a
better idea of where my character might be living, eating and
working, so I could use my time there efficiently.

And I keep plotting. Narrowing things down again. I worked
out there were diamonds in there somewhere and so read up
specifically about jewellers and forgers in Paris at the period.
I then went and bothered a nice man in Bond Street who
showed me huge (I thought) diamonds, saved me from an
embarrassing plot fail, and talked about how an expert spots
fakes. I read transcripts of trials, narrowed in on writers who
went where I wanted to go, and listened to their accounts of
the characters, language and attitudes in salons or dive bars.

Important side note here – call it a bauble on the research
tree: expressing the cultural attitudes of a different age,
including racism and misogyny, is hard. The danger is you
either sound like you are condoning those opinions, or sneering
about how rubbish people were in the olden days. As always,

the important thing is to take the time to research. Don't rely on stereotypes or what you've picked up from casual reading. Think hard about how those attitudes are expressed or challenged subtly in the contemporary accounts. See how they affect your characters. Use what you have learned so far to try and see the world through their eyes. Find a way to dramatize those attitudes, not just narrate or state them.

Now I have characters, plot, and a clear idea of the material and social worlds my characters are inhabiting. Time to write and complete the picture. The writing is not *quite* the top of the research tree though. There is a star, a big asterisk, to come.

When I start writing a scene I have a decent mental picture of the location where it is taking place, who the characters are, and what I want out of the scene in narrative terms, but I will not have every specific detail of the physical environment at my fingertips. I've learnt not to try. I remember once I thought a character was going to be putting on her boots as she talked to her friends, and before I started writing the scene I spent three frustrating hours finding out exactly what sort of boot and fastenings she'd be wearing. In the actual writing the character ended up not putting them on at all. Damn the woman. Now I've learnt just to follow the characters through the drama, and if I find I am lacking certain details I leave them out – then fill them in as I edit the scene the next writing day. For example, when I'm writing a chase scene through the back streets of Soho, I won't pause every other minute to check the name of the street my character is barrelling down, I'll just put in xx, concentrate on making the writing as good as I am able, then fill in the blanks later. Perhaps the characters are in a loft space in winter, it's cold. As I write the scene it seems proper that one of them puts her hands out to the stove. I know I'll need to see that stove a bit more clearly before I edit, so the next morning I'll go and find out what the stove would have looked like so I can look at it as I work. That might be an hour of research that turns into two words on the page, but if they are the right two words, then the reader will see what I see, and it's worth every second.

That's the star on top of the tree. So be curious, be empathetic, then be specific, and you will take your reader with you to your new world wherever, and whenever, it might be.

Historical Dialogue

L. C. Tyler

To get one point clear from the very beginning: in historical fiction, complete accuracy in dialogue is rarely possible and almost never desirable. Though the challenges of portraying the language of another age vary from period to period, there will always be a trade-off between authenticity and intelligibility.

The English language is, and has always been, in a constant state of change. The way people speak – not only the vocabulary but the rhythm of speech – has changed noticeably, even in my own lifetime. Where we would have once invariably phrased a compliment, 'I love the way you write historical dialogue,' it would now be common to say, 'I'm loving the way you write historical dialogue.' Whereas once you might have written, 'I was sitting beside my editor when they announced I'd won the Historical Dagger,' now people will say, 'I was sat beside my editor, when they announced I'd won the Historical Dagger.' If I flinch at both of these usages, I have to remind myself that a twelfth-century Englishman would flinch at almost everything I say. And everything he said would have sounded as natural – and as modern – to him as our speech does to us.

Let us look briefly at some actual twelfth-century narrative (from Layamon's *Brut* as it happens). 'Ther was Mordred of-slawe and i-don of lif-dawe'. (There was Mordred slain and the days of his life ended.) Here we have a phrase that may be of use to you in describing a twelfth-century crime scene, but I think you'll agree that a little of that sort of thing goes a long way. Too much authenticity in your early medieval dialogue and you'll have lost your readers before the end of the first paragraph. Late medieval is not much better. 'The scharp of the schalk schyndered the bones, and schrank thurgh the schyire grece, and scade hit in twynne' (the sharpness of the steel broke the bones, and sank through the soft flesh and sliced it in two) – not a quote from an early Val McDermid novel, but one of the bloodier bits of *Sir Gawain and the Green Knight*. Moving on to the early modern period, seventeenth-century speech rarely requires translation but still has a very different feel to it from modern English: 'Mrs Smith tells us of the great murder thereabouts, on Saturday last, of one Captain Bumbridge, by one Symons, both of her acquaintance; and hectors that were at play, and in drink: the former is killed, and is kinsman to my Lord of Ormond, which made him speak of it with so much passion, as I overheard him this morning, but could not make anything of it till now, but would they would kill more of them' (Pepys's Diary, 11 January 1668/9). The meaning of each word is clear enough, but the structure is very much of its time. I suspect that, by the end of the passage, you were struggling to see who was under threat of death.

This, then, is the problem. We want to use dialogue to evoke the period in question, add colour and flesh out our characters. We do not wish to send the reader scurrying for a dictionary or having to reread a passage in order to work out who was threatening to kill whom. The primary duty of the crime writer is to tell the story. It is not to teach the reader Middle English. Dialogue needs to be authentic enough to do the job, and no more than that. Moreover, if we wish the reader to see our characters as they would have seen themselves, we don't want them to appear as stuffed exhibits in a museum. We want the reader to identify with and, hopefully, like our characters, not view them as strange antique curiosities.

The solution chosen by most authors is to write historical

dialogue in good standard modern English, avoiding obvious neologisms, and to flavour it with some easily understood words and sentence structures from the period. Here is one example from Lindsey Davis, in a novel set in the seventeenth century (*Rebels and Traitors*):

> 'Nothing to it,' said Lovell. 'You must carry yourself like a fellow who has much gallant farmland of his own – but it is all temporarily entailed on your Anabaptistical second cousin.'

In this passage, the word 'gallant' takes us back nicely to the period – both in terms of its former use and, more subtly, as a reminder that we are in the middle of the Civil War. As a description of the second cousin, 'Anabaptist' would be fine, but 'Anabaptistical' gives even more of a flavour of the rhythm of seventeenth-century speech. One or two words can carry a lot of punch and are often enough.

Two further examples, both from books set in the fourteenth century. The first from Michael Jecks (*The Last Templar*):

> 'I suppose it must've been gone eleven by the time he went. It must've been getting close to the middle watches.'

The second from Susanna Gregory (*A Summer of Discontent*):

> 'No wonder so many Ely folk complain of agues in July and August,' said Bartholomew, taking a deep breath and coughing as the stinking odour caught throat. 'This fetid air must hold all manner of contagions.'

There are only a few words here to show we are in the past – 'the middle watches', 'agues', 'fetid'. But that is the point. It has to be done with a very light hand. The effect should be subtle and cumulative, rather than dumped on the reader in one go with a shovel.

As a warning what can happen if it is overdone, here is an example from Harrison Ainsworth's *Old St Paul's*:

'I cannot permit this, sir,' she cried. 'Your tarrying here
may, for aught I know, bring scandal upon my house. I am
sure it will be disagreeable to my husband. I am unacquainted
with your name and condition. You may be a man of rank.
You may be one of the profane and profligate crew who haunt
the court. You may be the worst of them all, my Lord Rochester
himself.'

This is, arguably, much closer to Pepys's seventeenth-century
English than Lindsey Davis's version, though to me it feels like
nineteenth-century English in fancy dress. You can get away
with a few passages of this sort if you wish (a point I expand
on below) but a whole novel of Ainsworth dialogue would, for
most modern readers, sit heavy on the stomach. It is not to
be recommended.

Historical dialect is another specific problem that the writer
may face. Standard English of a period may be well represented
in text books, and easy to study, but it may be harder to find
genuine written examples of, say, Essex speech in Stuart times.
The solution is usually to make it up, based on modern dialect
and standard English from the period (to the extent that it
existed, of course). This time, I offer up a passage from one
of my own books set in 1657 – the speaker specializes in selling
dead men's clothes, in this instance a doublet and breeches
required as evidence by my protagonist:

'You're lucky as I've still got 'em. I was going to Saffron
Walden Saturday. Sell 'em there. They've cleaned up nice, they
have. Nobody'd know the last owner had his throttle cut. Not
unless you look careful, and hopefully I'll be back here by the
time they do that.'

An accurate enough portrayal of seventeenth-century north
Essex speech? Who could possibly say for certain?

Happy perhaps are the authors of books on Roman or Saxon
England, where it is a question of straight translation into
modern English rather than attempting to imitate the language

of a particular period. At the other extreme, authors of books set in the nineteenth or twentieth centuries can get very close to the exact words and phrasing their characters would have used, without losing any of the sense, though even they still face the problem that narration entirely in authentic Victorian English (say) can come across as awkward and stilted. Complete accuracy could make the book feel like a pastiche, which may not be the writer's aim.

So, in summary, whatever the era you are writing about, be just accurate enough to convey a sense of the period without burdening the reader with too heavy a linguistic load. But that begs a lot of questions.

One difficulty is how you can be sure that you have stripped out all of the obvious neologisms, and how new a word or phrase has to be to disqualify it. My own rule of thumb is that if an expression was current in the first half of the twentieth century (and doesn't describe an object that wasn't actually in existence in the period in question), it's usually acceptable, because it won't immediately strike a discordant note with most readers. Even so, it's as well to err on the side of caution. Remember that words such as fabulous and awful have changed their meaning over the years. Likewise, beware of words such as 'sadism' or 'chauvinism' that are well-known to be derived from a particular person living at a particular time. But as a general rule, familiar, well-established words are OK. I once rejected the word 'loot' from one of my seventeenth-century novels, having discovered that it was not in use in the UK before the eighteenth century, but I am not sure I was right to do so. The replacement word I used was not as good, and in any case pedantry at that level takes more time than most of us have. I would, however, avoid any phrase that is *obviously* from this century or the late twentieth century. I would never have one of my characters, for example, deliver the put-down lines 'As if!' or 'End of.' I would not have any character urge the others on by saying: 'OK, let's do it!' Of course, as with everything, you'll inevitably fail to spot something before you send off the final manuscript and, if you are unlucky, your copy-editor may also let it go by. Rogue phrases are perhaps easier to identify than individual words, but I have caught a highly respected crime writer, whom I greatly admire, having his narrator say 'between a rock and a hard place' some two hundred years before the expression was first coined. (I shall not name him in the hope that he will in turn not point out any of my own historical inaccuracies.)

If the historical period is one you have lived through personally, then you will have an instinctive sense of what is right and what is wrong. If not, then the answer is to read as much as you can that was written in the time you are writing about and get a feeling for the style and for the individual words that were commonly used. After that, if it looks wrong, then it probably is. When in doubt, consult a good dictionary, or one of the more reputable internet sites, as to when a particular word or phrase became current.

In practice I find that I write my historical novels in three slightly different registers. When my protagonist is narrating, he speaks to the reader in something that is quite close to modern English. Dialogue contains more seventeenth-century words and phrases. Finally, with written documents in the book (a poem, a diary entry, a torn fragment of a message, the letter that provides the vital clue), I get quite close to authentic mid-seventeenth-century English, so long as the passage I quote is not so long that it will try the reader's patience. Of course, such is the way of dialogue generally, my characters do not all speak in the same way. My Quaker continues to use 'thou' when all of the other characters say 'you', because they did. My Essex characters use a local word or two (taken from an invaluable nineteenth-century book on Essex dialect) that my London characters don't. Some characters may be addicted to seventeenth-century slang – in *A Cruel Necessity*, Aminta has picked up the expression '*à d'autres*', which, along with other French phrases, was briefly in vogue in the 1650s and '60s. The older characters, of course, raise their eyebrows at the modern way these young people talk.

One final thought: however carefully you construct your

period dialogue, even if you ignore my advice and try for total accuracy, future generations will undoubtedly read what you have written and decide that it is all quaintly twenty-first century, just as the Ainsworth passage feels to me as much nineteenth century as seventeenth, because language will continue to change after us. I'd like to give the last word to Chaucer.

'Ye know ek that in form speech is chaunge
Within a thousand yeer and words tho
That hadden pris, now wonder nice and straunge
Us thinketh hem, and yet thei spake hem so
And spedde as well in love as men do now.'

Humour

'Crime and the comic; at first glance the two seem almost exact opposites', H. R. F. Keating said in *Writing Crime Fiction*, before proceeding to explain how often humour can be a vital component in a crime story. Agatha Christie's talent for humour has often been underestimated, but look at the deft way she pokes fun at jingoistic killers who deride the egotistical foreigner Hercule Poirot or sexist and ageist policemen who scorn the genteel old lady Jane Marple only to receive their just deserts when all is finally revealed.

From the gentle humour of Alexander McCall Smith to the witty wordplay in Reginald Hill's Dalziel and Pascoe series, from the savage irony of Anthony Berkeley's *Trial and Error* and many of Ruth Rendell's novels to the playful comedy often found in Simon Brett's work and the social satire of Julian Symons, Robert Barnard, and Ruth Dudley Edwards, crime writers have long employed humour to entertain readers and, very often, to make serious points about the world we live in.

Humour in crime fiction is often incidental, but even then it can be important to the story. David Williams, a Detection Club member who turned to writing after a highly successful career in advertising, pointed out that the humour in his books was not meant to be digressive or dispensable. A humorous interlude 'often provides a useful way of slipping across an otherwise awkwardly blatant, vital clue'. This method, often used in the past by John Dickson Carr, is a key technique for misdirecting the reader in a 'fair play' detective story.

Humour and Human Nature
Alexander McCall Smith

What's funny about crime? Nothing, really. Crime, especially
homicide – the central concern of most crime novelists – is a
tawdry business. There is no romance in the criminal law, even
if it provides fascinating intellectual challenges. For many years
I taught criminal law at a university and I took great pleasure
in teasing out some of the theoretical problems that it raised.
I often felt, though, a certain guilt at taking such an interest
in matters that were ultimately based on deeply distressing
human failings. In the real world, all crime has a human victim
– somebody whose life is disrupted and even wrecked by the
wrongful acts of another. It's difficult to see the humour there;
and yet, and yet . . .

Criminal lawyers often have a great sense of humour, just
as doctors do. You have to have that in order to survive daily
exposure to human nature's worst features. So crime, for all
its bleakness, can have its moments of humour, and these, for
the crime novelist, can be fertile ground. A good example of a
potentially humorous situation is the difference between aspi-
ration and achievement. Criminals are often not the brightest
of people. There may be smart operators who get away with
it – Patricia Highsmith's Tom Ripley is a fine example of that
sort – but for the most part those who commit a crime, and
get caught, have not thought out the odds nor been too clever
about the *modus*. So we get bank robbers who pass a threat
across the counter and then engage in a discussion with the
teller about the spelling or the grammar – I think Woody Allen
used such a device in one of his films. Or we get the burglar
who signs himself into the building, using his real name. Or,
and this seems almost too stupid to be credible, the thieves

who post pictures of themselves on Facebook – with the proceeds of the theft beside them.

The law reports are a fertile source of such incidents. I used to refer my criminal law students to what was known as 'the case of parking on the copper's foot'. What happened there was that a person inadvertently parked his car on a police officer's foot. When the police officer remonstrated with him, the driver did not move his car, but allowed the car to remain where it was, thus exposing himself to a charge of assault. The court put it in a somewhat amusing way, declaring that the accused had allowed himself to be in contact with the officer's foot through the medium of the car, and that this justified an assault conviction. The law reports are littered with such amusing, and sometimes absurd, instances of legal reasoning being used to justify the conviction of defendants who themselves are using every tactic to avoid obviously justified conviction. That dance between perpetrator and justice is often an amusing thing to witness.

I have written a number of novels of detection (in a very loose sense) set in Botswana. I also wrote a textbook on the criminal law of that country, and I have certainly taken inspiration from the research that I did for that. Trawling through the unpublished judgements of the High Court of Botswana I came across a number of cases that had a humorous side to them and that could be used in fiction. One, in particular, I used for an incident in the first volume of *The No 1 Ladies' Detective Agency* series. This involved a prosecution for culpable homicide on the grounds of negligence, the defendant being a minister of religion. He had taken seven new members of his flock to be baptized in the Limpopo River. It was a full immersion baptism, and the sinners (as I imagine they were described) were led into the river by the minister, with, I imagine, the appropriate accompaniment of hymns. Seven sinners went in, but only six emerged, a large crocodile having taken one of them. The result was the prosecution of the minister for negligent homicide in immersing his converts in a crocodile-infested river. Such events are, of course, tragedies for somebody, but it takes some effort to keep a straight face when recounting them.

So crime novels can be funny. They are about human nature, and human nature will always have its humorous side. And even *noir* can be lightened a bit with the odd humorous touch – with a focus on the quirks of the detective, for example. The genre itself, its conventions and expectations, may also be sent up, although that must be done carefully. Ultimately the author must respect the fact that what the reader wants is crime and its solution. That lies at the heart of the crime novel even if it can be decorated with pathos, romance, reflection, and a good dose of humour. So the detective may trip up over shoelaces or make ridiculous mistakes, but ultimately he or she is the hero or heroine and must get there in the end.

Character and Caricature

Robert Barnard

My books over the years have almost all been humorous in intention: darkly so in *Mothers' Boys*, more boisterous in *Political Suicide*. They are all more or less ironic in style, and they are populated by grotesques. The exception is *Out of the Blackout*, which I loved writing because the idea had grabbed me so irresistibly, though as it turned out I had considerable difficulty in finding an appropriate style for it. No doubt I shall return to the serious vein now and again in the future. Unremitting irony can get as tiresome for the writer as for the reader.

I do not apologize for the caricature nature of almost all my characterizations. Caricature is the basis of the humorous novel, from Fielding to early Waugh. Quite often I have stolen my pale shadows from those great masters, and in *Unruly Son* I cribbed the central figure from Waugh himself. The playwright

Joe Orton's mother, as described in John Lahr's *Prick Up Your Ears*, was the spark that ignited *Mother's Boys* (one of my favourite books, though my English editor dearly wanted to reject it on the grounds that matricide was not only repulsive – it simply didn't happen). The Sitwells and the Mitfords lie behind, though a good way behind, *Sheer Torture*. It will be seen that in life, as in literature, I like and admire grotesques and eccentrics, and listen avidly on buses and trains (no true writer ought willingly to travel by car) for conversations that reveal new depths of oddity or sheer dreadfulness.

The advantage of caricatures for the writer of the traditional whodunit are obvious. He has to establish a fair number of suspects, and establish them unequivocally in readers' minds; while leaving much of their natures unrevealed. A few broadly sketched characteristics of person or speech are invaluable. A caricature is essentially a shell, a performance. What is behind it is a mystery; its inner life is the subject of guesswork. A notable critic of Dickens has remarked how terrifying it would be to be admitted to the inner life of Mr Pecksniff, though acquaintance with the outer shell of the man is consistently delightful. So it should be with potential suspects in a detective story. The moment the writer enters my suspect's thoughts, the alert reader sits up: Is he cheating? Is he being deliberately ambiguous? Is he telling the whole truth? Could a murderer, so soon after his crime, think about *anything* without the murder obtruding? Such thoughts are often rather alienating. Best merely to *suggest* an inner life beneath the carapace of the public personality, and to use those suggestions when the time for a solution arrives.

Ian Rankin has already discussed the role of satire in crime fiction and on a similar note, in the mid-1990s, he floated the fascinating suggestion that 'at root all crime writers are satirists', quoting Muriel

Spark's argument, in a 1971 address, that 'the only effective art of our particular time is the satirical' and that given the rhetoric of that period, artists should 'contemplate the ridiculous nature of the reality before us'. Ian wondered if even the so-called 'cosy' detective novel was essentially a satirical form, 'deconstructing the most quintessential English values'. He noted, 'Though at the end of the book the status quo may be intact, it's been given a bloody good shake-up between times.' And the force of this argument is underlined when we reflect that several leading pioneers of Golden Age detective fiction, Anthony Berkeley, Ronald Knox, and A. A. Milne, all wrote humorous pieces for *Punch* when the magazine was in its heyday.

Whatever period one lives in, whatever the rhetoric of the day, there is scope for pungent satire. The crime story, as Ruth Dudley Edwards has often shown, is as good a vehicle for satirizing the absurdities of life as any.

Humour and Satire
Ruth Dudley Edwards

I agreed to contribute something on how to write comic crime and then found that when it came to dispensing practical advice, I was foxed. Seeing the funny side of things is a prerequisite for the job, and that isn't like learning a foreign language or taking up knitting. It has to be acquired in childhood.

So, with apologies, here are the mostly unhelpful tips I've come up with after thinking about why I'm on that that particular path.

Tip 1. Choose the right parents
My parents were Irish, but my father's English father had passed on to him a belief that unless you could laugh at

yourself you didn't have a sense of humour, and my mother's love of literary comedy was multicultural: she was as amused by Damon Runyon as she was by Evelyn Waugh and Flann O'Brien.

Tip 2. Secure the optimum place in the sibling pecking order

My sister was nine years my senior and my brother six, so mealtimes at home were full of debate, argument and the retailing of stories or the mocking of sacred cows, and I was frantic to understand what was going on. It was the early stage of my lifelong affliction with FOMO (Fear of Missing Out), which Wikipedia explains is 'a pervasive apprehension that others might be having rewarding experiences from which one is absent'. It's even worse if you're present but ill-equipped to join in.

It wasn't so bad when they were fighting about what seemed boring subjects like politics, but it was agonizing when they were laughing and I couldn't see why. At the age of five, every day I read the funnies in the newspaper and drove my brother crazy with questions like: 'What's the joke in *Blondie*?' – an unfunny strip about a suburban American family that bore no similarities whatsoever to mine. But I persevered and gradually began to get some of the one-liners and the point of some of the mocking anecdotes, many of which concerned academic colleagues of my father's, teaching colleagues of my mothers and, in the case of my brother, included parodies of sermons. My fate was sealed as my appetite for humour increased.

Tip 3. Have a misspent youth

I wasn't one of those children who desperately wanted to be a writer: I was one of those children who desperately wanted to be allowed to stay at home from school and read all day. In pursuit of this ambition I used to fake or exaggerate illness and I still feel a deep shame that in my early teens I worried my mother for months with mysterious undiagnosable fake headaches and occasional pretend faints. However, this gave me more time to make decent inroads into the lighter ends of the thousands of books that dominated the family home.

Besides, my criminality was to some considerable extent my mother's fault, since she had taught me to read long before I went to school, which meant consigning me to years of excruciating boredom as they taught me what I already knew instead of letting me sit at the back reading stories. Until my mid-teens, what I borrowed from my mother's and siblings' shelves – apart from English and American school stories – was primarily comedy or crime.

My mother was a fine practitioner of black Irish humour. When I was unmysteriously sick with childhood ailments, she read to me as a special treat nineteenth-century novels about Elsie Dinsmore, an irritating child of great piety who grew up on her father's plantation in the American South, initially cruelly persecuted because she put her Christian principles before his various ungodly demands, such as that she play secular music on a Sunday. Ultimately she converted him and everyone became pious. Mother could find fun in the most serious crises and sad occasions and the great Victorian tragic line – 'Dead! Dead! And never called me Mother!' – became family shorthand for grandstanding.

As I became fixated on comedy. I developed a lifelong passion for Richmal Crompton's priceless William Brown (of *Just William* fame), an anarchist who believed in living life to the full and despised and saw off the pretentious, the hysterical, the dreary, the patronising, the bullying, the snobbish, the self-important and many other kinds of deplorables in his English suburban world. And then I couldn't get enough of my mother's favourites, Stephen Leacock, James Thurber, Dorothy Parker, Robert Benchley, Leo Rosten, O. Henry, Saki and all the other usual suspects. Above all, there was the Great God P. G. Wodehouse, who bestrode our family intellectual collective like a colossus – sweeping up even my profoundly academic father who read little fiction – and was the source of endless quotes introduced with 'Do you remember when Bertie/Jeeves/Gussie Fink-Nottle/Madeline Bassett/Lord

Emsworth/Gally Threepwood/the Efficient Baxter/Psmith did X, Y or Z?'

Googling just now for family favourites, I was spoiled for choice: 'It is never difficult to distinguish between a Scotsman with a grievance and a ray of sunshine' (which became nationally popular in the UK during the prime ministership of the grim-faced Gordon Brown); 'Like so many substantial citizens of America, he had married young and kept on marrying, springing from blonde to blonde like the chamois of the Alps leaping from crag to crag'; 'on the occasions when Aunt is calling Aunt like mastodons bellowing across primeval swamps'; 'He looked haggard and careworn, like a Borgia who has suddenly remembered that he has forgotten to shove cyanide in the consommé, and the dinner gong due at any moment'; and the immortal exchange, 'There are moments, Jeeves, when one asks oneself, 'Do trousers matter?' 'The mood will pass, sir.'

Tip 4. It's the way that you tell them
I aspired to be funny but I couldn't compete at home and was too precocious for my contemporaries. I once went home triumphant at having seen on a public lavatory a poster from a Bible society from Matthew's gospel saying 'Come unto me and I will give you rest' and was crushed by my siblings' failure to find the way I relayed it funny. But becoming a university groupie in my mid-teens and listening to gifted speakers and hecklers in the debating society taught me something about what amuses people and what bores them. Timing, as with so much else, is all.

Tip 5: Nothing is sacred
What in retrospect I realize is that my enduring love for Wodehouse and Crompton would cause me to become the kind of crime writer I did. Both eschewed sentimentality or mawkishness and were irreverent and subversive. They laughed at everybody from tramps to the aristocracy. Vicars, writers, poets, intellectuals, dimwits, actors, policemen, teachers, spiritualists, people of all classes, communists, fascists and ideologues of

any kind were a source of mirth. There was nothing and nobody that you couldn't ridicule, including the dead. 'It was a confusion of ideas between him and one of the lions he was hunting in Kenya,' begins one of my favourite Wodehouse quotes, 'that had caused A. B. Spottsworth to make the obituary column. He thought the lion was dead, and the lion thought it wasn't.'

So it was no surprise that I approached crime fiction in the same spirit. Yes, I read all of Sherlock Holmes and the Golden Age authors my mother adored, and many were engrossing mysteries that never raised a smile. But I took the greatest pleasure in those that made me laugh, particularly those witty maestros Edmund Crispin and Michael Innes, especially when they made fun of academics. But there was wit aplenty to be found in the likes of Leo Bruce, who so brilliantly parodied Lord Peter Wimsey, Hercule Poirot and Father Brown in *Case for Three Detectives*, and indeed in a vast array of writers that I came to love who were as different as Raymond Chandler, Rex Stout and later my dear friend Reginald Hill. None was a respecter of persons.

Tip 6. Be kind to your ex-husband

My number one husband had had a difficult divorce second time around and rang me every day for solace. When all was resolved and he had met the lovely woman who was to be his third wife, he wanted to give me a thankyou present. Having been hired to set up a crime list at a small publishers he said he would commission me if I just sent him a brief outline. I had abandoned my job in the public service to be a full-time writer by then, but my beat was history, so I said 'Don't be silly, Patrick,' only to be reminded that I had idled my time away at school and university reading crime fiction and therefore counted as a crime buff. Being perennially hard up I took the bait: having embarked on what I thought was a conventional story, I found to my surprise that *Corridors of Death* was turning into a satire on the civil service department I had worked in. The murder weapon, for instance, was a sculpture with the title *Reconciliation*.

Tip 7. Choose your friends wisely

I have been blessed in my friends since my late teens, and with very few exceptions, the closest were all people who were short on self-pity, found much to laugh about and were creative in the art of discreet character assassination of ghastly people. Choosing contemporaries to send to a desert island has been one of our joyous games and an inspiration when I've been developing characters. We also rejoiced in making fun of each other and I was allowed open season on borrowing and exaggerating some of their characteristics, like Gordon's propensity to cover himself with snuff, James's paranoia about germs, and Paul's pedantry. Old friends and new have also been invaluable in providing me with inspiration and information, for *Corridors of Death* was well received and turned into a series. Gradually I became a satirist of the British establishment, which I knew reasonably well, for after leaving Ireland I experienced Cambridge University, a nationalized industry and the civil service, wrote books about the publisher Victor Gollancz (who had a wonderful crime list), the Economist magazine, and the Foreign Office, and made friendships in various respected institutions.

One of the many virtues of the English that has contributed to the stability of its society has been a long tradition of enjoying mockery of their betters. Think of the *Carry On* films. I never had any problems in finding pillars of the establishment to help me ridicule their institutions. My targets included gentlemen's clubs, Cambridge, the House of Lords, the Church of England, publishing, literary prizes, the Anglo-Irish peace process, and conceptual art. Along the way, I lampooned at every opportunity the political correctness infecting society, including a foray into Indiana college life in *Murdering Americans*. However, the absurdity of identity politics has caused me grief, for it is hard to satirize the unsatirizable.

Tip 8. Write it however you like, but do it

I have absolutely no suggestions as to how you should go about actually writing a novel. I have crime-writing friends who plot out every detail and some who are determined to get every last detail right, while I just decide where it is set and who is the first victim and then set off and see what happens. There is one rule, however: to be a crime writer you actually have to write a crime novel, so stop talking about it and sit down and do it.

Tip 9. Ignore the sensitive

I spent an hour once, in a queue in Toronto trying to register for the enormous crime festival that is Bouchercon, next to a bookseller who told me that she had had complaints from fellow-lesbians that I was a homophobe because of the lesbian couple I ridiculed in one of my novels. We got on fine otherwise though, and being fair-minded, she bought one, read it that night, came down to breakfast and said, 'It's OK. You're offensive to everybody.'

I don't care when people complain. It's quite simple. If you don't like it, don't read it.

Tip 10. Do it for the fun of it as there's no money

Crime writers are a broad church despite vast variations in our politics and our attitudes to violence. I am at what Reg Hill described as the Jane Austen end of the spectrum, while knowing that what sells these days is horror, gore, torture porn and gratuitous sex – all of which I hate. On comic crime panels, with friends like fellow *Howdunit* contributors Simon Brett and Len Tyler, we bemoan the fact that – with a very few exceptions – comic crime sells badly, doesn't translate, and is sniffed at when it comes to major prizes. But we take pleasure in knowing that we make people happy rather than give them nightmares. If you write torture porn, you might be chary of being in a room alone with the fan. We know that ours are lovely, share our sense of humour, and are a joy to meet. That's better than money.

In Short

The short crime story is an artistically rewarding form, so much so that despite its challenges, most crime writers find themselves unable to resist giving it a try. A short story offers the chance of a change of pace, and perhaps of subject and style. It may enable you to take a break from routine in between novels – a way of recharging the batteries before you embark on another full-length book.

Writing a short story is not, however, an easy option. If you try it simply because it seems easier to tackle than a novel, you're likely to be disappointed. It makes sense to read the great short stories (not just in the crime genre) and ask yourself what makes them great. It's also worth considering what effect you want the story to have upon the reader, and how you might achieve it. An arresting opening is a plus, and so is an ending that leaves the reader with a sense of satisfaction. In between the beginning and the end, don't waste a word.

Because most writers invest far less time in a short story than in a novel, you may be tempted to experiment in a way that might simply be too risky with a longer work of fiction. A failed attempt to write a different kind of novel may mean that you've sacrificed a year or more of your literary career. A rejected short story might only mean writing off the effort of a few days or weeks. In any case, you may be able to recycle the material effectively: for an author, nothing need be wasted.

Experiments sometimes result in striking success. In 'Don't Look

Behind You' by the American Fredric Brown, the reader of the story
is the criminal's victim; in Peter Lovesey's 'Youdunnit', the reader
is the culprit; in Reginald Hill's 'The Rio de Janeiro Paper', an
academic address turns into a confession of murder. The possibilities are as endless as your imagination. Recent years have seen
the publication of crime short stories composed, for instance, from
an extract from a book index; a set of acknowledgements in a book;
a set of expense receipts; and a series of tweets.

A short story may inspire a novel, or even a series. Reginald
Hill's short story about the private eye Joe Sixsmith preceded five
books about the character. When wondering whether to write a
novel set in the 1930s featuring an unorthodox female protagonist,
Rachel Savernake, I produced a short story about the character,
simply to see if I enjoyed writing about her. I found I did, and so
rather than try to publish the short story, I proceeded to write a
novel about Rachel, *Gallows Court*, and then another, *Mortmain
Hall* . . .

Of course, you don't need to break fresh ground. You might opt
to write a short story of psychological suspense or borrow the voice
of Dr Watson to join the hundreds of authors who have dabbled in
Sherlockian pastiche. Whatever type of short mystery you write,
you'll be following in a long tradition. It's often forgotten that detective fiction *began* with short stories rather than novels. Edgar Allan
Poe's 'The Murders in the Rue Morgue' posed a locked-room mystery
solved by the first fictional Great Detective, Chevalier C. Auguste
Dupin. Poe's other tales set templates (the story based on a real life
crime; the story in which the obvious answer proves to be correct;
the story based around a cipher; the story in which the 'least likely
person' is the culprit) that countless other writers in the genre have
followed. Sherlock Holmes' greatest cases were almost all recorded
in short stories, while Chesterton's Father Brown appeared in more
than fifty short stories, but not a single novel.

It was only after the First World War that the novel became the
dominant form in the genre. Paying markets for short mystery
stories declined, and that decline came to seem irreversible. In 1956,
the three Detection Club members (Josephine Bell, Michael Gilbert,
and Julian Symons) who edited the first anthology of fiction to

appear under the aegis of the CWA expressed their fear that the future of the short crime story was 'bleak'. Writing thirty years later, Harry Keating said that he was tempted to make his advice about writing short stories 'just one word – Don't'.

Against all the odds, the short crime story has survived. The CWA has for many years given an award, now known as the Short Story Dagger, for the best short story of the year, and in 2014 introduced the CWA Margery Allingham Prize, which is open to published and unpublished authors from all over the world. The judges take into account the extent to which the entries comply with Margery Allingham's definition of what makes a successful story: 'The Mystery remains box-shaped, at once a prison and a refuge. Its four walls are, roughly, a Crime, a Mystery, an Enquiry and a Conclusion with an Element of Satisfaction in it.' There are plenty of other competitions for short-story writers, usually funded by charging an entry fee.

The CWA has now published an anthology of members' work almost every year for more than six decades, and most of them focus on freshly written material. Other anthologies are published quite frequently, often but not always by relatively small independent presses. There is a wider range of markets for short stories in the United States. They include *Ellery Queen's Mystery Magazine*, which has published high-calibre work for more than three-quarters of a century, its stablemate *Alfred Hitchcock's Mystery Magazine*, and a glossy modern-day publication bearing a famous name, the *Strand Magazine*. In Britain, few print magazines offer space for short mysteries, but online sites offer an increasing amount of space to short crime stories, although payment (if any) is usually modest.

The challenges posed by the crime short story, and the opportunities the form offers, continue to excite writers. Countless members of the Detection Club have excelled at them, and the Club's recent anthology *Motives for Murder* included no fewer than four stories that were nominated for the CWA Short Story dagger, including the eventual winner.

Among Club members of the past, Roy Vickers was a prolific novelist over the course of four decades, but is best remembered as a master of the 'inverted' detective story, in which the reader

sees the crime being committed before the detective gets to work;
this form, invented by R. Austin Freeman before the First World
War, is most famously associated with the TV series *Columbo*.
Vickers' stories about Scotland Yard's Department of Dead Ends
include some classics of the genre, and these observations about
short stories come from his preface to the CWA anthology *Some
Like Them Dead* – a title suggested, according to Michael Gilbert,
by none other than Raymond Chandler.

Let's Pretend

Roy Vickers

There are no rules. But common sense and experience reveal
the existence of certain principles. The crime story is an art
form and therefore begins with an invitation: 'Let's pretend
. . .' We know that our social acquaintances do not commit
murder – except sometimes in their hearts. We invite you to
pretend that one of them carries his wishful thinking into action
– and off we go. But common sense indicates that we must not
extend that invitation a second time in the same story. Once
you have agreed to play, we must present you with a sequence
of events which you will accept as logically inevitable.

Thus, a problem story may include trickery by the villain,
but not by the author. In a whodunit, the suspects must exhibit
some trait of character to justify suspicion, beyond the accident
of time and place. A thriller must be reasonably accurate in
the matter of physical possibility – pocketable revolvers must
not be used as if they were precision rifles – and no situation
should be saved by chance.

On the other hand, the short story should not assume the
function of a documentary of police and legal procedure – you
require no general information which is not essential to the

human drama. Nor need it be hampered by the recorded behaviour of real-life criminals. Crime fiction owes virtually nothing to the real criminal – he cannot be used by an author in a manner comparable with that in which a painter uses a living model. For one thing, we are not on intimate terms with any more real murderers than you are. Like you, we are dependent upon the reports of trials – and these give only a foreshortened picture in which characterization has no place.

Some ideas seem better suited to development in a short story than in a novel. A holiday trip, for instance, may give you enough insight and information into an unfamiliar place to set a short story there, even if you lack the in-depth knowledge to sustain a full-length novel in that setting.

Despite his reservations about short stories, Harry Keating enjoyed taking advantage of the form's potential for variety. His best-loved detective, Inspector Ghote, appeared in short stories as well as novels, and he also wrote a series of stories about Mrs Craggs, a cleaning lady with a penchant for amateur detection, Sherlockian pastiches, and stand-alones. In his guide to the tech-niques of writing short stories, he recalled that his first short story won second prize in a competition run by *Ellery Queen's Mystery Magazine*, a success he attributed to the fact that 'its subject and setting were limited . . . But otherwise it had all the ingredients of a detective novel, down to a theme, the passion for justice.'

Switch-overs in Short Stories

H. R. F. Keating

Crime short stories . . . present a challenge to the writer. So, despite poor rewards, even the ultimate poor reward of death in the ever-shut drawer, they get written.

Yet their nature has, on the whole, changed. Detective short stories are still produced, but they have been thrust firmly into second place, both in the minds of writers and readers, by the crime short story. This, to use a definition of the American, Stanley Ellin, one of the writers to have given us short stories to equal any that have been written since crime and the short story met (read his 'The Speciality of the House'), is any story so long as it deals with 'that streak of wickedness in human nature' . . .

So much for the subject. But what about the way that the subject, that streak of wickedness, is handled? Let's hear from Stan Ellin again. He is talking this time of the short stories of Guy de Maupassant, only a few of which can perhaps be seized on as crime short stories before their time. Ellin says that he could tell even as a sixteen-year-old that 'here was a writer who reduced stories to their absolute essence' and, he adds, the ending of each de Maupassant story is, when you think about it, 'as inevitable as doom'.

Two tough precepts to follow. But they should be aimed at if you are writing in short story form the equivalent of the crime novel. Happily, there are what the ski people call 'nursery slopes'. There is a type of short story in crime fiction which does not make the highest demands on its writers, though it is not as easy as the gentlest of ski runs.

This is what I have called, in reviewing, the switch-over story. It is perhaps hardly more than an anecdote, generally quite short in length, in which towards the end the reader, who has been gently led along one seemingly well-defined path, is suddenly switched into seeing the situation in quite a different light . . .

A switch-over type of story can be written by doing what I have counselled writers of full-length detective stories not to do: by slipping in a tiny clue in the hope that readers will miss it. In this anecdotal kind of story the device is, on the whole, pleasing to the reader, even after being caught out by it, and so it is permissible. It might take the form of one small spelling mistake or an Americanism coming from someone stated as not being American or a supposedly deaf person repeating a quietly spoken remark; anything on those lines . . .

Where the detective short story had as its object the displaying of an act of detection, the crime short story or suspense short story has as its object to put a person or persons into danger and give a revelation to one or more people, be they the perpetrator of a crime, its victim or simply a witness. Where in the detective short story ingenuity was, in principle, the only quality called for, in the crime short story ingenuity has to be at the service of imagination. I say 'in principle' because, life being what it is, there are many occasions when it is impossible to say whether a story is a pure detection affair or one partaking of more of the crime element.

Among these borderline cases will come the short-story version of the inverted detective story we have already looked at, the story where the murderer is known to the reader from the outset and the pleasure lies in seeing how, inadvertently, he betrays himself, or she herself. Again, because of the shorter distance between premise and fulfilment, the inverted story at short length can be more pleasure-giving than in the more difficult book-length form. But otherwise all the rules for writing it apply, in miniature.

The same goes, too, for locked-room stories. At a length of between 2,000 and 5,000 words these are highly satisfying: at 60,000 words they can become tediously frivolous. Much the same comment can be applied to comic crime. Although in the hands of a master like Donald E. Westlake the full-length comic crime story can dazzle for 70,000 words or more, at the hands of a less expert practitioner the very repetition of good or goodish jokes can become fatiguing to the reader. Not so at the short story length, where humour can be used more gain-fully to put over the perhaps dull facts needed to lay out a situation leading to an ingenious switch-over ending.

Fiction and Fact

Crime fiction is very different from 'true crime' writing, but there has always been a close connection between fictional murder mysteries and events and people in real life, including actual murder cases. Fictionalizing fact is not, however, always straightforward. Peter Lovesey, an accomplished exponent of the art, examines the pros and cons.

Fictionalizing Characters and Crimes from Real Life

Peter Lovesey

Real-life crime has inspired fiction writers from the beginning. The father of the crime story, Edgar Allan Poe, based his 1842 detective story, 'The Mystery of Marie Rogêt', on the true case of Mary Rogers, a New York beauty whose body had been recovered from the Hudson River only the year before. Poe's interpretation of the facts, voiced through his sleuth, C. Auguste Dupin, and given a new setting in Paris, made an absorbing murder mystery out of a tragedy which, it later emerged, may

well have been more prosaic. The case officially remains
unsolved, but a deathbed confession declared that Mary Rogers
died as the result of a botched abortion and an attempt was
made to cover up the crime by disposing of her body in the
river. Whatever the truth, the innovative Poe used reality as a
creative spur.

Thousands of us since have drawn on true crime in a variety
of ways to bring extra authenticity to our writing. Some of the
most successful mysteries ever written originated with real
criminals, crimes and detectives: Robert Bloch's *Psycho* and
Thomas Harris's *The Silence of the Lambs* were both inspired
– for want of a better word – by the monstrous conduct of the
serial murderer Ed Gein; Stieg Larsson's *The Girl with the
Dragon Tattoo* by the unsolved murder of prostitute Catrine da
Costa; and James Ellroy's *The Black Dahlia* by another unsolved
killing, of Elizabeth Short. Agatha Christie used the kidnapping
of the Lindbergh baby as the core of the plot, thinly disguised,
of *Murder on the Orient Express*. It is well known that Sir
Arthur Conan Doyle based the deductive methods of Sherlock
Holmes on Dr Joseph Bell; and in the genre of espionage, John
Le Carré revealed that John Bingham, his former boss in MI5,
was a main inspiration for George Smiley.

True crime is generally regarded as a separate genre from
the novel, but one case in 1923, the Bywaters and Thompson
murder, became such a *cause célèbre* that it motivated writers
to tell the story in fiction. The lovers were brought to trial for
the murder of Edith Thompson's husband and although
Bywaters did the stabbing, Edith was found guilty of inciting
him in her love letters and both were hanged. E. M. Delafield's
Messalina of the Suburbs appeared the next year, identified by
all reviewers as a retelling of the case with changed names.
In 1930 the story was given a different treatment by Dorothy
L. Sayers and Robert Eustace in *The Documents in the Case*,
telling it through letters, telegrams, statements and press reports
and devising an original murder method, but this experimental approach failed to grip to the end. If nothing else, it
demonstrated that members of the Detection Club were not

wholly taken up with middle-class murders solved by eccentric amateur detectives. For me, the most successful novel inspired by Bywaters and Thompson was F. Tennyson Jesse's *A Pin to See the Peepshow* in 1934.

More recently, getting into the head of the accused was taken a stage further by Martin Edwards in his novel of Hawley Harvey Crippen, *Dancing for the Hangman*. Written in the first person as if by the condemned man himself in Pentonville Prison, the novel is an extended letter to his solicitor in hope of securing an appeal. Cold facts and fresh insights converge as Crippen tells the story of his marriage and its fatal outcome in a persuasive apologia that presents a different reading of the flawed, pathetic man whose name unjustly became a byword for cold-hearted killing.

The ultimate example of reality deployed in fiction is Truman Capote's *In Cold Blood,* proclaimed by Capote himself in a 1966 *Paris Review* interview with George Plimpton as 'a serious new art form, the "nonfiction novel"'. The book was six years in the making and based on numerous interviews with the main protagonists. The names were not changed, nor any of the details of the killing of four members of a Kansas family. The narrative drive never flags, from the back stories to the murders to the trial and the aftermath. The writing technique blends journalism and fictional devices, such as dialogue between the killers, in a convincing way. Capote, who was not known for self-effacement, kept himself scrupulously out of the book. It works equally well as a novel and non-fiction and was indisputably a breakthrough in the crime genre. For anyone wanting to create a realistic crime novel driven by suspense, *In Cold Blood* should be prescribed reading.

By now you may be thinking that six years of research is more than you are prepared to devote to the making of a novel. Truman Capote was already an established writer, with the success of *Breakfast at Tiffany's* providing confidence and a good income. Moreover, the effort of writing *In Cold Blood* must have been huge; after it, he never wrote another novel.

For most of us, it is enough if real crime can be used to

spark our creativity. Show a short newspaper report of a bank robbery to a class of students and ask them to set their imaginations to work and you get an amazing spectrum of results, from caper stories to heart-stopping suspense. Most of us have our own store of memories to draw on. My house was destroyed by a bomb during the Second World War at a time when I had just discovered the magic of reading. My parents had other priorities than buying books and when eventually I found one that may have been salvaged from the bombsite it was a battered copy of *The Life of Sir Edward Marshall Hall*, by Edward Marjoribanks. Not a promising title for a ten-year-old. But Marshall Hall had been the great advocate of the early years of the twentieth century, involved in such sensational trials as the 'Brides in the Bath', the 'Green Bicycle case' and the shooting of Prince Ali Fahmy in the Savoy Hotel. The power of Marjoribanks' writing and the fascination of the crimes gripped my imagination and certainly influenced me when I eventually became a writer myself.

Whenever possible in my Sergeant Cribb series about the Victorian police, I would get back to contemporary sources, spending many hours in the British Library's newspaper collection (this was forty years before much of it was digitised) checking on reports of crimes and trials. On a chance visit to a secondhand bookshop I was lucky enough to find *The Police Code*, by Sir Howard Vincent, the first Director of the CID, an encyclopaedia of policing covering everything from *A* for *Abandoned Children* to *W* for *Wrecking*. My first novel, *Wobble to Death*, was about murder during a six-day 'go-as-you-please' race at the Agricultural Hall, Islington, a vast building which by 1969 had become the Post Office sorting centre for overseas parcels. I talked my way in there and visualized the runners endlessly circling the track. I didn't think of it as research, but as a story coming alive in my imagination. My first piece of advice to anyone wishing to lend reality to fiction hardly needs stating: don't just check your source material – immerse yourself in it. These days the internet is a marvellous aid, but if possible get close-up. Visit your scene of crime, make notes and take photos. Every detail will become more real for you and will emerge in your writing.

Later in my career, I tested my mental agility in an exercise that any crime writer might find helpful, by speculating how a convicted criminal might have got away with the crime if he had planned it better. For *The False Inspector Dew*, I chose the case already mentioned of Dr Crippen, who poisoned his wife Cora and buried her in the cellar prior to trying to make his escape by ship to Canada with his mistress, Ethel Le Neve. Famously the couple were recognized and caught. Some lateral thinking came into play when I thought about Crippen's biggest error, the disposal of the body. I recalled the 1947 Gay Gibson case, when a ship's steward, James Camb, was convicted of murdering a young actress and pushing her through a porthole. The body was never found.

What if Crippen had invited his wife on the sea trip, murdered her early in the voyage, pushed the corpse through a porthole and then been joined by Ethel, who had stowed away and would pretend to be Mrs Crippen? This was the premise. I changed the names and, with a sense of irony, my protagonist fixed on the name of Crippen's nemesis, Inspector Dew, as his fake identity. This led to complications I must resist going into in case you read the book.

This brings me to a second piece of advice: look for creative ways of using real crime to stimulate your writing. You need not be constrained by the facts if you dress them up as fiction. Make the necessary changes of detail and you're at liberty to play with the plot because you are in charge.

But how much liberty should you take?

What do the following have in common, apart from the fact that they're all dead: Aristotle, Leonardo da Vinci, Queen Elizabeth I, Groucho Marx, and Elvis Presley? The answer is that they have all been put to work as crime solvers in detective novels. These examples are from memory, and an internet search will provide many more, surely above a hundred. Enough, I suggest, to make the celebrity sleuth a sub-species of fictional detective. But is it ethical? Allowing that you can't libel the dead, is any famous individual from the past fair game for some sleuthing? I'd better declare an interest and admit that I've taken the liberty myself with three books about Bertie, the Prince of Wales before he became King Edward VII; taken considerable liberties, in fact, because I made him an enthusiastic but inept amateur detective.

I must also confess that I can be offended when discovering that a favourite from my personal pantheon of heroes has been used or abused in this way by a fellow crime writer. If someone made a sleuth of Thomas Hardy or Edith Piaf, I wouldn't go near the book. However affectionate and true to life the portrayal might be, I would see it as trivializing the great, and I daresay most readers would agree that there are limits. So any writer about to hand a notebook and a magnifying glass to a real person should be aware that this may have a backlash. Numbers of potential readers will not be persuaded that this is a legitimate practice.

How did this aberration start? The earliest examples I'm familiar with are Lillian de la Torre's thirty-three short stories about Dr Sam Johnson, Detector. By her own account in *Twentieth Century Crime and Mystery Writers*, 'I began 'histo-detecting' for fun in 1942 when I was inspired to write mystery fiction featuring as a "detector" Dr Johnson, the real eighteenth-century lexicographer and sage, narrated by his biographer the fascinating rake, James Boswell . . . The mysteries, characters and settings are real but the solutions only rarely make any pretence of being other than fiction.'

De la Torre's innovation was brave, bold and stylish. You could say that everything about Johnson, from his life history to his mannerisms of speech, had been decided for her, but this wasn't necessarily an advantage. Anything that didn't chime with Boswell's version was liable to show. She took care to use eighteenth-century phraseology, idiom, and spelling, and she earned the loyalty of readers and the respect of reviewers.

Whether influenced by De la Torre or not, other crime writers were soon experimenting with detectives from real life. In 1949 the Dutch sinologist Robert van Gulik translated a book of

true-crime stories about an investigating T'ang dynasty magistrate, Di Renjie, and was encouraged to develop Judge Dee as
a fictional sleuth: three cases encapsulated in a single novel in
the Chinese tradition. Many more Judge Dee novels and short
stories followed over the next seventeen years.

The prolific and versatile John Dickson Carr was also one
of the first to dabble with a real-life sleuth in a 1950 short
story, 'The Gentleman from Paris', but as naming the gentleman
would be a spoiler, I can only recommend seeking the story
out for yourself. Carr used the celebrated Scotland Yard detective, Jonathan Whicher, in a 1959 novel, *Scandal at High
Chimneys*. And towards the end of his career, in *The Hungry
Goblin*, he made Wilkie Collins the detective, but Carr's biographer, Douglas Greene, found both novels unsatisfactory.

Of the numerous celebrity sleuths created since those
mid-twentieth-century pioneers, the majority are authors and
some are crime writers (I can think of Edgar Allan Poe, Arthur
Conan Doyle, Jacques Futrelle, Dashiell Hammett, Josephine
Tey, Leslie Charteris and Ian Fleming). We know our own kind
best.

The second main category is showbusiness performers. If
you're thinking of creating a celebrity sleuth, then you might
as well go for a 'celeb' who is universally known. How about
Humphrey Bogart, Greta Garbo, Marlene Dietrich, Noël Coward,
Mae West, Bette Davis, Alfred Hitchcock, Fred Astaire with
Ginger Rogers, and Clark Gable with Carole Lombard – all of
them recruited for a series of novels by one ingenious writer,
George Baxt? Other showbiz stars turned into sleuths include
Elvis Presley, Groucho Marx, Harry Houdini, Mabel Normand,
Steve Allen, Taylor Swift, and the entire 'rat pack' of Frank
Sinatra and friends.

Then there are people with power and influence. Various
US presidents from Lincoln to Obama have been put to work
in fiction as crime solvers. One of the Roosevelt family, Elliott,
the son of Franklin Delano, even wrote a series featuring his
mother Eleanor solving murders that mostly take place in the
White House. After the author's death in 1990, the series

continued for another twelve books until 2000, explained by
the publisher as a legacy of unpublished scripts. Suspicion was
aroused that a ghost writer was at work and he proved to be
William Harrington, who had collaborated with Roosevelt on
the early works.

Some really way-out sleuths have emerged in recent years.
Would you believe Beatrix Potter, Lizzie Borden, Louisa May
Alcott, Claude Monet or that less restrained painter, Francis
Bacon? Perhaps the ultimate in oddness was the series penned
by the ex-mayor of New York, Ed Koch, with assistance from
Herbert Resnicow and Wendy Corsi Staub, starring Koch himself
as the crime-solver.

I ask myself how an innocent traveller like me ever ventured
up this dangerous, overcrowded side street. As I recall, I was
midway through my career, having moved on from Victorian
stories. I had finished with Sergeant Cribb, who had featured
in books and television. Each of those stories had been set in
some form of sport or entertainment, but there was one I hadn't
used: horse racing. I found an account of the shocking death
of Fred Archer, the most successful jockey of the century, five
times the Derby winner, who shot himself at the age of 29. His
last words were, 'Are they coming?'

Could any writer resist such an opening?

I decided to write one last Victorian whodunit, but this time
with an amateur detective, the convention so much used by
early practitioners of the genre. And I saw straightaway that
my sleuth needed to be knowledgeable about racing and a friend
of the dead jockey. The biggest wreath on the coffin when it
was paraded along Newmarket High Street had been from
Bertie, the Prince of Wales. Archer had been the royal jockey,
well known to His Royal Highness. It didn't take long to decide
that Bertie must investigate. He was ideally placed, powerful
enough to keep Scotland Yard at arm's length if he chose, or
invite them in when he was at his wits' end. He had time on
his hands because his mother the Queen didn't trust him to
deal with affairs of state. It was all coming together nicely.

I read everything I could on Bertie and soon understood why

the Queen treated him as she did. He was somewhat deficient in the little grey cells, unlikely to deduce anything about the Archer mystery, and if he did it would be wrong.

Then why not make a virtue of necessity and have him as an over-confident but muddle-headed thinker? The mystery would get solved despite his best efforts and he would claim all the credit.

I went to Newmarket and got a sense of the real drama of 1886. I visited Falmouth House, where Archer had lived and died. At the National Horseracing Museum, I saw the silver pistol he had held to his head. I walked the funeral route and found the handsome headstone in the cemetery. I bought John Welcome's *Fred Archer: His Life and Times*. I do believe that if you write a story based on real people there's a responsibility to get everything as right as possible. The plot would require Bertie to go to Newmarket and attend the inquest, so I checked the Court Circular to make sure he was in the country at the time. I discovered it was held on the day of his birthday, when he was sure to be entertaining guests at Sandringham.

Sandringham was under fifty miles from Newmarket, so it was possible he could be back by the evening. Already I was getting myself into logistics you may think were unnecessary. Why not ignore his birthday for the purpose of the story? Grappling with the clash of dates enabled me to think as if I was Bertie myself.

Point of view is always a key decision. I swiftly realized this one needed writing in the first person as a memoir, and once I had the voice of Bertie the narrative flowed readily – so well that I eventually wrote three books: *Bertie and the Tinman*, *Bertie and the Seven Bodies* and *Bertie and the Crime of Passion*.

I'm still not sure I should encourage anyone to turn a real person into a sleuth, but I couldn't stop my own son from becoming a smoker, so here's my advice to anyone who won't be dissuaded. First, ask yourself if you really want to go through with this. If so, look at the approach of writers who already took the plunge and did it well: Margaret Doody's *Aristotle,*

Detective or Robert Barnard's *Dead, Mr Mozart* (under the pen name Bernard Bastable) would be a good start. Then do the research, and don't rely solely on the internet. Finally, respect your main character. The voice, pacing, settings, action and dialogue must be in keeping with the real person you have chosen as your sleuth.

Obvious, isn't it? But do you really want to try?

A key challenge when fictionalizing a real-life case is getting the facts right. This is especially tricky in areas such as the law, which is constantly changing. If your book is criticized by reviewers, the received wisdom is that there is little to be gained from complaining – even if what the critics say is mistaken or unfair. Anthony Berkeley, the witty if thin-skinned founder of the Detection Club, was not, however, a man to respond to criticism with a philosophical shrug.

His acclaimed novel *Trial and Error*, first published in 1938, involves a private prosecution for murder. Some legal experts expressed reservations about the accuracy of his technical research about the viability of a private prosecution for murder. When the novel was issued in paperback by Penguin, Berkeley seized the opportunity to fire back at the doubters by spelling out his justification in a new preface.

Incidentally, a Detection Club member of a younger generation, Michael Underwood (the pen name of John Michael Evelyn, a barrister who ultimately became Assistant Director of Public Prosecutions) wrote an essay in 1959 pointing out that the legal manoeuvres in Berkeley's entertaining novel were no longer possible. But the law keeps evolving, and since that time, there have indeed been private prosecutions for murder. One can imagine the ghost of Anthony Berkeley saying, 'I told you so.'

Trial and Error

Anthony Berkeley

As the legal points raised in this story seem to have caused some discussion, I am glad to use the opportunity of this new edition to make an explanation.

On the book's first appearance more than one newspaper went so far as to canvass the opinion of a legal pundit as to the 'law' involved; and the opinion was usually that my 'law' was pretty poor. Personal and highly interesting letters from eminent but strange barristers supported this view, in a kind but firm way. Unrepentant, I maintain that my 'law' is pretty sound.

So far as the outlines of the legal complexities go, these are founded on an actual case which occurred in 1866. As briefly as possible, the facts were these:

An Italian named Pellizzioni was convicted on a charge of murdering an Englishman, one Harrington, and wounding another in a tavern brawl in Clerkenwell. He had pleaded that, far from murdering anyone, he had been trying to quell the disturbance, and the fatal knife had actually been picked up at some distance from the rough-and-tumble in which Pellizzioni was involved. Nevertheless, before sentencing him to death, the judge observed that he had never known more direct or conclusive evidence in any case; and that appeared to be the end of Pellizzioni.

Certain of the convicted man's compatriots, however, were far from being as satisfied as the judge, and in the press the *Daily Telegraph* published a succession of articles attacking the verdict – though *The Times* considered that the evidence against Pellizzioni was 'undoubtedly as complete and as cogent as had ever been produced against a prisoner at the bar'. Mr H. Negretti, of the well-known optical instruments firm, took the lead in new and unofficial enquiries, which resulted in due course in a confession to the police by another Italian, named Mogni, that it was in fact he who had stabbed Harrington, though in self-defence.

The police viewed this statement with a marked lack of enthusiasm. They had one man convicted of Harrington's murder, and they did not want to be bothered with another. With difficulty could they be persuaded to lock the sobbing and now contrite Mogni up, and this they would only agree to do on a charge of aiding and abetting Pellizzioni. And they flatly refused to charge Mogni with the murder. The result was that when Mogni appeared in the magistrates' court, prosecuting counsel announced that he was acting on behalf of Mr Negretti, *and not of the Crown*, in charging Mogni with the murder.

In due course Mogni was committed for trial; Pellizzioni's execution was postponed to await the result; and the upshot was that, in spite of much caution on the part of the judge and every possible obstruction on the part of the police, Mogni was found guilty of the manslaughter of Harrington and sentenced to five years' imprisonment.

There were thus two men in prison at the same time, each of whom had separately been found guilty of the death of the same man; and the authorities clearly did not know what to do about it. One would have thought that a simple way out of the muddle might have been to accept the second verdict, based as it was on much clearer evidence, and grant Pellizzioni a free pardon. But that apparently was too easy. Pellizzioni was respited 'during the Queen's pleasure', and the authorities sat down to scratch their heads in earnest. The remarkable result was that Pellizzioni was put on trial a second time, but this time for stabbing and wounding another man; and of this, after three days of intensive forensic dialectics, he was acquitted, amid tumultuous plaudits both inside and outside the court. The way was thus free for the authorities to slip in with due dignity a free pardon for the other crime which he had not committed, and get rid of him out of prison. Even *The Times* observed, in a thousand or so polysyllabics, that it had all been a bit silly.

This, then, was the legal precedent which I followed, and followed fairly closely. It is true that I allowed Mr Todhunter bail – or rather, did not have him arrested at all until after the verdict, whereas Mogni did not get bail; but for this I plead novelist's licence.

The main point, however, to which legal exception is taken, is that I have termed Mr Todhunter's prosecution a 'private prosecution for murder'. I am told very firmly that such a thing is totally impossible, and was equally impossible at the time of Mogni; that it was not actually Mr Negretti who charged Mogni on indictment with murder, but that Mr Negretti was merely given permission to brief his own prosecuting counsel, who drew the indictment in the usual way as *R. v. Mogni*.

I am sure that this technical information is perfectly correct; but nevertheless to a layman these seem rather fine niceties. And when a private individual briefs counsel and charges a man with murder, and when the police not merely refuse to help but actually obstruct the prosecution, and when counsel informs the magistrates that he is acting on behalf of the private individual and *not* on behalf of the Crown, then I maintain that, even if the subsequent indictment was made out formally as *R. v.*, it is quite feasible to speak, in a loose, laymannish way, of 'a private prosecution for murder'. And if not, I am very, very sorry.

Partners in Crime

Writing in collaboration can be appealing. It offers a way of combating the isolation that writers often experience, and also as a way of combining talents, of making two plus two equal five. But writing in partnership with one or more colleagues also presents challenges.

Detection Club members have often worked collaboratively. The Club's two early BBC mysteries were each written by half a dozen members, while the Club's first novel, *The Floating Admiral*, was an exceptionally ambitious exercise involving thirteen contributors. There was no overriding plan; each author in turn took the story in a fresh direction. Anthony Berkeley, who was tasked with writing the final chapter, wryly called it 'Clearing up the Mess', but he pulled the strands of the plot together with such skill that the book has enjoyed lasting popularity. The Club's most recent joint venture, *The Sinking Admiral*, paid tribute to its literary predecessor, but was written in a different way, with Simon Brett orchestrating the overall structure of the book. As the story neared its climax, a 'Whodunit Dinner' was held at the Groucho Club in London, during which contributors plotted the resolution of the story and elected the brave individuals whose task was to write it up.

Writing a 'round-robin' novel can be hugely enjoyable, and in 1989 Tim Heald organized *The Rigby File*, a thriller compiled by a team of writers including several members of the Detection Club. Admittedly, such projects are not for the faint-hearted; nor are they suited to the inexperienced writer. But there are many examples of less convoluted literary collaborations that offer potential even for newcomers to crime writing. Michael Jecks and colleagues in the Medieval Murderers group of historical crime novelists have worked together on a series of books, starting with *The Tainted Relic*, comprising linked novellas by group members. The husband-and-wife team G. D. H. and Margaret Cole were founder members of the Club who wrote most of their books together, while in the modern era, Martyn Waites, a successful crime novelist under his own name, has co-written several books with his wife Lynda under the pseudonym Tania Carver.

In writing his novels, Dick Francis, a doyen of the Club, benefited from the input of his wife Mary and, later, his son Felix, in an example of a highly successful literary family enterprise. After Dick's death, Felix began a solo career publishing novels in the same vein and branded as 'Dick Francis novels', and was duly elected to membership of the Club. Meanwhile, the success of the American author James Patterson's partnerships with a host of authors has set a precedent for other bestselling collaborations. The Detection Club's Tom Harper has co-authored a book with South African thriller writer Wilbur Smith; so has Imogen Robertson, and it has recently been announced that she is collaborating on a thriller with former politician Tom Watson.

Margery Allingham's husband Philip Youngman Carter contributed ideas to some of her novels about Albert Campion, before completing her last book after her death, and then publishing Campion novels himself. Completion and continuation novels have become increasingly popular, and Jill Paton Walsh, as she describes elsewhere, took over Dorothy L. Sayers' mantle, completing an unfinished novel about Lord Peter Wimsey before continuing the Wimsey series. Stella Duffy has completed *Money in the Morgue* by Ngaio Marsh, who in the 1930s co-wrote *The Nursing Home Murder* with a doctor called Henry Jellett – who supplied medical know-how for the storyline. In recent years, Sophie Hannah has published a series of novels commissioned by Agatha Christie's estate and featuring Hercule Poirot.

The first Detection Club member to achieve success as a literary collaborator was Robert Eustace. This was the pen name of Eustace Robert Barton, a doctor who contributed scientific know-how to stories written by L. T. Meade, a prolific author of fiction for girls who turned to detective stories in the wake of the success of Sherlock Holmes. Eustace became friendly with Dorothy L. Sayers in the late 1920s after she asked permission to reprint one of the stories he'd written with Meade in an anthology, and it was no doubt thanks to her support that he became one of the founder members of the Detection Club. He collaborated with yet another Club member, Edgar Jepson, on a famous 'locked room' story, 'The Tea Leaf', but today he is best remembered for working with Sayers on her only novel not to feature Lord Peter Wimsey, *The Documents in the Case*. Again, Eustace came up with a clever technical idea, and Sayers did the writing. What is remarkable about their collaboration is that there is a detailed record of its progress, to be found in the first volume of Sayers' collected letters.

Sayers' correspondence shows very clearly the rollercoaster nature of the writing life: the lurches from excitement to despair; the thrill of coming up with fresh ideas; the frustration with publishers and the yearning for good publicity; the misery of receiving (mistaken, as it proved) criticism of the concept at the heart of the book when it was too late to do anything about it; and the joy of receiving an unexpected accolade from the scientific profession. Despite Sayers' downbeat assessment of the novel (a reaction common enough when a book has been finished), the correspondence provides a wonderful case study about the making of a detective story. *The Documents in the Case* remains an interesting and thought-provoking example of the 'casebook novel', a form popularized by novels such as Wilkie Collins' *The Moonstone*, and of a storyline and characters influenced by a real life murder.

Collaborative Writing
Dorothy L. Sayers' letters to Robert Eustace

7 May 1928

Dear Dr Barton
  . . . I am so glad you like Lord Peter. I certainly don't intend to
kill him off yet, but I think it would be better to invent a new
detective for any tales we do together . . . it would simplify
matters to have somebody with more scientific surroundings,
don't you think? Lord Peter isn't supposed to know a lot about
chemistry and that sort of thing, and it would mean inventing a
doctor or somebody to help him out. Also, I'm looking forward to
getting a rest from him, because his everlasting breeziness does
become a bit of a tax at times! The job is to invent a scientific
character of a new type. There have been so many of them –
thin, keen ones; short, sphinx-like ones; handsome, impressive
ones; queer, shabby ones; secretive, mysterious ones; aged, experienced ones; and even sturdy, commonplace ones – it's very hard
to think of any sort that hasn't been done . . .

15 May 1928

  . . . I have been thinking over the mushroom story, and the
more I think of it – the more I think of it! . . . In this story, as
you say, it is obvious that there must be a powerful love interest,
and I am going to turn my mind to making this part of the book
as modern and powerful as possible. The day of the two nice
young people, whose chaste affection is rewarded on the final
page, has rather gone by, and reviewers are apt to say, sneer-
ingly, that detective stories are better without any sentimental
intrigues. Since, in this case, we must have the love to help the
plot along, we must do our best to make it as credible and
convincing as up-to-date standards require.

29 June 1928

. . . I think we have got hold of a really fine theme for a story here, and I am most eager to get on to it . . . The religious-scientific aspect of the thing will require careful handling, but ought, I think, to be very interesting to people, if we can succeed in making it clear to them.

3 September 1928

. . . The scene in the laboratory will be very good. I think we might let the Great Scientist do a check experiment with genuine fungus poison first, so that the other bloke might exactly appreciate the difference between the two; it would add to the drama if, in the *first* instance, the observer could stand at the eye-piece and see the darkness change to light as the fungus-solution is put in the polariscope. It would prolong and work up the excitement a little and give the reader a feeling that he had seen the experiment worked for himself . . .

The big job now will be to introduce complications into the plot. As the whole thing is supposed, at first, to be an accident, we can't avail ourselves of the wrongfully-accused person or anything like that. We shall have to work it up powerfully on the emotional side. This is rather a new line for me . . . And we shall have somehow to work the scientific-theological interest solidly into the plot (I don't quite see how at the moment, but I expect it will come) . . .

I think *The Death Cap* would make an extremely good title in itself. It suggests murder and mystery, and to the person who isn't a mushroom expert it has a flavour of courts of law and the 'black cap' . . .

When the time comes, I am going to work up quite an interesting little item of news out of the collaboration of Robert Eustace and Dorothy L. Sayers and push it round to the press . . .

10 September 1928

. . . I will now devote my attention to the details of the crime,
and make suitable arrangements for the Villain to poison the
mushrooms without

    a) poisoning himself

    b) being obviously unwilling to share the poisoned dish

    c) being suspected of popping a genuine 'death-cap' into the
       dish.

If possible the trap shall poop off while the villain is away in
Town, or something. By the way, I shall want to know:

    1. What muscarine (artificial) solution looks like (whether clear
       or coloured, cloudy or transparent)

    2. What is the fatal dose

    3. What it smells and tastes like (like mushrooms?) in case I
       want to poison the dish, or the salt, or something other
       than the actual plants, as I rather want the villain to be out
       of the way when these are gathered and brought home.

19 November 1928

. . . I have decided, I think, how to administer the poison and
preserve the alibi intact. Also, I am introducing a valuable
witness to the death, who will be able to support the said alibi.

  I have also been considering the love-affair. I don't want to
make the villain too villainous – nor yet must the victim be a
villain. I think I shall (with your approval) make the victim a
harmless sort of bore, conceited and self-centred and always
twaddling about his cookery and so on, and have him married to
a sort of Edith Thompson woman, who eggs the villain on to get
rid of the husband. That will allow plenty of human nature and
furious frustration and all that kind of thing.

  Then I'm rather keen to try the experiment of writing the book
in a series of first-person narratives, à la Wilkie Collins. It will be
a new line to try, but I think I could manage it. My idea is that
somebody . . . gets his suspicions roused, and sets out to collect

statements and evidence, finishing up with the scientific experiment. Then . . . he bundles the whole lot off to the Public Prosecutor or the police, urging them to take it up. This gets over the difficulty which always confronts me in reading a Wilkie Collins book, namely, why, when all is settled and finished, anybody should have taken the trouble to collect and publish an account of the thing at all. It also gets over the tiresome business of an ending – whether one is to have the murderer tried, or make him confess, or allow him to commit suicide, or what!

26 April 1929

. . . I have just had a visit from our American publisher . . . I mentioned our idea about the publicity photographs of Miss Dorothy Sayers and her mysterious collaborator in the laboratory. He was absolutely entranced with the idea – he said: 'Oh, that's great! That's swell.' I fancy he will give us a really good show over there and get the book wide sales in the States. I am glad of this, because I'm afraid Benn will not do anything very brilliant on this side – Benns are all thyroid-deficient, dim and wombling imbeciles, damn them!

I am not at present intending, by the way, to make any very great secret about its being a murder, or about the identity of the murderer . . . This is a little different from the ordinary plan of the detective story, but it is much more like what actually happens in real life . . .

If only we can get this just exactly right, I do think the situation will be extremely powerful, and 'God's revenge against murder' very, very striking. I cannot tell you how enthusiastic I am about this plot, and how anxious I am not to spoil it by any crudity in the handling . . .

17 May 1929

. . . You need not worry about the coroner's inquest. Inquests have no legal importance at all, as far as that goes, and a case can be re-opened at any time after the verdict of a coroner's jury.

Thus, in the case of George Joseph Smith, who drowned his
three brides in a bath, though no suspicion was aroused until the
last murder, the murder for which he was actually tried was that
of the first wife, Annie Mundy, who had been peacefully buried
some years previously under a coroner's verdict of misadventure,
the two succeeding cases being admitted as collateral evidence of
design only.

20 November 1929

. . . The new idea for a story sounds very exciting, and I should
love to hear about it . . . But perhaps we had better wait a bit till
we see how this one turns out. At present I am being rather
dissatisfied with my work on it. I keep on seeing how I could
have done things better and having to re-write great chunks. I
think this is due partly to the change in style between this and
my other books, partly to over-anxiety – wanting to justify a new
departure and not let my collaborator down – and largely to the
generally unsettled feeling I have just at present . . . and with the
knowledge that I shall be leaving my permanent job at the end of
the year . . . The story is turning out rather grim and sordid, and
I am finding it hard to get a light touch into it. The miserable
domestic situation of the Harrisons, the mental aberrations of the
lady-housekeeper and the temperamental introspections of the
poet combine to produce an atmosphere of tense depression
which, though extremely suitable to the plot is not exhilarating,
either for author or reader!

11 January 1930

. . . You will, I am sure, sympathise when you hear that our
worthy friend Harrison passed away this evening in excruciating
agony. A particularly horrible circumstance is that the unfortunate gentleman was all alone when he met his death, in a remote
cottage. Mrs Harrison is naturally prostrated.

21 January 1930

. . . Just a line to say we are getting along nicely. The stepson is
suspecting the murder and is about to purchase a bunch of
compromising letters from a blackmailing charwoman! The
novelist is having a dreadful time, torn between his natural good
feeling and the fact that he was at the same public school as the
murderer. The wife is a dreadful person. The murderer (who has
my sympathy) has just discovered this and his feelings of misery
and remorse are dreadful, but nobody knows this yet but me . . .

Yours, with my mind full of fungi,

Dorothy L. Sayers

9 February 1930

. . . Yesterday morning at 3 ack emma I wrote the last words of
this here tarnation book and, drawing a squiggly line under them,
drank a large glass of Bovril-and-milk and staggered away to bed!

Today I took courage to review the first part of it, in which I
found much to displease me, but I think it will hold together
tolerably . . .

21 March 1930

. . . I am sending the book, but in my heart I know I have made
a failure of it. Really and truly I was feeling so nervous and
run-down last year . . . that I ought not to have been writing at
all. It has produced a mingled atmosphere of dullness and gloom
which will, I fear, be fatal to the book. As it was, the earlier half
was so bad, that I had to re-write great chunks of it, and it is
still bad. And during the second re-type, my typist was laid up
for a week with VIOLENT POISONING! I'm afraid there is a jinx
of some bad sort giving his attention to the book.

Please make any alterations straight on to the MS. I have 4
copies of it. I WISH I could have done better with the brilliant plot.

Yours very depressed

Dorothy L. Sayers

13 September 1930

. . . I enclose a little bit of trouble for you from the wife of a
learned gentleman who says the synthetic muscarine is all wrong.
I have written to thank her, and have said that muscarine is in
your department and that you will be happy to take up the
cudgels about it . . .

7 November 1930

. . . I have received a staggerer! A Harley Street physician has
written to ask my advice about synthetic gland-extracts! . . . I do
hope you will be able to put him on to what he wants – what a
scoop it would be! First time in history that a detective-story has
been of any serious use to anybody!

Adapting

The main focus of *Howdunit* is on writing novels, but crime writers also tackle other media – film, television, radio, theatre, and so on, sometimes producing original scripts, sometimes adapting their own novels or the work of others. Audiobooks have rapidly increased in popularity in recent years, while radio writing has long offered plenty of opportunities for crime specialists.

Val Gielgud, an actor (like his even more famous brother Sir John) and a broadcaster (he pioneered radio drama and also directed the first drama screened on British television) was a crime novelist in his spare time. He was also a member of the Detection Club whose novels included *Death at Broadcasting House*, co-written with Holt Marvell (the pen name of another BBC insider, Eric Maschwitz) and filmed in 1934.

Gielgud contributed occasional articles to *The Writer* magazine about writing plays for broadcast, and emphasized that the would-be dramatist's first priority was to listen to radio drama, so as to understand the medium. A radio audience is different from an audience in a theatre. The writer can't benefit from a mass reaction, whether it is amusement, horror, or applause. Listeners are usually people on their own or in very small groups, often at home and liable to be interrupted at any moment. Listeners, Gielgud said, are blind, so the worst fault of a radio drama is obscurity. Characters must be firmly realized, and not too numerous. The radio writer's aim, in short, was to grip the individual listener's attention immediately and never let it go.

More recently, Alison Joseph has combined a career as a crime novelist, featuring series protagonists as diverse as the nun Sister Agnes and Agatha Christie, with writing for radio. In addition to scripting original crime dramas, she has also written a five-part series about Sister Agnes and adapted four of Georges Simenon's Maigret novels and S. J. Watson's bestselling novel of domestic suspense, *Before I Go to Sleep*. She makes a case for radio as an ideal medium for crime fiction.

Writing for Radio
Alison Joseph

There has been crime drama on the radio for almost as long as there has been radio, as live theatrical broadcasts of the 1920s gave way to early (and experimental) made-for-radio plays of the 1930s, mostly in the USA. Let me start with a brief extract:

FRANCES	Dropping out of college? I won't have it. You need to do something with your life.
ELLA	SHRUG OF DEFIANCE
FRANCES	There's no point you rolling your eyes at me like that, young lady. You know I'm right.

Sharp-eyed readers will note that the second character doesn't actually say anything – and yet her response is made perfectly clear. Radio is about painting pictures in the mind of the listener, with sound, with speech and with music.

At the heart of this process is dialogue. Dialogue in radio plays can be divided into three categories: when people say what they mean; when they say one thing but mean something else; and when they say nothing at all. (Ella's line in the excerpt above is an obvious example of the third category.) And I would argue that for a play that centres around a crime story, all these categories are utterly essential. In fact, good crime writing in any form has as its key what the characters say and what they choose to hide, and radio just makes the most of this.

Here is another excerpt of dialogue. It comes from *Mitchener*, a 45-minute play broadcast on BBC Radio 4, where the detective is an air accident investigator. A plane has come down, killing all on board, and Meredith Foster, the wife of one of the passengers, has been insisting to Mitchener that it wasn't an accident, that she wants more investigation. Mitchener is talking to his own partner, Bridget, about it.

BRIDGET	The Wife—
MITCHENER	. . . Meredith.
BRIDGET	What's she like?
MITCHENER	Heartbroken. Angry. Efficient. Channelling all her work-self into finding out what happened. And not quite seeing, yet, that however much she finds out, it won't bring him back.
BRIDGET	I meant, to look at.
MITCHENER	. . . Oh. Um . . .
BRIDGET	Well-dressed?
MITCHENER	Don't know. Maybe. Trousers, you know. Jackets. Grey. Or is it cream. Pale colour. I think.
BRIDGET	You must know what she looks like.
MITCHENER	SHRUGS
BRIDGET	She's really good-looking. On the telly, she is.
MITCHENER	Look, I don't see her—
BRIDGET	As a woman?
MITCHENER	No.
BRIDGET	EXCLAMATION OF NOT BELIEVING THIS.
MITCHENER	It's about the facts. That's all.
BRIDGET	So is that what she wants to talk about?
MITCHENER	That's exactly what she wants to talk about.
PAUSE	

BRIDGET	It isn't that she's blonde.
MITCHENER	No?
BRIDGET	It's that she's getting a version of you that you hide from me. The man who loves his job. The man you used to be.

This extract shows examples of all three categories at work. When as a writer you only have what people say as your central tool, you have to rely on the listener to really hear what's going on between your characters. And in crime writing, that is at the core of the storytelling: that the audience, reader or listener, is aware that what people say to each other really matters – and that it may not be reliable.

A radio play is nothing without its actors. It is worth noting that care should be taken when writing instructions to the cast about how lines should be spoken. The notes above, for the silent lines, just convey what's going on, but it's best to avoid the temptation as a writer to describe exactly how the spoken lines should be performed, throwing in adverbs such as 'hesitantly' or 'angrily'. It's much better to trust your cast to find their own version of the lines.

Plot and structure

With a novel, you can flick back and forth between pages to check the story. But with an audio play, if it's broadcast live, the story has to work at first go and not get too tangled up with lots of characters and twists. It may also be serialized, and again, the listener tuning in will need clarification about what has happened so far (although with streaming, where you can listen again, this gives the audience more chance to catch up).

Beyond dialogue

Having said that dialogue is at the heart of radio drama, there are other ways of using speech to tell a story. Radio lends itself well to a character directly addressing the audience. It can be a way of introducing a different timescale or viewpoint: the wrongly accused suspect, a missing person, or even someone speaking from beyond the grave. It can be a flashback to a parallel but relevant part of the story that happened a long time ago (but perhaps without the whoosh of supernatural sound effects to signal this). Monologue can take different forms; it might be in the form of a letter, or a recording of a speech, or voicemail, or any other way which allows for a character to be a lone voice. It can also be . . .

Narration

This is often used in adaptation, so as not to lose the original authorial voice. It can work very well. As a listener, it's nice to feel that someone is telling you a story. There is a risk that it can distance the listener from the action, but used well, it can add a whole new dimension. Here's an example, from the Charles Paris series on BBC Radio 4 starring Bill Nighy, written by Jeremy Front, based on the original books by Simon Brett. In this scene, Charles is grumpily awaiting a call from his agent, and killing time by walking the streets in the rain.

SCENE 9 – STREET NARRATION

FX: THUNDER, RAIN, C. P. WALKS, OTHER SCUFFS

1 CHARLES:	Not even a monsoon stops millennials walking the streets, eyes glued to their phones.
2 MIL 1:	Ow.
3 CHARLES:	As I couldn't possibly get any wetter, I played a game I call 'Walk The Line'.
4 MIL 2:	Ow.
5 CHARLES:	The rules are simple:
6 MIL 3:	Ow.
7 CHARLES:	Choose a street . . .
8 MIL 4:	Ow.
9 CHARLES:	. . . and without malice or aggression, walk a straight line from A to B counting the number of screen zombies who bump into you along the way.

10 MIL 5:	Ow.
11 CHARLES:	Five points for an 'ow' and ten points for a 'sorry'.
1 MIL 6:	Sorry.
2 CHARLES:	Top score to date: forty-five not including the angry commuter who yelled—
3 COMMUTER:	LOOK WHERE YOU'RE GOING!
4 CHARLES:	. . . then collided with a food delivery cyclist who shouldn't have been on the pavement in the first place.
FX: BIKE CLATTER AND YELLS . . .	
5 CHARLES:	Schadenfreude or Darwinian natural selection – it restored my faith in universal karma.

Everything about the scene above is pure radio – it simply wouldn't work in any other form. It allows Charles to address the listener directly, while still being part of the story. Jeremy Front has said that he wanted to develop a 'Chandleresque, wry, world-weary yet self-aware character, commenting like a one-man Greek chorus. His intercessions must be funny, and they have to move the story on.'

Sound effects

The above extract shows another key aspect of radio drama, and that is sound effects. If writing, say, sci-fi, there is enormous fun to be had in raiding the sound effects library for rockets, spaceships, robots, spooky planet noises and aliens. But – even in sci-fi – none of this will work without a good story, decent writing and well-established characters. I would argue that in writing crime on the radio, less is more where sound effects are concerned.

However, there are times when they're absolutely essential: here is another extract from *Mitchener*, where the cockpit voice recording from the crashed plane is being played back.

GEORGE	Ah, there you are. Take a seat.
FX	ATC PLAYBACK SWITCHED ON

CO-PILOT	PK Four nine five to Tower . . .
AIR TRAFFIC CONTROL	PK four nine five, receiving . . .
CAPTAIN	We've got a small fire on board. Permission to land.
ATC	We've got you.
CO-PILOT	Coming in at two thousand . . .
ATC	Can you turn back towards Gatwick?
CAPTAIN	Yeah—
ATC	Cleared to land—

FX SMOKE ALARM CHANGES TO EMERGENCY

CAPTAIN	Where the hell is that— coming from?
ATC	Cleared to land in five—
CAPTAIN	Emergency—
CO-PILOT	We're losing—
FX	CRESCENDO OF ALARM NOISE
AIR TRAFFIC CONTROL	PK 495 . . . Come in PK 495 . . . they've gone quiet . . . We've lost them –

SILENCE

There is also music, a hugely important aspect of audio drama. Anyone who has listened to any good radio play will know how effectively music can be used.

And so to endings. Generally, a crime story overloaded with subplots and red herrings doesn't work too well on the radio, as there always comes the moment of resolution when we find out whodunit. Lengthy explanations from clever detectives tend to work better on the page.

Here is part of the end scene of *Mitchener*.

The truth has come out, and Meredith, the widow, has asked to meet Mitchener again.

MEREDITH	I wasn't sure you'd show up.
MITCHENER	Here I am.
MEREDITH	I've ordered champagne.
MITCHENER	Why . . .?
MEREDITH	Because I like it.

FX POURS TWO GLASSES.

MEREDITH	I've been so angry . . .
MITCHENER	I know.
MEREDITH	I'm— [STILL ANGRY, SHE'S GOING TO SAY]
MITCHENER	—Don't apologise.
MEREDITH	Apologise? I wasn't going to.
MITCHENER	Good. HE SIPS CHAMPAGNE. You owe me nothing.
MEREDITH	No.
PAUSE	
	You knew, didn't you?
MITCHENER	Knew what?
MEREDITH	You knew all along.
MEREDITH	PAUSE, THEN
	It's funny, isn't it. How you can know something and not know it at the same time. All that time I was demanding answers, and yet I think, from very early on, I knew. In my heart, I knew that something was very wrong. There I was demanding answers from your people, and all the time, the answer was there in front of me. In my husband's behaviour that day. In those weird sums of money. In those odd things he'd say, about his 'new friends' out there . . .
MITCHENER	I didn't, Meredith. I didn't know 'all along'.
PAUSE	
	When we were standing there, with the wreckage . . . something fell into place. But even then I wasn't sure what it was.
PAUSE	
	We both needed answers.
MEREDITH	Answers? It turns out that my husband, the love of my life, my straight-laced, God fearing, all-American husband, was shipping arms. What kind of answer is that?
PAUSE	

MEREDITH   There he was, providing for me. The beautiful
                flat . . . the designer clothes. And I used to
                say to him, even if we were dirt poor, I'd be
                happy with him. And I meant it.

PAUSE

                It turns out, he never trusted me enough to
                believe that I was telling the truth.

Whether your detective is a hard-bitten investigator, or a
washed-out actor trying to earn a living; whether she's a lone
heroic Detective Inspector, or a sweet old lady with a core of
steel, audio crime drama allows them to speak directly to the
audience. Most of all, crime fiction is a genre where the author
and the reader are intertwined; with its twists and turns, its
hidden secrets and unexpected reveals, it asks its audience to
pay attention. With radio, that audience has to listen; to find
the clues that are embedded in the dialogue. It makes it the
perfect medium for such a story.

Alison Joseph gives an example from a play featuring Charles Paris,
the most celebrated creation of Simon Brett, seventh President of
the Detection Club. One of Britain's most versatile writers, Simon
has published over one hundred books on a wide range of subjects.
He worked as a BBC radio producer before joining London Weekend
Television. As well as writing for radio and television, he has for
many years also scripted an annual play for the Arundel Festival.
He also had one of his stand-alone novels filmed. Yet the course of
adaptation doesn't always run smooth . . .

Adaptability

Simon Brett

Most crime writers are delighted that their books are published, but there are few who wouldn't wish for the additional exposure – and income – that would come from having their work adapted into another medium. A radio series? Nice. A stage play? Also nice. A television series? Even nicer. A feature film? Very nice indeed.

And almost everyone who's been active for any length of time in the crime-writing business will at some point have had producers sniffing around the dramatic rights in their works. Some may even get to the point of being paid money for options to develop their books in another medium.

The first time someone takes out an option, it's very exciting. The writer's imagination immediately leaps to visions of a top-rated Sunday evening series which runs for ever, sells round the world and ensures that every new book is catapulted immediately into the bestsellers' lists. After the first dozen options have come to nothing, a level of cynicism creeps in.

I've been through this a few times with my actor detective Charles Paris. The first of his investigations, *Cast, In Order Of Disappearance*, was published in 1975, and within a few years of that came the first interest in translating his adventures into another medium. Options were taken out, money changed hands, scripts were even commissioned, and I thought it was a matter of months before Charles's television incarnation would be on a screen near me.

That first one didn't work out, and nor did the many others which have emerged since. Various reasons were given. 'Television has always had a bad track record when it comes to series with a background of showbiz.' 'American audiences don't understand black humour.' There was always some excuse for it not to happen.

On occasions, the process got as far as scripts being

commissioned. I duly developed and rewrote my original stories. I got paid handsomely for my efforts. But at some point, between cup and lip, the project foundered. On one occasion, having delivered a final draft to the BBC script editor who'd commissioned it, I got an answering machine message saying: 'Perfect. I wouldn't change a word and be happy to go into the studio with it on Monday.' The next week, in a development familiar at the BBC, she lost her job. And, of course, the last thing the new broom who replaced her wanted to do was to pick up any of her projects.

The potential of Charles Paris appearing on television did lead to some very engaging encounters with producers and, particularly, actors. Some of them, under the illusion that I, the mere writer of the books, might have some power in the game, took me out for lunch. And trying to convince me that they were perfect casting for the notoriously bibulous Charles, then tried to drink me under the table. Entertaining, but not getting any nearer to a deal being done.

And all of the actors who were, at one stage, suggested as the ideal Charles Paris are either too old or, in most cases, long dead.

The one thing that has come out of all this is that the books do now have a new life on Radio 4, with the impeccable Bill Nighy playing the part. And, though that's very nice, and the adapter Jeremy Front does all the work and I get all the credit, it still isn't telly. To put it crudely, I get a lot less money for the radio. And only writers with private incomes don't think about money.

So, what advice would I give to aspiring crime writers who want to see their works in another medium? First, check out any producer who approaches you or your agent with enquiries about the dramatic rights in your books. The fact is that anyone can call themselves 'a producer', so make sure that the enquirer has some track record in the business – ideally, that they have actually produced a programme at some point. Agents can be very helpful here. They probably know the scene better than you do.

But one can still get caught out. I once spent four months working, under a contract which had been negotiated with my agent, adapting a novel into a screenplay for an extremely amiable producer. When, after many rewrites, I delivered a version he was happy with, my agent invoiced for the fee owing, only to be told by the producer, with charming candour, that he 'hadn't got any money'. The amount involved did not justify legal action, so that was four months out of my life. And, because the producer had the rights on the book I was adapting, there was no chance of selling the script elsewhere.

So, beware of people who call themselves 'producers'. Beware also of doing a lot of work on developing your project for nothing. This is a tricky area, and really depends on the relationship of trust between you and the producer. Such encounters often begin with the producer saying, 'Well, if you could just make a list of your books, with brief synopses, which will help me sell the idea and raise some development money.' That sounds reasonable, but it can all too easily escalate into your being asked to write detailed outlines of episodes and even complete scripts. To get that deeply into the project before the producer even has an option on your work is all too easily done. I would say that was always a bad idea, though I see its seductive appeal. For lonely writers, the idea of any kind of collaboration is attractive, as is the idea of presenting a united front in your attack on the media monoliths. And there are examples of that kind of unpaid collaboration resulting in successful series. But they are rare.

One thing that does frequently happen is that an unscrupulous producer will offer your works to a broadcaster for potential adaptation, *without actually having an option on the rights*. This has happened to me on more than one occasion, and there's not a lot one can do about it. Such behaviour is obviously unethical, and it can also have the effect of delaying any chance of the project getting off the ground. When someone who does have the legitimate right to offer the series idea to a broadcaster actually does so, they can get the response, 'Oh, someone else was offering this only six months ago, and we turned it down then.' The fact that that person had no right to make the offer doesn't register.

Incidentally, while on this subject, do not imagine that, if your project gets rejected by a major broadcaster, that it's forever dead in the water. Personnel changes at the top of such organizations are frequent and an idea that's been roundly rejected can, a couple of years later, be hailed as 'exactly what we need for Sunday evening'.

So, what can you do to make your crime novel or series of crime novels attractive to potential producers? Well, the most obvious answer is: be a huge global bestseller. Production companies like certainties and they operate in a world where there aren't many of them. So, they like to be able to say, 'This book has sold x million copies round the world, so that's x million people who might want to see the movie of the book.' It doesn't always work, of course. Some very duff movies have come out of bestselling books, but in the percentage game that is Hollywood they've probably still made a profit for the studios.

But if becoming a bestseller were simply a matter of will . . . well, we'd all have done it, wouldn't we? So, removing that option from the table, what else can you do to make your books suitable for adaptation?

Some of the answers are obvious and apply to any area of storytelling. Set your novels in places which are interesting in their own right. Invent intriguing plots and create characters whose actions and deliberations are going to engage the attention of your readership or audience.

Beyond that, in my experience, there's not a lot you can do. When I have an idea for something I want to write, I know from the start whether it's a novel, a short story, a stage play or a radio script, and once I begin writing I am obedient to the demands of the chosen medium. I often finish a project and think, 'Oh why didn't I make that more suitable for adaptation?' But that's the way I write, and I can't change it. And sometimes, when I have not seen any possibility of the work appearing in a different form, another mind has found the potential.

This brings me on to the big question. If the perfect scenario comes about – someone actually wants to turn your books into a television series – what should your level of involvement in the project be?

Every crime writer is proud and protective of their characters. And the history of adaptation is littered with inappropriate decisions being taken (the casting of 5'7' Tom Cruise as 6'5' Jack Reacher will serve as an example). So, can you keep more control if you write the scripts yourself?

The answer to this will vary from individual to individual. Traditionally, writers are not highly rated in the film industry. In Hollywood, they tell the story of the starlet who was so dumb that she slept with the writer. But that perception has changed a bit in recent years and it's very common now to see writers with executive producer credits on films and television series.

But if you want to go down the route of scripting your own series, there are a good few points you have to bear in mind. First – and I wouldn't mention this but for the fact that I do still meet writers who're doing it – under no circumstances start writing your own adaptation of your book if you haven't got a production company on board. The chances of something you've written on spec meeting the many demands of a commissioning broadcaster are absolutely nil. You will simply have wasted time that could have been better spent writing something new.

If you do want to get involved in production process, though, recognize from the start that it will be very time-consuming. If you imagine you're going to be able to get on with writing your next novel while the show is in production, think again.

Also, unless you're deeply interested in the process of film- or television-making, keep clear of it. The whole thing takes a hell of a long time, and can be very boring. People who can spend long days watching the snail-like progress of film-making must have been born with a very high boredom threshold.

I have this theory that the amount of interference you get with your writing depends on the percentage of the budget you are. With books, you may not get paid very much, but the author is a large percentage of the overall production costs, and my experience with publishers has been of minimal and very constructive interference. The same in radio. In television, the money paid to the writer seems very generous, but as a percentage of the whole series budget it is miniscule. And because of the financial stakes, a whole raft of script editors, producers, directors – and self-obsessed star actors – have the right to demand changes to your script. In the world of feature films all of the figures – and the levels of interference – grow exponentially.

Another point worth bearing in mind is that film and television are such technical media that producers want writers who have already shown themselves capable of meeting their demands. Studio time is so expensive that there are none available to teach an inexperienced screenwriter his or her craft. Also, at any given time, certain names of experienced adaptors will be flavour of the month. One of those names attached to your project might well speed it more quickly through development hell. Your insistence on scripting the series yourself could easily prove a deal-breaker.

My experience of adapting my own work has been mixed, but I have reached some conclusions about it. In the 1980s I turned my first two Charles Paris novels into two six-part series of half-hours for Radio 2, with the delightful Francis Matthews playing the part. I quite enjoyed doing that, though I was already began to find it quite boring . . . because for me the fun of writing is telling myself the story for the first time.

For that reason, when in the 1990s I was commissioned to write two one-hour television scripts featuring my widow sleuth Mrs Pargeter, I chose to write new investigations for the character rather than adapting any of the books. When the inevitable happened and the BBC decided not to commission the series, I economically recycled the storylines into the next two Mrs Pargeter novels. Nothing is wasted.

Since then there have been more options for both Charles Paris and Mrs Pargeter. More adapted scripts have been commissioned. With one of them, after endless rewrites, I found I had spent considerably longer writing the one-hour script than I had in writing the original book. I began to wonder if this was a fruitful use of my time.

Possibly my happiest adaptation experience was converting the scripts of my Radio 4 sitcom *After Henry* into half-hours for Thames Television. I found I could do two of them in a week, and for each I was paid more than six times my original radio script fee. Happy days.

Having my stand-alone thriller, *A Shock to the System*, turned into a feature film starring Michael Caine was also a pleasant experience. My only involvement in the production was bending down to the doormat to pick up an envelope containing what it still the largest cheque of my professional life. And I'm constantly reminded of it because with some of the proceeds my wife and I built on to our kitchen a conservatory, which we still call 'the Michael Caine Annexe'. He doesn't know that.

To sum up my advice . . . If someone takes up an option to turn your books into a movie or television series, don't hold your breath. Unless you have had a long-term ambition to be a screenwriter and understand the specialized skill set required, don't insist on doing the adaptation yourself. Do what most sensible writers do – take the money and get on with writing your next book (which can them in time can be adapted lucratively into another medium).

Oh, and a tiny technical tip . . . Try not to have more than one character in your book whose surname begins with the same letter. During television rehearsals, someone will be making notes of all the moves the director gives to the actors. If that beleaguered person only has to write one initial each time, they will think whoever's written the script is wonderful.

As I write this, there are currently paid-up options out on two of my series of books. And, in spite of all my adverse experiences, I'm afraid a tiny flicker of hope still springs eternal in my crime writer's breast. Maybe this time . . .

Challenges

Motivation, as Peter James has emphasized, is crucial for any writer. But how to keep motivated when the going gets rough? The writing life is full of challenges. When they threaten to become overwhelming, writers often feel isolated and struggle to cope.

A poignant illustration of what can go wrong emerges from *Bruce Montgomery/Edmund Crispin: A Life in Music and Books*, a biography by David Whittle of a prominent post-war member of the Detection Club. Crispin published his first detective novel at the age of twenty-three, and in the years that followed he earned widespread admiration as a novelist and composer. Within a decade, however, he was burned out as a writer. Ill-health and alcoholism took a heavy toll, and he found it almost impossible to write. His short story 'We Know You're Busy Writing, But We Thought You Wouldn't Mind If We Just Dropped In For a Minute' is a black comedy about an author suffering from writer's block.

Jessica Mann told the British Council in 2010 that she 'started writing crime fiction because it was what I most enjoyed reading and only later came to understand that I use writing as a way of dealing with fear. I am always aware of how precariously we skate on the thin ice of civilization and how easily things can go hideously wrong. In my stories, abnormal events intervene in a secure society where crime and violence, being unfamiliar, are all the more horrifying . . . Crime fiction is a genre chosen by writers who want to avoid self-exposure. So even when my writing seems to be candid or autobiographical, it is actually (to quote a book's title) *Telling Only Lies.'*

Simon Brett, author of over one hundred books and a long-serving President of the Detection Club, has written and spoken movingly about the intrusion of clinical depression into the writer's life. Thanks to the work of Simon and bodies such as the Society of Authors and the CWA, the importance of this issue is becoming more widely recognized, and initiatives are being put in place to help those in need of support. Here four authors talk with candour and positivity about challenges writers may face, and ways of rising to them.

Impostor Syndrome
Martyn Waites

Yeah. Impostor syndrome. It's a real thing. And it plays such a massive part in a writer's life, or indeed potentially any professional's life, and I don't think it's ever fully discussed or given its due as a massive impediment to being able to work.

Writing attracts people who are naturally thin-skinned. Being empathetic and both open to and interpretive of the emotions and actions of others and ourselves is what allows writers to inhabit characters and portray them on the page. In short, it helps us to be good at our job. But the flipside of this can be a nightmare.

Coping with bad reviews, for instance. If you're in any way sensitive this can be stressful and feel like a personal attack, especially if you define yourself by your work. A writer has to find a way to not let them impede that work, to dismiss them as just an opinion and not a particularly well constructed one at that. And yes, like all writers, I can memorize and repeat the bad reviews, as well as agree with them, but can't remember a single thing about the good ones.

Then there's social anxiety. Writers tend to enjoy their own company. It's a requirement of the job. So when you're asked to make public appearances, do events and signings, book tours and the like, it can be a daunting experience for someone who has deliberately chosen a career where they don't voluntarily have to leave the house. Yet it's part of the job and expected of a writer now. So we just have to deal with it, get on with it, and enjoy it. It's a privilege to be able to do what we do, to affect someone's life, so we should be grateful. And not complain.

But there's the other thing that will get you, no matter what. Impostor syndrome.

What is it? What it says. The feeling that you shouldn't be doing what you're doing. That you're not good enough to be paid to write. That it should be someone else, someone more talented, more incisive, wittier than you who should be writing. You have no penetrating insights to make about the human condition and you can't tell a story to save your life. And you shouldn't be allowed to be doing what you're doing. It can be crippling, a form of writer's block that can refuse to go away, because it isn't a question of working out what's wrong with the story, it's trying to work out what's wrong with the writer. Namely, that they shouldn't be doing what they're doing.

As I said earlier, it's a feeling that persists in many professions. The late actor, Don Henderson, was known to stalk rehearsal rooms of plays he was in, asking the other cast members sotto voce, 'Have they rumbled you yet?' The answers he received haven't been recorded. But I can guess the effect the question had. The other actor would have been thinking the same thought already.

Even now, after being a published writer for over twenty years, I go to events, whether they be parties, festivals or panels I'm speaking on, and still expect a hand on my shoulder accompanied by a voice informing me that I've had my fun and the real writers will be along in a minute, while guiding me to an exit. So why do I feel like an impostor? I've managed to keep a career going for over two decades in a very precarious business, I've been a bestseller, a critical success, I've won – and lost – awards. And yet. And yet . . . It persists. I think in part, certainly for me, it's a question of class and background. I come from a Northern working-class family. I was brought up in a tiny, dying community on the edge lands outside Gateshead. I was constantly told both at home and at school what my career options were – and acting (my original profession) and writing certainly weren't among them. We were given two options. If we'd done well at our O-levels, we could apply to the Civil Service. If we hadn't, we could go and work in the Komatsu factory. To a misfit kid with a love of books and comics, neither particularly appealed.

The thing that saved me was acting. I loved it. I went to work backstage at a theatre to see how it functioned. I auditioned for drama school and was accepted. After three years there I went straight into a play and wasn't out of work for the next two years. I had made it. And yet . . . It persisted. I was told by other actors that it was wonderful that I, with my regional accent, was allowed to be part of this world, because acting was a classless profession. No it wasn't and no it isn't: it's a middle-class one, even more so now, with opportunities to train and work in the profession more limited for those without money. And anyway, I didn't see myself as being an actor forever. I wanted to write.

So I wrote a novel. It got published. After five years' hard slog, I might add. And during this time I was still acting. But auditions and castings were hard. It's hard accepting rejection on a daily basis when it's for something you've got no control over. Too tall, too fat, too thin, hair all wrong, too Northern, not Northern enough. Impostor syndrome runs rampant then. You really start to believe you shouldn't be there. Especially when someone else always seems to get the parts you're up for.

I thought being a novelist would change all that. Actually having a copy of something I had accomplished, that I had made myself, a book, well . . . things would be different now. I could show people what I'd done. 'This is my novel. I wrote this. I've accomplished something that I was meant to do.' But I soon found out it didn't work like that. I initially signed a two-book deal. Writing my second novel was even more difficult than the first – because I had already been published. People (admittedly not very many of them) had paid money to read my words. And here I was, sitting at my keyboard daring to write another book, turning my thoughts and words into something people (hopefully more of them this time) would pay money to read. And it paralysed me, just the thought of it. Why would someone pay to read my words, to hear my opinions and thoughts? To see how inept I was at structuring a narrative, at creating characters? I looked on the bookshelf next to me. There were proper writers, ones I had loved, that had inspired and influenced me. They didn't go through all this. Do you think Graham Greene ever felt like he shouldn't have been doing what he was doing? Of course not. He was a proper writer. I was just pretending to be one.

Anyway, the second book was published and it had the same seismic effect on British cultural life that the first one had. But it did get some nice reviews and the attention of a bigger publisher. And no one told me I shouldn't be writing. Apart from a little voice inside my own head, that was.

Impostor syndrome gets worse with every book you publish, every good review you get, every big sale you make, every award you're nominated for, and especially those rare ones you actually win. You feel that this shouldn't be happening to you. That you're not worthy of all this praise, that they've got the wrong person. The hand will be on the shoulder soon guiding you to the door and the real writer will arrive. You've just been warming his seat, holding his contract or his award for him till he gets here.

I was convinced it was only me who ever experienced this. And I was also convinced that it was because I was Northern and from a working-class background. But here's the thing: I'm not the only one. I'm not even in a minority. I once mentioned it to a writer friend of mine to find he felt exactly the same. We were chatting after handing in our latest novels and noting with relief that they had been accepted. We've got away with it again, he said. And we had. We haven't been, as Don Henderson would have said, rumbled yet.

I've had similar conversations with other writers too, none of whom I'll name. And everyone I've spoken to has had it, continues to have it and will have it. Every one. A journalist once told me about meeting Graham Greene. There was a huge launch party for his latest novel back in the Seventies. It was, if I remember correctly, at the Metropole Hotel in Brighton. This journalist was eager to meet Greene, loved his work, had admired him for years. He got to the room, a huge, high-ceilinged ballroom, where the party was in full swing. Loads of publishing people there, all drinking, chatting, laughing. Enjoying themselves, celebrating the release of Greene's new book. But no Graham Greene. So this journalist wandered around the party, disappointed. He was at the far end of the room, away from the party guests and about to leave, when he noticed a man standing by one of the high windows, staring upwards. 'How many curtain rings do you think there are holding these curtains up?' the man asked. The journalist looked at him. It was Graham Greene. An impostor at his own party.

So what can we do about impostor syndrome, how can we address it? Well, there's nothing we can do about it. Just acknowledge it, work through it, live with it. And above all, keep going. It's part of what makes us sensitive enough to want to write in the first place. We just have to tell ourselves that we do deserve to be here, that we're privileged enough to be able to write. That it's our voice a reader wants to hear. Don't ignore the doubts; work with them. Use them to question what we're doing, help them to improve our work. If you think that you have some kind of God-given talent that needs to be shared with the rest of the waiting world, then good luck with your career; you won't be around long.

Writing is a balancing act. You have to be arrogant enough to want to write in the first place. To think you have a voice someone wants to hear, or insights to make, stories to tell. On the other side there's the doubt that inevitably comes – or should come – from wanting to do that. The trick is to get that balance right. To not let the doubts overwhelm you but welcome them, use them to improve your work. And at the same time be confident enough to sit down and write. And trust the words, the story, that emerges.

Ultimately, all a writer has is his or her own voice. And don't let anyone – least of all yourself – tell you that it shouldn't be heard.

Writing: A Painful Pleasure
Suzette A. Hill

The most acute pleasure is, of course, when your book is finished, passed and published. Hooray – relief, triumph and celebration! The converse is equally acute: the pain of rejection unleashes gloom, fury, a tearing of hair and a drowning of sorrows. However, between these two rather obvious and crude extremes, the author, whether budding or veteran, will experience a gamut of insidious delights, sudden joys and dark, nagging perplexities. Such mélange is the stuff of writing; and as with all artistic endeavours it contains a strong element of masochism. (Question: *Is* there an author who experiences no such masochism? If so, please reveal yourself. I shall be most intrigued!)

So in other words, writing is hard work. Do not expect otherwise. And please forgive me if I sound caustic or curmudgeonly when I say that those who declare they have a novel 'inside' them, waiting to be released, simply don't know the half of it! A novel is not something that lies dormant within, prefabricated and all ready to leap out at a convenient time; and strong thoughts about a topic, even one involving crime and detection, do not in themselves make a story. The abstract idea must become an artefact – and therein lies the rub.

Like any writing, a novel is fundamentally the manipulation of language for maximum effect. Nascent concepts have to be *transmuted* into a medium of words, sentences, concrete structures. They have to be developed through the creation of realistic characters, operate in contexts which are palpable, and be given a treatment sufficiently striking and evocative to convince and engage the reader. The writer will need to judge when and where to inject the elements of drama, pathos, surprise, action, reflection; when to increase or slacken the tempo, where to place dialogue and for what purpose . . . et cetera, et cetera. In short, he or she will not only have to *invent* and *present* the material but as with painting and music, or any art form, to select and orchestrate it. This is indeed the hard work – but also the challenge and excitement.

The foregoing general observations will probably be shared by most of my colleagues, but it would be wrong to assume that our writing styles, techniques, preferences, interests and methods are identical. Far from it! Each of us is different (thank goodness), and while there may be common links, the choosing and handling of data can vary enormously. Thus there are those authors for whom the *plot* is absolutely central and provides their greatest stimulus. Indeed it is the plot that calls the shots. Other aspects, while important, are there primarily to serve the necessities of that major element. For such authors, and indeed their readers, it is the puzzle itself that counts, and the way that the elements of plot are so woven as to produce an exquisitely complex spider's web to tantalize and intrigue. The deft treatment of plot, especially in crime fiction, is a wonderful skill . . . and how I envy those who have it!

By contrast my own tales are almost entirely character-driven and evolutionary. That is to say, the events and narrative twists grow out of the characters and their interaction. This is perhaps ironic, as long before I ventured into the fiction genre someone once said, 'You ought to write a novel', to which I gave the dismissive reply, 'Oh I couldn't possibly – besides, I'm not good on people.' And yet strangely when I eventually did take to writing, it was people – with all their quirks, oddities, problems and absurdities – that most engaged me. (And as a result, I suspect that despite the unfortunate corpses strewn around, my novels are nearer to social comedies than to full-blooded crime fiction.)

In this respect, and also before I had begun to write, I heard a novelist being interviewed on the radio. I can't remember who she was but I certainly found her talk illuminating – *until* she said something to the effect that she had little control over her characters; that they had a life of their own and she wasn't always sure what they were going to do next. At the time, and in my bumptious ignorance, I felt that was ridiculous. Surely, I thought, being the author she is the one in charge, the omniscient controller. Her claim that her inventions are somehow independent of their creator is pretentious hooey! . . . Not so. I have since discovered that characters, especially those which have become dear to you or whose personalities are strongly portrayed, do indeed seem to direct proceedings and slyly nudge you along paths you wouldn't normally have thought of. They exert a subversive power!

So, if creation of character (much of it through dialogue) is my pleasure, the plotting aspect is definitely not. This is probably because I cannot think in the abstract: before an overarching narrative structure can evolve there must be individuals, scenes and situations on the page – or at least in my mind's eye. Plots need plans. And alas, my plans are vague and readily collapsible. There is rarely a clear superimposed scheme.

In some ways such an ill-defined approach can be entertaining, in that it means I am telling *myself* a story and I never quite know how it is going to unfold, let alone resolve. Thus I write to find out. This process may be fun and intriguing, but it can also be painful. Building a preliminary framework is sometimes compared to producing a helpful skeleton: first put the bones in place and then fatten them with flesh. My problem is that I tend to reverse the order. It is not so much the flesh

– the texture – that bothers me but rather how to find the structure, that convenient and friendly skeleton. The beast is elusive, or at best crippled with arthritis. Thus to allay angst and boredom I will often compose in fragments – devising isolated scenes, conversations, random episodes. This gets me into the *spirit* of the thing and enables the creation of a world whose burgeoning reality compels further exploration, and from which directions and harmonies begin to emerge. Such an approach might be described as working from the particulars to the general, or from flesh to bone.

Because writing methods are so personal I hesitate to give specific advice (other than nil desperandum). However, there is one thing that I feel quite strongly about and believe is relevant to most novels: namely a tangible context. People do not operate in a vacuum; their feelings and actions occur within palpable settings. And if such settings – social and physical – are absent or only vaguely sketched, then credibility suffers. It is the author's task to ensure that the reader can see or *sense* the world (or living room) in which the protagonists act out their dramas. The context may be a figment but it needs fabric; without that fabric or sense of environment, situations lack substance. And if, as is often the case, the author chooses an actual location in which to place his/her characters, such as Barnsley or Bognor, then its features must be accurately portrayed. (NB. Get it wrong, and the locals object!) However, the danger here is that in one's eagerness to confer authenticity and bring the place to life, one can be overzealous. That is to say there is such a plethora of locational detail that the story sinks beneath its weight, and the whole thing achieves the subtlety of a travel brochure. As with most things, it is all a question of balance and nice judgement – a compound that the struggling author is endlessly trying to perfect.

In conclusion I can offer a further tip – in this case 'advice' being far too prescriptive a term. It is about the dreaded writer's block. The aspiring or novice author may be unacquainted with the condition. But be assured, sooner or later, in some form or degree, it will surely strike. Authors have different ways of coping with this malady, like a bracing walk with the dog, a break from routine (if such you have), the diversion of a book other than your own, or the old standby – consumption of strong drink. But this last resource, while palliative, is rarely curative, and one is still faced with an intractable blank page or screen.

As King Lear observed, nothing will come of nothing. And thus my own pet aid in such circumstances is to cover that yawning space with words. But *what* words? you may ask. After all, if ideas are being so elusive what precisely do you propose to write? To which I answer: broadly speaking anything at all – a snippet of a scene, a few lines of dialogue, a tiny episode; in fact anything that will get the mind moving again and oil the creaking Muse. We assume, rightly, that ideas generate words. But the converse is also true: words can stir, shape and determine thought. Thus, for example, one might jot down something like the following: *Entering the room, he lit a cigarette and stared disconsolately out of the window at the sodden lawn. The roses were lax and bedraggled; and the copper beech, blasted by sheets of rain, a ghostly blur . . . And yet from the blur something seemed to be moving. Yes, two figures walking slowly in the direction of the boathouse. Despite the foul weather they seemed lost in earnest conversation. Surely it couldn't be . . . oh yes it was! But they loathed each other, or so it had always seemed. How very extraordinary . . .* And so on, and so on.

Already such doodles have produced a mini-scenario, an incipient puzzle, images to spark the imagination and, with luck, to galvanize further pursuit. I do not suggest that such a piece be slotted wholesale into the existing narrative (though it might be), but it can be useful in striking chords; or, as is sometimes the case, it will goad the emerging tangent into making fresh paths. The essential thing is to get something down in front of you. It will rebuild confidence.

The process, of course, is not infallible; but with luck it can set you going again and ease you out of a tight corner into which, naturally, you had so blithely written yourself. However, as said, solutions will vary. And rather than push the pen in idle jottings, some people might simply prefer to walk the dog.

Writer's Block

David Stuart Davies

'How time flies; another ten days and I have achieved nothing. It doesn't come off. A page now and then is successful, but I can't keep it up, the next day I am powerless.'

Franz Kafka

The blank page – the curse of the creative writing profession. You sit down at your computer in readiness to produce something eminently readable, full of originality and verve – and suddenly freeze with fear. You cannot think of a thing to write. The imagination has dried up. The dreaded writer's block has struck.

Individuals whose occupation is writing depend on an active and fertile imagination fizzing with ideas, interesting plots and characters. If that lets you down, you are creatively impotent. It's like removing tools from a carpenter, paint and brushes from an artist, or access to a kitchen from a chef.

From talking to fellow crime writers, it's clear that this debilitating state is not as rare as one might suppose. It may strike at any time and even the most successful and prolific of authors can be affected. Writer's block does not only produce angst and bouts of depression but can also be responsible for severe physical conditions. One eminent crime novelist revealed to me that when he fell foul of the block he suffered with severe stomach pains as a result of not being able to write creatively.

So how does one cope with this crippling condition? It has to be said that overcoming its effects is not easy. One of the major problems with the onset of writer's block is that if you have a few sessions when the words will not come, it can trigger the belief that they never will again. Similar to insomnia, it can have a built-in cyclical trigger. However, the key to extracting yourself from this mire of despond is to force yourself to have a positive attitude and try various techniques recommended to help you to regain your inspiration and fluency.

In talking to fellow writers they have suggested a variety of approaches which have helped them individually to come through the tunnel and into the daylight once more.

One of the simplest suggestions is to give yourself a break from writing – a holiday from the page. Become involved in some other activity which will engage your brain and allow it to relax and refresh itself. It is often the case that when the mind is occupied with other things, fresh ideas spring forth. The release of the pressure of having to produce quality written material for a time may very well allow that block to crumble.

It's important not to suffer in silence or alone. Writers can feel embarrassed or ashamed if we are somehow failing in our task, but it is a mistake to bottle up the problem. One author observed, 'Set up a network of fellow writers with whom you can share the ghastliness and bliss of the business. When things get really bad, forget writing and meet someone for lunch.' Certainly, talking over your concerns with another writer is real medicine, which will not only ease the pain but will also help you recover.

In those periods when I've experienced the drying up of the creative juices, I've tried reading some of my previously published work in order to prove to myself, 'Yes, I can do it. On a good day I can do it and surely another good day will arrive soon.' It worked for me, but I have to admit the result was not instant – more a gradual reawakening of the spirit. Of course, this ploy could lead you into thinking that you'll never be able to write as well again – but above all you must force yourself to avoid those negative thoughts.

Another successful crime novelist with over fifty books to

his name suddenly found his latest novel was going nowhere. Various personal events, including the loss of a loved one, had brought on a clinical depression that affected his ability to write. However, he approached this problem in a very disciplined fashion – a technique which contradicts much of what has already been suggested in this piece. He kept to a routine, religiously going to his desk each day and writing for four hours. 'It was hard,' he told me, 'and you might think it was pointless since so many drafts went in the bin, but the discipline is what mattered and finally the problem eased.' It took him over six months to get back on track, but his dedication to his strict routine worked for him – and it may well for you.

It is clear, therefore, that one has to try various techniques – a suck-it-and-see approach – to find one that works for you and helps you to shrug off this darkest of black dogs. And talking of dogs, one writer even bought a puppy so that he had something to care for and make demands on him; walking the dog brought him into contact with fresh air and solitude, where ideas gradually began to percolate. Indeed, getting out of the house and taking the air was recommended by quite a few authors. To write well, you must be healthy and relaxed. A tired mind will only produce tired writing. Driving yourself to remain hunched over your computer for long hours is not healthy for body or prose.

For writers who create a series featuring a regular character, the challenge of coming up with something fresh and a little different for each new book can be daunting and bring about the dreaded block. There is always the niggling thought that the next novel has to be better or at least as good as the last. One writer who suffered from this creative blockage in their series solved it by writing something completely different from their usual work: new characters, new scenario. They found it a great release. It was stimulating and invigorating to try something outside their comfort zone, and it had the knock-on effect of bringing a freshness to their writing. Once the new book was finished, they felt ready to return to the series. Thanks to facing the demon with a positive and determined attitude, the shadows gradually disappeared. Fingers began flying over the keyboard once again.

Improvising
Stella Duffy

I came to writing from performance, first as an actor, then a stand-up, then an improviser. I still occasionally do some performance work, usually improvising with old friends who have companies that create work and perform regularly. I have always seen a clear link between improvising and writing: in its most basic form improvising is writing without pen and paper and writing is (in first draft at least) improvising alone. For many years, whenever I'm asked to teach a writing workshop, I have offered improvising for writers, and writing for improvisers. Improvising techniques help us to explore and play with the basic rules that every improviser uses to help us to create story, build characters, and develop scenes – above all, they help us to say *yes* to our own creative selves.

Starting with ourselves
The story does not tell itself – acknowledge your role in the making. At base, writing is a physical activity and we forget this at our peril. It doesn't matter if we are typing, writing longhand or using voice-activated software, we are using the body, the self, to create. In improvisation this is more obvious: a person is physically present, with or without other performers, and they are making stuff up, live, for a workshop or paying audience. We are physically present as writers too, whether we write alone or in a café; in silence, listening to music, or with the clatter of family life around us.

We use ourselves to make work. Our lives, our thinking, our

views all influence the characters we create and the stories we
tell with them. It doesn't matter how far removed from our
own lives our stories are, the person who is creating – you,
me – has nothing to create from but ourselves. Improvisation
helps us reconnect with the childlike imagination, the joy of
play, and the possibility of going beyond what we know to what
we can grow from the simple (but not at all easy) act of saying
yes. *Yes* to our own desire to create, *yes* to putting in the work,
yes to pushing through boredom or fear, *yes* to getting it done.

There is a self at the base of all creating. That self is not
static. In improvisation we encourage ourselves to pay attention
to where we are, to who we are on any given day, in any given
hour. To write when all is well is different from writing with
overdue bills on the table; with someone we love ill or unhappy;
if we are depressed or in pain or irritable or resentful.
Sometimes it is easier to write when the negative emotions
take over: we can give them to characters and play with them
on the page. Other times, it is difficult to the point of impossible.

Paying attention to ourselves will help us pay attention to
our characters. Allowing that our own moods and feelings and
physical condition affect how and what we do from day to day
will help us create full and viable characters with rich dimensions of their own.

Yes, yes and . . .
Also known as 'accept and build'. One improviser makes an
offer and another accepts it.

A   Gorgeous day, shall we go for a walk?
B   Yes, let's. There's something I want to tell you and it
      might be easier to talk while we're walking . . .

Person B has not only accepted A's offer of a walk, they've
built on it by adding some emotional content. They could also
have added action (*Yes, and let's take the dog, I fancy a big
run*) or intent (*I'd love that, let's walk to the beach*).

When people are learning to improvise we encourage them not to block like this:

A   Gorgeous day, shall we go for a walk?
B   No.

The block that is no makes it harder to move the action on, to develop the scene. This is not to suggest that an outright no is always wrong, but it's valuable to find an alternative offer even when saying no.

A   Gorgeous day, shall we go for a walk?
B   No, let's stay home and make mad passionate love.

We also have the choice of showing this build in action as opposed to dialogue

'Gorgeous day, shall we go for a walk?'
'No,' she said, smiling and leading the way back to bed.

There is another no that's harder to spot and therefore harder to deal with – that's the no we say to ourselves. The denial of the creative self, the rejection of ourselves as makers and artists. We do this every time we make an excuse not to write. 'I don't have time to write' is the most common.

You know this isn't true, don't you? Get off Twitter, Facebook or Instagram. Don't watch that thirty-minute TV programme. Write instead of reading the paper. Get up an hour before the children wake up and work then – Beryl Bainbridge did. Do it around your full time job like Chekhov, Dostoevsky and Trollope. Yes, they also had full-time wives and servants – that certainly helps – but there have been many women writers who were wives with full-time jobs and yet still made time to write. Spend your week's or fortnight's annual holiday writing. Write for an hour every weekend. Write for fifteen minutes every day. Make it as regular as cleaning your teeth. Make it a habit. For most people, 500 words a day is very achievable. Do that for a year (and keep moving forwards, don't go over and over the same few chapters) and you'll have a first draft. Then you'll have something to make better.

You do not need nine months of free time and a villa in Tuscany to write. You need an idea you want to work with and the determination to keep going. That's it. Stop saying no to your creative self and do the work.

Status

Status is key to improvising. When we pay attention to status, we create rounded characters without having to signal everything to the audience, without having to say everything out loud. Paying attention to status does so much for us, quickly and almost imperceptibly. Think of your own status, how comfortable or otherwise you feel at any one time in relation to other people and to place. It shows up in how you speak, move, stand, sit. Consider the differences when in your own home, in someone else's home, in a strange place that feels welcoming, in a known space that is uncomfortable. How are you with friends or among strangers?

We experience status interactions and alterations with respect to other people and to place at all times. Status can change over the course of a piece of work. Lady Macbeth is a great example, from medium status to high status to low in less than two hours. It can also happen within a scene – think of Blackadder believing he is in charge and learning that yet again he is definitely not. Malvolio's certainty in *Twelfth Night* that he is the beloved and his crushing disappointment when he realizes he is a figure of fun. A tiny addition such as how easily a character sits in a certain location or alongside another person can give your readers all the clues they need without you having to explain everything that they are feeling or experiencing. In this way the readers also dream into the character, making them more invested in the work.

There's magic in the mistakes

This is something improvisers learn by making those mistakes, live on stage, usually in front of a paying audience. The scene that falters and fades, going nowhere, but out of which one line feeds the next scene, which eventually makes a huge difference to the story. The performer who forgets the 'rules' of a game and creates an entirely new game in the process. The two performers who don't quite understand each other, to the delight of an audience that revels in their discomfort.

While it can be harder to sit with our discomfort as writers when a scene or a chapter or an entire piece of work isn't going well, it is exactly in staying with that discomfort that the magic lies. Other writers might tell you to go for a walk at this point, or have a drink, or do something – anything – else. They're all feasible suggestions, but I would suggest that it's also possible to stay with it – to sit in the discomfort of not being the brilliant writer you want to be, of being the barely adequate one who just can't make this scene fly, or write this dialogue so it feels real, or find the transitional scene that will bring together two important sections of a story. Sometimes it is in staying in the 'mistake', in working through it, that we find the gold.

Find the game

Despite what you may have seen on television, lots of improvisation is not formatted and doesn't have a game attached. One or more performers may simply come on stage and begin a scene. When we do this, we are looking for the 'game', the meat of the scene. We are looking for what else is going on, beyond the dialogue or the physical action. It can be useful to think about this when writing a scene: what else is going on here? If the character is getting ready to go to work, what else is going on for her? None of us is ever doing just one thing – we're also thinking, feeling, anticipating, daydreaming, remembering. This isn't relevant for every scene; some of them just are the action that shows on the surface. But in the build-up to a crucial moment, or at a point when you just need to get a character to

go from A to B, it is useful to pay attention to what else is going
on for them. It gives a welcome extra layer. When we pay attention in this way, it changes how we write the character's
physicality, their attitude to the physical space they are in, the
rhythm of their speech or how they speak at all.

Fear

Yes, improvising is scary. So is writing. It is scary to take our
precious time and decide we will use it to write. Scary to
commit to creating something and then to share it with others.
Most of us have impostor syndrome to some degree or another.
Very few people are utterly convinced of their own magnificence
(and those that are make very good villains). Most of us were
told as we grew up that we needed to be well-behaved, not
make too much of a fuss, not draw attention to ourselves and
certainly not to show off. Yet to make any work, to commit to
taking the time to create it, to edit it, to do everything you can
to make it as good as possible in this moment – and then to
send it out, to offer it up to strangers to critique, to agent, to
publish, to read – requires most of us to step out of a comfort
zone and risk being rejected, risk being not wanted. That is
scary. It brings up loads of fear for all of us – published or
unpublished.

On the other hand, it is a choice. You don't have to do this.
You are choosing to write, so you have to choose also to take
the tricky bits, the hard bits, along with the good bits. And it's
only writing – you're not Barbara Hepworth risking ruining a
perfect sculpture with one wrong chisel strike. You can always
start a new page.

Play

At heart, improvising is about playing, and playing is the perfect
counterpoint to the fear. Here's the truth – the world does not
need another book, not from any one of us. It doesn't need
yours and it doesn't need mine. There are already more stories
than we could ever read. Writers face inevitable difficulties.
Yet we can balance some of them with play, with joy. Children

run, dance, jump at will. They make up songs and stories, they turn tables into caves and chairs into elephants. We were all children once. We can be so again, on the page. We just have to say yes to ourselves and our possibility.

Say yes, make work, be brave. Easy – and also not easy at all – but very worthwhile.

Go and play.

Ending

In a crime novel, perhaps more than in any other branch of fiction, the way you bring your story to an end is crucial. H. R. F. Keating confessed in *Writing Crime Fiction* that, upon reading his draft manuscripts, his first reader, his wife Sheila, almost invariably pointed out that he had 'snatched at the end again'. The temptation to decide that a book is finished can seem overwhelming, but it is important to do everything possible to realize the full potential of the story. The key, Keating said, is to remember the story's *form*: 'You should aim for an effect similar to that of the final bars of a symphony.' In other words the climax, however startling, should be in keeping with the whole story, so as to give readers a sense of artistic satisfaction.

Harry Keating also favoured 'leaving things unsaid, by leaving your readers with the feeling that your people will go on living after they have reached your last page. There is no need to make a meal of this. A hint or two will do.' As Laura Wilson and Joanna Hines suggest, a wide range of questions arise about when and how a book is properly brought to an end.

The End of the Beginning
Laura Wilson

So, you have completed the first draft of your crime novel. Sit back, pour yourself a well-earned drink, and take what's left of the day off. You're going to need the rest, because, as Winston Churchill said about the Second Battle of El Alamein, where you are 'is not even the beginning of the end, but it is, perhaps, the end of the beginning'. Elsewhere he had something to say, too, about blood, toil, tears and sweat. Chances are, you will have completed your novel in the white heat of creativity, living and breathing with your characters, dreaming about them at night, and generally being utterly absorbed in their trials and tribulations. That's great; congratulations. But now you need to take a long, hard and objective look at what you've written. No matter how authoritative your first draft looks, all nicely typed up, it will contain flaws, and your job now is to identify and correct them. You need to learn to be self-critical in a whole new arena, no matter how inadequate it makes you feel – and, if you do it properly, it *will* make you feel inadequate, believe me. And it should; as Booker prize-winning author Anne Enright puts it, 'Only bad writers think that their work is really good.'

As bestselling novelist Michael Crichton (*The Andromeda Strain*, *Jurassic Park*) said, 'Books are not written, they're re-written,' and the truth is that quite a lot of them have to be re-written not once, but several times. When you read over your manuscript, pretend that you have never laid eyes on it before (yes, you can do this; you've got an imagination – that's why you started writing in the first place). Here is a checklist of things to look out for which will, I hope, make the process less arduous:

- First, the bleeding obvious: are you interested in the story? If you're not, nobody else will be.
- Have you started in the right place? Is there too much introductory background information? Will the reader be

instantly involved? If there is a prologue, is it really necessary – or, if there isn't a prologue, should there be?

- Does every scene advance the plot and/or give the reader important information about the characters? Particular pitfalls to watch out for are the character's childhood being recounted in detail to no purpose, and unintended red herrings.

- Are your major theme and plot elements introduced in the first quarter (or third if you must) of your novel? If not, they should be.

- Have you expressed everything you need to express in the best possible way? A good method of testing this is to read your work aloud, so that you can be sure that the rhythms of your sentences are OK, and that your work is correctly punctuated. It's also an excellent way to judge the effectiveness (or otherwise) of your dialogue. Now, about those bits that you think are really, really good . . . Nobody is sure who first used the phrase 'murder your darlings', but he or she was absolutely right. As Elmore Leonard said, 'If it sounds like writing, I rewrite it.' Alternatively, you could delete it, but either way, you should deal with it, because if you don't and your novel is accepted for publication, someone else will, further down the line. Be ruthless: is that beautifully crafted paragraph really necessary? I think you already know the answer, don't you?

- Is there enough conflict and tension? Too much exposition can get in the way of this. You need to *show* that there is conflict and tension, not just tell us about it. I've noticed, in work by unpublished writers of crime fiction, a tendency to set up conflicts and tensions and then back away from them, so that the carefully crafted build-up with its narrative 'hooks' ends not with a bang but with a whimper of the in-one-bound-Jack-was-free variety. Another surefire way to lose any suspense is to introduce irrelevant detail (see point about exposition below).

- Is there too much repetition? You should never use two

scenes to establish the same thing. You should also avoid
scenes where the characters have a long talk about all
the things they've done in the previous scene. In a detective novel, a re-cap is often necessary, lest the reader lose
sight of the various suspects and their possible motives
for murder, but keep it as succinct as possible. Also,
make sure your characters aren't telling each other stuff
that they would already know – find a different way to
get the points across to the reader.

- Is there sufficient variation in tone and pace? Unless you
  are writing a straight-down-the-line, underpants-over-the-
  trousers action thriller where everything takes place at
  warp speed and the characterization is paper-thin, you
  should intersperse action scenes with slower, more reflective ones.

- Does each chapter end with a hook to draw readers on
  to the next one?

- Are there too many coincidences? Or is there one huge
  one? Yes, I know they happen all the time in life, but in
  fiction they should be avoided as much as possible. You
  should also avoid such get-outs as having your protagonist's money problem solved by a miraculous lottery win
  or an inheritance from a hitherto unknown relative –
  unless, of course, this is going to lead to enormous
  trouble later on in the book.

- Are you confusing the reader with shifting points of view?
  If you are writing from the point of view of several
  different characters, it's best to stick to one point of view
  per chapter. If, for some reason, this isn't possible, at
  least allow a line break. Similarly, where there is
  dialogue, make sure you have identified your speakers.
  This is especially important if the conversation is between
  more than two people. You don't have to repeat the
  speech tags ('Jane said') after every single piece of
  dialogue, but you must do so enough to clarify who is
  saying what to whom. It is, incidentally, generally agreed
  (at least, I've never come across a single writer or editor

who disagrees), that it's best to keep to 'said' when you wish to indicate that a particular character is speaking, although 'shouted' and 'asked' are also acceptable. It's not a good idea to have people averring and opining and vociferating all over the place, and don't ever, ever, have them ejaculating – unless in a sexual context, and not always even then (see below). You should also avoid exclamation marks, which, as F. Scott Fitzgerald once said, 'are like laughing at your own jokes'. On no account use more than one font, and try to keep the italics to a minimum.

- Are your tenses consistent?
- Are there any clichés? There will be, of course. It's alarmingly easy for them to slip under the radar. It's fine to have a few in the dialogue, because that's how people talk, but if they are really piling up, you need to take action.
- Are there any inconsistencies? If your heroine has blue eyes on page 3, she'd better not have brown ones on page 76 (unless, of course, she's acquired some coloured contact lenses for the purpose of disguise).
- Have you checked all the facts? Are you sure about police procedure, historical details, and the rest? If you are writing a historical crime novel, you need to become positively paranoid about this. Are you sure that none of your characters are doing, saying, or even thinking, anything anachronistic?
- Is there too much exposition? Unless your character is going to witness a murder on the way to work, it's not necessary to include every detail of their bus journey. Even if they do witness a murder (or some other important incident takes place), it's probably still not necessary, and it certainly isn't necessary to tell the reader every detail of their morning routine. Cut to the chase.
- Is there anything else superfluous that needs to be cut? That fantastic description of a sunset on page 28 – what is the point of it? A bit of scene setting is fine, but

descriptions should avoid being simply ornamental. They
should be coloured by the person who is doing the
looking, so that the description is helping to define the
character at the same time (that's just one of the many
the reasons why eye-of-God narration is a bad idea). In
On Writing, Stephen King recounts a story about a rejection slip he received for one of his early efforts. On it was
written 'You need to revise for length. Formula: 2nd Draft
= 1st Draft minus 10%.' That is usually about right,
unless you have fallen into the trap of having too many
plot lines. If you suspect that this might be the case, ask
a partner or friend to read the manuscript. If, by around
chapter ten, they are shaking their heads in bafflement
and wondering what all the different characters could
possibly have to do with each other, you need a serious
re-think. If, on the other hand, your plot is too simple,
you may need to add a few more twists.

- Are your sex scenes really necessary? This is definitely
  one area where less is more. Only include details if they
  advance the plot or make a character point.

- As you near the end, ask yourself whether the plot is
  really working, and whether the murderer is the right
  person. Might it be more plausible if the killer turns out
  to be somebody else? The thing isn't cast in stone yet,
  and you can always change your mind.

- Is the ending plausible? Greek tragedies often used the
  deus ex machina – literally 'god out of the machine',
  whereby a seemingly inextricable problem is suddenly
  solved with the contrived and unexpected intervention of
  some new event. Even back then, it was criticized by
  Aristotle. It should never be used in crime fiction. If your
  plot isn't working, go back and change it; don't tack
  something on at the end. Similarly, make sure your villain
  doesn't give up too easily; it does need to be a fight to
  the finish. Also, make sure you haven't omitted any vital
  steps in the plot: however convoluted your novel, when
  there's a crime to be solved there must be a clear

sequence of clues, plausible deductions, and the rest.
Having said that, some things can legitimately be fudged.
A good example of this can be seen in the work of Simon
Brett, author of two excellent mystery series (the Charles
Paris series and the Fethering series). Both feature
amateur sleuths who unmask the killer without the aid of
the law. The police, of course, do have to be called at the
end to remove the miscreant, but as their exact method-
ology is wholly irrelevant to the story, Brett neatly
sidesteps the issue by writing something along the lines
of 'the police came, and they were very efficient'. That is
all that's needed – to go into details would entail a
confusing and unnecessary change from one sub-genre to
another.

- Make sure the ending is as dramatic as possible. If a
  character details a plan of action, such as a trap for the
  murderer, before he or she puts it into action, that plan
  must go wrong. Otherwise, the ending will be predictable
  and dull.
- Have you tied up all the loose ends? Remember Raymond
  Chandler, who forgot to tell the readers of *The Big Sleep*
  who killed the chauffeur. He got away with it – at least
  until Howard Hawks, who directed the 1946 film of the
  book, sent him a telegram about it, at which point he
  had to admit that he didn't have a clue. You won't get
  away with it.
- Last but not least, remember that, if your novel is set in
  the UK, the place where the dead people are taken is
  always called a mortuary, never a morgue.

Good luck! As Winston Churchill probably didn't say after all
– but it would have been jolly satisfactory if he had – 'Success
is not final, failure is not fatal: it is the courage to continue
that counts.'

In My End

Joanna Hines

Sometimes a writer learns most from her mistakes. When things go right, it can feel natural and instinctive – 'I'm a writer,' one thinks smugly. 'It just happens that way' – and it's only when things don't work out that you look at it and wonder why?

The end of my novel *Surface Tension* provided me with one of those 'oops' moments. It's a book that features a fairly whacky New Age cult, which was a great deal of fun to research and develop – creating a belief system based around the Mayan clock was intriguing. The Heirs of Akasha, as they were called, with their Questers and Acolytes and their belief that the world would end on 23 December 2012, were a mixture of charlatans and genuine believers. I didn't want to go down the stereotypical route of making the cult entirely evil and manipulative. It's the ambivalence that is interesting. After all, the Quakers were originally regarded as the most dangerous of loony cults. Now they have achieved salt-of-the-earth status.

But my indecision about the gloriously bonkers Heirs of Akasha went deeper. I wrote the book at a tricky time in my life, when all the signposts were blurred and the way ahead uncertain. So that when it came to the final chapter I was unable to provide any kind of real conclusion. It ends with more questions than answers. Had an early death been an accident or murder? Who was fake and who was lying? 'I don't know!' wails the narrator. The whole book ends with a question mark.

Which was OK for the fictional narrator, but probably the author should have got a grip on the whole business and made up her mind by the time she let the text out of her grasp.

So far as I know I was the only person who was bothered by this dithering. But it did set me wondering why the fuzzy ending made me so uncomfortable. I realized that when an author invites a reader, on page one, to accompany her for a number of hours along an imaginary path, then she is also offering a promise that the destination will deliver some kind of satisfying conclusion. A question posed at the beginning will be answered, so the reader can put the book to one side with a small sigh of satisfaction, the kind of pleasure in a puzzle solved that is so elusive in real life. Not all the i's have to be dotted nor the t's crossed, but the general sense of an arrival is important.

How to do this will obviously depend on several factors. 'And they all lived happily ever after' is probably best avoided as a bit simplistic. (Though the ritual ending can appeal just as much to adults as children, as the TV series *Yes, Minister* showed in every episode.) One should also bid farewell to the convention employed by so many old films where the villain – while keeping a firm grip on the gun, sabre, chainsaw, grenade or Death Star with which he intends to eliminate the helpless hero/heroine – is suddenly seized with an uncontrollable urge to unburden himself, pausing before the *coup de grace* to explain in minute detail exactly how his dastardly deeds were carried out. This not only explains the mechanics of the plot, but also gives the rescuers time to arrive, or enables the helpless hero/heroine to saw through the restraining ropes unobserved and leap to freedom. Today's narrator must devise a more convincing way to explain howdunit.

If the book is part of a series, it's possible to float a minor question that will assume greater importance in a later novel. Two narrative arcs are in play: the immediate mystery, which has been solved, and the ongoing drama of the characters' lives, which forms the extended arc of the series (a bit like the two Mayan clocks followed by the Heirs of Akasha, as it happens). The final sentence of the first Martin Beck novel, *Roseanna* by Maj Sjöwall and Per Wahlöö, is 'He was on his way home.' Which sounds positive enough, almost along the lines of 'and they lived happily ever after' – and the crime has been properly solved. Except that 'home' for Beck is a place of muddle and discomfort, and his wife and children are increasingly alienated – a theme which develops through all ten books in the series.

A brilliant example of a grappling hook thrown into the next book comes at the end of Aline Templeton's *The Darkness and the Deep*. Detective Inspector Marjory Fleming has been tough and effective throughout the novel, but in the final pages, with the crime solved and order re-established, she discovers her mother, on whom she has always relied, weeping over her husband's descent into forgetfulness and oblivion. 'She wasn't any more the person who knew all the answers.' Fleming is tempted to ignore the obvious signs, but instead she forces herself to become her mother's support. The final sentence tells us that, 'Reluctantly, with a terrible finality, Marjory Fleming said farewell to the last, precious vestiges of her childhood.' These few words expose the very human frailty at the core of Templeton's detective. The shift in the family dynamic will carry through into the next novel. It's the combination of a warm personal story with the bleak horrors of the criminal world that give this series its enduring appeal. In this book the pacing of the final pages, slowing up and allowing space in which to deliver the final punch, is near perfect.

Pacing is all. The accepted rule, often repeated, is that chapters and sentences should grow shorter as the end approaches. It's like that last burst of speed at the end of a race or the final fast movement in a symphony. Which may well be true, but it can be carried too far – and too fast. The challenge and satisfaction is often in setting up all the plot lines and dilemmas that will culminate in a high-octane climax. The danger for the writer is that, having toiled up the plot mountain and surveyed the view from the summit, the descent down the other side has a disconcerting tendency to run out of control. Unless you are one of those writers who plot every detail to the nth degree, there is always the possibility that one or two threads will be left out and have to be tied in awkwardly in a later draft. I've always found a degree of authorial uncertainty to be essential if I'm going to keep myself engaged. It's the surprises along the way that intrigue. Once it is all coming clear, the temptation to say 'This happened, then that happened and then it was all over, THE END!' can be quite strong, especially if a deadline is looming. Or is receding behind you. But the temptation must be resisted, at all costs.

Similarly, during the downward tumble towards the finish line, it's useful to space out the reveals. Minor dilemmas can be explained as the end approaches with just a final piece of information – like the last twist in a Rubik cube – to be dropped in right at the end. There can be death and destruction, but the reader needs to know that in crime fiction at least, some basic aspects of the puzzle will be solved. No drifting off into

Publishing

A distinguished editor of crime fiction once invited me to lunch to celebrate the publication of an anthology I'd edited. Towards the end of a convivial meal, I asked her what she thought of the current state of the crime writing market. Her expression became sombre. 'It's difficult,' she replied. 'Very difficult.' Then she thought for a moment and added, 'Mind you, I've been saying that to authors for the past thirty years'.

Since then, publishing has become even more complex. We have seen the rise of digital publishing and audiobooks. E-books (sometimes self-published, sometimes marketed with the benefit of sophisticated and expensive advertising campaigns) compete fiercely with mass market paperbacks, but an unexpected development has been that hardbacks have enjoyed something of a renaissance. After years of cost-saving, which resulted in cheaply made books whose pages soon browned and whose spines soon cracked, publishers are producing hardback books which are beautiful to handle and look at.

The British Library's Crime Classics include many novels written by Detection Club members that had been out of print and forgotten for up to three-quarters of a century. It's primarily a paperback imprint, yet so attractively designed that the books are widely collected, and sales figures for some titles dwarf the figures achieved by the original publication. Nobody involved with the project ever dreamed it would achieve such success. What the future holds for publishing, and therefore for authors, is likewise impossible to predict.

Several contributors to *Howdunit* have mentioned their agents. For beginning authors, it is often as difficult to find a literary agent as to find a publisher. Although most professional writers have agents, a minority prefer not to do so, sometimes because they have been scarred by past experience. As in every walk of life, one occasionally comes across agents who are lazy, incompetent, or unscrupulous. Conversely, a relationship with an agent who believes in your writing and is on your side in dealings with publishers may be of inestimable value. It is worth bearing in mind that if you are eligible to join the Society of Authors (whose website is a must-read), then the cost of the subscription is likely to be money very well spent, not least because they are willing to offer expert and unbiased advice on contracts with publishers.

At present, publishers still generally prefer to receive agented manuscripts and tend to relegate unsolicited submissions to the 'slush pile'. Small wonder that so many authors, including some who have been traditionally published with some success, contemplate self-publishing. Self-publishing can bring its own headaches and can also lead, at least once in a blue moon, to a nomination for the Booker Prize.

The four crime writers who contribute to this section of *Howdunit* all speak with authority. David Roberts was a publisher by profession and Antonia Hodgson a leading editor. Russell James has self-published with success and so has Jill Paton Walsh. Their personal views are informed by priceless experience.

The Changing Face of Publishing

David Roberts

Publishers, like farmers, never confess to having made money, and those who do have no idea how they did it.

William Goldman famously quipped that in Hollywood nobody knows anything: 'Not one person in the entire motion picture field knows for a certainty what's going to work. Every time out it's a guess but, if you are lucky, an educated one.'

It's equally true in publishing. The best most publishers can come up with is to have a new book as close in content and, more importantly, in its jacket and title as a book that has already been a bestseller. Ideally, the quotes on the jacket should be by the author whose work he is trying to rip off. If that's not possible, get another author to write for the jacket something along the lines of 'If you enjoy Tom Clancy, Lee Child or whoever is top of the *Sunday Times* Bestseller list, you will enjoy this.'

Of course, even better is to get the estate of some famous author like Ian Fleming or P. G. Wodehouse to let you write a pastiche or, as we authors like to say, a tribute – that is, a book you might mistake for the real thing in the bookshop until you get it home, open it, and discover your error.

I was a publisher for thirty years before giving it up to write. I thought that if I were asked to publish one more 'definitive' solution to the Jack-the-Ripper mystery or a 'definitive' *Does the Loch Ness Monster Really Exist?* (such books are always definitive until the next one) I would scream.

So I thought I could do better? Who was I fooling? I didn't want to trade on publishing connections, ask a favour and tumble into the real world that way. No, I would submit my typescript in the ordinary way and suffer the slings and arrows of outrageous fortune and . . . be rejected. Actors have it much worse because they are recognizable – no one knows or cares what an author looks like. But authors, too, are sensitive souls leading a lonely life and rejection slips saying 'not suitable for our list' are so many daggers in the heart.

There are no rules to writing novels – if there are, someone in this book will tell me. Some authors, for instance, plan every paragraph before putting pen to paper, but if I do that I soon get bored and go off-piste, possibly to be smothered by an avalanche. And yes, write from the heart about one's terrible childhood, unhappy love affairs and divorce; but give what you've written to someone you *don't* love and who doesn't love you so they can tell you are self-indulgent and – worst sin of all – boring. Above all, don't write a novel about someone writing a novel. It maybe the only thing you know about but don't let on to the reading public that you are barren of ideas.

Call me cynical but I still feel the bile rise when I read those fulsome acknowledgements in the novels of my more famous contemporaries. Along with 'dedicating this masterpiece to my long-suffering but admiring wife, husband or daughter', 'I must also thank my agent who read so many early drafts and suggested improvements . . . my editor who was like a mother/father to me', and 'I cannot thank enough the reading group who almost wrote this for me.' No, they didn't.

But surely publicity is the answer to the ingratitude of the reading public? If people only knew my book was published it would sell as well as Lee Child's. No, it wouldn't. As one publisher told me, 'Authors sometimes say, "If you spent half the money publicising my book you spend on your bestsellers, I too would be a bestseller," but of course they wouldn't be.' Publicity – especially paid advertising, which comes straight off the bottom line – only works to push a book already selling well onto the next level. A book which isn't selling is not worth spending a penny on – not in any sense. Only word-of-mouth recommendations will help, so make use of your friends and family.

Has publishing changed since the digital revolution? There's no point is bewailing what has already changed – the way books are read. Better to celebrate new ways of spreading the word. The more devices on which a book can be read the better. Before the internet, books were sold, remaindered and then disappeared. An American publisher I knew said most of his books were sold at O'Hare Airport, Chicago. The books in the racks were replenished every four hours and he expected to pulp half of every paperback print run. Now they continue to exist in the ether – ghostly but nevertheless real.

But it is not all gloom and doom. They said television would kill off the movies but it didn't – they live off each other. Did the movies kill off theatre? No – theatre just had to be better. Hardback books have to be more beautiful, better produced, and a pleasure to handle. The market for books worth fondling is bigger and expanding.

But what about plotting and dialogue? In my chosen area – I write crime novels set in the 1930s – there are no new plots but there are different way of packaging the plots. Context is all. The 1930s were as Auden said 'a low dishonest decade'. Politics was rancid and polarized – unlike today of course! A war was just round the corner. If this slice of history cannot provide the author with material in which to coat a crime – like chocolate round a peanut – what can?

No question, the historical crime novel is popular because the context is interesting and the reader maybe feels he or she is learning a little about the era in which the book is set. And for the author, the research is rewarding. My books are set in the 1930s not just because I have never been good at modern dialogue but because the letters and diaries of the time reveal how people lived, spoke and thought. Set your book in the Middle Ages and there is an immediate problem: we don't share their idea that God is, literally, the be-all and end-all. So we either have to leave out religion and be unfaithful to the reality; or – and this often happens – we add a hero or heroine who is 'modern', for the reader to identify with. Somehow the peasant girl knows all about modern doctoring, the spread of disease and how *not* to treat a patient. We know it is ridiculous, but it makes the reader comfortable and superior. The author is God, the reader is God, and so everything is possible.

Len Deighton, to whom this book is dedicated, is a brilliant researcher. Read *Bomber* and we know what it is to fly in such a contraption and we can feel the fear. *SS-GB* is so well researched we can surely *know* what it might be like to live in a world where the Nazis had conquered Britain. And Tom Clancy's *The Hunt for Red October*, in which he vividly describes what it must be like to sail a submarine, panders to every boy's – and girl's? – lust to know how complicated machines work. It is this technical mastery which can make an author's (perhaps unlikely) plot believable and involving.

So what about characters? Must there always be an 'odd couple' – preferably a man and a girl but for Conan Doyle two men? Someone to whom Sherlock Holmes can explain things and prove how clever he is? If there's a female, she can provide the love interest – call me old-fashioned. She may not fall at the hero's feet in the first chapter, because she's a modern girl regardless of the period in which the story is set. An example (I confess it) is my heroine, Verity Browne, based on the American journalist Martha Gellhorn. But the reader knows that the moment will come and she'll fall for the . . . well, the obvious. Yes, but when? For the reader, expectation is everything.

So how is writing a novel today different from what it was a generation ago? It is not. A good story, a strong plot, vividly drawn characters – the ingredients do not change. There are minor differences, of course. Today more sex, more explicit violence, more characters from diverse backgrounds; but could one write a better book than *War and Peace*, *Middlemarch* or *The Portrait of a Lady*? And none of these has explicit sex or violence – not even Tolstoy's dramatic telling of the disaster which was the Battle of Borodino. No one will live to see a day when these books gather dust on the bookshelves. True, and shame on us, that more libraries will close and we will read so much more online. But the magic that made these great books unforgettable is just what we need when we try to contribute our own bricks in the wall of literature.

So yes, publishing changes but nothing really changes. There is good luck and bad luck. *A Confederacy of Dunces* was published eleven years after the author, John Kennedy Toole, committed suicide believing he was a failure. It was published thanks to the amazing courage and conviction of his mother, and became a bestseller. Good luck or bad luck? How easy it would have been for her to give up and say this great book was unpublishable, and how wonderful that she did not. The moral, if there is one, must be never to give up. If you believe in your work then so will others – eventually.

What Editors Want

Antonia Hodgson

'*I can see you.*'

The voice on the phone sounds tense. Murderous, even.

I glance anxiously around the industrial-chic brasserie. I have already scouted the tables twice. If she's here, watching me, she must be a mistress of the shadows . . .

'Where are you?' I whisper.

'*Across the road.*'

I look out of the window, and there she is, separated by the passing traffic. It is a grey, muggy afternoon in Balham, south London. The air feels dirty, and everyone looks crumpled.

'*What,*' she says, '*are you doing there?*'

A good question.

Two weeks ago, the Detection Club handed me an assignment. They wanted to know what makes crime editors tick. My mission, if I chose to accept it, was to ask them. This was interview number one: Catherine Burke from Little, Brown. Catherine publishes her own authors and manages a team of crime editors, overseeing strategy for, oh, *you know*, Robert Galbraith, Val McDermid and Clare Mackintosh – to name a few.

Catherine has an exceedingly impressive job title, but life is short and publishing titles are long. Let's not dwell. We are good friends, which is lucky, as one of us went to the wrong restaurant. Cath is famed for her exceptional attention to detail, whereas I once thought I'd lost my phone *while on the phone*. Clearly, the fault was hers.

'I'm going to have a cocktail.' I've read the drinks menu several times, while waiting (in the correct restaurant). I order a pomegranate margarita.

'I'll just have water,' Cath says. She's not working today, but she's moving house soon and has stuff to do.

The cocktail arrives with the food. Cath looks at it. Looks at her water. Calls the waitress back. 'Actually . . . I'll have a gin and prosecco mimosa.'

I open my notepad. I've never interviewed anyone before, but I've seen *Line of Duty*. I'll be fine. 'What are you looking for when you read a submission?'

'It's an emotional reaction,' Cath says. 'You feel it in the pit of your stomach. You don't want to stop reading, you *have* to know where it's going next.' It's a rare, deeply personal feeling. 'The reading experience must come first. Then I put on my practical hat.'

'What if one of your editors loves a book, but you don't?'

'That's fine! In fact, that's really important – a variety of tastes. But I do want them to have a visceral reaction.'

'What are you looking for beyond the material itself?'

'More ideas,' she says, emphatically. 'I want to build careers. Most crime writers are expected to deliver a book a year, so I'm looking for a level of confidence, a plan of approach.'

'So what do you love most about your job?'

Cath's eyes light up. 'Seeing my authors' work recognized by readers and peers – and awards judges! Seeing books I care about resonate with people around the world . . .' She turns reflective. (I think the mimosa is kicking in.) 'Crime is a universal genre – it's human nature to take things that are out of our control into a controllable space and examine them. Explore them. Crime is reflective of the world, always changing, always interesting.'

I ask what advice she would give to an aspiring author.

'Write, write, write. The discipline of writing is what holds a lot of people back.'

I agree, although I'm not keen on the word 'discipline'. I think it's more of a vocation, or a compulsion. You just have to want to do it more than anything else.

'And the ending is vital,' Cath finishes, neatly. 'You have to know where you're going.'

We both nod sagely at this. After all, if you don't know where you're going, where on earth will you end up? Sitting in the wrong restaurant, that's where.

My second meeting is a breakfast meeting. When I worked in publishing, these were my favourite. You're fresh, they're fresh, the pastry is fresh. Perfect.

I'm catching up with Ed Wood, who also works at Little, Brown. The thing is, I hate cold-calling strangers for favours. I know everyone at Little, Brown because I worked there for a thousand years. (I did try to interview my editor at Hodder, but he said, 'Gosh, I'm terrible at these things,' then hid under a pile of manuscripts until the coast was clear.)

Ed is a creative thinker, who likes to come at things from a different slant, whether he's working with a new author or a long-standing bestseller. His authors include Mark Billingham, Chris Brookmyre, Stephen Booth and Jessica Fellowes.

'What are you looking for with a new book, Ed?'

'Three things. One is essential, two even better, three is perfect.'

Blimey.

He holds up a finger. 'Number one: high concept. I'm already publishing some of the great writers of procedurals, so anything else has to be really different.

'Number two: voice.'

Voice can be defined in several ways, so I ask what he means
by it.

'It might be a character's voice, or the authorial voice. Or it
could be that the author can pull the reader through the book
quickly – James Patterson and Dan Brown are brilliant at that.
The point is, it's something unique to this author, something
they are especially good at, and that draws the reader on.'

'Number three?'

'Something extra, that makes the author interesting. I know
this is controversial,' Ed adds swiftly, 'but it helps if an author
has a story behind the story. Anyway – if you have all three,
those books are especially exciting. And often end up in a huge
bidding war.'

Well, you can't argue with a huge bidding war.

I ask him about common, fixable mistakes.

'Rushed endings.' (Spoiler alert: *everyone* says this.) 'And
the middle! So many books dip after the first third. The second
third is *not* the bridge between the beginning and the end. It's
the *heart* of your story! This is where your character develops,
where they confront the hardest questions and are thrown into
conflict. You should be able to knock out the beginning and
the end and still have a fully functioning story – it's that important.'

I like this. 'So what advice would you give to an aspiring
author?'

'Know where to start, and where to end. Know what your
book is about, and make sure this runs clearly through the
whole narrative.'

When I ask what he loves best about his job, he smiles
broadly. 'I love the editing process, working with the author,
coming up with a fantastic solution to a problem together.
Authors always know what needs fixing – it's my job to coax
that out. It's incredibly rewarding.'

This makes sense. Ed is an enthusiast, who likes fresh challenges. I'm struck by how much an editor's personality informs
not only their approach to work, but their taste. This is why
one editor might turn a book down, only for another to snap

it up eagerly and turn it into a bestseller. Both will have made
the right decision, by the way.

'Don't shoot!' Joanne Dickinson raises her hands.

We're meeting for lunch at the Lady Ottoline, a Bloomsbury
pub famed for its pies. I've rushed over from Chinatown,
carrying a newly mended scroll rolled up under my arm. It
does look like a shotgun, to be fair – especially if you're used
to contemplating crime for a living. Luckily, while Jo is a
passionate campaigner for her authors, she's also the calmest
person I know. After six years at Simon & Schuster she is
moving to Hodder as publisher.

I ask what excites her about a new novel.

'Structure. Twists. Believable characters. I want to be taken on
a journey, surprised, kept on the edge of my seat. I'll know quite
quickly if I'm interested – often within the first twenty pages.'

The pies arrive. They are, as promised, delicious, but I'm
jotting notes, so mine congeals sadly on the plate. The sacrifices
we make for our art.

Jo talks about common structural mistakes. A first draft
might hold too much back to the end, or start with promise
then fall flat. 'But as long as the components are there . . .'

We chat about pitches and shoutlines. A lot of authors –
myself included – find it hard to distil their *precious baby* this
way. But as Jo says, 'A really good two-sentence shoutline can
sell a book around the world.'

Focuses the mind, doesn't it?

I ask what she loves most about the job. 'I love working
with an author, the editing process, creating something visually
exciting. And every day is different. I really like that element
of surprise.'

'Like someone coming at you with a Chinese scroll?'

She smiles serenely. *'Exactly.'*

INT. ROOFTOP PUBLISHING CANTEEN,
BLACKFRIARS, LONDON. DAY. JUNE 2019.

ANTONIA HODGSON, a writer in search of answers,
enters the canteen – a large, bright space with iconic
Thames views.
FOUR WOMEN sit around a table, eating lunch. They
work for SPHERE BOOKS, and have over thirty years of
editing experience between them. They've agreed to talk,
for a price.
ANTONIA slides a box of cupcakes across the table.
MADDIE WEST – who began her career at Mills & Boon
– is the most senior member of the team. She tests the
icing, nods. *Proceed.*

VIOLA HAYDEN   Ooh, Antonia, have you heard the
                     news?

VIOLA has been editing for five years, at Penguin, Random
House and now Sphere. In a fit of social awkwardness,
she once accidentally bowed to her boss, then decided
to commit to it with a deep flourish, like a Shakespearean
courtier. She is never allowed to forget this.

VIOLA (cont'd)   Abby is moving—
LUCY DAUMAN   —To Australia.

LUCY DAUMAN – whip-smart editor and punchline stealer
– has worked at Transworld and HarperCollins.

ANTONIA   So what are you looking for?
MADDIE   Something fresh and original. We're
                     seeing so many similar set-ups and
                     voices right now.

ANTONIA   Is a good pitch line important?
LUCY   Yes! Especially for commercial
                     fiction. That said, procedural crime
                     is different. You want to know much

more about the character of the
detective . . .

THALIA PROCTOR (legend within crime community,
Benedict Cumberbatch fanatic)

> When I first read a novel, I'm looking
> for how natural the writing feels.
> Genuine dialogue, nothing stilted.

EVERYONE gets very excited and starts talking over each
other.

EVERYONE   Nothing flowery! Nothing over-
                        written! No purple prose!

MADDIE WEST   You can't fix voice. You can fix struc-
                        ture, but the voice has to come from
                        the author.

LUCY   I'd rather something was under-
                        written than overwritten.

ABBY PARSONS (arriving and instantly slipping into the
conversation)

> Something extra you haven't seen
> before.

ABBY is an excellent, experienced editor. Everyone is
heartbroken she is leaving. [NB: rub ink into actor's
fingers to denote intellectual capabilities? Biro behind
ear?]

ANTONIA   What fixable problems do you see?

LUCY   Rushed endings. A great prologue
                        that doesn't tie in properly when
                        you're done.

ABBY (gnomically)   Sometimes you have to get to the
                        end, before you know how to begin.

EVERYONE nods.

VIOLA (almost singing) Plot holes, loose threads, too many
                        points of view.

ABBY (joining in)   Flimsy characters – often happens
                        with villains.

MADDIE   If you have a sprawling cast of char-
                        acters, you've probably lost track.

ANTONIA (muttering)	Try writing a coherent scene with five editors.
(to the room)	What are you looking for beyond the writing?
LUCY	Chemistry.
THALIA	Trust.
VIOLA (plaintive)	Gives due consideration to your well-meant notes.

EVERYONE laughs.

MADDIE	I do worry if they haven't read much within the genre. You don't have the same references when you come to the edit.
LUCY	Don't be a pushover, know your own mind. Consider the editor's suggestions, but if you disagree you should be able to explain why it needs to stay as it is.
VIOLA	And don't follow the trends just for the sake of it. Go with what feels authentic, even if it takes longer to break through – it will be worth it.
ANTONIA	Thanks, everyone. This has been really helpful.

She stands and performs a deep bow, directing it at VIOLA.

VIOLA	You'll never let me forget that, will you?
EVERYONE	Never.

Eight o'clock, Marylebone High Street. I've arrived at the café early to avoid rush hour. I'm so absorbed in my book it takes me half an hour to realize my date has had the same idea.

She's sitting three tables away, nose in her own book, vintage-print summer coat folded at her side.

Katherine Armstrong runs the crime list at Bonnier, editing Martyn Waites among others. She has a bright, can-do energy, and talks *very* fast.

I start with what she's looking for.

'I want to be completely drawn in, I want to be still reading at one in the morning! I don't have to like the characters, but I have to "get them". I'm investing my time, so I need to be completely absorbed.'

'Red flags?'

'Graphic scenes meant solely to titillate. I'm a big believer in the phrase "Stop at the door". It's usually better that way.'

'Common problems?' (Her quick delivery is rubbing off on me.)

'Cut straight to what it is you're trying to say. Let's not ramble.'

I laugh.

She laughs back, wags her finger. *'Let's not ramble!* An author should know what they're trying to achieve. Be clear what you're doing, what you're writing, what you want from a publisher.'

Her big piece of advice beyond the writing?

'If you take a meeting with an editor, have an honest, open chat. Listen to feedback. It saves trouble later. Also – it's great if an author is active on social media. Readers want that connection. They don't want some turret-prowling, pipe-smoking, whisky-drinking author.'

'They don't?' I feel sad. 'But that sounds great.'

'It does sound great,' Katherine admits. 'I think I have the concept brief for my next author photo.'

I ask her what she loves about the job.

'Finding a brilliant new voice. Sharing my passion for a book, sending it out into the world. Getting feedback from other authors and readers.'

'Great, thanks.' I settle back.

'That's it?' Katherine looks surprised. The interview has

lasted five minutes, max – but that's her own fault for being so precise. And *fast.*

Let's not ramble.

I meet my final interviewee in a café under a railway bridge, the crockery vibrating as we talk.

I've saved Clare Smith for last because she's one of my favourite people – funny, kind, incisive and wise. She has worked at Random House and HarperCollins, and is now Very Senior at Little, Brown. Clare reckons she reads about two hundred and fifty manuscripts a year, but she's *very* selective about what she commissions. What makes a book stand out?

'When I forget it's work. When I open up the manuscript and—' She brushes her arm. 'I get goosebumps, just thinking about it. The feeling is always the same, of being engrossed, like a child caught up. But then, something switches. I start thinking: how will I convince my colleagues to really go for this? How would I brief the cover? That initial feeling stays with you, but the publisher's voice gets stronger and stronger when you know you have something special.'

What regular problems does she see?

'Rushed endings,' she says, echoing everyone. 'And you must write what is true to you. Don't get distracted by the market or try to second guess your readers. Keep the focus on *your* story.'

I ask Clare what she loves about her job, and she positively glows. 'The sheer variety. It's creative and exciting, and surprising. You know: dreams really *can* come true at any moment and in unexpected ways. Imagine that – you can help someone achieve their dreams.'

How lovely. A good place to stop, I think. I close my notepad for the last time.

Here's what I've learned. Crime editors are motivated both

by passion and pragmatism. They want to be 'grabbed', 'engrossed', but their business minds run alongside, like a second narrative. *How will I pitch this? How would I brief the cover? Where does it sit within the market?*

There's only so much an author can do about that second part, but the first part is vital.

It's like this. Imagine some extraordinary, dramatic thing happens to you. You rush over to the pub, where all your friends are chatting away, distracted.

'Guess what just happened!' you shout.

Everyone turns to look at you.

Now – how do you keep their attention? How do you tell your story without them drifting off, turning to the match on the TV, checking their phones . . .

Come to think of it, why do you *really* need to tell them in the first place?

There's a powerful energy to the best commercial storytelling, a sense of urgency and purpose. *I am going to tell you this particular story, for this particular reason, and you will be utterly gripped, damn you, to the very end.*

Every editor I spoke to was hunting for this precious element, because they are, first and foremost, fans. Readers. They want to be enthralled.

So – write, write, write!

And don't rush the ending.

Traditional versus Self-Publishing

Russell James

Almost all books are digitally published now; that's not new. What *is* new is that you, the author, can digitally publish your-self. Who needs publishers when you can do it all yourself and, instead of earning a meagre royalty from each book (say 7½ or 10 per cent), you can take far more, perhaps 85 per cent of the selling price? Tempting, isn't it?

And how hard can it be? After all, when you wrote the book you almost certainly did so digitally. Practically nobody submits a typed or – heaven forbid! – a handwritten manuscript to a publisher. If you have spent all those hours at the keyboard researching, writing and rewriting your book in a digital format, haven't you already done most of the work? All the publisher has to do now is to take your digital text, the one from your very own PC, and feed it into their system to create the finished book. Can't you do that? Especially as you can download tools – free – from the internet to help you do the same.

Up to a point, Lord Cropper. Let's look at what's involved, how to do it, and how to do it properly. Let's then decide whether digital publishing is for you.

First, is digital publishing easy to do? It certainly appears to be and it's easier, of course, to produce an e-book than a printed one. To produce a Kindle version – which you are bound to do, as Amazon sells far more e-books than all other retailers put together – you have only to register with Amazon as an author and their software will take your word-processed text and reformat it for Kindle. You then produce the equivalent of a back-cover blurb and answer a few on-screen questions about the kind of book it is, its selling price, some basic points on rights and royalties – none of which you should find difficult – and you can move on to design (or be helped to design) a cover image. Which is not quite as easy as it may sound and which can, in fact, prove quite irritating. Perhaps the picture you want to use won't fit the space on their proforma, or isn't of sufficient quality. Perhaps your title, your subtitle, even your author name doesn't lie easily across the image. Perhaps the whole thing just doesn't look quite right. You are, after all, a writer, not a cover designer.

Although Amazon's tools are powerful, all of this set-up – creating and checking the text and cover – is not a process to be rushed. Traditional publishers know that the look of a book,

even the look of an e-book cover, can make the world of difference in terms of sales. That's why they employ professional
designers. You might choose to employ one too. Amazon will
encourage you to do so and (you'll not be surprised to hear)
can put you in touch with one of their designers at the touch
of a button. For what it's worth, I've always designed my own
covers, but who knows how many more copies I would have
sold had I paid a designer to make one for me.

Amazon's Kindle is not the only e-book reader, though it
does have by far the biggest market share. Wouldn't you like
to offer your book to other markets, such as Apple and Google
Books, to Sony, Nook and Kobo and all the smaller rivals, some
of which will grow while others die, but all of which added
together might add ten to twenty per cent to your e-book sales?
Members of the Society of Authors have found this additional
percentage varies greatly between writers. Some members find
non-Kindle sales well in excess of twenty per cent. Others find
them so insignificant that it is more worth their while to sign
into Amazon's exclusivity package (currently called KDP, though
this may change) and to forsake non-Kindle sales for other
benefits. It's something you can find out only by trial and error,
but your decision is not permanent; you can always change
your mind.

The easiest way to break into those non-Amazon e-book
markets is via one of the handful of companies happy to take
you through the process. At the time of writing, Smashwords
and Lulu are two of the most obvious companies to look at. In
return for a small commission (perhaps 15 per cent) they will
take your word-processed text and format it for all those
markets. What's more, they have a direct line into the retailers
and will ensure that, even if those companies have never heard
of you, they will offer your book to their entire marketplace.
With Smashwords and Lulu, cover design is handled slightly
differently: you create the whole thing (words and image) on
your PC and send it them as a high-quality jpeg. Alternatively,
they too can put you in touch with a professional designer.

It sounds simple and, to some extent, it is. But don't make

the mistake of assuming that your e-book pages will automatically replicate how the book looked upon your screen. Any images used in your text can be tricky, as can footnotes or text in odd fonts. Given that you're reading this in a Detection Club anthology, you probably write crime books and you may think you have no need for odd fonts or images – unless you're doing a Golden-Age style whodunit with diagrams of the crime scene. But does your story include diary entries or handwritten letters, or extracts from newspaper reports or, worst of all, small tables of information? Have you included lyrics or lines of poetry or anything resembling a script? For any of these you might have set the original piece in a particular style or format (depending on your word-processing program) which might not convert quite as you intended. For e-books it's best to write using as few line formats as possible. Use the tab key as seldom as possible, if at all. Don't use page numbers and don't justify the text.

From Smashwords you can download an excellent and free manual. Read it and do what it says. When you have uploaded your text (this applies to Kindle and all other e-book versions) take the time to check your conversion thoroughly. Expect to upload, correct, upload again and correct again several times. Don't rush this. You've uploaded your masterpiece but it isn't published yet; you're in the prepublication stage. Take the same care over this stage as you'd expect a traditional publisher to take on your behalf.

Do-it-yourself digital publishing is not confined to e-book publishing: modern print-on-demand companies will take a file produced on your PC and create a print-ready file from it. Most notably, again, Amazon will do this – or, to be more accurate, will provide the software to let you spend your time doing it – free of charge. (Smashwords won't; at present, they do e-books only.) Amazon will let you examine and adjust a screen version of the printed version, taking you through the entire publishing process (entire, that is, if you forget marketing and distribution). But joyful as it can be to sit at your screen and design a printed version of your book, you should keep in the back of your mind that a traditional publishing house will have a dedicated production department dedicated to this stage alone. If you want to turn your digital manuscript into a printed book, you'll have to become your own production department. It will take time; it will require a lot of close line-by-line perusal and attention to detail. You'll have to be as painstaking, in short, as you were when you wrote the thing.

At this stage you may be tempted to give up any thought of tangling with all this technological fiddle-faddle and use an intermediary company instead. There are a number of these seemingly friendly companies offering to 'help', 'guide' and 'assist' you through the process. No doubt they offer a service, at a cost, but I think it unlikely they'll increase your sales or find you new markets, and I'd strongly recommend you to feel your way (patiently!) with Smashwords or Amazon first. Their software is designed for writers, not for technocrats. And you will be in charge.

Paperbacks, though, are more tricky. I work in the book trade; I've seen a lot of self-published books – and almost all of them look slightly off (sometimes very off indeed). Yet using Amazon's software, you can, with care, produce professional-quality paperbacks. You are, remember, your own production department. You've already been your own editor and copy-editor, you will have designed your own book cover (or paid someone to do it for you), and you are now about to work on the book's internal design.

Take a handful of well-produced paperbacks and see how they've been laid out. They will vary slightly, and you can select the style that you prefer. The usual convention is to begin with a half title (a page containing nothing more than your book's title), the obverse of which has been left blank. This may or may not be followed by a page of promotional reviews, leading straight to the main title page. This must be on a facing (right-hand side) page, the obverse of which will comprise copyright information, year of publication, and perhaps a list of your other titles. There may then be a dedication page, containing nothing other than the dedication, perhaps along with some small epigraph. Again, the obverse will be blank, and the first page of the actual story must be on a facing, right-hand page.

Now for the main text, which you will examine minutely on screen. It is essential that you choose a page size your printer (probably Amazon) can work to, and you now reset your entire book text to pages of that size. Use a word processing program that allows you to set a page size and a book format, using right and left pages. Where your e-book text was supplied unjustified and with the pages unnumbered, this text is the opposite: numbered top or bottom as you choose, and with the book title, if you want it, as a header to each page. If your book has sections (Prologue, Book One, Book Two, etc.) you will want each of these to begin on a right-hand facing page. Once again I must stress: take your time. Take a lot of time.

And with all this emphasis on the time and effort you must put in, we must address the question: is this for you? Dispel the myth that self-publishing is for unpublished or no-longer published writers only. Stephen King and James Patterson are not in that category. Nevertheless, if you have secured yourself a 'proper' publisher or if your agent warns against, then you probably needn't bother self-publishing. But if rights have reverted to you on some of your earlier work, then here's a way to resurrect those books. And if you have not been published, or you are struggling to be republished, then here's an eminently feasible way to plunge into the pool.

But the unavoidable truth is that 'proper' publishers can do it better. Whether e-book or ink on paper, they'll usually produce a better-looking product. Plus they'll handle little things of great importance, like foreign publication rights, film and TV rights, audio rights, serialisation – and, most valuable of all, distribution, marketing and publicity. If you produce a beautiful paperback, how will you get it into a thousand bookshops? And as for e-books: there are hundreds of thousands out there, practically all of which will live forever (the tainted blessing of the infinite internet), so how will your little voice be heard? Publishers are there for a reason. They know what to do. If you have the luxury of choice, do-it-yourself versus traditional publisher, then your choice most probably comes down to this: do you want high royalties on low sales or low royalties on high sales?

One Thing Leads to Another

Jill Paton Walsh

Being a writer usually entails a fairly quiet life. However much travel one might do, however many tours and appearances, the job entails solitude: long hours in libraries, long hours at a desk. I worked for many years as a writer for children, and then wrote two adult novels of the kind they call 'literary' without any very great disturbance to this kind of life. Then something went wrong. My third adult novel was rejected by the publisher of the first two. And I could not understand the criticism offered. I was initially less cast down by this than I might have been because the book in question, *Knowledge of Angels*, felt to me the one I was born to write.

The germ of it had been in the back of my mind for maybe ten years and had got to me in a lecture about feral children. There I had heard of a child recovered from above the snow line on a mountain in eighteenth-century France who, according to the lecturer, had been kept in solitude while she was taught to speak French, in order to discover if the knowledge of the existence of God was innate. I asked the lecturer for references, but failed to find anything. If I looked for her now, I would find her easily, because a lot has been written since about feral children, but perhaps I am lucky I found so little then.

A day that changed my life was the day my husband was driving me in Mallorca in February 1992. As she so often did, the snow child tugged at my consciousness as I wondered if there was ever snow on the mountains there. And I thought:

'If that had happened here, I could write it!' In a blaze of excitement I realized I could extract the essence of the historical incident and tell it in an imaginary 'Grandinsula' so that its pungent relevance to the present day would more easily be seen.

What was that contemporary relevance? Well, if the knowledge of God is innate, all atheists are heretics. At the time this blazing illumination occurred to me, the whole Islamic world was being encouraged to murder Salman Rushdie. There were even some stupendously ignorant commentators congratulating themselves on the superior tolerance of Christianity. I provided my imaginary island with an atheist – shipwrecked, he swam ashore. And I wrote my book. It wouldn't let me stop, and was done very quickly.

And then the fun began. As I say, I was baffled by the comments of the rejecting editor. So I sent the manuscript to a friend in Massachusetts and asked her to tell me what was wrong. My wonderful agent, Bruce Hunter, sent the manuscript round London publishing houses, and it began to come back accompanied by interesting rejection letters. I particularly cherish one which said the book would still be read in one hundred years but was unpublishable now.

One evening my husband came to me in the kitchen to say that someone who said I didn't know him was calling from the American publishing house Houghton Mifflin. I was doing salmon in the microwave, a split-second affair, and I very nearly said, 'Tell him to push off.' Then I thought: 'Odd,' and went to the phone. I found myself talking to Peter Davison. He said: 'I'm reading your book.'

I said: 'You shouldn't be reading it. It hasn't been offered in the States.' He said: 'I need to know if I'm reading for pleasure or for possible acquisition.'

I worked out that the copy sent to Massachusetts for advice had got out and was wandering free. Icily I gave him the name of my New York agent and returned to the ruined fish.

Peter bought the book and London publishing houses continued to return it to my agent. The day came – another key day in my career – when Peter phoned to say they were printing the Houghton Mifflin edition next Monday. Did I want a few extra copies so that my British friends could read it? The nineteenth London rejection was on my desk. It was Friday.

My husband said: 'Fuck them all – we'll do it ourselves.'

We were not complete publishing virgins. We had published criticism of children's literature (about which my husband, John Rowe Townsend, was an expert) and non-commercial pieces of our own. We had an imprint name – Green Bay Publications (the wicked grow and flourish like the green bay tree). We rang Peter back and said: 'Can you make that a thousand?' In a burst of furious activity we got an ISBN, mocked up a British title page and Swift-aired it across the Atlantic, told Bruce what we were doing, and then, exhausted, went out to dinner with friends.

Among the friends were Robert and Linda Yeatman, who owned and ran Colt Books, a small publishing company. They carried no fiction. Linda fell quiet when she heard what we were doing, and the next morning Robert was in our sitting room expostulating with us. Linda had hoped that if nobody else would publish my novel, she would have a chance to publish fiction. He pointed out that we didn't have a rep, an invoicing programme on our computers or a warehouse. How did we propose to sell our copies? He added that he didn't like to see his wife upset.

At that point the four of us, with Bruce as godfather, agreed to share all expenses and any profits 50/50. If a reprint was required (we laughed at that idea) we would have a normal author's agreement, and the new copies would carry Colt Books' imprint. Linda said we needed a publicist. She rang four firms in London and only one, Julia Hobsbawm from Hobsbawm Macauley, rang back. Julia said to Linda's answerphone: 'One thousand copies? You can't possibly afford me on one thousand copies.' And then: 'You must have a lot of faith in this book – you'd better send me a copy.' Julia mounted a splendid publicity campaign for us for half her usual fee.

And it worked! The book began to get very good reviews; it

began to fly out of the shops. Radio 4's *Woman's Hour* wanted to interview me about self-publishing – they should really have interviewed John – and then they serialized it. Bill Scott-Kerr of Transworld bought the paperback rights; foreign rights began to sell. The Yeatmans had to reprint, so a second edition appeared with Colt Books on the title page.

And then *Knowledge of Angels* made the longlist for the 1994 Booker Prize; and then the shortlist. The phone began to ring at 7.30am and rang constantly until 10pm. We couldn't eat, dress or wash uninterrupted, and would have been in the madhouse shortly had a kindly top person at Transworld not known how to divert the calls from booksellers. The calls from newspapers were harder to deflect; the world had decided that 'Self-published book makes the Booker shortlist' was the story of the month. We really were besieged – a *Telegraph* photographer who turned up early contrived to photograph me so fresh out of the shower that my hair was soaking wet. His picture was on the front page; bad for my vanity, but good for sales.

I didn't win the Booker, but by then I really didn't need to; our action in self-publishing the book in Britain was vindicated. The experience left me with debts of gratitude to many people, some of them publishers. My book is still in print, of which I am of course glad; and still topical, which I bitterly regret.

And there was an unexpected consequence. 'Booker-shortlisted author' helped persuade the Trustees of Dorothy L. Sayers to invite me to complete the last Lord Peter Wimsey manuscript. I couldn't resist that challenge, and *Thrones, Dominations* was published in 1998.

Sayers had begun in 1936, but abandoned it, perhaps because the abdication of King Edward VIII affected her thinking about the storyline. She had written a number of complete scenes from the beginning of the story and a few diagrams, including a multicoloured representation of the interactions of the characters. The scenes were not numbered or ordered, and I had to arrange them in a way that seemed logical. At least in her notes she had made clear the murderer's identity.

In addition to my own detective novels, featuring Imogen Quy and set in Cambridge, I have published four books about Lord Peter: *Thrones, Dominations*, *A Presumption of Death*, *The Attenbury Emeralds*, and *The Late Scholar*. Now I'm working on a fifth. Lord Peter, though dreadfully frivolous compared to the dignified atheist on Grandinsula, is interested in the 'dream of justice' which is at the heart of so many detective stories, and he is not without his darker moments. He is, in terms of sheer enjoyment, the best company who has ever lived in my inner world.

Writing Lives

Anyone interested in writing is likely to be interested in understanding the challenges of the writing life – and contributors to *Howdunit* haven't shirked from talking about them. Of course, there's another side to the coin. It's a joy to have a book published and to hold the result of all that hard work in your hand. Even better if you come across someone who is actually reading your masterpiece, at least so long as their lips aren't pursed in disapproval. And while writing is a solitary occupation unless you write in collaboration, there are ever-increasing opportunities to mix with readers and fellow authors at talks or festivals.

Organizations such as (in Britain) the Society of Authors and the Crime Writers' Association offer members a wide range of benefits which more than justify the subscription cost, while smaller groups can provide not only mutual support but the chance to market your work to fresh audiences. A pioneering example in the crime fiction world was the Murder We Write touring group in the early 1990s, comprising four contributors to this book: Peter Lovesey, Liza Cody, Michael Z. Lewin, and Paula Gosling. Murder Squad, founded by Margaret Murphy in 2000, is a group of northern crime writers including Ann Cleeves, Martin Edwards, and more recently Kate Ellis, which has organized events throughout the UK and produced three anthologies and a CD; it is still going strong. These leads have been followed by a host of other groups, ranging from Medieval Murderers, who include Michael Jecks, to Killer Women, to which

Alison Joseph, Laura Wilson, and Elly Griffiths belong. Collaborations of this kind offer all kinds of opportunities, including the genuine pleasure of celebrating your friends' successes.

As Elly Griffiths explains, social media offers benefits (as well as challenges) for writers, while present-day technology offers a wide range of ways in which writers can reach out to readers. A website is probably a must and a blog may work splendidly, as long as you can keep refreshing them regularly with interesting content. Authors' newsletters have become increasingly popular. Readers around the world are now only a click or two away. The opportunities are infinite, and sometimes seem intoxicating.

Yet it's easy to become disheartened, whether by a mean-minded review or (perhaps even worse) apparent lack of interest in your work. Authors the world over moan to each other about the inadequacy of their publishers' efforts at publicity. There's always someone else who seems to be more successful, in terms of promotion, reviews, sales, awards, and so on. Celebrities who can barely string their own sentences together earn eye-popping book deals before leaving the hard graft to ghost writers, while people who can actually write for themselves struggle to achieve recognition. Even authors with a glass-half-full mindset may struggle to remain philosophical if they find themselves dropped by their publishers, for instance because their sales haven't justified the advance paid on their last book contract. It happens all the time.

Some of the anxieties of a writer's life brilliantly captured in these strip cartoons by the Detection Club's own 'Clewsey'.

So why do you want to write? If your main aim is to earn big bucks, there are easier ways to make money. On the other hand, if you really care about writing, you will write, whether or not you achieve publication. This leads to another important question, about how to finance your writing habit. When, if at all, should you take the plunge, give up the day job, and write full-time?

There is no 'right' answer. You need to decide what works for you. Personal and family circumstances play a crucial part. Money may not be your driver, but everyone needs to eat and a place to live. Even if you're one of the lucky few, offered a handsome deal by a high-calibre publisher, dare you risk giving up a secure job, if you have one, in order to pursue your dream? Financial pressures often mean that authors find themselves writing what publishers want them to write instead of what they want to write. If this becomes a way of life, it seldom ends well.

To combine writing with an outside job sometimes represents a realistic and reasonable compromise. It isn't easy but you might just achieve the best of both worlds, enjoying the privileges of the writing life without folding under its pressures. And it *is* a privilege to be asked to talk to readers, library users, and festival attendees. If Fortune smiles, there may be overseas trips and the chance of lecturing on cruises. Building a reputation that earns these invitations takes time, and that is another reason why it's important to try to hang on in there and not be knocked off course while trying to become established.

Take heart from the experience of Reginald Hill, creator of the Yorkshire cops Dalziel and Pascoe, and perhaps the leading British male writer of his generation. For years he combined work as a college lecturer with crime writing until his success as a novelist finally enabled him to take the plunge and write full-time. After many years and many books, he finally received the news that his series was to be adapted for television. The only snag was that Yorkshire TV cast the comedians Hale and Pace as his detectives; the result was calamitous. Undeterred, Reg regained control of the television rights and dropped lucky the second time around. The BBC made *Dalziel and Pascoe* a huge success and it ran for eleven series. But the TV deal didn't distract Reg from his work as a novelist. When the scriptwriters deviated from his vision and wrote out Pascoe's wife Ellie, Reg paid no attention. He simply stopped watching the shows and continued to write crime novels of distinction.

Like his friend and contemporary Robert Barnard, Reg never mastered typing, but although most writers of the twenty-first century can type, Reg's method of composing crime stories is a reminder of the importance of revision. In common with Kate Ellis and Andrew Taylor among others, he was quite prepared to change his murderer if the need arose, as he reflected in a piece written before his characters were brought to the small screen.

The Writing Process
Reginald Hill

In composition I fall somewhere between Gray's fantastic foppery and Trollope's exact measure, but rather closer to the latter. I know there will be days when writing will be impossible, either physically or temperamentally, so on all other days, weekends and holidays included, I'm sitting at my desk by nine in the morning and there I stay till one, by which time I may have produced a couple of hundred or a couple of thousand words. Afternoons are for reading, research, deep thought, correspondence, plus the odd game of golf or the even odder bout of gardening.

I'm still very much a steam-age writer. I can't type. I've tried and the noise distracts me, and besides, those regular little letters don't reflect what's going on in my mind anything like the spidery wanderings of black or blue lines of ink. I use a nylon-tipped pen, of a make which I'm not going to reveal unless they pay me. But I have used many a thousand of them and if I were ever the victim of an acid-bath murder and only the middle finger of my left hand remained, you could probably

identify it by fitting one of these pens into the groove just above
the top knuckle.

I generally start by reading through whatever I wrote the
previous day, revising it in some small detail perhaps, and
making marginal notes about any larger revision which I feel
may be necessary. This is because I want to get on with the
next bit and not finish the current session without any meas-
urable progress in terms of length. Often I will have scribbled
myself a note to remind me where I'm going next. Frequently
these notes are totally illegible, and I have to press on without
their help. Occasionally they are only half legible, and I am
sure there have been times when I have inadvertently misled
myself. I do, of course, have a broad idea of where a story is
going, but there is a constant process of modification in the
light of the opportunities that open up and the difficulties that
become apparent as I write.

Changes, of course, are nearly always retroactive as well as
anticipatory. To change a character or a relationship in
mid-book requires the whole build-up to be altered. Frequently
what seemed like a very small thing in the beginning involves
something like a complete rewrite. At other times, having
decided to modify a character, say, I discover as I work backward that this is not, after all, a sudden decision but something
I'd been nudging myself toward for a long time, and relatively
little needs changing in the earlier pages. I have on occasion
even changed the identity of the murderer, which might seem
so large a shift of direction as to be artistically disastrous. But
always it has been because the character first designated in
my mind has evolved into someone who could not have done
the killing, whereas someone else has emerged who could. Of
course the physical possibilities then have to be built in by an
alteration of details of time and place throughout the story, but
these are the mere furniture of a crime novel. I don't think
I've ever got them wrong yet, but I should much prefer to hear
the complaint that my perpetrator was in the wrong place than
that he was in the wrong personality.

Once a first draft is finished, I go through the whole book

and do a detailed revision and reshaping, still in longhand. At this stage I find scissors and Sellotape come in very handy. Then the draft goes to the only person in the whole world who has a more-than-even chance of deciphering it, my wife. She types it out and passes it back with comments, often unrepeatable. I then go through the typescript, revising once more, and above all attempting to trim the excess fat.

Characters, relationships, situations, backgrounds – I find that in order for me to get these right, I need to know far more than is necessary for the reader, and it's hard to keep this surplus out of an early draft. I should imagine that at this stage I cut between five and fifteen per cent of a book. Now comes the final typing, the script goes off to my agent, and the three-pronged anxiety syndrome familiar to all authors begins to prick at the gut. First the agent has to get it, second he has to like it, third he has to sell it. The first a telephone call or an acknowledgment slip takes care of, but it's a strong source of anxiety nonetheless, and I am always careful to ensure nothing leaves my possession unless I retain a back-up copy. The second is not automatic, not if you've got a decent agent. On the other hand, he won't be too brutally dismissive, not if he's got any soul and any sense! He'll tell you you're a genius, then he'll say he doesn't like it. But if he's enthusiastic, then you know the battle's half won. There may still be another round of revision if an editor feels strongly, and persuasively, that something needs changing. But these are the pains of the long-distance runner who sees the tape in view and knows that no blister on earth is going to stop him getting there.

Curiously, revision is a process I've come to enjoy more as time has gone on. Ideally, I think now I should like to hold on to my scripts for a couple of decades and keep on tinkering from time to time till I get them right. But when I started, the thought of altering those immortal words was like Moses taking a hammer to the tablets he'd just ferried down the mountain. I remember my first publisher-requested revisions consisted on my part of removing several *ands* and substituting commas. Things have changed and I am now able to wield the surgeon's

knife with a steady hand, not because I have less respect for
what I have written, but because I have got more.

The other advancement of learning which took place was also,
I suspect, common to most authors – the assimilation process
by which the raw material of personal experience is tested against
the needs of the story and not admitted until its colour, texture
and taste match that of the imaginative creation. What must go
is the self-indulgence of private jokes and personal references.

Particular research into backgrounds is one thing; the use
of what you already know is much more difficult. I went to
Italy to get background for *Another Death in Venice* and again
later for *Traitors' Blood* and a possible sequel. This process is
one of observing, selecting, discarding, and is, in fact, much
easier than writing a book set in milieus familiar from long
usage. In *A Clubbable Woman* I used a rugby club based upon
my own experience of the atmosphere and ethos of such a
club. In *An Advancement of Learning* I used a north-of-England
college not unlike the one I was then teaching in. In *Fell of
Dark* I used the city I had been brought up in and the area of
English countryside surrounding it. The dangers of close familiarity are not legal, though plenty of people claimed to
recognize enough characters and situations to fuel a chamberful
of lawsuits. (Interestingly, such identifications were nearly
always wrong and, happily, few people are objective enough
to spot themselves.) No, the real danger is artistic, that the
familiar reality should become more important than the
imagined story. We all know the type of tedious raconteur who
grinds through acres of nonessential detail and would pause
in his eyewitness account of the Crucifixion to inquire of himself,
'It was on a Friday . . . was it a Friday? . . . no, it could've
been Thursday . . . no, I'm wrong again, Thursday we had
that nasty shower . . . it was definitely Friday!' To the writer,
selectivity is all, and to the tyro, this is perhaps the most difficult process. Art should not simply hold a mirror up to life,
particularly to the author's own life. That way you get stuck
with one over-familiar face and a lot of uncontrolled background
detail, and in any case, it's all back to front . . .

I think that now after a couple of dozen books I am beginning to learn my trade . . . The ultimate stage of reputation,
of course, which comparatively few reach, would be to have a
name so powerful in market terms that it would sell anything.
Well, the money would be nice, but I don't know if I'm ready
yet for the irresponsibility.

Paula Gosling, one of the Detection Club's American-born members,
won the CWA's John Creasey Memorial Dagger for best first novel
with her debut, *A Running Duck*, and followed this a few years later
by winning the CWA Gold Dagger for best novel of the year with
Monkey Puzzle. Just as Reg Hill had the unhappy experience of
seeing his series cops played on television by two ill-chosen comedians, so Paula's first novel was filmed twice but in each case with
the story very loosely adapted and improbable casting: *Cobra* became
a vehicle for Sylvester Stallone, while the model Cindy Crawford
starred in *Fair Game*. As Simon Brett has explained, authors dream
of seeing their stories on the screen, but sometimes the reality
proves to be a mixed blessing. Meanwhile, the dedicated novelist
focuses on the current work-in-progress.

Keeping Track

Paula Gosling

Killing people for fun and profit has its upside. For me, it's the
research. I love that research. I pick a subject I find and go to
the children's section of the library and find all they've got on
it. Then I use the bibliography to progress to adult reading,

then expert reading, and so on, until I have it all in the palm of my notebook. Sometimes I even go and talk to experts face to face, and that's the most fascinating of all. If I could remember all the things I've had to learn about in order to write crime novels, I'd be as smart as Dickens.

Unfortunately, each successive book I write seems to obliterate the last. I knew something once about hunting, about solar astronomy, about Spain, about telepathy, about jazz, about survival in sub-zero environments – all that good stuff. I also knew characters named Malchek, Skinner, Cosatelli, Stryker, Abbott . . . oh, lots of folks. And I remember everything, absolutely everything about all of them – until somebody asks me.

Interviewers can be tough, but the fans are the toughest. Damn, they are smart cookies. They notice everything and forget nothing. There I am, full of excitement and information about my latest book, and they ask me something like 'Why did Professor Pinchman stay in his office that night?' Or 'Why did Malchek choose a Ruger rifle instead of a Remington?'

Who? What? *Monkey Puzzle*? *Fair Game*? Who wrote those? Me? Oh dear. Actually I think it's a matter of criminal capacity. I mean, books are big, lumpy things, full of words and images, and I have just this small, round, size-seven head. In *Fahrenheit 451* Bradbury had his characters of the future commit just one book to memory. One book each, right? So how can we be expected to remember eight? Oh, I see. It's our job to remember. We're writers. We get away with murder. True.

But we usually have to deal with just one murder at a time. All right, maybe two or three. Four? Well, certainly no more than ten. And we have to remember all the details of who was where and why they were there and what time it was and why the others weren't there and what the weather was like the previous Tuesday. And there are the noises and the smells and the colours, and how long the strychnine took to act, how much noise a .22 makes in a heavily-draped 20-foot by 18-foot room, how many men Drusilla slept with at college, why the floor creaked and why the mouse ran after the cat. Plus there's the rest of my life to think about: I have responsibilities, you know.

It's not easy being a woman with a career. I mean, what am I going to cook for dinner tonight and who's going to sort out the laundry and . . . and . . . no, I'm not getting shrill, I'm not, I'm *not*!

A good many Detection Club members have managed to juggle a demanding professional career together with a successful literary life. Among them is Jonathan Gash, best known for his books about the rascally antiques dealer Lovejoy, which were adapted for BBC television and ran for six series. In real life, as Dr John Grant, he achieved distinction in the field of medicine. Here, in a newly revised version of an article originally published in the *British Medical Journal* forty years ago, he muses on an important question in any author's life. To read in order to learn more about the craft of writing is one thing, but what about reading for pleasure?

Reading for Pleasure

Jonathan Gash

Writing fiction can actually dictate what one reads, a truth I discovered quite a long time after I first hit – well tapped – the literary scene. More, writing fiction may modify the pleasure one derives from reading.

To see how my illustrious predecessors went about it, I consulted all the Reading for Pleasure articles, and was at once struck by the poshness of their choices. I really mean it. Between *The Gulag Archipelago* and Neugroschel's translation of *Great Works of Jewish Fantasy* there's not a lot as far as I am

concerned, and in my days as a train-shocked commuter I
needed a minimum of five tomes a week to stay sane. Another
thing: there's an absence of stories in what my colleagues write
about, judging from their recommendations, but maybe I picked
back numbers 'with biasing unrandomness'. I wouldn't know.
But some books, such as those by P. M. Hubbard, do have the
peculiar hallmark of readability – which is about it, as far as
I can see.

Can the very labour of authorship, of itself and in some
subtle way, decide the choices one makes? Leaving aside the
business of 'collecting drop material for a book' and 'culling
for background' (I only learnt these terms recently), I actually
believe it can, and that very often such influences will make
one fly in the very teeth of learned critical opinion. And here's
the proof: Frederick Forsyth's *The Devil's Alternative*. Quite
unashamedly, I tell you I liked it. Fully aware of the risk of
biasing unrandomness again, I was quick to get through it
before that ghastly display appeared in Dillon's window and
brainwashed all pedestrians within bucket distance. The point
is that nobody ought to approve of it, presumably for the same
reasons that so many of us ought not to have approved of
Forsyth's *The Day of the Jackal*. We learnt from Robert
Robinson's book programme shortly after the book was
published that Forsyth suffers from a congenital form of the
Inadequate Characterization Syndrome. In fact, when the poor
author was called in to explain he got quite a drubbing from
the sixth-form-of-the-air for it. The story was seen as a routine
game of noughts and crosses, with the odd nought disguised
as a supertanker, and the odd cross exploding now and then,
but all really nothing but a game of OXO. Wrong, from one
who found himself reading it for no other reason than as a
kind of self-imposed duty, and who gained pleasure thereby:
interested, speculation pleasure this time.

Fiction, I feel, should be about recognizable 'selves', whether
they be people larger than life (Wilbur Smith's *Hungry as the
Sea* is an engrossing example) or even animals – and here I
strongly favour the gripping *Night of the White Bear* by

Alexander Knox instead of the much more vaunted and trendy
The Plague Dogs, or all those wee rabbits on Porton (sorry,
Watership) Down.

On a daughter's instruction I tackled the science fiction bestseller *Alien*, which ended up as a disappointingly mild curiosity
as to whether the beautiful space heroine would make it to
Earth, or whether her kitten, too, would turn out to be a Thing
in her space shuttle like all the rest. I didn't mind, though. The
spinoff of being able to exchange views with an offspring is not
to be sneezed at these days, and I'm on the lookout for more
of what young people read. The best of them is Frank Herbert's
interesting SF *Dune*, but E. M. Corder's *The Deer Hunter*, another
popular seller ('Now a Searing New Film'), proved a let-down.
I could not explain my sense of having read nothing once I'd
finished the book. The answer was in the cover – the book is,
in fact, that new phenomenon of the non-novel novel – that is,
a jolly good sequence of events but based on a screenplay, itself
based on the story by Cimino, Washburn, Garfinkle, and Uncle
Tom Cobley *et al*. I was reminded of Danny Kaye's famous joke
song about a film ultimately based on someone's inspirationally
profound punctuation mark.

Other production points can be as mystifying. All sympathy
for Peter van Greenaway's crime novel *Judas!* which was spoilt
for me by serious misjudgments in the printing and production.
This excellent story is based on the idea of the discovery of a
gospel written by Judas, no less, which discloses that Christ
was a nerk and a charlatan, St Peter a blackguard, St John a
fraud, and so on, while the only saving grace, as it were, is
Judas himself. I blame the publishers, who, for very little more
expense, could have italicised the 'gospel' flashbacks, and got
rid of those insanely narrow margins for top and laterals.
Unwise economies that seriously detracted from my enjoyment
of the book, a bright idea for a good story based straight on
the Nag Hammadi scrolls. Incidentally, the real Testament of
Judas Thomas found in 1945 laconically infers that Jesus
possibly had a twin called Judas . . .

A testy reader once wrote to me that I'd 'never got a police rank right yet', little knowing the neuroses she was generating. (Do I grovel? Do I keep it up, thereby enticing her to read me with even greater ferocity?) No such anxieties in N. J. Crisp's *The London Deal*, where his character Kenyon's difficulties are with his police superiors and inferiors alike, with every rank scrupulously stated and the story as interesting as it was cracked up to be. The only thing wrong is the dust jacket, which is of the sort over which the *Observer* critic recently perorated, calling them dull and unimaginative. One gets drawn in again, really wanting to know how Inspector Kenyon scores over that toad of a man in New Scotland Yard, as surely he must.

Doctors, however, must sometimes read for relaxation, which may actually be nothing to do with rest or pleasure. Doctors, therefore, must read Dick Francis. Little risk, I find, of being deeply drawn in here, but his evenly written novels may be started, resumed, or finished at any hour of day or night whether one is knackered or not, and put down in an untroubled frame of mind. I suggest *Risk*, *High Stakes*, and *In the Frame* for starters; the most likable crime books on the market.

Pleasurable reading from neat and concise analysis? A clear and somewhat unnerving possibility, after reading Julian Symons's *Bloody Murder*. Not a novel, but an erudite and readable account of the evolution of the crime novel which goes some way towards explaining why it is that one novel proves to be a turning-point in a genre and others not. (Incidentally, why *genre*? Will kind, clone, type, style, category, variant, or some other such not do? It sounds too affected for words.) A remarkable book, but it carries an important question for me: Mr Symons has an enjoyable knack of being able to follow that evolutionary thread when it lies buried among hundreds of thousands of titles, but where is the chap who will explore medical publications in a similar way? Analytic overscans (another new phrase I've been dying to use) seem to be the peculiar attribute of the non-medic.

But you can have too much analysis. In an effort to posh up the list of books I could cheerfully admit to having read and delighted in, I found a text wherein selections from modern poets were accompanied by various poets' comments on their works. The volume fell open at a spine-chilling paragraph written by a northern poet who received national acclaim for his *Terry Street*. It ended with a description of a gruesome futuristic vision of scurrying hordes of analysts of every sort, each with diplomas, heading intently for every known author, 'silent, and very fast'. It makes me think that reading for pleasure is merely the act of running like hell in the opposite direction. And writing too, at that.

Challenging as it may be to juggle writing novels with another demanding occupation, it can be done. The careers of two Detection Club members illustrate the point. Janet Neel is a solicitor who worked in the Department of Trade and then in merchant banking; she also spent five years as a governor of the BBC and in 2000, as Baroness Cohen of Pimlico, became a Labour life peer in the House of Lords. For good measure, her other appointments include a spell as a non-executive director of the London Stock Exchange. In the meantime, she published her first crime novel in 1988; it duly won the John Creasey Memorial Dagger for best debut, while two of her later books were shortlisted for the Gold Dagger.

Don't Give Up the Day Job
Janet Neel

I wrote my first detective novel when I was 27 and in a bad way, recovering from the failure of my first marriage and the realization that I had trained at huge trouble and expense for the sort of legal career that wasn't going to suit me. All my own fault: I had intended to be an international lawyer, swanking around pinning writs to oil ships like my mentors at Cambridge, but had changed tack to qualify as a solicitor so that I could earn good money while my then husband went to the Harvard Business School. As the marriage collapsed and I came home unable to go on with my job in the USA designing war games for their Defence Department, I found I could not decide what job to do or indeed to work at all. Rather than stay in the family home with my dismayed mother, I settled down in a flat with two nice women I had never met before and wrote a full-length detective novel in three months. I had always read crime novels for preference, majoring on the works of Marjorie Allingham and Josephine Tey.

I sent it to the late Celia Ramsay, a family connection who liked it but warned that substantial work lay between me and publication. Surprisingly this cleared my head. I understood that the solitary life of a writer was not what I needed at that moment; I wanted a good high-prestige job with lots of new people in it where I could be successful, as once I had been at Cambridge, England, and in Cambridge, USA. So I thanked Celia and filed the book and went to work on John Laing Construction sites, interviewing their labour force on behalf of a publicly funded consultancy to find out what they wanted out of life – stability or the best money and why. From there, much cheered by having been everyone's favourite thing on the sites, I got into the Civil Service as an experiment in which a dozen of us were taken into the administrative class at a senior grade.

I did thirteen years in the service, and was a success and found a good husband and had three children; then did four more years in a small merchant bank, headhunted to help them get government work in privatization before I went back to writing. Waiting for a substantial deal to come off – it was going to make my name – I found that writing stopped me fretting. Writing *Death's Bright Angel* – about the work of the Department of Industry in rescuing failing companies – I realized that my true *métier* was as a commercial lawyer; it won the John Creasey prize. Miles Huddleston of Constable helped me get there by giving me Prudence Fay – who has since edited all my crime novels – as well as one vital piece of advice. 'Do not,' he said over a good lunch, 'even think about giving up the day job.' He meant don't think about it until about book four, but I realized that I could not be a full-time writer – I needed people, activity, the chance to use my commercial skills, and the ability to make more money more easily than most writers ever do.

I also understood that like most writers I was better off writing what I knew and my usable experience was expanding very fast. The second book, *Death on Site*, is about murder on a construction site. I wrote it on holiday in Scotland, but what was before my eyes was the big Western Avenue site on an overnight shift – a ghoster – with the hard-drinking Laing's travelling men all around me as I watched them move huge concrete beams across the closed main road. The third book – shortlisted for the Gold Dagger – is about my old college Newnham and is based on my experience as an associate fellow and trustee of the Appeal Fund. And so on it goes; setting up a restaurant with my youngest brother provided the wherewithal for *A Timely Death*. My most recent book, *Ticket To Ride*, comes from my experience helping George Robertson, then Secretary of State for Defence, and thereafter Secretary General of NATO during the Kosovo war. There is another book to be written about the war in Iraq and another yet about my 12 years on the Board of the London Stock Exchange, but I could not have written any of these novels without my various day jobs.

In contrast to Janet Neel, Bertie Denham, the current Father of the House of Lords, is a hereditary peer who has served in the

governments of five different Conservative prime ministers. For him,
writing has offered welcome respite from the demands of political
life.

Writing to Relax

Bertie Denham

A handful of politicians have written thrillers and several
authors of crime fiction have been elevated to the House of
Lords. I suppose I am unusual in that I had a long career as
a whip in the upper house, and spent twenty years as Deputy
Chief Whip and then Chief Whip. The work of a whip is as
fascinating as that of a crime writer, and it requires just as
much understanding of human nature. What is perhaps less
obvious is that it's a highly pressured job, since in politics you
never know what is going to happen next. A whip needs to be
available seven days a week and can be called upon at very
short notice to deliver (or at least, try to deliver) the necessary
votes.

For me, therefore, writing crime fiction became a form of
relaxation. It has helped me to escape from the demands and
stresses of my unorthodox 'day job'. There are literary connections in my family – one of my Christian names is Mitford,
reflecting the fact that my mother was a first cousin of Nancy
Mitford. I'd always enjoyed reading thrillers, but it was many
years before I felt inspired to write a book of my own. Really,
the urge to become a thriller writer came out of the blue,
during the later stages of my career as a whip.

From the 1960s onwards, Dick Francis, Gavin Lyall, and
John Le Carré were favourite authors, long before I met them
in person and was elected to join them in membership of the
Detection Club. The help and support that established writers

give to aspiring novelists is, and has always been, immensely valuable. When I was working on my first book, I was lucky to benefit from the encouragement of the Labour peer Lord Ted Willis, who is now perhaps best remembered as the creator of *Dixon of Dock Green*.

That first book was *The Man Who Lost His Shadow*, which introduced my 'series detective', Derek (Viscount) Thryde, a young Conservative whip. The story was set against a background of parliamentary life, country houses, and country sports, so I was following the traditional advice of 'write about what you know'. As my writing developed, though, I tried so far as possible to vary my approach; for instance, my settings ranged from Scotland to the Caribbean. As a result, I found myself needing to research a wide range of settings and activities with which I was much less familiar.

The fascination of this research (for instance, exploring the River Orwell and the Suffolk coast while planning a chase scene) added to the pleasure I took from more generally from my writing career. It represented such a contrast – a complete break from my principal working life – and because of that, I found the company of fellow crime novelists delightful, just as I found that writing crime fiction was unexpectedly therapeutic.

It's tempting to take the view that the author's job is to write the book and it's the publisher's job to sell it. Tempting, but high-risk. Yes, marketing one's work does not come easily to a good many writers, and it is certainly wise to steer away from crass self-promotion. Yes, it's reasonable to expect publishers to do their utmost to sell their books, rather than give the impression (and this is a familiar feeling to many authors) that they have sworn to observe a code of *omertà* as regards one's latest masterpiece. But most publishers expect authors to help with the promotion of their books, and there is nothing new or unreasonable about this.

Dorothy L. Sayers worked in advertising in the 1920s and she was not only alert to the importance of marketing books, she was very good at it. Her belief that murder writers must advertise influenced the approach of members of the Detection Club in its early days; even the popular magazine *Weekly Illustrated* was invited into the club's premises in Soho to take photographs of Sayers and Helen Simpson drinking beer and their colleagues trying to look suitably mysterious.

In an age of self-publishing and social media, more and more authors are finding that promoting their wares, although time-consuming and far from straightforward, is not only worthwhile but essential; it may even prove enjoyable. Elly Griffiths offers perceptive observations on the pros and cons, and the merit of 'lighting small fires'.

Social Media and the Death of Nancy

Elly Griffiths

You've written a brilliant book, now it will sell itself. You can retire to your desk, sharpen your quill and start on the next one. Well, even in the days of quills it wasn't that easy. Charles Dickens promoted his books tirelessly. He toured America, on one occasion earning over ninety-five thousand dollars for seventy-five readings, and was so famous that people recognized him in the street (an almost unheard-of experience for a writer, even in this age of social media). In fact, it was a reading that killed Dickens. He suffered a stroke after an over-enthusiastic rendition of the death of Nancy in *Oliver Twist* and died shortly afterwards, aged just fifty-eight.

Do we have to promote our books until it kills us? Is writing a great book – as Dickens undoubtedly did many times – enough? Or is there a middle way between acting out gruesome death scenes to an enthralled audience and keeping your book a delicious secret?

Dickens was lucky (a near-fatal railway accident and Bill Sykes aside). He was naturally gregarious and an enthusiastic actor. But writers are not necessarily like this. After all, we have chosen a profession that involves spending a lot of time on our own. There is no guarantee that we can keep an audience entertained with witty and erudite anecdotes, though a surprising number of authors can. And, even if we do venture out, does this really help to sell our books? We have all slogged miles to a library or bookshop, only to find an audience of four people, two of whom are employed by the establishment and one of whom is lost. I once did an event with three other crime writers to find a room full of empty chairs and an audience of one, a woman who then proceeded to tell us about her own (mysteriously still unpublished) dystopian novel. Scottish author James Oswald recalls reading to an audience of three, one of whom rushed out halfway through, muttering something about not being able to take it any more. James never worked out what caused such a violent reaction, though when he met one of the other audience members a few years later, he said that he'd never forgotten the event. Simon Brett tells the story of an author on an Arts Council tour who arrived at the venue and found there was only one man waiting. The author suggested to his lone auditor that, as there were only two of them, they might just repair to the pub. 'No,' the man insisted, 'you must do your talk.' It turned out that he'd been employed to play the piano in the interval.

Performing to an audience of one grumpy pianist doesn't sell books but it might well bear fruit in other areas. Travelling to an event shows goodwill and it's great to support libraries and bookshops. My first editor once described it to me as 'lighting small fires'. Maybe our dystopian novelist went home to Mr Dystopia and enthused about our books, maybe he recommended them to his book group, maybe someone tweeted about them – it all helps. But lighting small fires can be expensive. Few libraries can afford to pay speakers and you can quickly find yourself out of pocket after paying for fares and a consoling Twix or two on the journey home. It's sensible to group a few such events together but then, before long, you are 'on tour', a gruelling slog around Travelodges and Premier Inns that saps the soul and, crucially, cuts into your writing time. Of course, book events can be fantastic. Libraries and bookshops are beautiful places; book people are always nice people; and it's wonderful to meet those most wondrous of beings, your readers. But the hard fact is that you need a roomful of such deities, all willing to buy a book, before your trip makes commercial sense.

Is there anything you can do to promote your book without leaving home? Of course there is. Even writers have heard of the internet, right? So you do the basics: you create a website, set up a Twitter account and a Facebook page, maybe even go crazy and add Instagram. Now what? Do you add a photo of yourself, looking mistily glamorous and writerly? Do you add a picture of your dog/cat/guinea pig? Do you immediately start talking about your book #buyitnow #specialoffer? Do you ignore vulgar consumerism and start talking about favourite films or enter into a spirited *Doctor Who* vs *Blake's 7* debate? The answer is, probably a mixture of all these things. It's nice to see what authors look like but, frankly, it's even nicer to see their pets. If you don't have a pet, borrow one or persuade your neighbour's chihuahua to stand winsomely beside your laptop. You need to tell people about your new book – that's why people are following you in the first place – but please don't make this your only interaction. It's very tedious to be harangued all the time. Instead, talk about your friends' books. This has several advantages. One, it will make you look like the nice person you are. Two, your friends will be pleased and, if you're lucky, they will return the compliment and talk about your new publications. Three, it makes you look good to have wide-ranging and eclectic tastes and, who knows, you might even enjoy the books for their own sake.

Equally, don't be afraid to talk about something other than books. Twitter, in particular, is a good place for entertaining but meaningless debates (and, of course *Blake's 7* is better, it goes without saying). Readers will like to see that you have a hinterland and you can spend many a happy hour ranking Bruce Springsteen's studio albums in the company of other obsessives. But there's the rub. Social media is the thief of time. You can disappear down a rabbit hole and not return for the best part of a day. Also, it is easy to get into petty arguments and nothing says 'don't buy my book' like a thread full of veiled insults. It seems a sensible strategy to limit your social media time to an hour in the morning or evening. On Instagram it's meant to be an advantage to post at the same time every day, preferably in the early afternoon when America starts to wake up. So post a nice picture of your chihuahua friend and don't look at the comments until later. However, once you do look, make sure you answer or at least 'like' everything. Interaction is the key. Build up a relationship and soon you will have that most valuable of things: an online following.

But does having an online following sell books? I conducted a brief, unscientific poll amongst my crime writer pals and the consensus was that the single most valuable thing you can do is create a mailing list. Once you have collected the names of people who actually want to hear about your books, you can then send them newsletters, special offers and details of events. People are also talking about 'street teams', key readers around the country who will evangelize about your books. You can set up special Facebook chat groups for these fans or, better still, meet them in person. But this all takes time and a certain amount of technical know-how. I have never mastered Mailchimp with its annoying monkey. While I do send out a monthly newsletter, I have to admit that it is administered by my publisher. This is not ideal, say those who know, because your mailing list should belong only to you. Of course, self-published writers have always been better at this sort of thing. To be a successful independent author you don't only have to understand the Amazon algorithms, you have to know how to connect with your readers. The indies are way ahead of traditional publishers in this area. It's a strange thing; no one has ever walked into a shop and asked for 'a HarperCollins book' but authors have been slow to understand that they, not the publishers, are the brand.

What can you do if your time and inclination are severely limited? If you only do one thing on social media I think it should be this: tell people when your book is published and say something interesting about it. Don't just post a link to Amazon or a bookshop, say something about the research or the history behind your latest literary offering, say you enjoyed writing it, post a picture of your neighbour's chihuahua sniffing the pages. Ian Rankin on Twitter is a good example of a high-profile writer who makes you feel as if you are interacting with the real person. He doesn't just tell sell his books, he posts pictures of himself in Edinburgh's Oxford Bar, he shares music links, he recommends other writers, he always responds to comments. This is why people follow writers on Twitter.

But be careful. At its best, social media is a community but at its worst it can be a dark place. Remember, your aim is to be visible but the downside is that you're now visible. It's not just your loyal readers who can contact you. It makes sense to protect yourself a little. This is where your trusty animal friend helps again. You can post pictures of your pet cat in lieu of photographs of yourself and your children. This will foster a sense of intimacy without giving too much away. Ditto chat about music and books. Try to steer away from politics, though I know it's hard sometimes. Don't respond to anything offensive, just block them and move on. Think before you post and never, ever go on Twitter when drunk.

So what should you post and where? The received wisdom is that Facebook is a network of people while Twitter is a network of ideas. It's not an accident that Facebook has 'friends' and Twitter has 'followers'. Facebook and Instagram posts last longer. Twitter is ephemeral – which is sometimes a good thing because it also doesn't have an 'edit' button. So, if you spell book 'boko', as I often do, simply post again with a rueful smiley face. Instagram is a visual medium so this is the place for your most artistic photographs. Purists like their Instagram 'feed' to look curated, so some users stick to limited palettes and themed pictures, such as artful shots of books and coffee cups. For me, this is slightly boring. I appreciate a nice picture as much as anyone (I follow several landscape and cute animal accounts) but I like my authors to be more interesting and multifaceted. The demographics show that younger people prefer Instagram and also that they are quite prepared to spend money on the basis of an attractive post, so add buying links. Facebook is still the best place to chat with your readers but you should respond to all messages on Twitter and Instagram too, even if it is just to like them.

Just for you, this is my brief guide to publication day on social media:

1. Post a video on Facebook with buying links. Author-opening-box-of-books is cheesy but effective. Make sure you have an animal in the video.
2. Post several times on Twitter with different messages each time. Add a key line from the book or, better still, an audio link. Thank people who have helped you. Add an amusing animal gif.
3. Post a beautiful picture of the book on Instagram. Include a buying link and hashtags but don't go over-board. Sign up as a business account so that you can see your statistics (though they are often very depressing).

And, if you really can't stomach doing any of this, don't worry too much.

The only thing that you, and only you, can do is write the books. So just keep on doing that – though if you want anyone to read them, investing in a chihuahua might be a good move.

As Elly Griffiths says, the key to a writing life is to keep on writing the books. And to keep remembering that, whatever the ups and downs, it's a vocation that can offer a great deal of joy. John Le Carré has enjoyed a long and distinguished career as a novelist and in his recent book *The Pigeon Tunnel* he emphasizes that his love of writing endures.

The Joy of Writing

John Le Carré

I love writing on the hoof, in notebooks on walks, in trains and cafés, then scurrying home to pick over my booty. When I am in Hampstead there is a bench I favour on the Heath, tucked under a spreading tree and set apart from its companions, and that's where I like to scribble. I have only ever written by hand. Arrogantly perhaps, I prefer to remain with the centuries-old tradition of unmechanized writing. The lapsed graphic artist in me actually enjoys drawing the words.

I love best the *privacy* of writing, which is why I don't do literary festivals and, as much as I can, stay away from interviews, even if the record doesn't look that way. There are times, usually at night, when I wish I'd never given an interview at all. First, you invent yourself, then you get to believe your invention. That is not a process that is compatible with self-knowledge.

On research trips I am partially protected by having a different name in real life. I can sign into hotels without anxiously wondering whether my name will be recognized: then when it isn't, anxiously wondering why not. When I'm obliged to come clean with the people whose experience I want to tap, results vary. One person refuses to trust me another inch, the next promotes me to Chief of the Secret Service and, over my protestations that I was only ever the lowest form of secret life, replies that I would say that, wouldn't I? After which, he proceeds to ply me with confidences I don't want, can't use and won't remember, on the mistaken assumption that I will pass them on to We Know Who. I have given a couple of examples of this serio-comic dilemma.

But the majority of the luckless souls I've bombarded in this way over the last fifty years – from middle-ranking executives in the pharmaceutical industry to bankers, mercenaries and various shades of spy – have shown me forbearance and generosity. The most generous were the war reporters and foreign correspondents who took the parasitic novelist under their wing, credited him with courage he didn't possess and allowed him to tag along.

Finally, to Len Deighton, the dedicatee of *Howdunit*. Like the other contributors to this book, his talents as a writer have been complemented by his work ethic. 'Even on Christmas Day', an essay he wrote in 1982 about the need for writers to keep writing, even (or especially?) when they might be doing other things, has probably influenced me more than any other essay on the craft of writing. Here he reflects on a long career of outstanding achievement.

Different Books; Different Problems; Different Solutions

Len Deighton

We all have our own way of writing our books and each book is likely to bring new demands. What works for me might not work for you but you might find some of my experience useful. Bear in mind that I have been described as a very slow worker who is addicted to research.

My research has taken me to many foreign countries. I like to be with my wife and sons and so we usually have had to rent somewhere to stay. Shopping and conversations with neighbours enrich one's understanding in a way that a single man in a hotel could never hope to find. My wife is fluent in many languages and nowadays my sons – who acquired their language skills at schools in France, Germany and Austria – manage Japanese and Mandarin too. My linguistic family has greatly helped for my research. And their presence has created friendships with many interesting people in many countries.

But before research there must be preparation. Is your proposed story interesting: with a firm structure and satisfying end? Is the substance of your story enough to sustain a book? Is the story best told in the first person? Once writing starts I need the momentum that comes from writing and revising every day.

The preparatory stage brings decisions about where the story takes place, and at what season of the year. Are there technical aspects of the story and if so can you handle them? I have abandoned three books halfway through and it is a miserable experience. One was an espionage story centred upon an orchestra travelling behind the Iron Curtain. I could read a score, and tap a few bars on a piano, but it didn't take long for me to admit that I didn't know enough about music. Another abandoned book came after I had spent months with the US Air Force. They sent me to a fighter base in East Anglia. They equipped me with a flight suit and all the paraphernalia; they gave me an air-crew

*Lunch with Ian Fleming. At his suggestion we went to a private
room in his favourite restaurant, 'The White Tower' in Percy Street.
He had been a regular customer since his wartime days
at the Admiralty.*

*The date was March 1963. The previous November Ian had
chosen* The IPCRESS File *as one of the books of the year for the*
Sunday Times *Christmas Selection. We both had roast duck –
a speciality of the house.*

*The photo was taken by Jack Nisberg, an American freelancer
who was a close friend from my own days as a photographer.*

physical exam and countless jabs. They gave me a seat in the ready room and let me fly backseat in their Phantom fighter planes and live with the pilots, among whom I formed friendships that still flourish. Suddenly North Vietnam sought peace; The US President sought re-election and the fighting ended just as I was about to join a tactical fighter squadron in the war zone. Everything changed and I put all the work aside.

The third abandoned book was to be about world-wide revolutionary movements. I did a considerable amount of research on Russian Bolsheviks and I mixed with trouble-makers, Trotskyites and terrorists. I talked to various police specialists and a retired MI5 officer. But with a detailed outline and two or three false starts I gave up.

The time span of your story will have an effect on the pace of the narrative and the interaction of your characters. *Bomber*, about one RAF bombing raid, its German target, and the radar and night-fighter interception, covers exactly 24 hours, providing a concentration of time but a dispersion of place. For writing *Bomber* I had the advantage that my service in the RAF included flying in Avro Lancaster bombers and De Havilland Mosquito fighters. The RAF Museum staff allowed me to climb around inside their precious Junkers Ju 88 and the Imperial War Museum let me sift and scan hours and hours of Junkers instruction film.

In contrast, *Winter* describes a Berlin family from 1900 until 1945. The family is torn to pieces by Europe's recent history. Both books required a carefully researched and cool look at the past, but from an author's point of view they were completely different. Eyewitness accounts (including diaries and memoirs) have always been my first choice for research. Many history books restate and endorse the myths and errors of previous accounts, repeating wartime propaganda. It was exasperation that impelled me to write three military history books, *Fighter*, *Blitzkrieg*, and *Blood, Tears and Folly*, to blow away some of the nonsense.

History books, and fiction reliably based on history, bring a need for efficient reference systems. For *Bomber* I used coloured

papers for my typescript to distinguish between chapters about
the RAF, German air force, German radar and the German
civilians. By looking at the coloured edges I could see if the
story was sufficiently balanced. *Bomber* required a great deal
of research and for easy reference my workroom walls were
covered in maps and diagrams. Revisions, corrections and edits
are always a part of my writing process; and scribbling between
the lines on typewritten pages, as well as cutting them up and
rearranging paragraphs, kept me on my knees brandishing the
glue pot. The engineer who came to service my IBM electric
typewriter once said, 'Your poor secretary; she says she has
retyped one of your chapters twenty-five times!'

'Yes,' I said trying to look penitent. 'But what can I do?'

'Let me take you to Shell head office' – the Thames-side
office block also on his beat – 'and see how they produce their
instruction manuals.'

The answer was a computer. It was 1969 and the name
'word processor' had not been coined. Within a week one of
these massive IBM machines was swinging on a tall crane to
get it through the second-floor window of my little house in
Merrick Square, London SE1. Many years later an American
researcher wrote a history of word processing and acknowledged that I was the first person – by many years – to write
a book using such a contraption. It was *Bomber*, and in my
acknowledgements I thanked the people at IBM for their
wonderful machine. This established the date of my claim. At
this point I must give credit to my old friend Edward Millard
Oliver who spotted some pre-publication material on the
internet and contacted the American writer. And I must also
admit that it was my brilliant Australian secretary Ellenor who
mastered the machine's fits and starts and temperamental
tantrums.

If preparation is the most vital part of writing a book, it is
still more a saving of time and money for anyone producing a
film, which is what I did in the Sixties after buying the screen
rights of *Oh! What A Lovely War* from Joan Littlewood. (The
show was composed of words sung, spoken or written by the

participants, and so were my additional sequences.) Moviemaking is a multifarious business. The producer buys the screen rights of a book or play, writes a screenplay (or has it written), finds someone to put up the necessary millions of dollars (in my case Paramount Pictures) decides about the cast (whether they are available and affordable in the film budget), engages a director and other vital employees such as casting director, costume designers, location manager and lighting cameraman. It is useful to have an executive producer and I was lucky enough to have a brilliant and experienced one, a wartime Spitfire pilot named 'Mack' McDavidson. He was in effect my partner and the film owes a great deal to his skills and faultless administration.

It was winter. My screenplay brought the centre of action to the Brighton Pier. It was obvious that I could not start shooting until the seasonal weather changed. With expensive offices in Piccadilly and a bank balance severely depleted by my personal purchase of the *Oh! What A Lovely War* screen rights, I urgently needed a deal and some money to pay my rent and the bills.

My agent, William Morris, took my script to Charlie Bluhdorn, the Anglophile boss at Paramount. It was Charlie's enthusiasm and faith in me that brought the project into life. But to bridge the winter gap, William Morris obtained additional finance for *Only When I Larf*, a book about confidence tricksters that I had recently completed. *Larf* was mostly an indoor shoot. My art director, John Blezard, built an amazing penthouse suite in a dilapidated warehouse near Tower Bridge (so attractive that it featured in February 1968 *House & Garden*). Locations in New York City and sunny Beirut provided outdoor scenes.

For *Oh! What A Lovely War* I borrowed a locomotive, rented and renovated both Brighton piers and hired the band of the Irish Guards. There is no need to tell you how vital preparation was in such a double production schedule. I worked night and day and checked out everything, from the sets and costumes to cloaking Brighton's municipal rubbish dump with fake snow (for the Christmas truce sequence) and arranging with a friend for the flight of a vintage World War One aeroplane. I was concerned about the movements of all the cast, because clumsy movements marr a film. Eleanor Fazan the choreographer made a vital contribution to the action and I learnt a great deal while watching her at work.

Having spent seven years as an art student, I was keen to make *Oh! What A Lovely War* visually satisfying. It was a chance to bring into my films people whose work I knew was exceptional. May Routh, an art school friend, worked on the costumes and later made a name in Hollywood; another art student colleague Ray Hawkey designed the stunning titles. I engaged Pat Tilley, an accomplished artist friend to keep the untried director (Richard Attenborough) supplied with story-boards that sketched camera positions for each day's shooting.

When I was a student at St Martins School of Art in Charing Cross Road, I shared a postbox address with several others, including some congenial confidence tricksters. They were amusing people and amazingly self-righteous as they explained that they only outwitted greedy victims. Several years later I recalled their stories and wrote *Only When I Larf*. For me every book offers a chance to experiment. In this book I gave each of the three main characters – a young man, a middle-aged man and a woman who changes her affection – a first-person chapter. Each character tells their story, which often contradicts and overlaps the other two. It was fun to write and revealed to me how useful it can be to have your characters 'remember with advantages', as Henry V puts it on St Crispin's Day. Or sometimes tell whopping lies.

Like most writers I begrudge wasted experience (even my abandoned revolution research was used in a South American locale for *MAMista*). *Close-Up* revisited my many and varied experiences in the movie business. I was on friendly terms with the top men at Paramount and saw the tough commercial decisions being made. I signed renowned actors and actresses: Laurence Olivier, Maggie Smith, John Gieldgud, Ralph Richardson and all the Redgraves. And I bargained at length with their unsentimental agents. My journey through the jungle left me with abundant material for a book. *Close-Up* is a story about the vendettas, coercion and backstabbing social politics that I had seen at first hand. I wrote of the bitterness and stress that haunts the acting profession. To focus the drama, I depicted a film star battling against the impending downturn of his box-office value. I wanted the intimacy of a first-person plus an overview. So I entwined the story of the actor with a commentary by his biographer.

Some stories nag at one's brain. Several readers who had read *Bomber* wrote to suggest a book about the US 8th Air Force. One Malcolm Bates sent me many long letters, photos and books; his enthusiasm was inspiring. The American airfields were like small towns: not only hangars and well-equipped workshops but pharmacies, libraries and prisons; chapels and ice-cream parlours; dental surgeries, hospitals, movie theatres and tailors' shops.

Anecdotal episodes were added when an ex-RAF officer, Wing Commander 'Beau' Carr, infiltrated me into a group of American veterans of the 91st Bomber Group on a visit to England the bases where they had been stationed.

'That's where I lived', one of them told his wife. It became the first page of *Goodbye Mickey Mouse*.

Initially I proposed to write each chapter in the first-person viewpoint of each of the major characters. My American editor, Georgie Remer, expressed alarm. She knew of no writer who could successfully manage the many varied American regional accents and speech patterns that I would need to master. I drastically modified my plans. I would still focus each chapter on a character but I would write it in the third person and look over their shoulder.

Goodbye Mickey Mouse was the result of numerous suggestions but the birth of *SS-GB* is easier to explain. I was drinking coffee in the office of Tony Colwell, my editor at Jonathan Cape, together with Ray Hawkey the designer. It was quite late and we had just finished choosing photos and captions for *Fighter*, a history of the Battle of Britain.

'No one knows what would have happened had we lost', said Tony.

'The Germans had plans ready', I said. 'I have a shelf filled with books and official papers that reveal their ideas.'

'Would it make a book?' said Ray.

'It never happened,' I reminded him.

'It's called an "alternative world" story', said Ray.

I had never heard of this category and it didn't appeal to me at first. But I went to my library and the more I read, the more interesting it became. In the event I didn't use much of the German material. It was a fascinating subject and I wrote it in the format of a detective story; murder on page one and solution on the last page. The central character was a Scotland Yard detective, 'Archer of the Yard', and I used locations that I remembered from my wartime days in London.

I like to write in the first person despite the limitations it brings (such as having the same person present in every chapter). So I told the story through the eyes of Archer. But as I was typing the final chapters I hit a brick wall. No matter what twists and turns I considered, there was no way out. So I dumped the whole typescript: converting it to third-person narrative would end-up lumpy and crude. Instead I took a new ream of paper and started all over again. It was a sobering example of poor planning, but the rewrite taught me a lot about story construction and about characterization too.

So where are all those spies? We authors know that readers will not tolerate the use of coincidence to facilitate our plots. But in real life, coincidence pops up time and time again: and that's how my life has been in regard to the espionage community. During the 1960s our next-door neighbours in Merrick Square were Mr and Mrs Nicholas Elliot. He was a senior spook who had come back from Beirut, where he had been talking to Kim Philby, the KGB spy. Philby was offered a pardon in exchange for a complete and detailed confession. Elliot was tipped to become head of MI6 and Merrick Square was conveniently close to his office in Vauxhall Bridge Road (which was next door to my publisher). Elliot did not get the confession nor the top job. Many years afterwards we were living in a small village near Cannes while I worked on *Yesterday's Spy*,

which is set in that region. Elliot's wife was again our neighbour.

There were other coincidental encounters with the espionage
world. Visiting a friend held in HM Prison Wormwood Scrubs
on a sunny day when visitors and inmates were gathered in
the grassy interior lawn, I found George Blake, one of Russia's
most successful agents, seated at the next table. Maxwell Knight
of MI5 and Sir Maurice Oldfield, the head of MI6, were friends
of friends. They were everywhere. One didn't have to look
beyond our writing fraternity to find men who had worked in
the service.

It all began in May 1940 when, in the middle of the night,
my parents and I watched the police arresting Anna Wolkoff,
our next-door neighbour in Gloucester Place Mews. Anna was
the daughter of Admiral Wolkoff, who had been the Russian
naval attaché until the Revolution. She was a friendly neighbour
and her success as a fashionable milliner enabled her to give
dinner parties to which influential people were invited. My
mother cooked and served at those dinners. Anna was bitterly
resentful about the communists who had taken over power in
Russia. This was a time when communists abounded.
Encouraged by gullible nincompoops such as George Bernard
Shaw and H. G. Wells, many otherwise sensible people betrayed
their country to support Stalin's empire, where a million
Russians were being murdered each year and countless others
sent to labour camps.

Others believed that Hitler's totalitarian and militant Germany
was a bulwark against Stalin's expanding communist empire
and should be tolerated if not helped. It was mostly people of
this belief who were guests at Anna's dinner parties. From the
table talk Anna sifted useful information, assisted by Tyler Kent,
the cipher clerk at the US Embassy, who lived nearby at 47
Gloucester Place. Anna's notes of the chatter revealed the
political sympathies and prejudice of Westminster, Whitehall
and beyond. It was valuable material and it all went to Berlin
by means of Tyler's access to the American diplomatic bag.

The trial was held in camera and the names of Anna's dinner

guests were never made public. Anna was sentenced to ten years in prison; Kent to seven years. Later I was shown some records of the arrest. The story had been changed so that Anna was arrested in her parent's home in South Kensington. There was even a handwritten notebook page from the arresting police officer. It was all an official fake. The authorities had decided to obliterate all mention of her real home and the dinner party guests. My mother was never questioned and neither were the other neighbours in the mews. Some said that Joseph Kennedy was one of Anna's regular guests. His widely expressed political views suggest that he would have fitted in to the conversations well.

Whether any of this influenced my first book, *The IPCRESS File*, I am still not sure. I don't know why I wrote it. Most successful authors seem to have had the writing bug since childhood. I didn't have such a driving ambition; I scribbled and fumbled. I threw away more pages than I kept. It started as a pastime and even when it was completed I put it aside and forgot about it.

The critics were kind to me. But the mood of *The IPCRESS File* that distinguished it was its ordinariness. The main character was not a hero; he was like the people I grew up with, and I didn't know any heroes of the sort found in books. It was this ordinariness that I wanted to explore more fully when many years later I began the *Game, Set and Match* trilogy that became the nine Bernard Samson books.

Samson would have worries about money. He would also have two small children, an erudite wife, an unsparingly candid schoolfriend, a vivacious sister-in-law and her long-suffering workaholic husband, with whom Bernard would share a dislike of his rich and pompous father-in-law. Bernard's upbringing in Berlin would enable him to pass as a native but this achievement would not be greatly admired by his Whitehall superiors, who were to include a ruthless rival and an avuncular superior. And the story would depict them all as they grew older and weaker but not much wiser. Well, I wasn't going to be able to cram that cast of characters into a normal-sized book. So I

Me and my toys:

Starting in the bottom left corner there is the IBM 72 (the electric typewriter is a part of it). On it is my screenplay for Oh! What a Lovely War.

Beyond that there is a twin-spool video-recorder, then me, and the camera for the video recorder. To the right there is a teletape machine, used mostly for my travel pieces for Playboy *magazine in Chicago, where I was the Travel Editor.*

drew a large wall chart depicting the whole project, the main events in Samson's life

Next, I stared long and hard at my chart and started to divide it into book-length episodes. There would have to be two trilogies; no! three, as I incorporated Samson's professional life. Would they be continuous? No. I would need time gaps and at some point in the series I might have to move from first person to third person in order to give the reader an overall view of the story.

Looking back on the writing of the nine 'Samson books' (ten if you include *Winter*, the prequel) my biggest regret is that I killed the sister-in-law far too early. She was a valuable character and the ongoing mystery of her death was not enough to compensate for her loss. I should have killed someone else. But there it is; we all make mistakes.

The Contributors:
Biographical Notes

Dates are given for Detection Club members who are no longer living.

Catherine Aird is the pen name of Kinn McIntosh. She is the author of the Calleshire Chronicles, a series featuring Detective Inspector C. D. Sloan, which began with *The Religious Body* in 1966 and has been running for more than half a century. She has received the Golden Handcuffs award and in 2015 the Crime Writers' Association awarded her the highest honour in British crime writing, the Diamond Dagger, in recognition of the sustained excellence of her body of work.

Margery Allingham (1904–66), an undisputed 'Queen of Crime' during the Golden Age, published her first novel at nineteen and introduced Albert Campion, her principal series detective, in *The Crime at Black Dudley*. At first a minor character, he became one of the most enigmatic and interesting of Golden Age detectives – though cut out of the 1956 film of *The Tiger in the Smoke*, regarded by many as one of the finest detective novels. In 1989–90 Campion was portrayed on television by Peter Davison.

Eric Ambler (1909–88) is widely credited with revolutionizing the spy and thriller novel by introducing elements of realism and by focusing on protagonists who were not professional spies. *The Mask of Dimitrios*, arguably his finest work, was filmed in 1944, while *The Light of Day* became the movie *Topkapi*, starring Peter Ustinov. *Journey into Fear* was also made into a film, while Ambler wrote the screenplays for *The October Man* and *A Night to Remember*.

Desmond Bagley (1923–1983) was born in Kendal and moved to South Africa after the Second World War. Over the years he made a transition from unskilled printer's apprentice, aircraft engineer, mine worker, nightclub photographer and radio scriptwriter to become a multimillion-selling author of adventure thrillers. Returning to the UK in the 1960s, he lived with his wife Joan in Devon and then on Guernsey, where a blue plaque was unveiled in his honour in 2018. Five of his novels were adapted for television or film, and 2019 saw the publication of *Domino Island*, based on a draft manuscript found among his papers after his death.

Robert Barnard (1936–2013) had a distinguished career as an academic before he became a full-time writer. His first crime novel, *Death of an Old Goat*, was written while he was professor of English at the University of Tromsø in Norway, the world's most northerly university. Under the name of Bernard Bastable he also wrote novels featuring Mozart as a detective. He regarded Agatha Christie as his ideal crime writer and published an appreciation of her work, *A Talent to Deceive*, as well as a book on Dickens and a history of English literature. He received the Diamond Dagger in 2003.

Anthony Berkeley was, like Francis Iles, a pen name of Anthony Berkeley Cox (1893–1971), the founder of the Detection Club. His first two detective novels were originally published anonymously, but he achieved widespread recognition with his masterly whodunit *The Poisoned Chocolates Case*. The first

Iles novel, *Malice Aforethought*, has been televised twice, while *Before the Fact* was filmed by Alfred Hitchcock as *Suspicion*. After 1939, he wrote no further novels but under the Iles name became a highly influential reviewer.

Mark Billingham was born and brought up in Birmingham. Having worked for some years as an actor and more recently as a TV writer and stand-up comedian, he published his first crime novel in 2001, launching a sequence featuring London-based detective Tom Thorne. A television series based on the Thorne novels starred David Morrissey, while another based on the novels *In The Dark* and *Time Of Death* was screened in 2017.

Nicholas Blake was the pen name that Cecil Day-Lewis (1904–72) adopted for writing detective fiction. The first Blake novel, *A Question of Proof*, introduced Nigel Strangeways, who became a popular series character. He appears in Blake's most renowned mystery, *The Beast Must Die*, although that story (filmed twice, including by Claude Chabrol) is structured very differently from the stereotypical whodunit. Although Day-Lewis became Poet Laureate, he is today at least as well remembered for his detective fiction as for his verse.

Christianna Brand (1907–88) published her first book, *Death in High Heels*, in 1941, and although she was not a prolific novelist, she remains widely admired for the style and ingenuity of her detective stories, mostly in the classic vein. Her most famous book is the wartime mystery *Green for Danger*, which was successfully filmed with Alastair Sim playing Inspector Cockrill, her main series character. Her Nurse Matilda stories for children were also very popular.

Simon Brett is the author of over one hundred books and many plays for radio and the theatre. He has published four series of detective novels (the Charles Paris, Mrs Pargeter, Fethering, and Blotto & Twinks mysteries) as well as stand-alone novels such as *A Shock to the System*, which was adapted into a film with Michael Caine. President of the Detection Club from 2001 to 2015, he masterminded the Club's round-robin novel *The Sinking Admiral* and in 2019 wrote a play for BBC Radio about the Club's origins, *Eric the Skull*, which was broadcast on Radio 4 in 2020.

John Dickson Carr (1906–1977) is widely regarded as the most gifted of all exponents of the locked-room mystery. A native of Pennsylvania, he relocated to Britain after marrying an Englishwoman and pursued a career as a detective novelist with a taste for the baroque. His first great detective, the French examining magistrate Henri Bencolin, was succeeded by Dr Gideon Fell, a rumbustious character modelled on G. K. Chesterton, whom Carr much admired. As Carter Dickson, he wrote primarily about Sir Henry Merrivale, a baronet and barrister who shared Fell's penchant for solving baffling impossible crimes. Carr also created Colonel March, based on Carr's friend and fellow Detection Club member John Rhode (Major Cecil John Street, who also wrote as Miles Burton and Cecil Waye). A 1955–56 television series, *Colonel March of Scotland Yard*, starred Boris Karloff as March.

Kate Charles is the pen name of Carol Chase, who was born in Cincinatti but moved to England in 1986. Her novels are mostly set against the background of the Church of England, and her work also shows the influence of Barbara Pym. In 2012 she was awarded the George N. Dove Award by the Popular Culture Association for outstanding contribution to the serious study of mystery and crime fiction, in recognition of her work as co-organizer of the annual St Hilda's Crime and Mystery Conference in Oxford.

Gilbert Keith Chesterton (1874–1936) was the first President of the Detection Club. He was an extraordinarily prolific and versatile writer of fiction, literary and art criticism, poetry, journalism, essays, and biography, and also found time to run his own weekly newspaper and become a well-known broad-caster and controversialist. Today he is best remembered as the creator of the unassuming priest and amateur detective Father Brown, whose real life model was Father Joseph O'Connor. The stories have been adapted for film, with Alec Guinness as the priest and for television.

Agatha Christie (1890–1976) is to this day the best selling novelist the world has ever seen. Her first novel, *The Mysterious Affair at Styles*, introduced the legendary Belgian detective Hercule Poirot, who has been played in film and television adaptations of the books by actors as diverse as Peter Ustinov, Albert Finney, David Suchet, John Malkovich, and Kenneth Branagh. Christie also created Jane Marple, the unlikely amateur detective who lived in St Mary Mead. Christie's detective novels are said to have sold two billion copies worldwide, while her stage play *The Mousetrap* opened in the West End in 1952 and is still running. She was elected President of the Detection Club following the death of Dorothy L. Sayers and she remained in post until her own death.

Ann Cleeves published her first crime novel in 1986. A series about the bird-watchers George and Molly Palmer-Jones was followed by a series about Inspector Ramsay. Her books about DCI Vera Stanhope have been televised as *Vera,* starring Brenda Blethyn, while the Gold Dagger-winning *Raven Black* launched her fourth series, featuring DI Jimmy Perez and the basis for the TV series *Shetland*. Her fifth and latest series is set in Devon. She received the Diamond Dagger in 2017.

Liza Cody is an artist trained at the Royal Academy Schools of Art as well as a crime novelist. *Dupe*, her first novel, won the John Creasey Memorial Dagger, and launched a series about the female private investigator Anna Lee, televised with Imogen Stubbs in the lead role. She has also published the Bucket Nut Trilogy featuring professional wrestler Eva Wylie, as well as stand-alone novels such as *Rift*, *Gimme More*, *Ballad of a Dead*

Nobody, and *Miss Terry*. She has won a Silver Dagger, an Anthony award, and a Marlowe in Germany.

J. J. Connington was the name under which Scottish chemist Professor Alfred William Stewart (1880–1947) wrote fiction. In 1908 he published a successful textbook on inorganic chemistry; his dystopian novel *Nordenholt's Millions* appeared fifteen years later. He switched to detective fiction and created Sir Clinton Driffield, a memorably ruthless chief constable who became his principal series character. Many of his mystery plots make effective use of his expertise in science and technology.

Natasha Cooper is a pen name of Daphne Wright, who worked in publishing before becoming a novelist. She began with historical fiction and then, as Natasha Cooper, started a light-hearted crime series featuring Willow King. A series about barrister Trish Maguire followed. Adjusting her pseudonym slightly to N. J. Cooper, she has subsequently produced a series featuring Karen Taylor, a forensic psychiatrist. She is also a well-known reviewer.

Edmund Crispin was the name under which Robert Bruce Montgomery (1921–78) wrote detective fiction and edited science fiction anthologies. Montgomery was a successful composer of concert music and soundtracks for films including six *Carry On* films, the thriller *Eyewitness*, and *The Brides of Fu Manchu*. Today he is remembered principally for his detective stories. *The Case of the Gilded Fly* introduced the Oxford don and amateur sleuth Gervase Fen, who appeared in all nine of Crispin's novels and the overwhelming majority of his short detective stories.

Freeman Wills Crofts (1879–1957) wrote his first detective novel while convalescing from his job as an Irish railway engineer after a serious illness. *The Cask*, published in 1920, became a bestseller and before the end of that decade Crofts retired to England to write full-time. His principal detective was the affable but relentless Inspector Joseph 'Soapy' French, who specialized in breaking down ingenious alibis. Crofts also published 'inverted detective novels' such as *The 12.30 from Croydon* and *Antidote to Venom*.

Lionel Davidson (1922–2009) published a mere eight thrillers, but three of them won Gold Daggers. The first, *The Night of Wenceslas*, was filmed as *Hot Enough for June*, while *The Chelsea Murders* was adapted for television. After a sixteen-year break, he published his final book, *Kolymsky Heights*, which received widespread acclaim; a posthumous reprint enjoyed even more success, becoming an international best-seller. Davidson, who also wrote young adult fiction as David Line, received the Diamond Dagger in 2001.

David Stuart Davies worked as an English teacher prior to becoming a full-time novelist, playwright, and editor. He is a leading expert on Sherlock Holmes, and has published novels and non-fiction about the great detective as well as a one-man play, *Sherlock Holmes – the Last Act*. His crime fiction includes a series about private investigator Johnny One Eye. Formerly the editor of *Sherlock* magazine, for twenty years he edited *Red Herrings*, the CWA members' monthly newsletter.

Lindsey Davis left the civil service to pursue a literary career, and after publishing romantic fiction, she turned to historical novels, and created the Roman detective Marcus Didius Falco, who first appeared in *The Silver Pigs* in 1989. His British-born adopted daughter, Flavia Alba, takes the lead in a series that began in 2013 with *The Ides of April*. She has received numerous prestigious awards, including the Historical Dagger, the Dagger in the Library, and the Diamond Dagger.

Len Deighton's career as a spy novelist began in 1962 with the bestselling *The IPCRESS File*, which broke fresh ground in the genre. His unnamed protagonist was called Harry Palmer in the films adapted from his early books, and played by Michael Caine. Deighton is also a military historian, cookery writer, and graphic artist. In 2017 the BBC adapted his alternate history novel *SS-GB* for a five-part series.

Bertie Denham is the writing name of Bertram Stanley Mitford Bowyer, 2nd Baron Denham. He first served as a Conservative party whip in the House of Lords during the premiership of Harold Macmillan, and is currently the Father (longest-serving member) of the House of Lords. Although a hereditary peer, he was elected to continue to serve following the reforms introduced by the House of Lords Act 1999. His novels include *Foxhunt*, *Two Thyrdes*, and *Black Rod*.

Stella Duffy was born in London but grew up in New Zealand before returning to Britain. She is an actor, playwright, and novelist whose work includes a series of crime novels featuring Saz Martin. She was commissioned to complete *Money in the Morgue*, a Roderick Alleyn mystery which Ngaio Marsh began but failed to finish. A prolific writer of short stories, she won the Short Story Dagger for 'Martha Grace'. She was Stonewall Writer of the Year in 2008.

Marjorie Eccles is the author of thirteen contemporary novels about Inspector Gil Mayo, adapted for BBC television in 2006 with impressionist and actor Alistair McGowan as Mayo. A prolific short-story writer, she has won the Agatha award and currently writes crime novels set in the first half of the twentieth century.

Martin Edwards is President of the Detection Club, consultant to the British Library's Crime Classics imprint, and recipient of the Diamond Dagger in 2020. He has published series set in Liverpool and the Lake District as well as stand-alone novels such as *Dancing for the Hangman*. His latest novel, *Mortmain Hall*, is a sequel to *Gallows Court*, which was nominated for the eDunnit award for best crime novel and the Historical Dagger. He was honoured with the Dagger in the Library for his body of work and has received the Edgar, Agatha, H.R.F.

Keating, and Poirot awards, two Macavity awards, and the Short Story Dagger.

Ruth Dudley Edwards, a former academic, teacher, marketing executive and civil servant, has been a freelance writer for forty years. A historian and prize-winning biographer, she has won the Gold Dagger for Non-Fiction and was shortlisted for the John Creasey Memorial Dagger for best first crime novel. She has also won the Last Laugh award for funniest novel of the year.

Kate Ellis launched the long-running DI Wesley Peterson series set in Devon with her first novel, *The Merchant House*. She has also written five crime novels featuring another cop, Joe Plantagenet, set in a fictionalized York; a trilogy set in the immediate aftermath of the First World War; and many short stories. *The Devil's Priest* is a stand-alone historical mystery set in Liverpool. She won the Dagger in the Library in 2019.

Felix Francis is the younger son of Dick Francis, the National Hunt champion jockey who became a bestselling thriller writer and long-standing member of the Detection Club. Felix's mother Mary assisted with both the research and the writing of many of Dick's novels, and Felix was also involved. Dick drew upon Felix's knowledge and experience as a physics teacher in *Twice Shy* and his time as an international marksman in *Shattered* and *Under Orders*. With the publication of *Dead Heat* in 2007, Felix took on a more significant role in the writing, and since his father's death has continued to write books in the Francis tradition, starting with *Gamble*.

Anthea Fraser's first professional publications were short stories. Her first novel was published in 1970, and she wrote books with paranormal themes as well as romantic suspense stories before turning to crime fiction. She has created two mystery novel series, the first featuring DCI David Webb and the second featuring biographer and journalist Rona Parish. She has also published novels under the pseudonym Vanessa Graham.

Richard Austin Freeman (1862–1943) was a doctor who put his medical and scientific expertise to good use in his novels about Dr John Thorndyke. He is widely credited as inventing the 'inverted detective story' in the tales collected in *The Singing Bone*; his meticulous research gave his crime fiction an air of authenticity. Raymond Chandler called him 'a wonderful performer' and said, 'He has no equal in his genre, and he is also a much better writer than you might think, if you were superficially inclined, because in spite of the immense leisure of his writing, he accomplishes an even suspense which is quite unexpected.'

Celia Fremlin (1914–2009) was born in Kent and educated at Berkhamsted School for Girls and Somerville College, Oxford, where she read classics and philosophy. During the Second World War she worked for the Mass Observation project, an experience that resulted in her first published book, *War Factory*, which recorded the experiences and attitudes of women war workers in a radar equipment factory outside Malmesbury, Wiltshire. Her first published novel of suspense was *The Hours Before Dawn*, which won the Mystery Writers of America's Edgar Award for best crime novel in 1960. Over the next 35 years she published a further eighteen titles, including three collections of stories.

Frances Fyfield worked as a solicitor for the Crown Prosecution Service, thus 'learning a bit about murder at second hand'. Later, writing became her vocation, although the law and its ramifications have influenced many of her novels. Her Helen West books have been adapted for television, and she is a regular contributor to BBC Radio 4. Her non-series novel *Blood from Stone* won the Gold Dagger.

Jonathan Gash is a pen name of John Grant, who has also written one novel as Graham Gaunt. A doctor who has worked both as a general practitioner and a pathologist, he won the John Creasey Memorial Dagger for his first detective novel,

The Judas Pair. This introduced Lovejoy, who later became a popular figure on television, played by Ian McShane. Jonathan Gash's other novels include a series featuring Dr Clare Burtonall.

Michael Gilbert (1912–2006) received the Diamond Dagger in recognition of his outstanding achievement as a crime writer and was also made a Grand Master of the Mystery Writers of America. His experiences as a prisoner of war in Italy provide background material for 1952's *Death in Captivity*, one of the finest British 'impossible crime' stories of the post-war era, filmed as *Danger Within*. Gilbert was a partner in a leading law firm and wrote during his morning commute. His urbanity is reflected in the smooth, readable prose of his whodunits, thrillers, spy stories, legal mysteries, and police stories. He was equally adept at writing novels, stage plays, radio plays, and television scripts.

Robert Goddard worked in journalism, teaching, and as an educational administrator in Devon before becoming a full-time novelist. One of his Harry Barnett novels, *Into the Blue*, was the inaugural winner of the WHSmith Thumping Good Read Award, presented to the best new fiction author of the year, while *Long Time Coming* won the Edgar for Best Original Paperback. *Into the Blue* was adapted for television, with John Thaw in the lead. He received the Diamond Dagger in 2019.

Paula Gosling is American but moved to England in the 1960s. A former copywriter, she received the John Creasey Memorial Dagger for her debut, *A Running Duck* (filmed twice, including as *Cobra* with Sylvester Stallone), and the Gold Dagger for her first Jack Stryker novel, *Monkey Puzzle*. She is also the author of the Luke Abbott and Blackwater Bay series, and of several stand-alones.

Ann Granger worked for the Foreign Office in embassies around the world and wrote romantic fiction before deciding to concentrate on the crime genre. Her series about Mitchell and Markby, launched in 1991, was followed by three further series, featuring respectively Fran Varady, Lizzie Martin, and Campbell and Carter. The Lizzie Martin books are set in the nineteenth century.

Elly Griffiths is the pen name adopted by Domenica de Rosa when she turned to crime writing, having written fiction set in Italy under her own name. As Griffiths, she has written two series, featuring forensic archaeologist Ruth Galloway and the Brighton-based duo of DI Edgar Stephens and Max Mephisto respectively. *The Stranger Diaries* is a stand-alone Gothic thriller. She has won the Dagger in the Library and has recently begun to write crime stories for children.

Sophie Hannah's bestselling crime fiction has been published in forty-nine languages. In 2014, with the blessing of Agatha Christie's family and estate, Sophie published a new Poirot novel, *The Monogram Murders*, which was a bestseller in more than fifteen countries, and she has subsequently written further Poirot novels. In 2013, *The Carrier* won the Crime Thriller of the Year Award at the Specsavers National Book Awards. She has also published two short story collections and five collections of poetry.

Tom Harper is the pseudonym of Edwin Thomas. He was a runner-up for the Debut Dagger award for *The Blighted Cliffs*, published under his own name, which launched a series set during the Napoleonic wars. As Harper, he has written a series set during the First Crusade among other novels, and has also collaborated with Wilbur Smith.

Cynthia Harrod-Eagles wrote her first novel while at university and in 1972 won the Young Writers' Award with *The Waiting Game*. She has now written more than ninety books in a variety of genres and has won the RNA Novel of the Year Award. Her main series are the historical Morland Dynasty and War At Home series, and the Inspector Bill Slider Mysteries, set in the present day.

Michael Hartland is the pen name under which Michael Leonard James writes thrillers and for radio and television. He worked for many years in the government service, and for five years in Vienna on the staff of the United Nations organization, the International Atomic Energy Agency. He has published five spy novels featuring David Nairn and is also the author of a stand-alone novel under the name Ruth Carrington.

John Harvey has published over one hundred books under various names, and has worked on scripts for TV and radio. He started writing in the 1970s when he produced a variety of pulp fiction including westerns. He also ran Slow Dancer Press from 1977 to 1999, publishing poetry. His own poetry has been published in a number of chapbooks and two collections. His crime fiction includes the Charlie Resnick series, which was televised, and the Frank Elder books. His awards include a Silver Dagger, a Short Story Dagger, and the Diamond Dagger.

Mick Herron is a novelist and short story writer whose books include the Sarah Tucker/Zoë Boehm series and the stand-alone novel *Reconstruction*. He is the author of the acclaimed Jackson Lamb series, the second of which, *Dead Lions*, won the Gold Dagger. His novels have regularly appeared on award shortlists and *Spook Street* won the Steel Dagger and the Last Laugh Award.

Reginald Hill (1936–2012), the son of a professional footballer, was educated at St Catherine's College, Oxford and pursued a career in teaching. In 1980, he retired as senior lecturer at Doncaster College of Education in order to pursue his crime writing career, which had begun ten years earlier with the first Dalziel and Pascoe novel, *A Clubbable Woman*. He wrote a wide range of other novels, including several thrillers originally published under the name Patrick Ruell. He received a Gold Dagger for *Bones and Silence* in 1990 and the Diamond Dagger five years later.

Suzette A. Hill worked as an English teacher before becoming a crime novelist. Her light-hearted mystery series about Reverend Francis Oughterard is set in 1950s Guildford; she self-published the first book, *A Load of Old Bones*, only for it to be taken up by a commercial publisher. She has followed it up with the Rosy Gilchrist series.

Joanna Hines has written psychological thrillers as well as historical novels. She has also reviewed crime fiction for the *Guardian*. *Dora's Room* was chosen by WHSmith for its first Fresh Talent promotion and *Improvising Carla* was adapted for television. Writing as Joanna Hodgkin, she has produced narrative non-fiction and an account of her mother's marriage to Lawrence Durrell.

Antonia Hodgson worked in publishing for nearly twenty years, rising to become editor-in-chief at Little, Brown before her own first novel appeared. This was *A Devil in the Marshalsea*, set in the early Georgian era, which won the Historical Dagger. It has been followed by *The Last Confession of Thomas Hawkins* and *A Death at Fountains Abbey*.

Michael Innes was the pen name of John Innes Mackintosh Stewart (1906–94), who enjoyed a distinguished academic career, culminating in a professorship in English at Oxford University. Innes' debut, *Death at the President's Lodging* was bought by the leading publisher Victor Gollancz, and the front cover of the dust jacket of the first edition in 1936 announced, 'This is the best "first" Detective Story that has ever come our way.' This bold claim was justified by the cleverness and wit of the story, and the novel established both Innes and his detective, Inspector (later Sir John) Appleby. The Appleby series continued for half a century.

Bill James is the principal pen name of James Tucker, a former journalist. *Protection*, the fourth Harpur and Iles novel, won the Le Point prize for the best European novel of 2004, and was televised by the BBC in 1996 under the title *Harpur & Iles*. He has also written spy fiction, comedy, satire, and non-fiction, writing under his own name, as Bill James, and as Judith Jones and David Craig. The Craig novel *Whose Little Girl Are You?* was filmed as *The Squeeze*, starring Stacy Keach, Edward Fox and Carol White.

P. D. James (1920–2014) worked from 1949 to 1968 in the National Health Service and subsequently in the Home Office. She was a Fellow of the Royal Society of Literature and of the Royal Society of Arts and served as a governor of the BBC, a member of the Arts Council (chairing the Literary Advisory Panel), on the Board of the British Council, and as a magistrate. She won awards for crime writing in Britain, America, Italy and Scandinavia, including the Diamond Dagger, the Mystery Writers of America Grandmaster Award and the US National Arts Club Medal of Honor for Literature. She received honorary degrees from seven British universities, was awarded an OBE in 1983, and was created a life peer in 1991.

Peter James has written thirty-five novels, including a best-selling series featuring Brighton-based Detective Superintendent Roy Grace, which have sold more than twenty million copies worldwide. In 1993, Penguin published his novel *Host* on two floppy discs (in addition to conventional print formats); this has been called the world's first electronic novel, and a copy is in the Science Museum. He has written supernatural thrillers, spy fiction, science-based thrillers, a children's novel, and the novella *The Perfect Murder*, which was adapted by Shaun McKenna into a stage play.

Russell James has written more than twenty books, fact and fiction, crime and historical. His early novels included thrillers set in London such as *Underground*, and he has also published satirical fiction and a police procedural. His non-fiction includes two companion volumes, *Great British Fictional Detectives* and *Great British Fictional Villains*.

Michael Jecks has written a long series of novels featuring former Knight Templar Sir Baldwin Furnshill, as well as a trilogy centred on the Hundred Years War. He has also published collections of his short fiction. He founded the Medieval Murderers, a speaking and entertainment group of six historical writers which has developed to collaborate on books written as linked novellas, each book with a consistent theme.

Alison Joseph began her career as a documentary director, making programmes for Channel 4. Her principal crime series features a nun, Sister Agnes, and her other books include stories about Agatha Christie. She has written extensively for radio, adapting Maigret novels by Georges Simenon and books by S. J. Watson and Craig Russell, as well as writing original dramas.

H. R. F. Keating (1926–2011) published five stand-alone novels before introducing the Indian policeman Inspector Ghote in *The Perfect Murder*, which won the Gold Dagger. The Ghote series continued for over forty years. Another novel set in India, *The Murder of the Maharajah*, also won a Gold Dagger, and Keating received the Diamond Dagger in recognition of his lifetime achievements in the genre. He served as President of the Detection Club. As a leading critic and commentator, his books include *Writing Crime Fiction* and studies of Agatha Christie and Sherlock Holmes.

Mary Kelly (1927–2017) was educated at a convent and at Edinburgh University, where she met her future husband, Denis. After marriage and graduation, she worked as an auxiliary nurse and then, like Denis, as a teacher. Her first three novels featured a police officer called Brett Nightingale but her breakthrough came with her fourth book, *The Spoilt Kill*, which won the Gold Dagger in 1961. She was elected to the Detection Club and served as its Secretary, but after her last novel appeared in 1974 she devoted herself to other pursuits.

Janet Laurence, a former Chair of the Crime Writers' Association, has published ten contemporary novels featuring cookery writer Darina Lisle and policeman William Pigram, as well as one non-series crime novel and four historical crime novels. She has also written contemporary women's novels under the pen name Julia Lisle, a book on how to write cookery books, and a book on how to write crime fiction.

John Le Carré is the pen name adopted by David Cornwell for his novels. He is a distinguished author of spy fiction, but his first two novels were detective stories that introduced George Smiley, a character inspired in part by John Bingham, a fellow crime writer, secret service agent, and Detection Club member. Then followed an international bestseller, *The Spy Who Came in from the Cold*, which was made into a film starring Richard Burton. Many of his subsequent books have been adapted for film or television (or, in the case of *Tinker Tailor Soldier Spy*, both). Le Carré was ranked by *The Times* as one of the fifty greatest writers since 1945 and received the Goethe Medal in 2011. He has also received the Diamond Dagger.

Michael Zinn Lewin is an American-born author perhaps best known for his series about the private detective Albert Samson, based in Indianapolis. Lewin grew up there but has lived in England for more than forty years. Much of his fiction continues to be set in Indianapolis, including a secondary series about the cop Leroy Powder. A series set in Bath, England, features the Lunghis who run their detective agency as a family business.

Peter Lovesey had already published a successful book about athletics when he won a competition with his first crime fiction novel, *Wobble to Death*, which launched a series about the Victorian detective Sergeant Cribb, later televised with Alan Dobie playing Cribb. His books and short stories have won or been shortlisted for nearly all the major prizes in the international crime writing world. He has received the Diamond Dagger and became an Mystery Writers of America Grand Master in 2018.

Alexander McCall Smith was born and educated in Bulawayo, and studied law at Edinburgh University. He later helped to found the law school at the University of Botswana, and also taught there. The first entry in his No. 1 Ladies' Detective Agency series, set in Botswana, appeared in 1998 and the books rapidly achieved bestseller status. He has also created the 44 Scotland Street series, the Sunday Philosophy Club series, the Corduroy Mansions series, and the Detective Varg series, as well as writing numerous children's books and academic texts.

Val McDermid, an internationally bestselling novelist and recipient of the Diamond Dagger, is a former journalist and the author of four series, featuring Lindsay Gordon, Kate Brannigan, Tony Hill and Carol Jordan, and Inspector Karen Pirie. *The Mermaids Singing*, the first Hill and Jordan book, won the Gold Dagger and the series was televised as *The Wire in the Blood*. Her stand-alone novels include *A Place of Execution*, *Trick of the Dark*, and a new version of *Northanger Abbey*. Her nonfiction includes books about female private eyes and forensic science.

John Malcolm is the pen name under which antiques dealer, businessman, and journalist John Malcolm Andrews writes crime fiction, notably the Tim Simpson series of art mysteries. A former chair of the CWA, he has also written two stand-alone crime novels. As John Andrews, he was author of the first *Price Guide to Antique Furniture* and managing editor of *Antique Collecting* magazine.

Jessica Mann (1937–2018) read archaeology and Anglo-Saxon at Cambridge University before taking a degree in law. She was a columnist, reviewer, and broadcaster whose non-fiction books included *Deadlier than the Male*, a study of female crime writers. Her first novel, *A Charitable End*, appeared in 1971; her last came out forty-five years later. Her main series character was the archaeologist Tamara Hoyland. *A Private Enquiry* was shortlisted for the Gold Dagger and featured another recurrent character, psychiatrist Dr Fidelis Berlin.

Ngaio Marsh (1895–1982) was born in Christchurch, New Zealand. She studied painting and became an actor and theatre director. Her first detective novel, *A Man Lay Dead*, introduced a gentlemanly Scotland Yard sleuth, Roderick Alleyn, who featured in a long-running series of novels that often reflected her love of art and drama. In 2018, Stella Duffy published a completed version of an Alleyn novel, *Money in the Morgue*, which Marsh had abandoned after writing a few chapters while working as an ambulance driver during the Second World War.

Priscilla Masters writes both series and stand-alones. A former nurse whose late husband was a doctor, she has made use of her medical knowledge in a wide range of novels. Her DI Joanna Piercy books feature a Staffordshire cop, the Martha Gunn series a Shrewsbury coroner, and the Claire Roget books a forensic psychiatrist.

Susan Moody's first crime novel, *Penny Black*, was published in 1984, the first in a series of seven books featuring amateur sleuth Penny Wanawake. She has written a number of suspense thrillers, and in 1993 introduced a series of crime novels with a new central character, Cassandra Swann. *Misselthwaite* was shortlisted for the Romantic Novelists' Association Award in 1995, while *The Colour of Hope*, the story of a family struggling to cope with the loss of their daughter in a boating accident, was written under the name Susan Madison, as is her recent title, *Touching the Sky*.

Patricia Moyes (1923–2000) was born in Dublin and educated in England. During the Second World War, she served in the Women's Auxiliary Air Force, and her experiences subsequently provided background for her novel *Johnny Under Ground*. She worked in the film business as Peter Ustinov's assistant for eight years and later lived in Virgin Gorda with her second husband; several of her books are set in the Caribbean.

Janet Neel is a solicitor who worked in the Department of Trade and then in merchant banking; she also spent five years as a governor of the BBC and in 2000, as Baroness Cohen of Pimlico, became a Labour life peer in the House of Lords. Her other appointments include a spell as a non-executive director of the London Stock Exchange. She published her first crime novel in 1988; it won the John Creasey Memorial Dagger for best debut, while two of her later books were shortlisted for the Gold Dagger.

Michael Pearce was raised in Anglo-Egyptian Sudan. During the Cold War he trained as a Russian interpreter; he subsequently became involved with Amnesty International. His first novel, *The Mamur Zapt and the Return of the Carpet*, appeared in 1988. A later book in the same series, *The Mamur Zapt and the Spoils of Egypt* won the Last Laugh Award for funniest crime novel, while *Death of an Effendi* was shortlisted for the Historical Dagger.

Ian Rankin's Rebus series has been televised and translated into twenty-two languages and the books are bestsellers on several continents. In addition to his Rebus and Malcolm Fox novels, he has written stand-alone novels, a graphic novel, and a play, as well as novels under the pseudonym Jack Harvey. He has received four Dagger awards, including the Diamond Dagger, and an Edgar, together with awards in Denmark, France and Germany.

Michael Ridpath worked in the City after graduating from Oxford, but became a full-time author after his first novel, *Free to Trade*, was published. He wrote seven more books featuring the world of business and finance before launching a series set in Iceland. He has also published a spy novel and *Amnesia*, a stand-alone thriller.

David Roberts was an editor at Chatto & Windus, editorial director at Weidenfeld & Nicolson, and a partner at Michael O'Mara Books, prior to becoming a full-time writer in 2000. His series of crime novels set during the 1930s, starting with *Sweet Poison*, features Lord Edward Corinth and Verity Browne, a character based on Martha Gellhorn.

Imogen Robertson directed for film, television, and radio before becoming a full-time writer. She won a *Daily Telegraph* competition with the first thousand words of the book that became *Instruments of Darkness* and launched a historical series featuring the detective duo Harriet Westerman and Gabriel Crowther. She has also collaborated on a novel with the bestselling author Wilbur Smith.

Peter Robinson is an English-Canadian crime writer best known for his crime novels set in Yorkshire featuring DCI Banks, which gave rise to a popular TV series with Stephen Tompkinson in the title role. He has also written stand-alone novels, many short stories, and poetry, and has received awards for his crime fiction in the UK, US, Canada, and Denmark.

James Runcie is a writer, director and literary curator. He is the author of *The Grantchester Mysteries* (televised with James Norton as Sidney Chambers) a Fellow of the Royal Society of Literature and commissioning editor for arts at BBC Radio 4. He was a founder member of *The Late Show*, and made documentary films for the BBC for fifteen years before going freelance to make programmes for Channel 4 and ITV.

William Ryan, a former barrister, is the Irish author of five novels, including the Captain Korolev series set in 1930s Moscow and a stand-alone book, *The Constant Soldier*. His latest novel, *A House of Ghosts*, set in 1917 and published as by W. C. Ryan, is a non-series book with a supernatural element. His books have been shortlisted for several awards.

Dorothy Leigh Sayers (1893–1957) was a renowned English crime writer, poet, playwright, essayist, translator, and Christian humanist. She was also a student of classical and modern languages. She is best known for her mysteries, a series of novels and short stories set between the First and Second World Wars that feature English aristocrat and amateur sleuth Lord Peter Wimsey. Sayers herself considered her translation of Dante's *Divine Comedy* to be her best work. She is also known for her plays, literary criticism, and essays.

Julian Symons (1912–1994) was an eminent crime writer and critic of the genre as well as being a biographer, poet, editor, and social and military historian. His early detective novels were relatively orthodox, but he soon became dissatisfied with the conventions of the classic form and began in the early 1950s to develop the British psychological crime novel. He received the Gold Dagger for *The Colour of Murder* and an Edgar from the Mystery Writers of America for *The Progress of a Crime*. In 1990 he received the Diamond Dagger in recognition of his outstanding career in the genre; he was also a Grand Master of the MWA. He wrote an influential history of the genre, *Bloody Murder*, and served as President of the Detection Club.

Andrew Taylor's crime novels include a series about William Dougal, starting with *Caroline Minuscule*, which won the John Creasey Memorial Dagger; the Roth Trilogy, televised as *Fallen Angel*; the Lydmouth series; stand-alone novels such as *The American Boy*; and much else. He has won the Historical Dagger three times and also the Diamond Dagger, along with awards in Sweden and the US.

Aline Templeton grew up in the East Neuk of Fife and was educated at St Leonards School, St Andrews and Cambridge

University. She has worked in education and broadcasting and has written numerous stories and articles for national newspapers and magazines. After publishing seven stand-alone books, she started a series set in Galloway and featuring DI Marjory Fleming. Her latest series character is DI Kelso Strang.

June Thomson, a former teacher, published *Not One of Us*, her first novel about Inspector Finch (renamed Rudd in the US) in 1971. The series continued for thirty-five years, but in 1990 she began to publish collections of short stories about Sherlock Holmes and Dr Watson, and this series has become her main focus. She has also written a biography of the Baker Street duo, *Holmes and Watson*.

L. C. (Len) Tyler worked for the British Council before becoming Chief Executive of the Royal College of Paediatrics and Child Health. He is the author of a series of humorous mysteries featuring crime writer Ethelred Tressider and his literary agent Elsie Thirkettle, and a historical series about seventeenth-century lawyer John Grey. He received the Short Story Dagger for 'The Trials of Margaret', published in the Detection Club anthology *Motives for Murder*.

Roy Vickers was the best-known pen name of William Edward Vickers (1889–1965), who also wrote as David Durham, Sefton Kyle, and John Spencer. A prolific writer of novels and short stories alike, he is best remembered as the creator of the Department of Dead Ends, a branch of Scotland Yard dedicated to solving eccentric cases, often as a result of chance. He was a prominent figure in the early years of the Crime Writers' Association and edited several anthologies of short fiction.

Martyn Waites has turned his hand to many occupations: market trader, bar manager, stand-up comic and teacher of drama to teenage ex-offenders. Following this last job he decided to go to drama school and became a professional actor, playing both policemen and villains in *Inspector Morse*,

Spender, *The Bill*, and *Harry*. As a theatre actor he appeared as a lead in Catherine Cookson's plays and had a go at stand-up. He won the 2014 Grand Prix du Roman Noir Award for his novel *Born Under Punches* and has enjoyed further success with his later books, including the Brennan and Esposito novels written under the pseudonym of Tania Carver.

Jill Paton Walsh is the author of many non-crime novels for adults: the fourth of these, *Knowledge of Angels*, was shortlisted for the Booker Prize. Before writing for adults she made a career as a writer of children's books and has won many literary awards, including the Whitbread Prize. *The Wyndham Case* was the first of her detective novels about Imogen Quy. Her books about Lord Peter Wimsey have taken Dorothy L. Sayers' character into the 1950s and she is President of the Dorothy L. Sayers Society.

Laura Wilson has worked as a teacher and editor of non-fiction. Many of her novels have either a historical setting or a distinct historical connection, and often have split or dual narratives. Her fifth novel, *The Lover*, won the Prix du Polar Européen in 2005, and her eighth, *Stratton's War*, won the Historical Dagger. Both books were also shortlisted for the Gold Dagger. She is the crime fiction reviewer for the *Guardian* newspaper, and teaches on the City University Crime Thriller Novel Creative Writing MA course.

The Detection Club: Presidents

Given in chronological order.

1930–1936

G. K. CHESTERTON

1936–1949

E. C. BENTLEY

1949–1957

DOROTHY L. SAYERS

1958–1976

AGATHA CHRISTIE

1976–1985

JULIAN SYMONS

1985–2001

H. R. F. KEATING

2001–2015

SIMON BRETT

2015–

MARTIN EDWARDS

LORD GORELL served as Co-President 1958–1963.

The Detection Club: Members

Given in chronological order of joining the Club.

1930–2
G. K. CHESTERTON
H. C. BAILEY
E. C. BENTLEY
ANTHONY BERKELEY
Dame AGATHA CHRISTIE
G. D. H. COLE
M. COLE
J. J. CONNINGTON
FREEMAN WILLS CROFTS
CLEMENCE DANE
ROBERT EUSTACE
R. AUSTIN FREEMAN
LORD GORELL
EDGAR JEPSON
IANTHE JERROLD
MILWARD KENNEDY
RONALD A KNOX
A. E. W. MASON
A. A. MILNE
ARTHUR MORRISON
BARONESS ORCZY
Mrs. VICTOR RICKARD
JOHN RHODE
DOROTHY L. SAYERS
HENRY WADE
VICTOR L. WHITECHURCH

HELEN SIMPSON
HUGH WALPOLE

1933
ANTHONY GILBERT
E. R. PUNSHON
GLADYS MITCHELL

1934
MARGERY ALLINGHAM

1935
NORMAN KENDAL
R. C. WOODTHORPE

1936
JOHN DICKSON CARR

1937
NICHOLAS BLAKE
NEWTON GAYLE
E. C. R. LORAC
CHRISTOPHER BUSH

1946
CYRIL HARE
CHRISTIANNA BRAND

RICHARD HULL
ALICE CAMPBELL

1947
VAL GIELGUD
EDMUND CRISPIN

1948
DOROTHY BOWERS

1949
MICHAEL INNES
MICHAEL GILBERT
DOUGLAS G. BROWNE

1950
MARY FITT

1951
JULIAN SYMONS

1952
ANDREW GARVE
ERIC AMBLER

1954
JOSEPHINE BELL

1955
ROY VICKERS
GLYN CARR

1957
MACDONALD HASTINGS

1958
EDWARD CANDY
G. BELTON COBB
E. H. CLEMENTS
J. C. MASTERMAN
JOHN TRENCH
CLIFFORD WITTING

ELIZABETH FERRARS
KATHARINE FARRER

1959
MICHAEL UNDERWOOD
MARGOT BENNETT
DOROTHY EDEN
GEORGE MILNER

1960
WILLIAM MOLE

1961
GUY CULLINGFORD
JOHN SHERWOOD

1962
MARY KELLY

1963
JOAN FLEMING
CELIA FREMLIN
ANTHONY LEJEUNE

1964
JOHN BLACKBURN

1965
WILLIAM HAGGARD

1966
DICK FRANCIS
H. R. F. KEATING

1967
FRANCIS CLIFFORD

1968
JOHN BINGHAM
HENRY CECIL
GAVIN LYALL
MILES TRIPP

1969
LEN DEIGHTON
PETER DICKINSON

1970
COLIN WATSON
DOUGLAS RUTHERFORD

1971
JOAN AIKEN
PATRICIA MOYES
ANTHONY PRICE

1972
P. D. JAMES
JEAN STUBBS

1973
KENNETH BENTON
JEAN BOWDEN

1974
GWENDOLINE BUTLER
JOHN LE CARRÉ
PETER LOVESEY
Dame NGAIO MARSH

1975
PATRICIA HIGHSMITH
MICHAEL KENYON
LAURENCE MEYNELL
ROBERT PLAYER

1976
GEOFFREY HOUSEHOLD
JAMES McCLURE
ANNE MORICE
MARGARET YORKE

1977
RUTH RENDELL

1978
DESMOND BAGLEY
SIMON BRETT
CELIA DALE
REGINALD HILL

1979
LIONEL DAVIDSON
MARTIN RUSSELL

1980
COLIN DEXTER

1981
CATHERINE AIRD

1982
JUNE THOMSON,

1983
JOHN WAINWRIGHT

1985
JESSICA MANN
ANTONIA FRASER

1986
JAMES MELVILLE

1987
TIM HEALD
JONATHAN GASH

1988
DAVID WILLIAMS
GEORGE SIMS

1989
SUSAN MOODY

1990
ANTHEA FRASER

1991
LIZA CODY
ROBERT BARNARD

1992
BERTIE DENHAM

1993
JOHN MALCOLM
MICHAEL Z. LEWIN

1994
LINDSEY DAVIS
FRANCES FYFIELD

1995
ANDREW TAYLOR

1996
RUTH DUDLEY EDWARDS

1997
MICHAEL HARTLAND

1998
IAN RANKIN
JOHN HARVEY

1999
ANN GRANGER
ROBERT GODDARD

2000
JANET NEEL
VAL McDERMID

2001
JANET LAURENCE
DAPHNE WRIGHT
RUSSELL JAMES
FRANK DELANEY

2002
PAULA GOSLING
MICHAEL RIDPATH
BILL JAMES

2003
CLARE FRANCIS
MICHAEL PEARCE
ALINE TEMPLETON

2004
MARIAN BABSON
STELLA DUFFY
JOANNA HINES

2005
JILL PATON WALSH
MICHAEL JECKS

2006
ALEXANDER McCALL SMITH
MARK BILLINGHAM
PETER ROBINSON

2007
LAURA WILSON

2008
MARTIN EDWARDS
ANN CLEEVES

2009
DAVID ROBERTS
SOPHIE HANNAH

2010
KATE CHARLES
MARTYN WAITES

2011
PETER JAMES
EDWIN THOMAS

2012
FELIX FRANCIS

2013
LEN TYLER
IMOGEN ROBERTSON

2014
ALISON JOSEPH
KATE ELLIS
MARJORIE ECCLES
SUZETTE A. HILL

2015
CYNTHIA HARROD-EAGLES
DAVID STUART DAVIES
WILLIAM RYAN

2016
MICK HERRON
JAMES RUNCIE

2017
ELLY GRIFFITHS

2018
PRISCILLA MASTERS

2019
ANTONIA HODGSON

Copyright and Acknowledgements

As mentioned in the Introduction to *Howdunit*, the generous co-operation of all the living contributors and also the family members and heirs of deceased contributors has been both essential and invaluable and is gratefully acknowledged. For a book as eclectic as this, identifying sources and rights correctly involves complex detective work. We hope we have come up with all the right answers, but in the event of any error or omission, please advise the publishers so that a correction may be made. The thanks of Detection Club members and HarperCollins go to all the literary agents whose help and support of various kinds has made it possible to feature such a wide range of contributions. They include Georgia Glover, Jane Gregory, Becky Brown, Joanna Lee, Ciara Finan, Jonny Geller, Peter Buckman, Euan Thorneycroft, Carol Heaton, Alisa Ahmed, Lisa Moylett, Norah Perkins, Olivia Maidment, Vickie Dillon, Sharon Rubin, and Sarah Baxter of the Society of Authors.

Index of Authors

Subject Index